1738 21330 3/29

D0576143

AVIATION CENTURY

WORLD WAR II

AVIATION CENTURY

WORLD WAR II

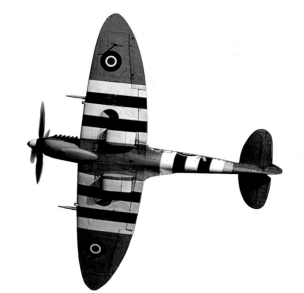

RON DICK AND DAN PATTERSON

The BOSTON MILLS PRESS

A BOSTON MILLS PRESS BOOK

© Ron Dick and Dan Patterson, 2004

First printing 2004

National Library of Canada Cataloguing in Publication

Dick, Ron, 1931-
Aviation century World War II / Ron Dick and Dan Patterson.

Includes bibliographical references and index.
ISBN 1-55046-426-4

1. Aeronautics--History. 2. World War, 1939-1945--Aerial operations.
I. Patterson, Dan, 1953- II. Title.

D785.D43 2004   940.54'4   C2004-900964-8

Publisher Cataloging-in-Publication Data (U.S.)

Dick, Ron, 1931-

Aviation century World War II / Ron Dick ; and Dan Patterson. _ 1st ed.

[352] p. : ill. , photos. (chiefly col.) ; cm. (Aviation Century)

Includes bibliographical references and index.

Summary: The aerial conflict during World War II covered in two parts:
1, Europe and the Middle East; 2, the Pacific, China, Burma and India.

ISBN 1-55046-426-4

1. Airplanes _ History. 2. Aircraft industry – History. 3. Aeronautics—History.
4. World War, 1939-1945 -- Aerial operations. I. Patterson, Dan, 1953- II. Title.
III. Series.

629.13'009   22   TL670.3.D52Avc   2004

Published in 2004 by BOSTON MILLS PRESS
132 Main Street,
Erin, Ontario N0B 1T0
Tel 519-833-2407
Fax 519-833-2195
books@bostonmillspress.com
www.bostonmillspress.com

IN CANADA:
Distributed by Firefly Books Ltd.
66 Leek Crescent
Richmond Hill, Ontario L4B 1H1

IN THE UNITED STATES:
Distributed by Firefly Books (U.S.) Inc.
P.O. Box 1338, Ellicott Station
Buffalo, New York 14205

Aviation Century series editor: Kathleen Fraser
Design: PageWave Graphics Inc.

The publisher acknowledges the financial support of the Government of Canada through
the Book Publishing Industry Development Program (BPIDP) for its publishing efforts.

HALF-TITLE PAGE *An Italian S.M.79 at Sidi Barrani Aerodrome after it was forced down by RAF fighters.*

PAGE 2 *From inside the ball turret of a restored B-17 Flying Fortress, the four-engined bomber leaves its shadow on the runway.*

TITLE PAGE *A restored Spitfire IX, showing its invasion stripes.*

PAGE 6 *From the collection of the United States Air Force Museum, the trombone, hat, glasses and music of Major Glenn Miller. His band became part of the USAAF and offered a welcome break from the air war. The airplane he was in while flying over the English Channel on December 15, 1944, was lost and no trace was ever found.*

FRONT JACKET

MAIN IMAGE *A rare fighter, the Hawker Typhoon on display at the RAF Museum, Hendon, England.*

BOTTOM ROW

FAR LEFT *The P-47 Thunderbolt flown by Butch Schroeder of Danville, Illinois, warms up the Pratt & Whitney R-2800 engine.*

CENTER LEFT *From dead ahead, the 30 mm cannon in the spiral-painted nose of a Bf 109G-10.*

CENTER RIGHT *The distinctive vertical stabilizer of the B-26 Marauder, on display at the United States Air Force Museum, Dayton, Ohio.*

FAR RIGHT *A very rare Japanese Zero displayed at the National Museum of Naval Aviation, Pensacola, Florida.*

BACK JACKET *The unmistakable tail of the B-24 Liberator.*

Dedicated to aviators,
past, present
and of the future.

Contents

ACKNOWLEDGMENTS

WHEN WE BEGAN THE work of research and photography for the *Aviation Century* series in 1998, we were vaguely aware that we were embarking on a project of considerable magnitude, but it was as we approached the third volume, *Aviation Century World War II*, that we were really confronted by the scale of the problem. Whole libraries could be devoted to the use of air power in World War II, and we proposed to cover the subject in one book. Answering the question "What do we leave out?" was a burdensome task, but it would have been far more so without the advice and guidance of many friends on both sides of the Atlantic. Our gratitude for their help is heartfelt. We are deeply indebted to them all, and hope that in preparing these acknowledgments we have remembered everyone. If we have inadvertently missed someone, we hope they will let us know, so that we may put that right in the next book.

Many names and organizations have been thanked before in earlier volumes. Their repeated appearance on this page underlines their continued willingness to offer us their support throughout the *Aviation Century* series. We are most grateful for their tolerance of our endless questions and frequent cries for help. Our particular thanks go to the directors and staffs of the Smithsonian's

National Air & Space Museum, Washington, D.C.; the Museum of Flight, Seattle, Washington; the Virginia Aviation Museum, Richmond, Virginia: the USAF History Office; the United States Air Force Museum, Dayton, Ohio; the Museum of Naval Aviation, Pensacola, Florida; the U.S. Marine Corps Museum, Quantico, Virginia; the Canada Aviation Museum, Ottawa; the Canadian Warplane Heritage Museum, Hamilton, Ontario; the Royal Aeronautical Society, London; the Imperial War Museum, Duxford, U.K.; the Royal Air Force Museum, Hendon and Cosford, U.K.; the Fleet Air Arm Museum, Yeovilton, U.K.; the Science Museum, London; the Shuttleworth Trust; the Musée de l'Air et de l'Espace, Le Bourget, France; the Museo Storico Aeronautica Militare, Vigna di Valle, Italy; the Museo Caproni, Trento, Italy; the Flygvapenmuseum, Linkoping, Sweden; the Muzeum Lotnictwa Polskiego, Krakow, Poland; and the Royal Australian Air Force Museum, Point Cook, Victoria, Australia.

Archive photographs in this volume came from the collections of Wright State University; the Smithsonian National Air & Space Museum; the Museum of Flight, Seattle; the USAF Museum; the National Museum of Naval Aviation, Pensacola; the Imperial War Museum; the Royal Air

Force Museum, Hendon; the Royal Aeronautical Society; the Museo Caproni, Trento; and from the private collections of the Caproni family and the authors. In London, the staff of *Aeroplane Monthly* went out of their way to offer their expert advice and free use of the magazine's archives. We are grateful to Michael Oakey, Tony Harmsworth, Tanya Caffrey, Nick Stroud and Lydia Matharu. David Brown of KJP, London, (now Calumet Photo) offered generous support and advice in the provision of photographic equipment while we were working in the United Kingdom.

A number of distinguished artists generously agreed to contribute their work to *Aviation Century*. This third volume includes paintings or drawings by Gil Cohen, Bob Rasmussen, Roy Grinnell, Gerald Coulson, Jim Dietz, R. G. Smith, Robert Taylor, Nicolas Trudgian and Michael Turner. Gil Cohen's paintings are from the collection of Eugene Eisenberg. The authors are again most grateful to Pat Barnard, formerly of the Military Gallery, Bath, U.K., for all his help and encouragement. The present owners of the Military Gallery, Colin Hudson and Rick Taylor, have continued to offer support and have been kind enough to grant permission for the reproduction of works by many of the artists. We are grateful to

Burleigh Presss, and to Andy Moon in particular, for providing us with the image of Gerald Coulson's painting of the Dambusters, and to Gregory Thompson, at the United States Air Force Art Collection, for R.G. Smith's *Silver Wings*.

Special thanks for their individual contributions go to Dr. Richard Hallion, Trish Graboske, Tom Allison, Scott Wiley, Dennis Parks, Katherine Williams, Bob Rasmussen, Hill Goodspeed, Irene Grinnell, David McFarland, Floyd McGowin, Donald Nijboer, Michael Fopp, Henry Hall, Phil Jarrett, Graham Mottram, Ted Inman, Colette Byatt, Clive and Linda Denny, Paddy Worth, Contessa Maria Fede Armani Caproni, Lieutenant General Antonino Lenzo, Dr. Orazio Guiffrida, Colonel Marco Scarlatti and Lieutenant Egidi.

The years since we began this project have demanded a great deal from our wives, Paul and Cheryl. They have tolerated our idiosyncrasies and borne the burdens we have placed on them with quite remarkable grace. When occasionally we slumped under the weight of the project, our backbones were stiffened by their encouragement and our sweating brows cooled by their caring hands. We again offer them our love and thanks for looking after us so well.

RON DICK AND DAN PATTERSON

FOREWORD
Major General Ramsay D. Potts

THE U.S. STRATEGIC BOMBING SURVEY concluded that the contribution of the U.S. Eighth Air Force to the Allied defeat of Germany in WWII had been decisive but that operations might have been conducted better or differently. The U.S. Army Air Forces bombing campaign against Germany in WWII was conceived as a strategic campaign against different components of the German war machine: that is, oil, ballbearings and aircraft production. Because of the exigencies of the war itself, however, the targets became more general in nature and involved many tactical targets.

The two principal strategic targets were oil and the German transportation system. Air Chief Marshal Tedder, who was General Eisenhower's Deputy Commander, favored an attack on the German transportation system while General Spaatz, who commanded the U.S. Strategic Air Forces in Europe, favored a campaign against Germany's oil targets. As it turned out, the bombers struck both targets and both campaigns were successful. By late 1944, oil and gas production were reduced to 16 percent of normal and the German rail system was rendered virtually inoperative. I had the good fortune to participate in both campaigns and to live to tell the story.

Perhaps the bombers' most important and valuable role was as a decoy to force the German fighters into the fight. This enabled the Allied fighters, and particularly the P-51s of the Eighth Air Force, to engage the Luftwaffe in aerial combat resulting in the defeat of the German Air Force and air power superiority over the beachhead on D-Day.

Most of the assessments of the RAF bombing campaign against German cities have been negative but I disagree and think that the lasting effect on attitudes in Germany since WWII must be considered. The head of RAF Bomber Command, Sir Arthur Harris, has been severely criticized for concentrating on city bombing, but it must be remembered that top-level British authorities, including Prime Minister Churchill, approved the RAF bombing plan. One side of the story of air power in WWII that has not been sufficiently described in other publications was the remarkable recovery of the Soviet Air Force after it was practically wiped out in the early days of the German offensive against Russia. This book details that occurrence in remarkable detail. Coincident with the battle of Stalingrad, the Soviet Air Force began making a significant contribution to the Russian war effort and joined with the Soviet ground armies in the later counteroffensive that battered the Germans into submission.

It is evident that air power was essential to victory in many different venues. The Battle of Britain was a clear victory for Britain over the Luftwaffe and prevented the Germans from invading Britain. Equally significant was the Battle of Malta. Malta was battered time and again by the superior air power of the Luftwaffe, but the RAF held on by the skin of their teeth and averted an invasion of the Island. This enabled reinforcements to reach the Middle East and gave the British Army at El Alamein time to build up superior forces and to defeat Rommel's Afrika Corps in that decisive battle.

The Normandy invasion itself that took place on June 6, 1944, is an example of the ground operations that could not have taken place without air superiority first being established over the invasion bridgeheads. On D-Day 1944, there were over 7,000 Allied sorties in or near the invasion sites, while fewer than 100 enemy aircraft were able to make their presence felt over the beachheads. Perhaps one of the clearest examples that a lack of air power could be a major contributing factor to defeat occurred at Stalingrad. In the early days of the battle, the Luftwaffe sustained significant support of the German armies, but this critically waned, and in the end, the Luftwaffe could not sustain this support and General Von Paulus was forced to surrender his armies to Russia.

This book provides a panoramic sweep of the role of air power in Europe in WWII and provides a wealth of detail about air actions both large and small.

MAJOR GENERAL RAMSAY D. POTTS, USAF RESERVE (RETD.)
ARLINGTON, VIRGINIA
JANUARY 2004

FOREWORD
Colonel Donald S. Lopez

IN THIS VOLUME OF the Aviation Century series, authors Ron Dick and Dan Patterson attempt the monumental task of covering aerial warfare as it was fought between 1939 and 1945. My own experience was with the 23rd Fighter Group in China, and I can testify to the vastness of the Pacific theater and the ferocity of combat with the Japanese.

Japanese aggression in Asia began with the occupation of Manchuria in 1931, followed by the invasion and capture of most of the northern and coastal China in 1937 marked by the infamous "Rape of Nanking." On December 7, 1941, Japan launched a sneak air attack on the U. S. Naval base at Pearl Harbor, Hawaii, destroying most of the surface forces of the Pacific Fleet except for the aircraft carriers. This freed Japan to attack much of Indo-China, the Malay Peninsula, the Philippines, and the Dutch East Indies. By April 1942, they had conquered most of this territory, including the British stronghold of Singapore, Java, the Philippines and were advancing in Burma.

The Japanese Air Force had been bombing with little or no opposition in Burma and especially in China where the Air Force was poorly trained and poorly equipped. In late 1941, the American Volunteer Group, later to achieve fame as the Flying Tigers, arrived in Burma. Within a short time, both in Burma and China, these American pilots flying Curtiss P-40s began to inflict heavy losses on the Japanese Air Force, which had seemed invincible up to that point. In just six months of combat, under the leadership of Colonel, later Major General Claire Chennault, they compiled the remarkable record of almost 300 Japanese planes destroyed in the air with the loss of only eight. Their achievements were a major shot in the arm to Allied morale since this was the first the Japanese had been defeated.

In May and June 1942, two naval battles took place that turned the tide of the war, the Battle of the Coral Sea and the Battle of Midway. These were the first naval battle in which the opposing fleets never came within sight of one another since all of the attacks on both sides were by aircraft.

In the Coral Sea the losses were about equal, but Japan abandoned its plan to invade Australia. At Midway, Japan lost four fleet carriers and hundreds of its top pilots while the U.S. lost only one carrier. Japan never fully recovered from this defeat.

The Allies decided on a two-pronged attack to retake the captured Japanese territories, with General Douglas MacArthur commanding in the South West Pacific area and Admiral Chester Nimitz the Central Pacific. There were many bloody battles over the next two years as the Allies moved inexorably forward on both fronts. MacArthur's goal was to retake the Philippines while Nimitz made amphibious landings on fanatically defended islands, finally capturing the Marianna islands of Guam, Saipan and Tinian, which were within B-29 range of the Japanese mainland. During the air combat in this area, known as "The Marianna's Turkey Shoot," more than 350 Japanese aircraft were shot down.

Following some fierce fighting, the islands of Iwo Jima and Okinawa were taken, and in desperation the Japanese resorted to kamikaze attacks on U.S. ships with some success. These two islands were used as fighter bases and emergency landing fields for combat-damaged B-29s engaged in the bombing of the Japanese mainland. The fire bombing of Japan in the spring and summer of 1945 devastated most of the major cities of Japan and virtually destroyed its industrial capability. In August atomic bombs were dropped on Hiroshima and Nagasaki, and on August 15, Japan surrendered, ending the largest war in history.

All of these aspects of the Pacific War and more are covered in this book. The comprehensive text is admirably illustrated both by archive images, many previously unpublished, and by Dan Patterson's dramatic new color photography.

COLONEL DONALD S. LOPEZ, USAF (RETD.)
DEPUTY DIRECTOR, NATIONAL AIR & SPACE MUSEUM
WASHINGTON, D.C.
FEBRUARY 2004

PHOTOGRAPHER'S PREFACE
Dan Patterson

SOME OF THE GREAT photographs that have defined the experience of World War II were made by some of the countless GIs who labored in combat with large and often unwieldy cameras to record the often amazing and historic events in which they were participating. The photographers who were also aircrew had the additional burden of high-altitude clothing, working in temperatures somewhere around 30 to 50 degrees below zero, and when the combat got hot there was nowhere to hide while the action was all around them. These men did their jobs and the images they left for us are compelling and unique. There had never been an air war like this before.

These soldiers also recorded the everyday life of the air force. They made images of the maintenance necessary to keep the warplanes in the air, the press release portraits to send home with stories of the exploits and accomplishments of their units. In England, early in the actions of the Eighth Air Force, when the rate of losses was high, some Bomb Group commanders had these unit photographers make photos of the replacement crews before their first mission. The loss rates for the newer crews was even higher, and the commanders at times did not even have time to know who these men were before they were lost in combat. These photographs served as the only visual record of their presence.

I got to know one of these men, Gunther "Dutch" Biel. He was a unit photographer with the 390th Bomb Group, Eighth Air Force, stationed at Framlingham in Sussex, northeast of London and close to the North Sea. I knew Dutch late in his life, and had been aware of him most of mine, as he was a friend of my dad's and a longtime commercial photographer here in Dayton, Ohio. Dutch was a larger-than-life figure whose reputation for quality photographs was huge as well as his ability to enjoy life. He always was willing to answer any questions I had and we developed a professional respect. Until he discovered my interest in aviation history and let me know about his

service, I never had any idea of his experiences in the Eighth Air Force. I learned an entire new side of Dutch Biel and began to understand why he didn't suffer fools very well.

Gunther Biel was born in Germany; his family moved to the U.S. in the 1930s as Hitler came to power. They settled in Dayton, Ohio, and "Dutch" developed an early interest in photography. When the U.S. entered the war, he enlisted and was sent to the Army Air Forces, who recognized his talents in photography and assigned him to the 390th Bomb Group, also appreciating his fluency in German. During his tour in the U.K., he flew thirteen missions over occupied Europe as a photographer. Dutch told me that he and other photographers we not welcomed by the aircrew, as his weight and the weight of his equipment meant that much less ammunition they could carry. At one point a German Ju 88 overflew the 390th's base at night. Thinking they were about to be attacked, the base had blacked out the field. The German pilot had seen enough of the field to land his bomber, and surrendered. Dutch was called to interpret, as the now captured pilot spoke no English and was very agitated. Fifty years later Dutch recounted this story to me. "The German pilot was pretty damn angry. He told me that he was trying to come over to our side, give us this new Ju 88, and they turned all the lights off. 'What are they trying to do, fucking kill me?'"

I spent some time with Dutch before he died; he allowed me access to all of his photos from the war, and there were a lot. Many of the historic images in this book whose subjects are B-17s and the Eighth Air Force are from his files. He underplayed his role in the war effort and said that he was just doing his job. I am not sure which of the famous images from the war he made — he wouldn't say — but his files were a rich treasure of images. So, for Dutch and the other men who fought the war with a camera, thank you.

Dan Patterson
Dayton, Ohio
January 2004

The navigator's table of the B-17 Shoo Shoo Baby, *now preserved at the USAF Musuem. The map in the photo was used by the crew of this airplane on an actual mission.*

INTRODUCTION
Air Vice-Marshal Ron Dick

IN 1939, WHEN THE curtain rose on the first act of WWII in Europe, none of the major powers had clear ideas on how air power might best be used to influence the conflict. The predominant interwar theories had suggested that strategic bombing would be air power's most significant role, with fleets of bombers assaulting the essential structure of an enemy nation, thereby undermining the morale of its people and destroying its capacity to wage war. Strongly represented though these ideas were, they were set aside by most nations. By 1939, only the United States and Britain were making serious attempts to establish strategic bombing forces. However, both had officially left behind the original concept of attacking civilian populations and were proclaiming that their bombers would strike with rapier-like precision at specific targets. Unfortunately, the Anglo-Americans had paid insufficient attention to the practicalities of such a policy. The available instruments of aerial destruction were soon shown to be inadequate for so demanding a task.

The strategic air power theorists were wrong, too, in that it proved impossible to bring an enemy nation to its knees by using air power alone. The relentless and increasingly heavy pounding of Germany from the air over six long years failed by itself to force a surrender, vital though it was as an element of the combined Allied offensive. Nevertheless, in 1945 the theorists felt justified in claiming that their principal conclusion had been correct; it was the timing of its application that had been wrong. They could point out that the practitioners had jumped the gun in 1939 by reaching for the ultimate goal before the necessary equipment was at hand. Once the intercontinental bomber and the atomic bomb arrived, the theory and the means to prove it came together. The destruction of Hiroshima and Nagasaki from the air finally broke the Japanese will to resist. Would that not still have been the case if such a Draconian response from the United States had been possible four years earlier, immediately after Pearl Harbor?

Wherever the truth of the strategic argument lies, it is undeniable that few of those involved in the use of air power in 1939 could have predicted the extent to which aircraft would contribute to the Allied victory. Interwar emphasis on the bomber had perhaps veiled the real versatility of air power. In the event, beginning in 1939–40 with the German "blitzkrieg" and the Battle of Britain, aircraft turned the tide of war again and again. Their worth was proved in many roles besides bombing, including such varied tasks as air defense, close support of ground operations, interdiction, airborne assault, maritime patrol, shipping strikes, transport support, and reconnaissance. The flimsy, unarmed and often scorned contraptions of 1914 grew into indispensable items of military hardware. In the process, they revolutionized the character of warfare and influenced every aspect of the worldwide struggle.

Ron Dick
Fredericksburg, Virginia
January 2004

> *For I dipt into the future, far as human eye could see,*
> *Saw the vision of the world, and all the wonder there would be;*
> *Saw the the heavens fill with commerce, argosies of magic sails,*
> *Pilots of the purple twilight, dropping down with costly bales;*
> *Heard the heavens fill with shouting, and there rain'd a ghastly dew*
> *From the nations' airy navies grappling in the central blue.*
>
> ALFRED, LORD TENNYSON, *LOCKSLEY HALL*, 1842

B-17 serial number 44-83868 flew with the U.S. Navy as a PB-1W until July 1956. Some years after its Navy career was over it was converted into a fire bomber and flown from Sequioa Field, California. In 1983, it was acquired by the Royal Air Force and restored by TBM Inc. as a B-17G of the 94th Bomb Group, USAAF. Author Ron Dick, with co-pilot/engineer Ken Stubbs and navigator Dave Fox, then flew it from California to the United Kingdom. It is now on display in the Bomber Hall of the RAF Museum, Hendon.

PART I

Europe and the Middle East

"Born of the spirit of the German airmen in the first World War, inspired by faith in our Führer and Commander-in-Chief, thus stands the German Air Force today, ready to carry out every command of the Führer with lightning speed and undreamed of might."
HERMANN GÖRING, REICHSMARSCHALL, AUGUST 1939

The large globe from the Pentagon office of General H. H. "Hap" Arnold, Chief of Staff of the United States Army Air Forces during World War II, now preserved at the USAF Museum, Dayton, Ohio. It is turned to show the European theater of operations, where the prewar borders of Germany are outlined in red grease pencil.

CHAPTER 1

Europe, 1939–41

THE GERMAN FORCES LAUNCHED across the Polish border on September 1, 1939, had been molded by the experiences of the Spanish Civil War. To perhaps a greater degree than any other nation, Germany had grasped the importance of combined arms operations, using highly mobile ground forces strongly supported from the air. Hermann Göring's bombastic order of the day to the Luftwaffe opened with a hint about the bravura part he had played in the origins of German air power and closed with a phrase bearing a prophecy that would prove to be only too accurate: "Born of the spirit of the German airmen in the First World War, inspired by faith in our Führer…thus stands the Luftwaffe today, ready to carry out every command of the Führer with lightning speed and undreamed of might."

Blitzkrieg

Swift attack and crushing strength were qualities that the Luftwaffe was to exhibit repeatedly in the months which followed. As the German armies rolled forward into Poland, the Luftwaffe quickly gained air superiority, waves of Messerschmitt Bf 109Es overwhelming the few obsolete open-cockpit PZL P.11 fighters that rose to oppose them. Over 360 Junkers Ju 87 dive-bombers gave close support to the ground offensive, blasting ways through the Polish defenses. Some 300 Heinkel He 111s and 400 Dornier Do 17s penetrated more deeply, attacking lines of communication and airfields, where they caught many Polish aircraft on the ground. Reconnaissance aircraft were everywhere, reporting on the disposition of Polish forces and identifying likely targets. Adolf Galland, in his book *The First and the Last*, recalled these heady days for the Luftwaffe: "After a few heavy strategic blows by the Luftwaffe, which gave the Germans absolute air supremacy, the splendid coordination and cooperation between the fast-moving mechanized army and the Luftwaffe began. It was something completely new in modern warfare. Everything went off with the precision of clockwork."

For this kind of warfare, termed "blitzkrieg" (lightning war), the German forces were ideally suited. The Luftwaffe was particularly well prepared, with experienced aircrew and modern equipment, and in Poland they outnumbered their opponents by about ten to one. Even so, they did not have it all their own way. The Poles fought magnificently, hurling their PZL P.11 fighters time and again against the Luftwaffe assault, and responding as best they could with daylight attacks on the advancing German troops in outdated PZL P.23B light bombers, which were easy meat for both the Bf 109s and the Wehrmacht's gunners. Hajo Herrmann, flying a Heinkel He 111 with KG4, had reason to remember the persistence of the

OPPOSITE PAGE
Developed from an original 1930 design by the talented Polish aerodynamicist Zygmunt Pulawski, the gull-winged PZL P.11 was the first fighter to face the Luftwaffe in combat in WWII.

Ahead of their time in 1930, the PZL series fighters were obsolescent by September 1, 1939. Hard though the Polish airmen fought, they were quickly overwhelmed by the Luftwaffe's superior numbers and more advanced technology. A surviving example of the PZL P.11C is exhibited at the Muzeum Lotnictwa Polskiego in Krakow, Poland. Its radial engine is a Bristol Mercury built under license in Poland by Skoda.

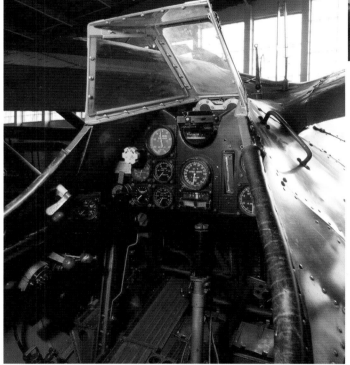

Polish airmen: "Still the fighter pilots in their PZLs came at us even more aggressively and courageously. One brave airman attacked me head on and shot out my port motor, so that I had to crawl homeward on one engine."

Courage alone was not enough, however. Over 100 Polish fighters were destroyed in five days, and within two weeks the Polish Air Force had effectively ceased to exist. The Luftwaffe, too, was licking its wounds; about 150 of the almost 1,400 German combat aircraft were lost, many to

ground fire. In the light of the campaign's crushing effectiveness, this was seen as a small price to pay.

In the initial stages of the war, German airmen adhered strictly to the principle of striking only at targets of military significance. As Polish refugees began to flood eastward, however, the Luftwaffe continued to attack the roads, and the horrors of aerial warfare were inflicted on thousands of civilians. More carnage followed in the Polish capital. With Poland overrun and the remnants of the Polish Air Force ordered to Rumania, resistance continued in Warsaw. To force an end to the conflict, the Luftwaffe was ordered to bomb the city, which endured a series of heavy indiscriminate attacks and suffered massive destruction. It was a portent of the total war the peoples of the world could expect in the years ahead.

The message to those intending to oppose Nazi ambition was only too clear — nothing would be allowed to hinder the advance of the Nazi cause. Combined with the deadly efficiency of the German military envelopment of Poland, this raised apprehensions all over Europe, especially in France and the United Kingdom, which, in accordance with their treaty with Poland, had declared war on Germany on September 3, 1939. The German leaders were naturally euphoric, a state of mind that blinded them to some aspects of their victory that would not necessarily

ABOVE *Small antipersonnel bombs are mounted under the P.11's high gull-wings.*
BELOW *Germany's Fuhrer, Adolf Hitler, and the Chief of the Luftwaffe, Hermann Göring, were exhilarated by the rapid success of the German forces in their assault on Poland.*
BELOW RIGHT *The Messerschmitt Bf 109E was much faster and more heavily armed than its Polish opposition.*

apply to future campaigns. The Ju 87 Stukas, for instance, had had a shattering effect, both physically and psychologically damaging, but it had been achieved against slight fighter opposition. The supreme confidence Göring had in his ungainly dive-bombers would be shaken when he launched them against a better-equipped foe.

The RAF Goes to War

On September 3, 1939, the day that Britain declared war on Germany, RAF bombers were in the air to attack the German Navy at Wilhelmshaven. All talk of using the bombers for strategic strikes against the enemy heartland was forgotten. Instead, the RAF found itself carefully restricted to operations that supported the navy and the army, or to the unconvincing business of dropping leaflets over German cities at night. In his history of the RAF at war, Denis Richards commented on: "The over-optimistic view of what might be achieved; the care taken to avoid harming the German civil population; the large proportion of aircraft failing to find the objective; the ineffective bombs and inconsiderable results; the expectation that crews would be skillful enough to find and bomb in atrocious weather a hotly defended target on the other side of the North Sea; and the unflinching courage with which the attacks were pressed home — all these were typical, not merely of September 1939, but of many months to come."

The attacks launched in bad weather on September 3 failed to find their targets. The next day the RAF tried again with fourteen Wellingtons and fifteen Blenheims. Some aircraft found and attacked ships, causing minimal damage while losing a quarter of the force. On September 29, eleven Hampdens set off across the North Sea but only six came back after a clash with Messerschmitt Bf 109s. Bad weather restricted operations for two months, but in December the

LEFT *Originally designed as a light bomber, some Bristol Blenheim Is were adapted for use as "heavy fighters." They proved to be inadequate performers in both roles.* RIGHT *In 1939, No. 19 Squadron was one of the few RAF squadrons to be equipped with Spitfire Is.*

future employment of RAF Bomber Command was decided in two encounters that brought home the realities of the air war with a vengeance. Of twelve Wellingtons attacking ships at Wilhelmshaven on December 14, five were shot down and another crashed on its return. Four days later, twenty-two Wellingtons entered enemy air space and fought a running battle with Bf 109s and Bf 110s. Twelve of the bombers were shot down and three more crashed in Britain. Bomber Command's chiefs began to question whether operating unescorted bombers against heavily defended targets in daylight was a sensible use of their resources.

Fury in Finland

In preparation for the assault on Poland, Germany had signed a nonaggression pact with the Soviet Union in August 1939. Soviet forces now moved forward to partition Poland with their German allies. However, the Soviets remained rightly suspicious of future German intentions and tried to bully Finland into giving up land for bases that could guard the Baltic approaches to Leningrad. The Finns refused, so on November 30, 1939, Soviet Tupolev SB-2 and Ilyushin DB-3 bombers struck at Helsinki and Viipuri, at the

same time launching almost a million men across Finland's frontiers. So began the Winter War, which proved to be a humiliating and very costly experience for the Soviets.

It was assumed, both by the Soviets and in the wider world, that little Finland would not be able to withstand the onslaught of such massive forces. In terms of air power alone, the Soviets had some 900 combat aircraft to take on a Finnish Air Force front line consisting of forty-one Fokker D.XXI and fifteen Bristol Bulldog fighters, seventeen Bristol Blenheim light bombers, thirty-four Fokker C.X reconnaissance aircraft, and six Junkers W.34 bomber/transports. However, the careful dispersal of this small force defeated early attempts to destroy it on the ground, and the vigor with which it defended Finnish skies surprised its enemies. Finnish fighter pilots began accumulating aerial victories, some of them at a remarkable rate. On January 6, 1940, Captain Jorman Sarvanto, flying his D.XXI, attacked a formation of seven DB-3s and shot down six of them in just four minutes. Another Finn despatched the seventh. The redoubtable Sarvanto went on to claim seven other victories during the Winter War.

Valiant and resourceful though they were, it was inevitable that the Finns would succumb to the superior strength of the Soviets eventually. The Winter War lasted 105 days before Finland had to concede. In the process, the Soviet Union had been forced to increase the number of aircraft being employed against Finland, transferring units from other regions to bring the totals to 1,500 in January and 2,000 in February. Reinforcements of Gloster Gladiators, Morane-Saulnier 406s, and Fiat G.50s arrived in Finland too late to affect the issue. When the fighting stopped, the Finns had lost sixty-two aircraft from all causes, but the Soviets had lost ten times that many, half of them in aerial combat and the rest to ground fire. In the ground war, the figures were even more startling. The Finns reported some 25,000 dead and 43,000 wounded. The Soviets had suffered far more severely, with 200,000 killed and 400,000 wounded. It had been a costly victory, and it had unforeseen consequences. Hitler and his generals drew the conclusion that the Soviet forces were ill-equipped, badly organized and poorly led. They assumed that they would not be capable of offering serious resistance to the German war machine.

Striking North

Before launching his major European campaigns, Hitler turned north. In a directive issued on March 1, 1940, he gave his reasons for so doing: "This operation should prevent British encroachment in Scandinavia and the Baltic. Further it should guarantee our ore bases in Sweden and give our Navy and Air Force a wider starting line against Britain." (Of the 15 million tons of iron ore used by Germany in the first year of the war, 11 million tons were mined in northern Sweden and shipped from the Norwegian port of Narvik.) In the early hours of April 9, 1940, German forces attacked Denmark and Norway. Junkers Ju 52/3m transports began operations by dropping paratroops on Danish coastal forts, bridges and the principal airfields near Aalborg. Denmark was overrun on the first day.

The invasion of southern Norway was more difficult, distance and the sea presenting challenges that could not be overcome without the Luftwaffe. The threat of serious opposition from Norwegian fighters was negligible, consisting as

A rare example of the Hawker Fury biplane fighter survives at Linkoping, Sweden. Shown in Finnish markings, it is powered by a radial engine instead of the more usual Rolls-Royce Kestrel.

HMS Courageous *seen from the rear cockpit of a departing Fairey Swordfish.* Courageous *was a sister ship of* Glorious. *Both aircraft carriers were sunk in the early days of WWII.*

it did merely of a single squadron of Gloster Gladiators. The composition of the air component for the operation (about 1,000 aircraft) therefore reflected the priority of moving troops and supplies by air in quantity. More than 500 Junkers Ju 52/3m transports were supported by 290 Heinkel He 111 and Dornier Do 17 bombers, forty Junkers Ju 87s, seventy reconnaissance aircraft, seventy Messerschmitt Bf 110s, and only thirty Messerschmitt Bf 109Es. After paratroops had captured the Norwegian airfields at Stavanger and Oslo, the Junkers Ju 52/3ms flew in a constant stream of men and supplies. (By the end of the Norwegian campaign, Junkers Ju 52/3ms had flown over 3,000 sorties to deliver 29,280 men, 259,300 gallons of fuel, and 2,376 tons of supplies.) Seaborne landings at various points around the Norwegian coast were generally unopposed, except in Oslo Fiord, where the resistance was spirited. Here and in a number of actions at sea, the Germans suffered significant naval losses, including the sinking of the cruiser *Königsberg* by Blackburn Skuas of the Royal Navy. This was notable as being the first time a major warship was sunk by air attack in an act of war; it was far from being the last. Sorties by RAF Bomber Command were less successful. On April 12, twenty-four Hampdens, thirty-six Wellingtons, and twenty-three Blenheims were sent unescorted to attack shipping and Norwegian coastal targets. They were intercepted by Luftwaffe fighters, and six Hampdens and three

Wellingtons were shot down. Taken together with the losses experienced during unescorted daylight raids in the first weeks of the war, this ensured that Hampdens and Wellingtons would from then on be restricted to night operations only.

British plans to establish a force in Norway had been overtaken by events, but in mid-April, British, French and Polish troops were landed at the ports of Namsos and Andalsnes, and at Harstad, 30 miles north of Narvik, in a belated attempt to bolster Norwegian resistance. It was a feeble and poorly planned intervention. In a decision suggesting that the air power lessons of Spain and Poland had escaped the Allied planners entirely, the troops were committed without supporting aircraft. Junkers Ju 87s demonstrated the folly of this arrangement immediately by reducing the port facilities of Andalsnes and Namsos to rubble. On April 23, the Allies tried to put things right by sending in eighteen Gloster Gladiators of the RAF's No. 263 Squadron. They were flown off the aircraft carrier HMS *Glorious* to land on the frozen Lake Lesjaskog, near Andalsnes. Again, the Luftwaffe was waiting. Although several of the raiders were shot down, within twenty-four hours the frozen lake had been rendered unusable and 263 Squadron was down to only five flyable aircraft. By the end of the month, they had none. German forces, secure under their air umbrella, controlled the southern half of Norway, and the Luftwaffe was making life so intolerable for the Allied forces at Andalsnes and Namsos that they were withdrawn.

Further north, at Narvik, it was not over quite so quickly. The Royal Navy had been successful in sinking the enemy ships in the area and isolating the small German occupying force, and some 25,000 Allied troops, advancing from Harstad, were intent on recapturing the port. By May 22, No. 263 Squadron, restored to full strength with new Gladiators, was back in Norway to provide air cover, this time reinforced by the Hurricanes of No. 46 Squadron. In the course of the next two weeks, the two squadrons between them accounted for thirty-seven enemy aircraft. On May 28, the Allies took Narvik, but it was a hollow victory. With the main German offensive in western Europe now in full cry, the decision had already been taken to withdraw from Norway.

On June 7, No. 263 Squadron took its eight remaining Gladiators back aboard HMS *Glorious*, but No. 46 Squadron was ordered to destroy its ten Hurricanes. None

The Fairey Battle light bomber entered service with the RAF in 1937. It was slow, cumbersome and lightly armed, and its shortcomings were ruthlessly exposed in combat. During the Battle of France, many Fairey Battle squadrons were effectively destroyed.

of the 46 Squadron pilots had ever landed on a ship and, in any case, it was thought impossible to land modern fighters without arrester gear on a carrier. However, the CO, Squadron Leader "Bing" Cross, elected to attempt "the impossible." All ten Hurricanes were flown out to HMS *Glorious* early on the morning of June 8, and all ten arrived safely on the deck. The pilots were jubilant. They had shown that modern fighters could be taken aboard ship and they had saved ten priceless fighters. Their jubilation was short-lived. That afternoon HMS *Glorious*, escorted by two destroyers, was surprised by the German battle-cruisers *Scharnhorst* and *Gniesnau*. In an extraordinary lapse that reflected the casual attitude of many senior naval officers of the time to the uses of air power, the captain of the carrier had not taken the precaution of launching air

patrols to cover his passage through the Norwegian Sea. The radar-directed gunfire of the German ships made short work of sending the carrier, the destroyers and the precious Hurricanes to the bottom of the ocean. In total, 1,474 officers and men of the Royal Navy and forty-one of the Royal Air Force died, including all but two of the pilots from 46 Squadron.

Western Europe Invaded

On May 10, 1940, German forces swept across their western frontiers in a whirlwind invasion of the Netherlands, Belgium, Luxembourg and France. Some seventy-five Wehrmacht divisions were supported by Luftflotten 2 and 3 of the Luftwaffe with about 4,000 aircraft. These included 1,260 fighters and 1,600 bombers. They were opposed on the Allied side by about 650 serviceable fighters and 400 bombers belonging to the air forces of France, Belgium, the Netherlands and Britain, but few of these were modern types. In addition, whereas the Luftwaffe was acting under a single national command and was able to concentrate its efforts to support the invasion plan, the Allied air forces had no such unity and were inconveniently dispersed. The French Armée de l'Air, in particular, had many units held in areas well away from the front. Some of the best French fighters, Dewoitine D.520s, were defending the Toulouse region, 400 miles to the southwest.

The Luftwaffe opened its campaign with a series of raids on twenty-two Allied airfields, and the ground offensive was given strong support by both bombers and transports. Paratroops seized vital airfields and bridges, and the "impregnable" Belgian fortress of Eben Emael fell to a spectacular assault by fifty-five glider-borne troops who landed on its roof. The forces of the Netherlands fought fiercely, but half of the air force's front-line strength was gone in twenty-four hours and the country was overwhelmed in just five days. In one of the great tragedies of the war, the heart of Rotterdam was destroyed by Heinkel He 111s (of KG54, the "Death's Head" Geschwader) even as surrender negotiations for the city were taking place. Hitler had authorized the attack to hasten the Netherlands' capitulation. There were 800 people killed and 80,000 made homeless because recall orders seeking to stop the raid were not received in time. Rotterdam joined Guernica and Warsaw in illustrating the frightful results of unleashing a bomber force against a civilian population. Its destruction also served as the catalyst that at last released RAF bombers from all restrictions, freeing them to

The Junkers Ju 87 "Stuka" acquired a fearsome reputation in the early days of WWII. Used by the Luftwaffe in combined offensives with the German army, and facing little effective opposition in the air, the Ju 87 was a terrifying and effective weapon. During the Battle of Britain, its limitations became apparent, and it was withdrawn after heavy losses. This example is preserved in the RAF Museum at Hendon.

attack targets inside Germany. On the night of May 11, in the first raid of the war on a German town, thirty-seven bombers took off to strike at targets in Mönchengladbach.

The Battle of France

Responding to the invasion, Allied light bombers made desperate attempts to stem the tide of the German advance. Both the Armée de l'Air and the RAF suffered fearful losses in the process. On May 10, thirty-two Fairey Battles first faced the impressive intensity of German light antiaircraft fire. Thirteen were shot down and every one of the others damaged. Six Bristol Blenheims, sent against the German held airfield of Waalhaven, ran into Bf 110s, and five of their number were lost. The following day, seven out of eight Battles were lost, four Blenheims out of eight were shot down and two more damaged, and all the Blenheims of No. 114 Squadron were put out of action on the ground. On May 12, things got even worse. Nine Blenheims of No. 139 Squadron attacked a German Army column on the road from Maastricht, and seven were shot down. Ten of twenty-four Blenheims failed to return from a raid on

Hurricane Scramble, *by Michael Turner. The Hurricanes of 85 Squadron operating from Merville in May 1940, during the Battle of France.*

bridges over the Maas River. Five Battles struck at the Albert Canal bridges and all five were lost. (In this action, a Battle of No. 12 Squadron, flown by Flying Officer D.E. Garland, pilot; Sergeant T. Gray, observer; and Leading Aircraftsman L.R. Reynolds, gunner, was shot down after pressing home an attack at low level under intense fire. Garland and Gray each received posthumous awards of the Victoria Cross, the first of very few to RAF personnel during WWII.) Six more were destroyed out of fifteen attacking in the Ardennes. On May 14, one of the most disastrous days ever for the RAF, seventy-one Battles were sent into action and forty shot down. Such a calamitous rate of loss quickly reduced the striking power of Allied air to negligible proportions.

At the same time, the Luftwaffe was giving lessons in the art of the blitzkrieg. On May 13, the German Army columns poured out of the Ardennes, aiming to cross the Meuse River between Sedan and Dinant. To prepare for a crossing, the Luftwaffe began pounding the French Army defenders, the Stukas and medium bombers attacking both the front-line troops and the areas immediately behind the battle zone. The results of this unceasing onslaught were profound. Headquarters lost touch with the forward units, and the men at the front became increasingly isolated and demoralized. Deprived of their command structure and terrified by the attentions of the ever-present Stukas, the French troops were unnerved. A German sergeant who witnessed the

bombardment from the other side of the Meuse gave a dramatic account of its effect: "[The attack of the Stukas] is one of the most powerful impressions of this war…. We can see the bombs very clearly. It becomes a regular rain of bombs that whistle down on Sedan and the bunker positions. Each time the explosion is overwhelming, the noise deafening. Everything becomes blended together; along with the howling sirens of the Stukas in their dives, the bombs whistle and crack and burst. A huge blow of annihilation strikes the enemy…"

The reputation of the Stuka, already established by its performances in Spain and Poland, now assumed legendary proportions. Stories of its terrifying capabilities went before it and were magnified in the telling. Dread of its appearance overhead became discernible in Allied troops, and that affected their performance on the battlefield. There was no denying that the Ju 87 Stuka was a formidable dive-bomber, able to deliver its weapons with an accuracy of 30 yards or less and, at this stage of the war, fitted with a siren to add to its powerful psychological effect. Not so readily apparent was its vulnerability. It was slow and had poor defensive armament, but in Spain, Poland and France it operated in ideal conditions. German air superiority was assured and serious opposition minimal. Its capacity to spread fear and wreak destruction was therefore almost unlimited. It would not always operate under such favorable conditions. In May 1940, however, the Stuka squadrons were at the height of their powers and there was no doubting the effect of their bombing. Their will to resist broken, many French soldiers fled or surrendered. A huge gap was torn in the French line, and the German armor raced through it toward the Channel, driving an enormous wedge between the British and French forces in Belgium and the rest of the French Army to the south.

RAF Fighters in France

To honor a prewar agreement, four Hurricane squadrons (Nos. 1, 73, 85 and 87) were deployed to France in September 1939. In response to requests from the French government, two more fighter squadrons (Nos. 607 and 615, equipped with Gladiators) were sent in November. Four more Hurricane squadrons (Nos. 3, 79, 501 and 504) crossed the Channel on May 10, the first day of the German offensive. At the same time, the two Gladiator squadrons were reequipping with Hurricanes. More frantic appeals from France led to the equivalent of two more Hurricane squadrons leaving the United Kingdom on May 13, to be used principally as replacements rather than reinforcements. By May 14, with the German armored columns racing across northern France, the French premier, Paul Reynaud, was pleading with Winston Churchill for ten more fighter squadrons.

British army commanders, pressed to the limit by the German advance, supported his appeal. Churchill was inclined to agree, but at this point the Commander-in-Chief of RAF Fighter Command, Air Chief Marshal Sir Hugh Dowding, intervened. In a meeting with the British War Cabinet on May 15, he presented his arguments for not deploying more fighter squadrons to France, where they were being consumed piecemeal in a battle of attrition. He held that Fighter Command's principal responsibility was the defense of British air space, and reminded the government of their acceptance of his estimate that fifty-two fighter squadrons were needed to do that effectively. Sending further squadrons to France in support of

Artifacts and a pilot's personal flying kit displayed on the tailplane of a Hurricane. From the left, an Irvin sheepskin-lined jacket, "Mae West" life vest and parachute harness. At right center, leather gauntlets. Below, a flying helmet fitted with goggles and an oxygen mask of chamois and fabric.

what he believed was a losing cause would seriously threaten the security of the United Kingdom.

The following day, Dowding put his convictions in writing in one of the most remarkable letters ever written by a C-in-C to his political masters. He first included another reminder of the fifty-two squadron minimum, and added a warning that Fighter Command had now been reduced to some thirty six squadrons. In his closing paragraphs he wrote:

> I must point out that within the last few days the equivalent of ten squadrons have been sent to France, that the Hurricane squadrons remaining in this country are seriously depleted, and that the more squadrons which are sent to France the higher will be the wastage and the more insistent the demands for reinforcements.
>
> I must therefore request that as a matter of urgency the Air Ministry will consider and decide what level of strength is to be left to the Fighter Command for the defence of this country, and will assure me that when this level has been reached, not one fighter will be sent across the Channel however urgent and insistent the appeals for help may be.
>
> I believe that if an adequate fighter force is kept in this country, if the Fleet remains in being, and if the Home Forces are suitably organized to resist invasion, we should be able to carry on the war single-handed for some time, if not indefinitely. But, if the Home Defence Force is drained away in desperate attempts to remedy the situation in France, defeat in France will involve the final, complete and irremediable defeat of this country.

Churchill, alarmed by news of the French collapse, went to Paris on May 16 to see for himself. He was deeply moved

"I realized just how lucky a fighter pilot is. He has none of the personalized emotions of the soldier, handed a rifle and a bayonet and told to charge. He does not even have to share the dangerous emotions of the bomber pilot who night after night must experience that childhood longing for smashing things. The fighter pilot's emotions are those of the duelist — cool, precise, impersonal. He is privileged to kill well. For if one must either kill or be killed, as now one must, it should, I feel, be done with dignity. Death should be given the setting it deserves; it should never be a pettiness; and for the fighter pilot it never can be."

RICHARD HILLARY, *THE LAST ENEMY*

by the French predicament and, despite Dowding's warning, sent back messages authorizing the transfer of four more squadrons, later adding another six. The War Cabinet, all too conscious of Dowding's arguments, was relieved to find that the practicalities of the situation in France, forced by the rapid German advance, made such generosity impossible. There were no longer the airfields to support another ten squadrons, so a compromise was reached. Three squadrons would fly from England to France each morning and another three would relieve them in the afternoon, returning across the Channel to their bases at the end of each day. It was to no avail. Hard though the fighter squadrons of the Armée de l'Air and the RAF fought, the Allies were overwhelmed. Dennis David of 87 Squadron remembered that "Whatever we did in the air, and no matter how many German aircraft we destroyed, it seemed to make no difference; the German forces kept advancing and seemed invincible." By May 19 the deployment of RAF fighters across the Channel was in reverse, and two days later only the remnants of Nos. 1, 73 and 501 Squadrons remained in France, retreating steadily westward toward the Atlantic coast ports, from where they eventually withdrew to the U.K. Meanwhile, dramatic events were taking shape on the Channel coast, near the Franco-Belgian border.

Dunkirk

By May 26, 1940, some 400,000 British and French troops were trapped with their backs to the sea in a small pocket round the port of Dunkirk. Much to the surprise of the Allies and the frustration of the German battlefield commanders, the Wehrmacht units that had pursued them there were standing back. Hitler, concerned that the armor of the Panzer divisions would become mired in the low-lying canal-ridden country near the French coast, and fearing the possibility of a French counterattack from the south, had agreed to Göring's suggestion that the

A pilot of the 21st century, Glenn Denney, recreates a scene from 1940. The young RAF men who fought the Battle of Britain were often rushed into combat with very little flying experience. The dark-colored Mae Wests worn were difficult to see in the waters of the English Channel, so many pilots painted theirs yellow. The Air Ministry took the hint and began manufacturing them in yellow.

the first time, the RAF was operating from its own bases and was able to concentrate its strength on the achievement of a single objective over one area. It was the first time, too, that significant numbers of Spitfires were committed to the battle alongside the Hurricanes. While the RAF fighters held center stage, Fleet Air Arm Skuas and Rocs played their part, Bomber Command Blenheims attacked German troop positions in daylight,

Luftwaffe should be allowed to pound the Allies into submission. During the pause in the ground offensive, the Allies did what they could to protect the Dunkirk pocket by setting up a defensive perimeter, and, in an operation code-named Dynamo, gathered together an armada of small ships on the British side of the Channel to attempt an evacuation.

On the evening of May 26, Operation Dynamo began. Hundreds of vessels — destroyers, ferries, tugs, launches, fishing boats, small sailing boats and almost anything else that would float — started shuttling across the narrow waters of the Channel to pick up the soldiers crowding the piers and beaches of Dunkirk. Waves of Luftwaffe bombers did their best to frustrate the evacuation, but the character of the air war had changed. For

and heavy bombers struck at road and rail communications during the hours of darkness.

The air battle over Dunkirk was fierce, with the Luftwaffe facing much stiffer opposition than before and unable to impose its accustomed superiority. Dynamo lasted from May 26 to June 4, and in that time RAF Fighter Command flew 2,739 sorties in support of the evacuation. The German bomber pilot Werner Kreipe wrote afterward: "The enemy fighters pounced on our tightly knit formations with the fury of maniacs…on this one day, out of twenty-seven planes in one wing eleven were put out of action. The days of easy victory were over. We had met the Royal Air Force head on." The Luftwaffe, nevertheless, did get through to the beaches and the ships, killing many soldiers and sinking six destroyers, five minesweepers, a hospital ship, and over 100 assorted

TOP *The restoration of this Hurricane, finished in the colors of the legendary legless fighter leader, Douglas Bader, was completed by Hawker Restorations in the year 2000. It is now a regular performer on the air show circuit.*

BOTTOM *A classic fighter aircraft, the Messerschmitt Bf 109E was a formidable opponent for the RAF during the Battle of Britain. Its most serious shortcoming was a lack of external fuel tanks. On internal fuel alone, the 109E could reach the London area from its French bases, but could stay there only a few minutes before being forced to turn for home.*

other vessels. They could not, however, stop the evacuation. By the time Dynamo ended on June 4, over 338,000 troops had escaped across the Channel. It was a deliverance made possible by the courage of the sailors, the discipline of the troops, and the determination of the airmen.

At the time, the soldiers did not appreciate the scale of the battle being fought far above them. Bombed and strafed by those Luftwaffe aircraft that reached Dunkirk, they saw few friendly fighters over the beaches and were angry at being left, as they believed, unprotected. Al Deere of 54 Squadron, shot down over the Belgian coast and trying to find his way back to the U.K., joined the masses of troops at Dunkirk and was surprised at his icy reception. A British major sneered, "For all the good you chaps seem to be doing over here you might as well stay on the ground." Churchill, concerned to put the record straight, told the House of Commons: "Wars are not won by evacuations. But there

was a victory inside this deliverance. It was gained by the Royal Air Force."

Operation Dyanamo cost the RAF 145 aircraft, of which ninety-nine were fighters. There were 132 Luftwaffe aircraft shot down. Taken together with the Battle of France, the losses suffered by both sides during the months of May and June had been surprisingly high. The Luftwaffe records show 1,401 aircraft destroyed by the Allies, including 477 medium bombers, 123 dive-bombers, and 371 fighters. The Armée de l'Air lost over 750 aircraft, and the RAF 959, among them 453 of Dowding's priceless fighters — 385 Hurricanes and 67 Spitfires. (Well over 100 of the Hurricanes lost in France were either destroyed on the ground or were under repair and had to be abandoned during the withdrawal.) Even more serious for the RAF was the loss of 915 aircrew of all categories, including 320 pilots killed and 115 taken prisoner.

This Messerschmitt Bf 109E is on display in the RAF Museum at Hendon.

SPITFIRE IIA

The Spitfire IIA flown by the Battle of Britain Memorial Flight is the oldest airworthy Spitfire in the world. It saw action during the Battle, survived the war at a gunnery school, and was restored to flying condition in 1967 for the movie *The Battle of Britain*. When Dan Patterson photographed this aircraft at RAF Coningsby in 1997, it was painted as *Enniskillen*, an aircraft provided by the Belfast Telegraph Spitfire Fund.

The Battle of Britain

"The battle of France is over. I expect that the Battle of Britain is about to begin. Hitler knows that he will have to break us in this island or lose the war. Let us therefore brace ourselves to our duties, and so bear ourselves that, if the British Empire and its Commonwealth last for a thousand years, men will still say: 'This was their finest hour.'"

Stirring words — and in the circumstances they needed to be. Hitler believed he had won his war in the west and that the British would behave rationally and negotiate a peaceful settlement. He had made no provision to cope with the possibility that the islanders might be stubborn. It

was not until July 2, 1940, in the face of continued British recalcitrance, that he even asked for a study of a possible invasion. On July 16, Hitler at last ordered his forces to prepare for such an invasion, which he set provisionally for mid-August. He called it Operation Seelöwe (Sea Lion). His hope remained, however, that Britain could be convinced that further conflict was unwise, and that a settlement could be forced by means of a Luftwaffe bombing campaign alone. In any event, it was agreed that an invasion could not be mounted unless the Luftwaffe could keep British warships from interfering, and could provide the necessary air support over the beachheads. This, Göring insisted, would

Achtung! Spitfire, *by Roy Grinnell. A Spitfire of 64 Squadron dives through a formation of Heinkel 111s during the Battle of Britain in 1940.*

not be a problem — once the RAF had been defeated. The essential prerequisite for the invasion of Britain was established, and the stage was set for a clash between air forces that would influence the whole course of the war.

Göring's opponent for the Battle of Britain, Sir Hugh Dowding, was one of the few senior airmen to have had serious reservations about strategic air power theories. For him, at least, it was not written that the bomber would always prevail, and he had devoted the prewar years to ensuring that Britain would have an effective defense against air attack. An integral part of his defensive system was a minimum of fifty-two fighter squadrons. After Dunkirk, he was down to thirty-six, of which only twenty-eight were combat ready, and only twenty-three had Hurricanes or Spitfires.

The Dowding system depended on first detecting an incoming raid by radar. The radar plot was passed by landline to Fighter Command Headquarters, and from there to the appropriate Group and Sector operations rooms. Once the raids penetrated inland, radar could no longer follow them, so the reporting was picked up by Observer Corps posts. The senior controller at Group scrambled and allocated fighters to raids as he thought best, and once they were airborne, control was passed to the Sector operations rooms at principal airfields to bring about the interceptions. The system was the best that could have been devised at the time, and it proved to be remarkably effective, especially as used by the commander of No. 11 Group, Air Vice-Marshal Keith Park, whose squadrons were in the front line, defending the southeast of England. The eventual outcome of the struggle owed much to his qualities as a battle commander. To Park's north, commanding No. 12 Group, was AVM Trafford Leigh-Mallory. Apart from defending eastern England, Leigh-Mallory's squadrons flew in support of 11 Group.

On the other side of the Channel, Göring was on the crest of a wave following the Luftwaffe's successes and he held immense political power. However, he was no general, and he had little idea of the nature or limitations of air power. Both he and Hitler were firmly wedded to the idea of the blitzkrieg using Stukas and fast light bombers, and

Göring saw the proposed invasion of the United Kingdom in terms of nothing more than a large river crossing. His principal commanders for the battle, however, were professionals. Hugo Sperrle had Luftflotte 3. Although he had a reputation to rival Göring's for enjoying the luxuries of life, he was experienced in the use of tactical air power and had commanded the Condor Legion in Spain. "Smiling" Albert Kesselring of Luftflotte 2 was one of the war's most resilient commanders. He went on to become C-in-C of German forces in Italy and then in the west during the closing months of the war.

These Luftwaffe men commanded complete air forces containing all the specializations — fighters, bombers, reconnaissance, air-sea rescue, and so on. Cooperation between these varied units was often poor. Fighter leaders hardly ever talked to bomber leaders, either on the ground or in the air. The RAF's functional arrangement simplified things on the British side of the Channel. Fighter Command had only one responsibility — the defense of U.K. airspace — and (with one notable exception) the elements of the command combined together well to achieve that single purpose.

RAF Fighter Command's principal weapons were the Hurricane and Spitfire. The workhorse of the battle was the Hurricane, which outnumbered the Spitfire by about two to one throughout. Inferior to the Luftwaffe's Bf 109 in speed, acceleration and rate of climb, it could out-turn its opponent and was a good steady platform for its eight .303-inch machine guns. The Spitfire was a fighter pilot's dream. Even in its original Mark I form, it was almost the Bf 109's equal for speed

A Spitfire apparently caught by a German photographer as it zooms by the nose of a Heinkel 111. The helmet of a Luftwaffe crewmember fills the foreground. If this is a real combat shot, the photographer was both extremely cool and very quick. Is it genuine?

The Heinkel He 111 formed the backbone of the Luftwaffe's bomber force at the outbreak of WWII. Production continued throughout the war: almost 7,000 in ten variants had been delivered by 1945. This example at the RAF Museum, Hendon.

and was as quick to accelerate. It was light on the controls and more than a match for the Bf 109 in maneuverability. A disadvantage for both RAF fighters was that their splendid Merlin engines were fitted with carburetors. In negative G maneuvers, this meant that the engine cut out until positive G was restored. German pilots soon found that they could gain temporary respite from pursuit by bunting down out of a fight, gaining a second or two while the Spitfire rolled to follow.

Another Merlin-engined fighter on the strength of Fighter Command when the Battle began was the Boulton Paul Defiant. Conceived as an aircraft capable of delivering Nelsonian broadsides at bomber formations, it was equipped with a four-gun turret aft of the cockpit and was without fixed forward-firing guns. Heavy and cumbersome, it proved incapable of defending itself against conventional fighters.

The Luftwaffe's principal fighter was the Messerschmitt Bf 109E, a classic single-seater, blooded in Spain and flown largely by battle-hardened pilots. In the early days it could claim to be faster than its RAF opponents. It was a steady gun platform and it had the advantage of having armament that included a 20 mm cannon. The Daimler Benz DB 601 engine was fuel injected and would not cut out under negative G. Effective though it was in the hands of pilots such as Adolf Galland and Werner Mölders, however, the Bf 109 had weaknesses. The cockpit was cramped and its canopy offered little headroom; the controls were not well harmonized and became extremely heavy as speed increased. Perhaps even worse was the narrow, spindly undercarriage; because of it, more Bf 109s were lost in landing and taxiing accidents than in combat in the course of the war. However, an even more serious shortcoming was the limited fuel capacity, which allowed the Bf 109 only a few minutes of combat over London even when operating from bases near the French coast.

Three medium bomber types were available for the assault on Britain, of which the He 111 was the most numerous, the Do 17 the least effective, and the Ju 88 the fastest and most versatile. Göring's unwavering faith in the Ju 87 dive-bomber, so feared as an element of blitzkrieg, was to be tested in the summer of 1940. His favorite was slow, and its single rearward-facing gun was inadequate protection against the RAF's fighters, who regarded it as easy meat. The Luftwaffe was also to be disappointed in its long-range escort fighter, the twin-engined Messerschmitt Bf 110. While the basic idea of the long-range escort fighter was sound, the realization of it in the Bf 110 was not. In combat with modern single-engine fighters, it proved sluggish and poorly armed defensively. Formations of Bf 110s were often driven to flying in defensive circles and relying on help from the Bf 109s. Flown in roles for which it was not primarily intended, as a night fighter and a low-level fighter-bomber, the Bf 110 was later more successful.

At the beginning of July, Dowding had 532 serviceable single-engined aircraft available and some 1,200 pilots. Just 347 Hurricanes and 160 Spitfires were ready to go. He did not think it was enough, but it was better than the two Hurricane squadrons he had had at the time of the Munich appeasement less than two years before. On the other side of the Channel, Luftflotten 2 and 3 had 1,935 aircraft serviceable between them. Of these, 769 were twin-engined bombers, 248 were dive-bombers, 168 were Bf 110s, and 656 were Bf 109s. Another 32 Bf 110s and 95 bombers were available from Luftflotte 5 in Norway.

In the official British view, the first phase of the Battle of Britain opened on July 10 and lasted until August 7. Called Kanalkampf by the Luftwaffe, it consisted of attacks on convoys in the Channel or coastal targets, and of fighter sweeps over the English coast aimed at tempting the RAF into an attrition battle. Dowding and Park were not interested. RAF squadrons were ordered to avoid combat with German fighters whenever possible. The RAF's first priority was the bomber force. It was all a prelude to the real battle, but a number of lessons were learned in July by both sides.

The RAF found out the hard way that its tactics were out of date. Most squadrons were still trying to fight in the old-style close formations. To say the least of it, this was foolish. In close formation, only the leader's eyes are of any use for spotting the enemy, and maneuvering is ponderous. The Luftwaffe had long since adopted the loose "finger four" for its fighters, and had thereby gained mutual support, flexibility and maximum impact for their attacks. Then there was the demise of the RAF's aerial battleship. On July 19, nine Defiants of 141 Squadron were patrolling over the Channel. They were jumped by ten Bf 109s led by Hannes Trautloft, who sensibly attacked from below and behind. The Defiants broke and tried to bring their turret guns to bear, but within the first sixty seconds, four of them fell into the Channel in flames. Two more crashed on the cliffs, and a seventh was so badly damaged that it never flew again. One Bf 109 was shot down by Hurricanes that arrived just in time to save 141 Squadron from complete extinction. The RAF took the hint and Defiants were withdrawn from daylight combat. Another more serious problem was also making itself felt. The RAF's experience level was declining noticeably. During the Battle of France and the skirmishing of July, no fewer than eighty squadron and flight commanders had been lost.

On the other side, the Luftwaffe had it confirmed that the Bf 110 was useless against modern single-seat fighters, and any lingering hopes that day bombers might not

A Bf 109E that became part of the harvest in September 1940. Curious British servicemen examined the almost intact machine.

need fighter escort were shown to be false. It dawned on the Luftwaffe that Bf 109s would be needed in greater numbers to cover more tasks. In operations against the United Kingdom in daylight, where the Bf 109 could go, so could others. Outside the Bf 109's limited radius of action, it was hazardous to fly. This single fact multiplied the Luftwaffe's difficulties considerably, hamstringing German operational capabilities before battle was seriously joined.

On August 1, 1940, Hitler finally issued a directive that the Luftwaffe was to "destroy the British air force as quickly as possible." So Adlerangriff (Attack of the Eagles) was devised, and Göring settled on August 13 as Adler Tag (Eagle Day). His order to the Luftwaffe included the remark: "Within a short period you will wipe the British air force from the sky."

Dowding had a copy of that message as quickly as Kesselring had his. Even at this stage of the war, British eavesdropping was very efficient. Most of the Luftwaffe's signals traffic was being read, and the RAF had a fairly accurate picture of the Luftwaffe and its operations throughout the battle. The Luftwaffe's intelligence on the RAF, however, was poor. On July 16, Göring's staff presented an evaluation of the RAF that correctly estimated the front-line strength of Fighter Command. However, it seriously underestimated the production capacity of British industry, and when this error was combined with the natural over-estimation of kills in combat that always occurs, the result was the daily expectation that the RAF was at death's door. This increasingly confident prediction

was freely transmitted to the Luftwaffe's squadrons, producing a rising feeling of disillusionment among the aircrew. A common sarcasm of the time was contained in the report of a bomber crew during the latter part of the Battle. "Crossed the Kent coast at 5,000 meters," it said. "Promptly intercepted once more by the RAF's last fifty fighters." German intelligence summaries did not even mention the RAF's defense system. There was nothing about radar stations, operations rooms or the reporting network. Indeed, when the Luftwaffe worked out that the RAF squadrons were being controlled, they drew the wrong conclusion. The system was inflexible, they said, and could easily be swamped. They even suggested that such close control made it impossible to concentrate powerful forces at any particular point. That was wrong, as the Luftwaffe was to find out.

On August 12, the day before Adler Tag, an effort was made to do something about those puzzling radar stations. Raids were launched against the towers and their accompanying buildings, and several more were directed against forward airfields. Particularly effective precision strikes were delivered by Bf 110 fighter-bombers, and their efforts were largely responsible for considerable damage done to four radar sites and Manston airfield. However, German signals units noticed that transmissions from the radar stations hardly missed a beat. The Luftwaffe drew false conclusions from that. They assumed that the radar stations were too difficult to attack effectively and they did little to follow up. Actually, the radar units were lucky. Their control rooms were exposed above ground, but they had, for the most part, escaped serious damage. Curiously, having made an incorrect assumption about their capacity to hurt the radar stations, the Luftwaffe made another by going to the other extreme over airfields. The damage inflicted on

Intended as a long-range escort fighter, the Messerschmitt Bf 110 was no match for the Spitfires and Hurricanes of the RAF. Caught by these single-engined fighters, Bf 110 formations were often forced to fly in defensive circles, or had to rely on their smaller cousins, the Bf 109s, for protection.

The Boulton Paul Defiant was an aberration in fighter design, conceived for attacks against bomber formations with little regard for the problem of coping with escorting enemy fighters. Equipped with a heavy four-gun turret but no forward-firing guns, it was incapable of defending itself against the Luftwaffe's Bf 109s and was withdrawn from daylight operations.

Manston was seen to be great. The base was left apparently in ruins, covered in a cloud of smoke and with its airfield pockmarked by craters. The Luftwaffe commanders drew a line through Manston and wrote "destroyed" against it. In fact, following Herculean efforts from the base personnel, Manston was operational again the following day.

The Luftwaffe was not alone in failing to appreciate the need for following up attacks. If a target was struck but not destroyed, it was deemed too difficult and left alone. If it was apparently hurt badly, it was said to be destroyed, and so, again, it was not put down for re-attack. Neglecting the need for follow-up attacks was a serious error, destined to be repeated by other air forces.

Adler Tag dawned with fog covering the Luftwaffe's bases. Göring himself issued a postponing order. One bomber wing did not get it. At 05:00 hours, seventy-four Do 17s of KG2 took off from France for targets in the Thames estuary. Their Bf 110 escort got off, too, and joined the Dorniers over the French coast. The Bf 110s now got a recall on their radios, but the Dorniers did not have that frequency, nor any common radio channel by which the fighters could contact them. After flying some fairly high-spirited maneuvers across the bomber lead's bows in an effort to make him turn back, the Bf 110s gave up and went home. The Dorniers plodded on, protected to some extent by the cloud cover, and succeeded in bombing their targets. However, five of the bombers were shot down and five more struggled home badly damaged and with casualties. The Luftwaffe's poor communications had let them down.

HURRICANE

Sydney Camm's classic fighter, the Hurricane, rebuilt to flying condition by Hawker Restorations and finished in the markings of Douglas Bader, the Duxford fighter leader, accompanied by a typical fighter pilot's car, a 1927 Bentley. In the cockpit, the firing button is prominent on the spade grip joystick. This shot was taken at the Shuttleworth Collection. Archive photographs show armorers rearming a Hurricane after combat — four of the eight machine guns can be seen in the open gun-bay of the port wing — and pilots running to their aircraft in response to a "scramble" order.

Dennis David, seen here with the Hurricane I *at the RAF Museum, Hendon, in 1999, was a fiery young Welshman in 1940. He was a Hurricane pilot with No. 87 Squadron in the Battles of France and Britain, achieving twenty-one aerial victories.*

Adler Tag finally dawned in the afternoon, at 1530, when the mists had cleared, and the Luftwaffe flew 1,485 sorties by the end of the day. Raids were flown against targets all over the south of England, and several airfields were hit hard by Stukas. At Detling, in Kent, twenty-two aircraft were destroyed on the ground. It was claimed as a great success, but in the context of the effort to defeat Fighter Command, it was meaningless. Luftwaffe intelligence had struck again. A glance at the German target lists for the period shows that they did not know which were fighter airfields and which were not. Detling was a Coastal Command airfield, and the aircraft destroyed were of little consequence to the outcome of the Battle.

For all their efforts, the Luftwaffe achieved very little on Adler Tag, and it cost them thirty-four aircraft. Göring was pleased, however. German crews claimed to have destroyed eighty-eight RAF aircraft, including seventy Spitfires and Hurricanes. Unfortunately for the Luftwaffe, the actual RAF loss had been thirteen, with just three pilots killed. Such inflated claims in the confusion of battle are understandable, and were common to all air forces. In aerial combat, aircraft are often shot at by more than one person, and each man claims the victory as his. During the Battle of Britain, the Luftwaffe's claims were more exaggerated than the RAF's because there were many gunners in the bomber formations. The problem for the Luftwaffe was that, in believing their inflated figures, they deluded themselves into a daily expectation of victory, and so fell into a downward spiral of depression when the victory did not occur. RAF pilots, on the other hand, felt only fierce satisfaction. They did not expect to achieve the complete destruction of the Luftwaffe forces ranged against them. They knew they were outnumbered, and their losses were made bearable by the thought that they were giving more than they got.

The second phase of the battle lasted until August 23. This was the period when Göring had the aim right — the destruction of Fighter Command in the air and on the ground. Two days were particularly significant — August 15 and 18. Forewarned by intelligence, Dowding was ready for the Luftwaffe's maximum efforts on both days. On August 15, Göring took advantage of good weather to launch all three Luftflotten against the United Kingdom

Pete Brothers flew as a flight commander with Nos. 32 and 257 Squadrons during the Battle of Britain. By mid-September 1940, he had eleven aerial victories to his credit, eight of which were against Luftwaffe fighters.

(Luftflotten 2 and 3, plus 5 from Norway). It was wrongly believed that the RAF was concentrated in the south, and that the north would be open for Luftflotte 5's attack. Luftflotte 5's bombers, with only a Bf 110 escort, ran into a veritable hornet's nest and were cut to pieces. Unable to cope with Hurricanes and Spitfires, the Bf 110s fled, and the bombers struggled on to suffer a loss of almost 20 percent. One Hurricane was slightly damaged. Luftflotte 5 withdrew in confusion across the North Sea — and from the battle. The lesson about operating without Bf 109s was forcibly driven home.

In the south, the Luftwaffe had more success. In a succession of raids with large numbers of aircraft, severe damage was done to a number of airfields and an aircraft factory. On occasion the defending squadrons were overwhelmed by sheer numbers. By the end of the day, the

ABOVE *Pilots of No. 92 Squadron display their Battle of Britain scoreboard in September 1940.*
LEFT *"Sailor" Malan, a South African, was an outstanding and implacable fighter leader for the RAF. His attitude to the enemy was encapsulated in his statement that he "preferred to send bombers home shot to pieces and full of dead and dying." It sent a message to the Luftwaffe that was difficult to forget.*

Luftwaffe had flown over 2,000 sorties to Fighter Command's 974. Losses were in a similar ratio — seventy-one to twenty-eight, with twelve RAF pilots killed. It was also apparent that the RAF pilots were getting to the bombers. Only six of the seventy-one Luftwaffe aircraft shot down were Bf 109s. It should be remembered also that many of the bombers that did make it back were carrying dead and wounded men. "Sailor" Malan, one of the RAF's most outstanding fighter leaders, went so far as to say that he preferred to send bombers home shot to pieces and full of dead and dying. He believed it sent a message to the Luftwaffe that they would find difficult to forget. Churchill was much encouraged by the day's results, commenting that "Dowding's generalship must be regarded as an example of genius in the art of war."

On August 18, a cloudless summer Sunday, the Luftwaffe delivered several tremendous blows against principal airfields. Kenley and Biggin Hill, both vital sector stations, were hit by coordinated raids from high and low level, and hangars and many station facilities were destroyed. The Bf 109 escort for these raids was massive, and the defenders were often outnumbered by as many as five to one in the air. Many were caught on the ground between sorties, and No. 615 (County of Surrey) Squadron was effectively eliminated when it lost four Hurricanes in the air and six more on the ground during the few minutes of the attack on Kenley. One Bf 109 pilot, Gerhard Schöpful, could hardly believe his luck. He caught No. 501 Squadron's Hurricanes climbing out over Kent in the RAF's old-fashioned formation. He came at them out of the sun and from the rear and shot down four Hurricanes in less than two minutes. He was so close to the fourth one that his aircraft was damaged by debris and he had to break away. Incredibly, 501 Squadron never saw him from start to finish.

The other side of the coin was the havoc wreaked on the massed Stukas that struck at airfields further west. The Luftwaffe War Diaries recorded that thirty Junkers Ju 87s were either destroyed or damaged beyond repair. It was too high a price to pay, and Göring reluctantly withdrew his Stukas from the battle. In doing so, he suffered a defeat for no gain because, yet again, the airfields attacked by the Stukas did not belong to Fighter Command.

On August 18, the RAF lost thirty-five fighters in combat, and the Luftwaffe sixty aircraft, over thirty of which were bombers. The attacks on the Luftwaffe's bombers were beginning to tell — on both sides of the Channel. RAF fighter pilots felt exposed to the attacks of their Luftwaffe counterparts while charging through to the bombers, and Göring decided that every raid had to have at least twice as many Bf 109s as it had bombers. The German fighter pilots, for very good tactical reasons, preferred to escort their charges loosely. To ensure the maximum advantage over the RAF's fighters, they needed height, speed and the freedom to pounce when they chose. The bomber pilots did not see it that way. They protested that they were not being escorted closely enough, and pointed to their losses as evidence of that fact. Over the protests of fighter leaders such as Mölders and Galland, Göring agreed with the bombers. He criticized the fighter units for not doing their job, and ordered not only that the bombers were to be more heavily escorted in future, but that a large proportion of the fighter force would fly closed up to the bombers at the same height and speed. The fighter pilots were not amused.

After a short lull brought on by the weather, the Luftwaffe launched a furious assault in an all-out attempt to force the RAF to its knees. This phase of the battle lasted from August 24 until September 7. During these two weeks, the Luftwaffe launched thirty-three major raids, twenty-four of them against airfields, many of which were badly damaged and forced to operate under makeshift arrangements. Lost were 295 Spitfires and Hurricanes and another 171 were badly damaged. Only 269 replacements arrived. However, the real nightmare for Dowding was the pilot problem. In two weeks, 103 pilots were killed and 128 wounded. A squadron's official complement of pilots was twenty-six. By September 6, they were down to an average of nineteen, and there were no experienced replacements. New squadrons, posted in from

> *My TEN RULES for AIR FIGHTING*
>
> 1. *Wait until you see the whites of his eyes.*
> 2. *Fire short bursts of 1 to 2 seconds and only when your sights are definitely "ON."*
> 3. *Whilst shooting think of nothing else; brace the whole of the body; have both hands on the stick; concentrate on your ring sight.*
> 4. *Always keep a sharp lookout. "Keep your finger out"!*
> 5. *Height gives you the initiative.*
> 6. *Always turn and face the attack.*
> 7. *Make your decisions promptly. It is better to act quickly even though your tactics are not the best.*
> 8. *Never fly straight and level for more than 30 seconds in the combat area.*
> 9. *When diving to attack always leave a proportion of your formation above to act as top guard.*
> 10. *INITIATIVE, AGGRESSION, AIR DISCIPLINE, and TEAM WORK are words that MEAN something in Air Fighting. Go in quickly — Punch Hard — Get out!*
>
> ADOLPHUS G. "SAILOR" MALAN,
> RSAAF, AUGUST 1941

At the Imperial War Museum's airfield at Duxford, the station operations room has been restored to the way it was for the Battle of Britain. The plotting table is covered with a map of southern England marked with the Fighter Command group and sector boundaries. Counters showing the position and strength of enemy raids and RAF squadrons are on the table. Note that the room is above ground, so the windows are taped to provide some protection from flying glass if bombs fall nearby.

the north, were full of raw young men who could barely fly their aircraft. No. 501 Squadron, hardened by weeks in the front line, lost nine aircraft and four pilots during these two weeks. No. 253 Squadron, newly arrived, lost thirteen aircraft and nine pilots in *one* week.

When any organization functions under such enormous pressures, it is inevitable that the strain will show. Things will go wrong and there will be recriminations as to why. This was the case in Fighter Command. Statistically

living on borrowed time, many RAF pilots had the impression that they were being fed piecemeal into the battle and that they were predestined to fight heavily outnumbered on every occasion. There is a lot of truth to that, but there were good reasons for it. The proximity of 11 Group to the enemy meant that Park had to react quickly to counter a threat. He also had to guard against feints and follow-up raids by holding squadrons in reserve. As a result, he had no time to assemble large fighter formations, and he could never launch all his squadrons at once. History suggests that Park was right, but 12 Group's commander, Leigh-Mallory, was convinced that Park had got it wrong. He believed that every effort should be made to confront the Luftwaffe with overwhelming strength as often as possible. This was the "Big Wing" theory, promoted by 12 Group fighter leaders who were chafing at being used most of the time as a covering force for 11 Group's stations when their squadrons were in action. Douglas Bader at Duxford wanted his wing of five squadrons to be launched early and used as a single instrument. He said that he would rather get properly organized and attack bombers on their way home than commit single squadrons in an effort to break up raids before they bombed. The argument went on raging on long after the battle, but on balance, events support the view that Park had the tactics right. Certainly, 12 Group's methods of operating caused him some heartache at the time. More than once, Park claimed, 11 Group stations had been left uncovered and attacked when 12 Group had been asked for support. The Duxford Wing had confused 11 Group controllers by appearing unannounced in the south and being reported as another big raid. Bader's insistence on gaining maximum height before engaging often meant that the Duxford Wing became embroiled in a purely fighter battle with the top cover Bf 109s — just what Dowding did not want to happen.

At this stage, there were still many British people who expected a German invasion of Britain, and there were some extraordinary last-ditch measures under active consideration. Light aircraft, such as the RAF's primary trainer, the de Havilland Tiger Moth, were to be given racks so that they could bomb enemy troops attempting a landing. One Tiger Moth was fitted with a scythe-like blade known as a "paraslasher" for cutting paratroops' canopies as they descended to earth, and another, known as the "human crop-sprayer" used a tank fitted in the front cockpit connected to powder dispensers under the wings. The tank was to be filled with "Paris Green," an extremely poisonous insecticide. Low-flying Tigers were to dust the German troops as they waded ashore.

The turning point, and the decisive phase of the battle, began on September 7. On the night of August 24/25, a Heinkel He 111 crew got lost and dumped its bombs on the City of London. This was strictly against Hitler's

Undercarriage and flaps down, two Spitfires return to base after combat.

specific orders, but accidents will happen. The shockwaves of those explosions echoed all the way to Hiroshima. Churchill immediately ordered a reprisal raid on Berlin, and the following night, eighty-one aircraft of Bomber Command scattered their bombs over that part of Germany. Hitler ranted about paying back the British for terror bombing and Göring smarted with embarrassment. He had, after all, gone so far as to say that "No enemy aircraft will ever fly over the Reich." As a result, Hitler lifted his ban on bombing London, and Göring took the hint. Encouraged by Kesselring, who maintained that London was the one target the RAF would sacrifice itself to preserve, Göring ordered a massive attack on the London docks for September 7.

This was to be the start of the final push. Göring was confident that the RAF really was down to fewer than 300 fighters, and he arrived on the French coast to gaze across at the cliffs of Dover and watch his air armada sally forth to victory. He announced grandly: "I have taken personal command of the Luftwaffe's battle." It was all coming together at once. The Channel ports were filling with invasion barges, the German army was ready to use them, and the RAF was about to be defeated. By the end of the day, Göring had every reason to believe that it was indeed all going to happen. The Luftwaffe had done well. Over 300 bombers hemmed in by an escort of 600 fighters hit East

Developed from the unsuccessful Blenheim I, the Blenheim IV was a more effective aircraft. It sported a longer nose, had more powerful engines and was more heavily armed. The Blenheim IV remained in service with RAF Bomber Command squadrons until 1942, when it was replaced in the front line by the Douglas Boston and the de Havilland Mosquito.

London almost unhindered. The RAF fighters had been positioned to defend their airfields as usual, and the Luftwaffe reached London almost without opposition. Those RAF squadrons that did make contact were impressed by the size of the German formations and had difficulty in penetrating the immense fighter screen to get at the bombers. London burned, and that night 250 more bombers came to stoke the fires. Göring was well satisfied and said confidently: "They have had enough."

The truth was that both sides were showing considerable wear and tear. Dowding's pilot establishments and aircraft reserves were at their lowest ebb. However, they were not nearly so low as the German leaders thought — and the shifting of the Luftwaffe's aim to London was a bad mistake. With the pressure removed from its airfields and command centers, Fighter Command recovered rapidly. On September 9 and 11, the Luftwaffe again struck at London in strength — at least, Luftflotte 2 did. Luftflotte 3 was now bombing London by night only. The defenses were ready for them, and many bomber formations were broken up or turned away before they reached London. The RAF fighters suffered at the hands of the massive escorts, but there was a glimmer of light at the end of the tunnel.

It is generally accepted in Britain that the glimmer became a beacon on Sunday, September 15. On a sunny autumn day, Luftflotte 2's weary bomber squadrons once more dragged themselves toward London. They had again been told that the RAF could not last more than a few days. They were met by a rejuvenated and full strength 11 Group, and the bombers were disintegrated as an organized force by a series of massive head-on attacks. At the climax of the action, with the Luftwaffe already in disarray, Bader's Duxford Wing appeared, and for once there was no argument about its impact, particularly in the minds of the German airmen. They had been told that the RAF was on the verge of defeat; they had suffered a savage mauling at the hands of an apparently endless stream of 11 Group squadrons; now they were confronted by another huge formation of Hurricanes and Spitfires. Their world was turned upside down. The boundless optimism of July gave way to despair.

There were other big days when fierce battles were fought over southern England before the Luftwaffe finally abandoned its daylight offensive, but it was on

In 1940, Hitler and Göring were exhilarated by the fall of France and confident that Britain could be forced into submission.

the skies of Britain since the Luftwaffe continued to attack by night. This misses the point. The threat was invasion. To defeat the threat, the RAF only needed *not to lose.* Fighter Command's continued existence was enough to ensure Britain's survival. The cost to both sides was grievous. The RAF claimed 2,700 German aircraft. The real figure was closer to 1,700. The Luftwaffe claimed over 3,000 RAF fighters. They actually destroyed 915. Such bald statistics can only give a general idea. They take no account of aircraft damaged, aircrew wounded, RAF pilots shot down but unhurt — nor do they say anything about RAF losses elsewhere, in Bomber and Coastal Commands, during this period.

Whatever the physical damage, both sides knew they had been engaged in a struggle of epic proportions; a struggle in which the Luftwaffe, despite the courage and determination of its aircrew, did not prevail. The irony may be that the Luftwaffe was given a task that was always beyond its capabilities. It is difficult to imagine that the Luftwaffe could have destroyed Fighter Command without destroying itself in the process. Mutual immolation was avoided by Hitler's turn to the east. Fighter Command was triumphant, and yet its victorious commanders, Dowding and Park, were immediately removed from their posts. Looked at dispassionately, their departure was perhaps justifiable — both were exhausted — but it was done in a manner that reflects little credit on those who brought it about. Although laurels for Dowding and Park were eventually forthcoming, they were long delayed, and that was shameful.

Churchill was jubilant. For the first time, the German military machine had been brought up short. People all over the world began to wonder if it could possibly be that Churchill had been right when he said: "Hitler knows that he will have to break us in this island or lose the war." Well might he say in the House of Commons: "Never in the field of human conflict was so much owed by so many to so few."

September 15 that a decision was reached. The RAF claimed 185 aircraft shot down; a vast, if understandable, overestimate, reduced to sixty by later research. The figure was unimportant. The events of the day exhilarated Fighter Command and the British people. Confidence radiated from the island, and the Luftwaffe licked its wounds. On the other side of the Channel, Hitler took it all in and postponed Operation Seelöwe indefinitely. He dispersed the invasion fleet and settled for a night offensive against British cities. Then he turned to studying maps of the Soviet Union.

(German sources do not attach any particular significance to September 15. The period from September 6, 1940, to May 10, 1941, is regarded as one phase of the Luftwaffe's assault on Britain, involving bombing operations by day and night against the British economy and retaliatory strikes on British cities.)

It has been claimed that it was not a complete victory; that the Luftwaffe had been exhausted and repulsed but not defeated. The RAF could not yet claim complete control of

The Blitz

Repulsed by day, the Luftwaffe sought to impose Hitler's will on the British people by continuing the assault at night. During the hours of darkness the German bombers were almost immune. The RAF's night-fighting techniques had hardly progressed since WWI, and interceptions of enemy aircraft relied more on luck than judgment. Night fighter squadrons were equipped initially with Blenheims and the unfortunate Defiants, hastily diverted from their daytime disasters. Toward the end of 1940, these were joined by some Hurricane squadrons, including No. 85, commanded by Peter Townsend. He later wrote that he was "dumbfounded" that he should be asked "to transform 85 from a seasoned and successful day fighter squadron into a specialized night-fighter squadron." They faced, he said, an "almost hopeless task, lacking as we did the proper equipment, above all airborne radar and an effective armament." He might have added that, in 1940, there was no possibility of being helped to find the enemy by Ground Controlled Interception (GCI) radar. The Fighter Command system then looked only outward, over the sea.

The Luftwaffe's night bombers, on the other hand, did have help in the form of three navigation and bombing aids, all of which relied on radio beams from ground stations. Knickebein could be used by any bomber fitted with the Lorenz blind approach equipment. More specialized aids were X-Gerät, installed in the He 111H-4s of KGr 100, and Y-Gerät, carried by those of KG 26. Both the X- and

A comparison of the different calibers of bullets and shells most often used in aerial warfare in WWII gives some idea of the impact they made on their target. The rifle-caliber .303 at the top is noticeably less massive than the .50 caliber beneath it, and is dwarfed by the 20 mm cannon shell at the bottom. All rest on the uniform jacket of a Royal Canadian Air Force sergeant pilot.

Y-Geräts were capable of delivering bombs on target with reasonable accuracy.

Over the winter of 1940–41, the Luftwaffe maintained the longest continuous offensive conducted by either side against a single (if very large) target. At one stage, London endured heavy attacks on fifty-seven consecutive nights. During one especially concentrated effort of five nights, beginning on October 9, the Luftwaffe launched 487, 307, 150, 303, and 320 bomber sorties against the British capital. It was confidently predicted that the civil population would panic and force its government to negotiate, but the Germans (and the Allies later in the war) seriously underestimated the resilience of ordinary people under heavy bombing. In November, Göring shifted the weight of the Luftwaffe offensive to include a wider assault on ports and industrial centers, with special emphasis on aircraft factories. On the night of November 14/15, KGr 100 used its X-Gerät equipment to lead a force of 449 bombers to Coventry. That night 394 tons of high explosive, 56 tons of incendiaries and 127 parachute mines fell on the city. The center burned fiercely and was largely destroyed, with 380 people killed and 800 seriously injured. Twelve aircraft factories and nine other industrial facilities were hit, and

In 1941, a new Luftwaffe fighter made its appearance. The Focke Wulf Fw 190 came as an unpleasant surprise for the RAF, since it could outfly the fighters then in service with RAF Fighter Command.

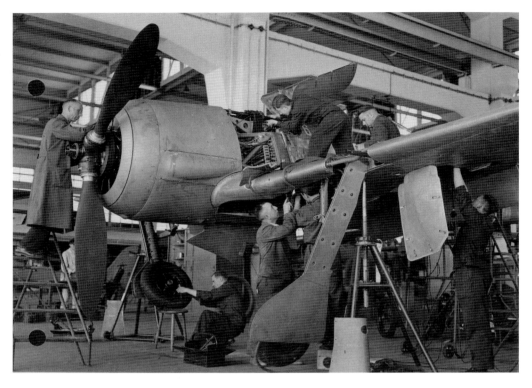

the city's infrastructure — railways, roads, electric power lines, water and gas mains — was severely disrupted. Other heavy raids followed on Birmingham, Bristol, Plymouth, Liverpool, Southampton, Sheffield, Newcastle, Manchester and Glasgow. The assault on London continued too, reaching new heights in the spring of 1941, with raids by 685 and 712 bombers on nights in April, and another by 507 on May 10. These onslaughts signaled not an intensification of the Blitz, but its dying fury, as the Luftwaffe sought to do as much damage as possible in the time it had left before being called to action on another front.

When the night offensive against Britain began, the nation's defenses were almost powerless to intervene. As the weeks of winter went by, things started to improve. First came jammers to bend and confuse the Luftwaffe's radio beams, and a host of dummy targets to mislead the bomber crews. The number of antiaircraft guns and searchlights increased sharply, and new radars of all types began coming into service. Some offered the AA guns unheard of accuracy, and others formed the basis of the inland coverage needed to guide night fighters to their targets. Most importantly, the first airborne intercept (AI) radars were giving the fighters a chance to see in the dark. A new fighter was being introduced, too: the Bristol Beaufighter, a fast, powerful twin-engined aircraft equipped with a fearsome battery of four 20 mm cannon and six machine guns and carrying AI Mk IV, which could pick up an enemy bomber at 4 miles.

These countermeasures had their effect. In January 1941, the night fighters claimed three bombers shot down, and the AA guns, twelve. In February, the figures were four and eight. March brought a marked change as the fighters got into their stride — 22 to 17. In April, it was 48 to 39, and in May the total destroyed was a much more telling 138, of which the fighters claimed 96. The No. 604 Squadron Beaufighter crew of Squadron Leader John Cunningham and Sergeant C.F. Rawnsley was the most successful night fighting team. Extracts from their combat report of April 11, 1941, give an idea of the Beaufighter's devastating impact. Having been guided toward the enemy bomber by GCI control, Rawnsley made radar contact at maximum range. Cunningham, following his AI operator's instructions to close in, "obtained a visual at 2,500ft range and about 30 degrees up. Identified E/A [enemy aircraft] as He 111 which was flying just beneath cloud layer and occasionally going through wisps which allowed me to get within 80 yards and about 20–30 feet beneath before opening fire. Immediately there was a big white flash in the fuselage center section and black pieces flew off the fuselage. E/A went into vertical dive to the right and about half a minute later the sky all around me was lit up by an enormous orange flash and glow. Bits of E/A were seen to be burning on the ground…. One He 111 destroyed. Rounds fired 64."

At the same time that the British defenses were raising the stakes for the Luftwaffe, Hitler was planning his turn to the east. By the end of May, the whole of Luftflotte 2 had been transferred to bases in Germany and Poland in preparation for the invasion of the Soviet Union. The attempt to force the British to their knees by air attack was over. In the eight months of the Blitz, the Luftwaffe had failed in its primary objective, but had nevertheless inflicted considerable harm on Britain and its people. Aircraft production was slowed, and industry generally affected to some degree. More than half a million men had been forced to involve themselves in antiaircraft and civil defense. Over 40,000 civilians had been killed and another 46,000 injured. This had all been achieved at a cost of some 600 aircraft, a figure that represented only 1.5 percent of the sorties flown. Damaging and cheaply conducted though it was, the campaign might have been even more effective if the

aim had been more precise and consistent. The Luftwaffe vacillated between targets, attacking first British morale, then the industrial heartland, then the ports, and sometimes all three in succession. In the end, the German airmen had to leave the job unfinished.

Cross-Channel Operations

Even before the Blitz came to an end, the RAF began to "lean forward into France" in a conscious attempt to wrest the initiative from the Luftwaffe. Fighter sweeps, known as "Rhubarbs," penetrated northern France at low level, attack-

In later years a legendary test pilot for de Havilland, John Cunningham became the RAF's first night fighter ace in 1941 while flying the Bristol Beaufighter equipped with AI Mk IV, an airborne radar capable of detecting an enemy night bomber at 4 miles. He later helped to develop the de Havilland Mosquito, and is seen here with the yellow prototype at the small de Havilland Museum near Hatfield, north of London, in 1999. INSET A Hurricane of 85 Squadron prepares for a night patrol.

The Spitfire V was a marked improvement over earlier versions, but its pilots found that they could be outflown by the Fw 190 and the new Messerschmitt Bf 109F.

ing airfields, ports and communications. More ambitious operations, called "Circuses," involved large numbers of fighters escorting a few bombers. Although the sweeps aimed to cause as much damage and disruption as possible, they were also intended to force the enemy to maintain strong defenses in the west, diverting German resources from the Mediterranean theater and later from the campaign against the Soviet Union. That they accomplished these aims to some degree is undeniable, but at considerable cost. The disadvantages suffered by the Luftwaffe during the Battle of Britain — operating at extreme range over enemy territory — were now felt by the RAF. Pilots shot down but not killed became prisoners, and damaged aircraft were often forced to land on the wrong side of the Channel. RAF Fighter Command aircrew (now commanded by Air Marshal Sholto Douglas), like the Luftwaffe before them, tended to believe their own exaggerated claims and were suitably encouraged. From mid-June 1941 to the end of the year, 731 enemy aircraft were reported shot down for an RAF loss of 411. The actual German figure was 154, and that included 51 noncombat losses. Far from being favorable, therefore, the balance sheet was about four to one against the RAF. The technological edge was swinging to the Luftwaffe, too. RAF pilots in their Spitfire Vs were finding

the improved Messerschmitt Bf 109F a handful, and in the latter half of 1941 they were being outflown by a superb new fighter, the Focke-Wulf Fw 190. As had been the case with the RFC's unrelenting offensive policy in WWI, carrying the war to the enemy proved to be an expensive business.

Cross-Channel activity for the RAF also began to include joint operations with other services. In February 1942, a commando raid was launched against the German radar station at Bruneval, on the French coast near Le Havre. This was a site for the large, long-range radar code-named Freya, but RAF reconnaissance revealed that a smaller Würzburg aerial was close by. Not much was known about the Würzburg, so it was decided to get a closer look at its component parts. Details of the local defenses were obtained from the French Resistance, and on the night of February 27, twelve Whitleys of No. 51 Squadron dropped paratroops on Bruneval. During a brief, sharply fought action, the raiders managed to overpower the station guards and remove the most essential elements of the radar before withdrawing to the coast to be picked up by the Royal Navy. The captured parts gave scientists much valuable information about the Würzburg, and useful countermeasures were devised.

Raiding on a much grander scale followed six months later, but with far less successful results. It was felt by the

Allies that a large-scale landing on the French coast should be attempted with the object of gaining experience for an eventual invasion. It was also hoped that such an action would force the Luftwaffe into a major battle for aerial supremacy over the landing site. Fifty-six fighter squadrons, flying Hurricanes, Spitfires and the new Typhoons, were entrusted to Air Vice-Marshal Leigh-Mallory. He also had at his disposal four squadrons of Mustang I tactical reconnaissance fighters, and five squadrons of light bombers (Blenheims and Bostons). The raid took place on August 19, 1942, and was disastrous. Some 6,000 men, drawn principally from the Canadian Second Division, assaulted the port of Dieppe and were cut to pieces by devastating crossfire from German strongpoints ringing the harbor. Two-thirds of the troops were killed or captured. The story in the air was not much better. Although the Luftwaffe was largely prevented from intervening in the ground action, the German port defenses seemed unaffected by the suppressive fire of the RAF fighters and the results of the air battle were very much in the Luftwaffe's favor. The RAF lost 106 aircraft and had 71 pilots reported either killed or missing. The Luftwaffe had 48 aircraft shot down and 24 damaged. The operation was an object lesson in how not to conduct and support a landing on a hostile coast. The seeds of experience planted by that painfully learned lesson were eventually to bear fruit on the beaches of Normandy two years later.

A much less overt RAF cross-Channel activity began with the formation of a special duties unit in the latter part of 1940. Its job was to transport agents to and from France and to supply them with the tools of their trade. Initially comprising a single flight of Westland Lysanders, the force in the United Kingdom later grew to become two squadrons, Nos. 138 and 161, adding Whitleys, Halifaxes, Hudsons and Stirlings to its strength. While the larger aircraft were used only for dropping agents and supplies by parachute, both the Lysanders and Hudsons regularly landed in German-held territory, principally in France but occasionally in other parts of Europe, too. At a time when the squadrons of Bomber Command were having difficulty in finding cities, the special duties aircrews were making their way at night to rough fields in the countryside, marked only by handheld flashlights. Between the end of 1940 and June 1944, there were 219 successful landings made in France, 183 by Lysanders and 36 by Hudsons. In the course of these operations, four Lysanders were shot down, four crashed on landing, and two had to be abandoned after becoming inextricably bogged in French mud. The losses were relatively light, but it was a hazardous business, demanding remarkable piloting and navigational skills besides considerable nerve.

The Westland Lysander was designed specifically for army cooperation duties, including tactical reconnaissance, artillery spotting and supply dropping.

RIGHT *The remarkable slow-flying capabilities and rugged construction of the Westland Lysander made it particularly suited for clandestine missions, allowing it to operate from unprepared fields to deliver and collect secret agents in enemy-occupied territory. This example is kept in flying condition by the Shuttleworth Trust at Old Warden in Bedfordshire.*
BELOW *Aircraft and crews of a Lysander squadron lined up and ready to go flying in the days before WWII.*

Scattering Bombs by Night

After the disasters of the war's early months, RAF Bomber Command took the hint and did not again commit its pre-war twins (Wellingtons, Whitleys and Hampdens) in raids against targets in Germany by day. As Air Vice-Marshal Coningham of No. 4 Group said, "If Bomber Command was to remain in the war it had no alternative but to fight in the dark." Unfortunately, only Coningham's Whitley squadrons had been trained for night operations.

Another problem was that it was difficult for most of the RAF's commanders to accept that their cherished interwar theories were misguided, even in the face of mounting evidence. They had created and now believed Bomber Command's public image. In 1940, the idea that the Germans could be cowed into submission by "massive

blows" delivered by the Command as it then stood was still very much alive. The first of those blows against the German homeland fell on May 15, 1940. Fewer than 100 twin-engined bombers struck at the industrial area of the Ruhr, and the limited strength of this relatively minor foray was diffused among sixteen assorted targets.

Similarly scattered attacks on the cities of the Ruhr and elsewhere in Germany, as far afield as Hamburg and Berlin, followed throughout 1940, the largest being the 134 aircraft sent against Mannheim in December. Loss rates remained low, at 2 percent or less, and crews did what they could with inadequate equipment. They flew for hours over enemy territory in all weathers, freezing in drafty turrets and cockpits, using the rudimentary navigation techniques available to them to search for precise targets in the blacked-out countryside. Enduring monotony, discomfort and fear, they were buoyed by the thought that they were striking at the enemy and confident that the targets they attacked were being hit hard.

The same pattern of operations was repeated at intervals during 1941, but it also became possible during the year to discern hints of major change. For one thing, the evidence of post-raid photography had become too clear to ignore. The bitter truth was that targets were not being hit hard. Even when conditions favored Bomber Command (as they had on the Mannheim raid), it was apparent that the bomber force did not have the capacity to destroy a specific target. Reconnaissance showed that heavy concentrations of bombs were never achieved and that the damage inflicted on a chosen area was usually light. In August 1941, Churchill was handed a document known as the Butt Report that brought together all the half-formed doubts and fears about the conduct of the bombing offensive. Among its conclusions, this scientific study contained the assertion: "Of those aircraft attacking their target, only one in three got within five miles." Over the Ruhr, an area consistently covered in industrial haze, this proportion fell to one in ten.

Although he was concerned over the conclusions of the Butt Report and urged the Chief of the Air Staff to give them his "most urgent attention," the Prime Minister had never felt strongly that the ability to achieve great precision was an essential prerequisite for a bombing offensive. As early as July 1940, Churchill was writing about the need for "an absolutely devastating, exterminating attack by heavy bombers from this country upon the Nazi homeland."

Three months later he was urging that "a whole-hearted effort shall be made to cart a large number of bombs into Germany." The words "exterminating" and "cart" do not suggest a wish for accuracy: they speak to Churchill's insistence that the German nation and its people should be hurt by whatever means was available.

In 1940 and 1941, Britain's situation was often desperate. German U-boats were causing havoc in the Atlantic, the Luftwaffe bombed British cities at night with impunity, and the British Army had been defeated in Europe and suffered serious reverses in the Mediterranean theater. Only one light shone in the otherwise unrelieved gloom. For all its limitations, Bomber Command was Britain's sole means of retaliating against its enemy, and the vast majority of the British people listened to reports of its "devastating" attacks on Germany with satisfaction. With no immediate prospects of success either on land or at sea, Bomber Command's persistent offensive action during the dark days of the war was the first essential step on the long road to victory, a fact that Churchill knew very well. He therefore approved of the sentiments expressed in a directive to the Command in July 1941. Besides singling out the German

At the outbreak of war in 1939, the only RAF bomber squadrons trained in night operations were those flying the Armstrong-Whitworth Whitley. Unfortunately, the Whitley was not adequately equipped to undertake a strategic bombing campaign against Germany. Unsuited though it was for its principal role, the Whitley was important in helping to maintain Bomber Command's offensive until the arrival of more effective four-engined aircraft in 1942.

transportation system for special attention, the directive included the instruction to "direct the main effort of the bomber force…to destroying the morale of the civil population as a whole and the industrial workers in particular." The reality of what the bombers could really be asked to do had begun to be accepted, even before the revelations of the Butt Report.

The other changes seen in 1941 heralded both good and bad news for Bomber Command. The good news was that a few of the long-awaited four-engined "heavies" appeared in the front line; on the debit side was the fact that losses were increasing. Besides the heavier concentrations of flak and searchlights around prime targets, bomber crews now had to face the Kammhuber Line, a wall of flak and searchlights along the continental coastline, backed by a chain of radar stations controlling Luftwaffe night fighters. While this stiffening opposition could hardly be welcomed by bomber crews, even that had its positive side. It showed that Hitler was being forced to take the RAF's persistence seriously, and that the Germans were necessarily committing valuable resources to the defense of the Third Reich's airspace.

The Axis Prevails in Southeast Europe

As Hitler made his preparations for attacking the Soviet Union, he was conscious of weaknesses along his southern flank. It was important to ensure that opposing forces could not use the territories of the Balkans as footholds on the European continent. Hungary and Romania proved willing partners to the Tri-Partite Pact (signed by Germany, Italy and Japan in September 1940), and German troops were established in both countries by November 1940. Bulgaria followed in March 1941, as did Yugoslavia, until its government was overthrown by a coup that rejected the alliance. In the meantime, Mussolini, somewhat piqued by the successes of his ally and anxious to gain some glory for Italy, had invaded Greece from Albania in October 1940. Undertaken by ill-prepared and poorly led forces, the Italian adventure was soon in trouble. The Greeks repelled the invaders and also appealed to Britain for help. By the end of November, several squadrons of RAF Blenheims and Gladiators, diverted from the fighting in North Africa, were operating in Greece, alongside the PZL P.24s, Bloch MB.151s, Potez 63s and Fairey Battles of the Royal Hellenic Air Force.

Concerned by the events in Yugoslavia and Greece, Hitler decided to intervene. On April 6, 1941, German forces invaded both countries, strongly supported by some 1,200 modern aircraft of Luftflotte 4. They were opposed in the air by no more than 500 aircraft, most of which were hopelessly outdated, although the Gladiator squadrons had reequipped with Hurricanes. The German assault began with a series of massive bombing attacks on Belgrade, punishing the Yugoslavs for their recalcitrance; 17,000 civilians died. By the end of April, both Yugoslavia and the mainland of Greece had been overrun, and the remnants of the Allied forces had been withdrawn to Crete and Egypt.

In the course of the campaign in Greece, the nonstop action produced some of the highest scoring Hurricane pilots of the war. Richard "Ape" Cullen of 80 Squadron achieved six kills in the Gladiator before undertaking a swift and informal conversion to the Hurricane in the front line at the end of February 1941. Five days later he was a Hurricane ace, having shot down a Fiat B.R.20, two Savoia-Marchetti S.M.79s and two Fiat C.R.42s in one day. Three days later he destroyed four enemy aircraft in one sortie, but on the following day he was bounced by several Fiat G.50s and was not seen again. No. 80 Squadron's combat record includes many more aces. William Vale achieved ten victories in the Gladiator; and by the end of April, when the squadron had withdrawn to Crete, he had added another thirteen in the Hurricane. Four more followed in May before he was rested from operations. Ted Hewitt had sixteen kills, and Roald Dahl (the celebrated author of children's books) was also an 80 Squadron ace. The most outstanding figure of the campaign, however, was "Pat" Pattle, who first fought with the Gladiators of 80 Squadron before commanding No. 33 Squadron's Hurricanes. Remarkable by any standards, Pattle was described by a distinguished former squadron commander of his as being "of the bravest; an exceptional fighter leader and brilliant fighter pilot." With fifteen confirmed victories in the Gladiator, Pattle converted to the Hurricane in February 1941. His score mounted rapidly during March and April, including several instances of multiple kills in one day against such formidable opposition as the Luftwaffe's Bf 109s. On April 20, flying his third sortie of the day while suffering from influenza, he shot down two Bf 110s. He was then seen to be going to the

The Fiat C.R.42 was the last of the front-line biplane fighters. It was introduced to squadrons of the Regia Aeronautica in 1939, and production was maintained until the Italian Armistice in June 1943. Among the export orders were seventy-two C.R.42s for Sweden. The aircraft shown here in Swedish markings is on display at the Swedish Air Force Museum in Linkoping.

could launch raids against the Rumanian oil fields. The job of subduing Crete was given to the Luftwaffe, using General Kurt Student's paratroopers. In all, 650 combat aircraft, 700 troop transports and 80 gliders were made available for the operation. On May 20, with air superiority assured, the Ju 52/3ms and DFS 230 gliders (Deutches Forschungsinstitut für Segelflug — German Reseach Institute for Gliding) began delivering troops to capture the two principal Cretan airfields, but the assault did not go according to plan. Resistance was fierce, and most of the first waves of paratroopers were destroyed, either shot down by ground fire or wiped out at their landing sites. Student was not to be denied, however. In the face of mounting losses, he continued to pour troops onto the island until a foothold was gained on Maleme airfield by soldiers of the 100th Mountain Rifle Regiment. They hung on while Ju 52/3ms landed behind them and offloaded reinforcements, eventually delivering some 30,000 men. Crete was fully in German hands by the end of the month. Though Crete was claimed as a creditable victory, the huge losses suffered by the paratroopers and the transports (170 Ju 52/3ms shot down) shocked the German High Command. Large-scale airborne assaults were never again authorized by Hitler, but the Allies studied the campaign and took from it some useful pointers for their own operations later in the war. (It was claimed that the resistance to the Axis forces in the Balkan campaign was futile and unnecessarily costly in men and equipment. However, it diverted the Germans from their main aim and delayed the attack on the Soviet Union for six vital weeks, a period that may have been crucial to Soviet survival.)

assistance of one of his flight commanders when he was in turn shot down and killed by fire from a Bf 110. In the evacuation from Crete, No. 33 Squadron's records were lost, but it is clear that Squadron Leader Marmaduke Thomas St. John "Pat" Pattle was the highest-scoring RAF fighter pilot of the war. The exact number of his victories will never be known, but some estimates have been as high as fifty-one, all of them after the first fifteen being achieved in the Hurricane.

Even though Greece had fallen, the Germans knew that it would not be sensible to ignore Crete and give the British the opportunity to establish bases there from which they

CHAPTER 2

The Mediterranean and Middle East

INEFFECTUAL THOUGH THE EARLY efforts of the Italians were both in the Balkans and North Africa, their forces nevertheless posed a significant threat to Allied, particularly British, interests in the Mediterranean theater. The naval base of Malta was within easy reach of bombers based in Sicily, and large Italian ground forces (in Cyrenaica and Abyssinia) were uncomfortably close to the Suez Canal and, at the southern entrance to the Red Sea, the port of Aden.

Maltese Crossroads

Malta's strategic importance at the crossroads of the Mediterranean was readily apparent. The island's long siege began on June 11, 1940, when fifty-five S.M.79 bombers left their bases in Sicily escorted by eighteen Macchi MC.200 fighters and made a daylight raid on the Maltese docks and airfields. It was Italy's first belligerent act following Mussolini's declaration of war on the Allies the day before, and it was made against what was arguably the most poorly defended of Britain's overseas bases. In the summer of 1940, the primary responsibility of the RAF was the defense of the United Kingdom, and it was impossible in the circumstances to supply other theaters with the modern aircraft they so desperately needed. In June 1940, Malta had only a few Sea Gladiator biplane fighters held in packing crates as reserves for the Royal Navy. Several were hastily assembled and used with limited success against the Italian raids. (The defense of Malta in June 1940 spawned the legend of *Faith, Hope* and *Charity,* reputedly the three Sea Gladiators flown daily against overwhelming odds. While it may be true that only three fighters were available on any given day to oppose the Italian raids, it is probable that they were not always the same aircraft. The names, created perhaps to build morale, appeared in stories of the struggle only after the event.) At the end of the month, Malta's resistance was stiffened slightly by four Hurricanes commandeered while on their way to North Africa. Early in August, more Hurricanes were brought in by the aircraft carrier *Argus* to form an operational squadron, No. 261. By the end of 1940, Malta was keeping an eye on its tormentors with reconnaissance Martin Marylands and was striking back with naval aircraft and the Wellington bombers of No. 148 Squadron. Italian convoys with supplies for their forces in Libya were preyed upon, and targets in both Italy and North Africa were regularly attacked.

OPPOSITE PAGE Gladiators Over Malta, *by Michael Turner. Sea Gladiator N5520 joined the Hal Far Fighter Flight in April 1940. Piloted by Flight Lieutenant J.L. Waters, RAF, N5520 (later christened* Faith*) shot down and destroyed an Italian S.M.79 on June 11, 1940, and another S.M.79 the next day. The fuselage of* Faith *is preserved on Malta.*

In April 1942, the USS Wasp *carried much-needed Spitfires into the Mediterranean for the defense of Malta. The normally sleek outline of the Spitfire Vs was broken by the addition of a dust-catching air intake under the nose.*

they drew attention to themselves. In the last two months of 1941, Malta-based aircraft sank over 70,000 tons of enemy shipping while several Allied convoys reached the island unscathed. Hitler resolved to eliminate this nettlesome problem by recalling Luftflotte 2 from the Eastern Front and placing it under Albert Kesselring's command. He unleashed a campaign of unprecedented fury with daily attacks against the island by large bomber formations. Allied shipping was harassed continually and, at one time, three out of four ships in every Malta convoy were being sunk. An important weapon in the maritime confrontation, both at this time and throughout the war in the Mediterranean, was the S.M.79 torpedo bomber. The courageous Italian aircrews engaged in shipping attack were the Regia Aeronautica's elite, and they proved to be a thorn in the Royal Navy's side as long as Italy remained an Axis partner.

Two Sunderland flying boats arrived to conduct maritime patrols, and Flight Lieutenant W.W. Campbell's crew sank two Italian submarines in their first three days. These offensive operations proved so successful that they invited Axis retribution. It came at the end of 1940, when the Luftwaffe's Fliegerkorps X arrived in Sicily.

On January 10, 1941, sixty Ju 87s and He 111s attacked a British convoy, scoring six direct hits on HMS *Illustrious*. The carrier survived and limped into Malta's Grand Harbour. Thereafter, the Luftwaffe began a massive campaign against Malta that continued unabated for the first three months of the year. No. 261 Squadron and a few Fleet Air Arm fighters struggled to cope with the assault. The island's airfields and the harbor area were repeatedly attacked and severely damaged. HMS *Illustrious* was hit several more times but was patched up sufficiently to set off for Alexandria, Egypt, on January 23. However, other priorities in Europe and North Africa arose to divert the Luftwaffe, and by May the onslaught had eased. The Malta squadrons, reinforced with Blenheims, Beaufighters and three more Hurricane squadrons, resumed the offensive. Once more the measure of their success could be gauged by the way

> *"Who said a wasp couldn't sting twice?"*
> WINSTON CHURCHILL, IN A SIGNAL TO THE CARRIER USS *WASP* AFTER HER SECOND DELIVERY OF SPITFIRES TO MALTA, 1942.

By April 1942, the Maltese people were seriously short of food and fuel, and the number of defending fighters was dwindling rapidly, many of them destroyed on the ground. On March 15, fifteen Spitfires arrived on HMS *Eagle* to bolster the defense, followed by another forty-seven aboard the U.S. carrier *Wasp* on April 20. The Luftwaffe welcomed them the same day, and by the evening of April 21, only seventeen Spitfires were serviceable to fly. This was the worst period of the blitz on Malta. During the month of April, the Luftwaffe flew 4,900 sorties against the island and dropped 6,278 tons of bombs. The destruction was immense, but the RAF buildup persisted, and sixty-two more Spitfires reached Malta from *Wasp* and *Eagle* on May 9. Further deliveries of fighter aircraft continued during the summer months of 1942, and a number of RAF pilots gained reputations in the course of endless dogfights, notably Canadians George "Screwball" Buerling and Wally McLeod, and Rhodesian Johnny Plagis, who respectively scored twenty-six, thirteen and sixteen aerial victories over the island in their Spitfires.

Vacillations in German priorities again drew off the Luftwaffe to support Field Marshal Rommel's last desert offensive, allowing the Malta squadrons to return to the business of harassing the Axis sea lines of supply, which they did to great effect. The Axis efforts by sea, intended to sustain Rommel's Afrika Corps, both during his advance and in retreat after his defeat at El Alamein in October 1942, were seriously diminished. According to Vice Admiral Weichold (German liaison officer at Italian naval headquarters), the October losses of Axis shipping were 45 percent of the Italian and 59 percent of the German tonnage dispatched. It was clear that Rommel's defeat was achieved as much behind the lines as on the battlefield, and that Malta's part in the Allied victory was crucial.

Cooperation in the Desert

When Italy entered the war on June 10, 1940, the British situation in North and East Africa immediately became critical. Both on the ground and in the air, the Italian forces considerably outnumbered the British and were at least as well equipped. The RAF's Middle East Air Force, with its headquarters in Egypt, was responsible for operations in an area covering four and a half million square miles, stretching from the Balkans to East Africa and from Iraq to Gibraltar. Spread across this vast region were little more than 300 assorted RAF aircraft, almost all of them obsolescent. The most modern type in the theater was the Blenheim IV, but it equipped only a single squadron. The rest of the front line included Gloster Gladiators, Westland Lysander army cooperation aircraft and Bristol Bombay transports fitted with bomb racks. East Africa was watched over by even more limited machines, among them Vickers Wellesley bombers, and biplanes such as the Gloster Gauntlet, Hawker Hardy, and the Vickers Vincent and Valentia. The Italians had some 480 combat aircraft based in Libya and East Africa, and those in Libya were backed by readily available reinforcements from Italy.

U.S. sailors on board the USS Wasp *gather to watch the departure of a Spitfire for Malta.*

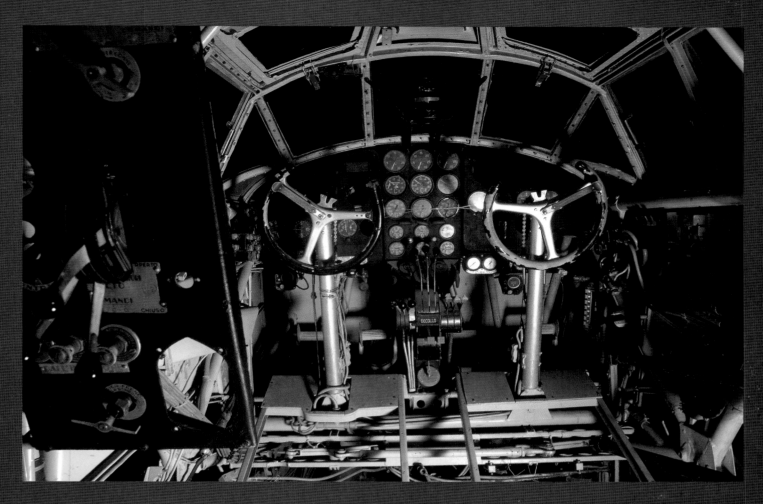

SAVOIA-MARCHETTI S.M.79

The Savoia-Marchetti S.M.79 was an excellent torpedo bomber and was used to good effect against the Allied convoys in the Mediterranean. An S.M.79 in Syrian markings is on display at the Caproni Museum in Trento, Italy.

LEFT In 1999, Dan Patterson photographed the distinguished Italian pilot, Francesco Volpi, in front of the type in which he completed so many operational sorties. Volpi flew the S.M.79 as a conventional and torpedo bomber, and also as a transport aircraft during the Battle of Stalingrad.

ABOVE AND RIGHT The cockpit and gun position of the S.M.79 were photographed during a visit to the Italian Air Force Museum at Vigna di Valle in 1999. Under restoration at the time, the aircraft is now exhibited fully restored.

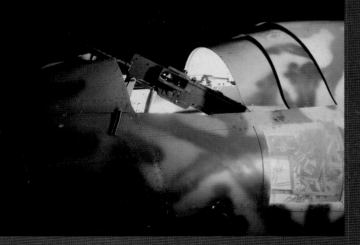

In theaters of operation other than Europe, the campaigns were generally on a smaller scale, but were often of great significance. In North Africa, Erwin Rommel was a thorn in the Allied side from the moment he arrived to take command of Axis forces. On India's northwest frontier, leaflets in two languages sought local support against the Nazis.

THIS LEAFLET MIGHT HAVE BEEN A NAZI BOMB! DEFEND THE PUNJAB BY HELPING TO BUY WAR 'PLANES

GIVE WHAT YOU CAN AFFORD TO·DAY

Lacking adequate numbers and modern types, the RAF made up for its shortcomings by being aggressive. Commanding No. 202 Group in Egypt was a forceful Canadian, Air Commodore Raymond Collishaw, the third-ranking British ace from WWI. (See *Aviation Century, The Early Years,* Naval Air Operations in Chapter 2.) At first light on June 11, the morning after the Italian declaration of war, his Blenheims attacked Italian airfields in Libya, seizing the initiative from the Regia Aeronautica. Nor was Collishaw above using subterfuge to keep the Italians off balance. For a time in 1940, there was only one Hurricane in his command. Kept constantly on the move between landing fields, "Collie's Battleship" created the illusion that the RAF had plenty of modern fighters in North Africa. Even so, by September the Italians had recovered their equilibrium sufficiently to launch an offensive.

It soon emerged that the North African campaign was going to be one in which armies and air forces had to work closely together. The long, narrow lines of communication that grew behind an advancing army invited aircraft attack, and ground forces offered airmen tempting targets as they moved over the open desert. Airfields ranked with the few small ports as objectives of paramount importance, and were among the principal objectives of the struggle between the armies. That the British Secretary of State for War, Anthony Eden, recognized all this is shown by his remarks in his report of a visit to the Middle East in October 1940: "Liaison between the Army and Air Force is excellent and the RAF are giving support for which no praise can be too high within their limited resources. Reinforcement of the RAF is the pressing need of the hour here and will, I am convinced, prove to be the decisive factor."

Eden's words brought some results. By the end of the year, the RAF's Middle East Air Force had been reinforced with eighty-seven Hurricanes, eighty-five Blenheim IVs, and forty-one Wellingtons. As the supply lines of the Italians lengthened and their advance ran out of steam, Collishaw used his new assets to good effect, firmly establishing air superiority and giving strong support to a counteroffensive brilliantly directed by Lieutenant General Richard O'Connor. In just ten weeks, O'Connor effectively destroyed the Italian Tenth Army, driving it back 500 miles and taking 130,000 prisoners. It was described by the Commander-in-Chief, General Wavell, as a triumph of interservice cooperation. So it was, and it set the pattern for all that followed in the desert war, in good times and bad.

The victorious O'Connor was robbed of total victory by the decision to withdraw forces from North Africa to aid Greece against German invasion. His headlong advance across Libya was checked, and at this critical juncture the situation changed significantly. Hitler decided to intervene in the desert, and in February 1941, General Erwin Rommel arrived in Tripoli. Before the end of March, Rommel was on the move against his weakened enemy, his air force strengthened during his advance by the arrival of some fifty Messerschmitt Bf 109Es. By April 11, his German and Italian troops had recovered almost all the ground so recently lost to O'Connor. (The shift in fortunes was obvious when O'Connor himself was taken prisoner during Rommel's advance.) However, Australian troops held out under siege

in Tobruk, and unable to use any major port closer than Tripoli, Rommel began to suffer the problems that had bedeviled his Italian predecessor. His supply lines became dangerously attenuated and were subject to continual attack by British air and sea forces. The German offensive in the Soviet Union consumed units that could have made all the difference to Rommel's drive to Cairo and the Suez Canal.

The year 1941 was one of fluctuating fortunes, characterized by periods of fierce fighting and lulls during which both sides were forced to back away and try to rebuild their strengths. In November, a new British C-in-C, General Claude Auchinleck, launched Operation Crusader, and by December, Rommel had been pushed back to his starting point, but not for long. The inexorable military law of overextension now worked against his opponent. It did not help Auchinleck's cause, either, that British troops were being diverted to counter Japanese aggression in the Far East. Rommel's forces surged forward again, this time taking Tobruk and overwhelming the gallant stand of the Free French fortress at Bir Hakim. In July 1942, they crossed into Egypt, reaching a point near the railway station at El Alamein, at the edge

RAF fighter squadrons in North Africa were delighted to see Hurricanes arriving by the end of 1940, even though the accomodation and cooking facilities were a little rustic. During the siege of Tobruk, efforts were made to get the valuable Hurricanes out of sight in makeshift hangars.

of the Qattara Depression and less than 150 miles from Cairo. There they came to a halt, faced by a formidable defensive line, to gather themselves for the final assault that would clear the way to the Suez Canal and the oilfields of the Middle East. That the temporarily victorious Axis forces on the ground were nevertheless feeling the sting of air power was recorded in the Afrika Corps diary with comments such as "The day was notably lively with many successful bombing attacks by the

Hurricane IIDs fitted with four 20 mm cannons proved most effective in strafing attacks against Axis forces in the North African desert. The aircraft illustrated is the last Hurricane ever built and is flown by the RAF's Battle of Britain Memorial Flight. Originally known as "The Last of the Many," it was painted in desert markings for the 2000 display season.

British," and "The continuous raids by day and night are hindering the troops seriously."

The desert air war never approached the scale of the struggle in Europe, east or west, and it was essentially different in many ways. No element of the air campaign could be identified as strategic, nor were civilians deliberately targeted. Tactical air power's influence on the land battle was the overriding consideration, and the importance of achieving air superiority over the battlefield was repeatedly demonstrated. It was during the desert war that sensible principles of close cooperation between Allied air and surface forces were devised and put into practice. In June 1941, command of the Middle East Air Force passed to Air Marshal Sir Arthur Tedder, a man with definite ideas about interservice cooperation. Soon after taking over, he wrote: "In my opinion, sea, land and air operations in the Middle East Theatre are now so closely inter-related that effective coordination will only be possible if the campaign is considered and controlled as a combined operation in the full sense of that term."

Selected to serve with Tedder was a man who fully supported those views. Air Vice-Marshal Arthur Coningham replaced Collishaw as commander of the Western Desert Air Force in July. A forty-six-year-old New Zealander (known as "Mary," a corruption of Maori), he and his army counterpart immediately began to cooperate in the fullest sense of the word. They established a joint headquarters, and they and their staffs shared a common mess. At a time when the high command of the RAF in London still clung to the prewar idea that the only proper roles for fighters were to combat enemy aircraft and look after bombers, Coningham was tasking them for low-level bombing and strafing attacks on shipping and military vehicles. Fighter-bombers such as Hurricanes and Curtiss P-40s (first as Tomahawks, later as Kittyhawks) proved to be far more effective than the Blenheim and Maryland light bombers. Flying from rough airfields closer to the battle, they were quicker to respond to the Army's requests and better able to tackle small, mobile targets when they arrived on the scene. Using aircraft in this aggressive manner at low level did expose them daily to concentrated antiaircraft fire, and also gave Luftwaffe fighters the advantage of height, and losses were understandably high. During the period of Operation Crusader (November 18, 1941, to January 20, 1942), the RAF in the Middle East (North Africa and Malta) lost some

440 aircraft of all types. However, the soldiers were appreciative of the efforts being made in the air. As Tedder subsequently wrote: "It was clear that the Army, for once, was pleased with the RAF."

Aces of the Desert

It was in 1942 that the desert fighter aces rose to prominence. On the Allied side, Neville Duke, Billy Drake and Clive "Killer" Caldwell, Australia's top-scoring pilot with $28\frac{1}{2}$ victories, led the way in their P-40s. Skillful though they were, they still needed a certain amount of good fortune to survive. To quote Duke (28 victories) on his combat experience: "The Curtiss' greatest asset was its ruggedness. On one occasion I lost my elevator, an aileron, my flaps and was full of holes. The lowest speed at which I could control the Tomahawk in that condition was 150 mph. I crash-landed it at Tobruk and walked away without a scratch. Another

Joachim Marseille, known to the Luftwaffe as "The Star of Africa," was the highest-scoring German pilot against the Western Allies. By the time of his death in September 1941, he claimed to have destroyed 158 Allied aircraft, including one incredible day on which he is said to have destroyed seventeen of his enemies.

time a 109's cannon shell exploded in my wing while I was in a very tight turn at low altitude. The impact flipped the aircraft over on its back and when I recovered we hit the ground at very high speed, smashing the aircraft flat on the desert floor. Again I walked away."

For the Axis air forces, the leading marksmen were Hans-Joachim Marseille and Werner Schrör. Marseille was an exceptional fighter pilot, often called "The Star of Africa." If his combat claims are accurate, he shot down more RAF aircraft than any other pilot. He first saw combat during the Battle of Britain, where he claimed seven enemy destroyed while being shot down four times himself.

Marseille arrived in North Africa to serve with JG 27 in April 1941 and began where he had left off, shooting down a Hurricane in his first week and then being shot down in turn. However, when his unit was reequipped with the Bf 109F, his true abilities were revealed and his score increased dramatically. On February 22, 1942, with fifty kills to his name, he was awarded the Knight's Cross. That summer, he claimed multiple victories during a sortie on numerous occasions, expending an average of only fifteen rounds on each victim. After downing six P-40s in eleven minutes on June 3, he received the Oak Leaves to his Knight's Cross. On June 17 he repeated the feat, shooting down six more fighters in seven minutes near his own airfield, bringing his total to 101 and being rewarded with the Swords. On September 1, during a day of almost continuous combat, Marseille apparently surpassed even his own remarkable achievements. In the course of three sorties he claimed the destruction of seventeen RAF fighters, an exploit that brought him the Diamonds to the Knight's Cross, a level of recognition reached by very few. By the end of the month, he was dead, killed not by an enemy bullet but by accident. Returning from a mission, Marseille reported an engine problem and dense smoke in the cockpit. He chose to bail out and was struck by the tail of his aircraft as he did so. He fell to the desert below, parachute unopened. Fighter pilot extraordinaire, Marseille had flown a total of 382 combat sorties and claimed to have destroyed 158 aircraft.

Billy Drake flew Hurricanes in the Battle of France and scored four aerial victories before being shot down. His reputation as a fighter leader was made as commander of 112 Squadron flying Curtiss Kittyhawks during the North African campaign. By 1943, he had raised his score to twenty four and a half in the air, and had added thirteen more destroyed on the ground.

On to Tripoli and Beyond

The final move in the ebb and flow of the desert war began on the night of October 23, 1942, when General Bernard Montgomery, the new commander of the British Eighth Army, unleashed his forces at El Alamein, opening with a devastating artillery barrage, bombing raids by Wellington squadrons (aided by flare-dropping Albacores of the Fleet Air Arm), and strafing attacks by Hurricane night fighters.

This time the British assault had been preceded by a massive buildup that ensured ample reserves of men and material. The Middle East Air Force had been transformed, and now comprised some 1,500 aircraft, 1,200 of which were deployed in the desert. They were equipped largely with modern aircraft, including Kittyhawks, Spitfire Vs, Beaufighters, Beauforts and Halifaxes. Now that the United States was in the war, there were also some very welcome American squadrons flying P-40 Warhawks, B-25 Mitchells and B-24 Liberators. The international character of the MEAF was reflected in the breakdown of its ninety-six

The Hurricane IIC of the Battle of Britain Memorial Flight airborne over the Lincolnshire countryside near its base at RAF Coningsby.

squadrons: sixty British (including airmen from the Dominions), thirteen American, thirteen South African, five Australian, two Greek, and one each from Rhodesia, France and Yugoslavia. Against this formidable array, the Axis air forces could deploy in the desert about 700 aircraft, only half of which could be counted on as serviceable to fly.

During the morning of October 24, as the Eighth Army surged into battle, swarms of RAF fighter-bombers began an endless series of attacks on enemy troop positions. Allied air superiority was assured and was never again relinquished during the desert campaign. So dominant were the Allied fighters over the battle area that, on several occasions, Luftwaffe attempts to intervene were broken up and Ju 87s jettisoned bombs on their own troops. On November 4, 1942, the stubborn German defense at El Alamein was finally broken. Allied aircraft harried the retreating Axis columns unmercifully as they streamed west along the coast road. Against the enemy armor, the recently introduced Hurricane IID tank-busters were outstanding. Familiarly known as "flying can-openers," they were fitted with two 40 mm cannons. The Hurricane's top speed fell to 286 mph when encumbered with such enormous guns, and its lively maneuverability was seriously impaired, but there was no doubting its ability to destroy tanks.

The Axis forces had begun a retreat which would con-tinue for almost 2,000 miles, all the way to Tunis. Field Marshal Rommel commented ruefully: "British air superiority threw to the winds all our operational and tactical rules. The strength of the Anglo-American air force was, in all the battles to come, the deciding factor."

Operation Torch

As Rommel began his long retreat, word reached him that Allied forces had landed at the other end of North Africa. Initial American reluctance to become involved in what they saw as a peripheral theater had been disposed of, and in the hope that they might be welcomed by the resident French, U.S. troops were in the vanguard of the landings on November 8, 1942. Conducted under the overall command of Lieutenant General Dwight Eisenhower, Torch was the first large Allied combined operation, and it was as complex and potentially hazardous as any that followed. Over 500 ships from the United States and United Kingdom made their way through the dangerous waters of the Atlantic to land more than 100,000 men on the North African coast, at Casablanca, Oran and Algiers. Air cover was provided initially by aircraft operating from carriers and from the RAF bases at Gibraltar and Malta, but it was not long before RAF Hurricanes and U.S. Twelfth Air Force units joined the battle against the French colonial forces resisting the landings.

The commander of the Twelfth, Major General Jimmy Doolittle, arrived at Gibraltar on the afternoon of November 6, his B-17 bearing the scars of a brisk encounter with four Junkers Ju 88s over the Bay of Biscay. He was therefore on hand on November 8 to order the 31st Fighter Group to fly its Spitfires into Tafaraoui airfield near Oran. Their arrival there was eventful, some Spitfires silencing French artillery shelling the airfield, while others took on four Dewoitine fighters that shot down one of the 31st's aircraft during its landing approach. Three of the Dewoitines were destroyed. Within hours, the 52nd Fighter Group's Spitfires and the 33rd Fighter Group's P-40s were added to the Twelfth's strength ashore. The 60th Troop Carrier Group's C-47s also arrived carrying paratroops from the United Kingdom, although bad weather and communications failures scattered them all over the northwest shoulder of Africa.

By November 10, the French Air Force in North Africa had been destroyed or captured. The Twelfth Air Force had lost six Spitfires (two to friendly fire) and three C-47s. In the next ten days, the Twelfth's strength in Algeria grew to include four fighter groups (the 1st and 14th with P-38s,

and the 31st and 52nd with Spitfires), a light bomber squadron (the 15th with A-20s), the B-17s of the 97th Bomb Group, and two troop carrier groups. In Morocco, the buildup went more slowly, but there were still the P-40s of the 33rd Fighter Group, some B-25s of the 310th Bomb Group, and parts of the 62nd Troop Carrier group. Further east, the RAF flew in Spitfires, Beaufighters and Bisleys (Canadian-built Blenheim Vs).

Once established ashore, the Allied forces turned east to move on Tunisia, aiming to crush Rommel between themselves and the British Eighth Army, now driving the Axis armies steadily westward. The Germans reacted quickly, pouring reinforcements into Tunisia and checking the forward Allied units. To make things worse, the heavy winter rains set in, bogging down the inadequate transport of the Allied armies and turning their dirt airfields to soup. The Luftwaffe was operating from hard surfaces and was not affected. The winter months proved a trial for the Allied forces, with the Luftwaffe generally having the upper hand over Tunisia. Nevertheless, Allied bombers continued to harass the enemy whenever possible, with B-17s, B-26s, A-20s and Bisleys attacking airfields and port facilities.

Black Six, *a Messerschmitt Bf 109G, photographed by Dan Patterson in flight over the English Channel in 1997.*

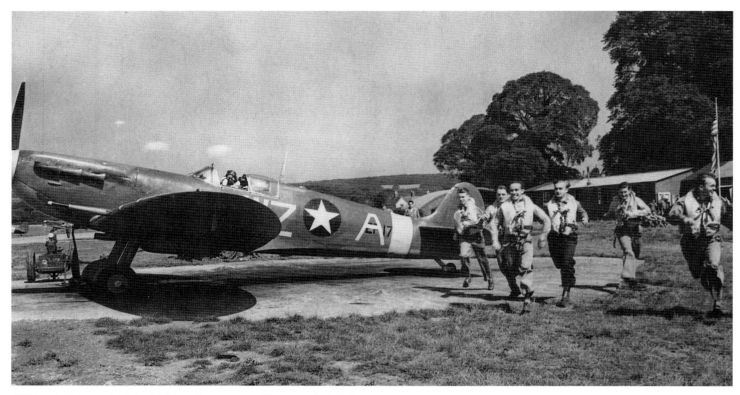

USAAF pilots of the 31st Fighter Group scramble to their Spitfires.

They were joined in these efforts by RAF Wellingtons based in Malta and the western desert, and by B-17s and B-24s of another recent arrival in the Mediterranean theater, the U.S. Ninth Air Force. Allied losses were sometimes frighteningly high, as on December 4, when ten Bisleys of No. 18 Squadron, unescorted, attempted to attack an enemy airfield in daylight; all were shot down by Bf 109s.

Not all of the hardships endured by the Allied air forces were inevitable. Many were self-inflicted. When the command arrangements for Operation Torch were made, no account was taken of the experience gained at some cost by the British in over two years of desert warfare. An impractical structure divided along national and geographical lines was imposed, with an American Western Air Command in Morocco and western Algeria, and a British Eastern Air Command in eastern Algeria. Putting air power into such arbitrary compartments is contrary to its nature, which essentially ignores artificial demarcations, especially those drawn on maps. Nor was any attempt made to take advantage of the hard-won expertise of Tedder when considering the problems of army/air force cooperation. The result was that much of the Allied potential in the air was wasted in

the early weeks of the campaign. This changed after the Casablanca Conference in January 1943, when the Allied air forces were combined as part of a sweeping reorganization. Air Marshal Sir Arthur Tedder became Commander of the Mediterranean Air Command, which had three elements: the Malta and Middle East Commands, and the Northwest African Allied Air Forces (NAAF). The NAAF was given to General Carl Spaatz in a shuffle that still left him with the overall responsibility of commanding U.S. air forces in the European theater while moving to Africa.

The NAAF was functionally subdivided into three: a strategic air force commanded by Jimmy Doolittle; a tactical air force, the North African Tactical Air Force (NATAF) under Air Marshal "Mary" Coningham; and a coastal air force led by Air Marshal Hugh Lloyd. The new arrangements placed the two officers who had been most closely involved with the development of army and air force cooperation during the war in the desert, Tedder and Coningham, in command positions, and their record of success profoundly influenced their USAAF colleagues. The NAAF was a new experience for American airmen. USAAF and RAF officers were intermingled at every level, and the importance of eliminating interservice rivalries and working closely with their army opposite numbers was constantly emphasized. These principles, although not always strictly adhered to, were afterward always in the minds of USAAF officers. Functional divisions also became common, with whole air forces being designated "strategic" or "tactical." Significantly, too, the belief that air forces cooperating in the land battle should fight under a single air commander was firmly established.

The Luftwaffe Struck Down

As the winter weather eased, Coningham issued a directive to the NATAF. In it, he stressed the importance of achieving air supremacy before becoming heavily engaged in the land battle. His priorities were, first, "a continual offensive against the enemy in the air," and second, "sustained attacks on enemy airfields." In conclusion, he emphasized that "The inculcation of the offensive spirit is of paramount importance." Concentrated offensive operations were unleashed in March 1943, and the days of Luftwaffe superiority were over. German aircraft losses rose rapidly, both in air combat and on the ground. Much to the relief of Allied troops but probably the regret of the fighter pilots, the notorious Ju 87 Stuka had to be withdrawn from combat in Africa after

> *"We'd have shot down more only we ran out of Stukas."*
>
> MOON COLLINGWOOD, NO. 1 SQUADRON, SAAF, AFTER THE DESTRUCTION OF FIFTEEN JU 87S NEAR EL ALAMEIN ON JULY 2, 1942.

crippling losses, notably on April 3, when the 52nd Fighter Group intercepted twenty Ju 87s and, brushing aside their escort, destroyed fourteen for the loss of one Spitfire.

From March 1943 until the end of the North African campaign in May, the Allied air forces kept a constant pressure on the enemy's airfields, ports and troop concentrations. B-17s introduced themselves to Italy, achieving an impressive success in sinking the cruiser *Trieste* at its anchorage, as well as destroying 30 acres of Palermo's docks and several ships in an explosion felt by the bombers at 19,000 feet. The principal Axis line of defense in Tunisia, the Mareth Line, was broken after relentless pounding by tactical aircraft. Luftwaffe fighters became hunted creatures, moving continually from one airstrip to another and adopting extreme dispersal measures. Operating in what was, for him, a target-rich environment, one of the Luftwaffe's great aces, Heinz Bär, fought on to some effect, shooting down a total of nineteen enemy aircraft in defense of the Mareth Line. (Heinz Bär ended the war credited with 220 victories, including thirteen during the Battle of Britain, ninety-six in the USSR, and sixty-one in North Africa. His last sixteen came while flying the Me 262 jet fighter.)

A Hurricane fitted with a desert air intake in flight over North Africa.

The excellent Macchi MC.202 Folgore became operational in Libya during November 1941. Powered by a Daimler-Benz 601 engine of 1,175 horsepower, it was fast and had a good rate of climb. More than 1,100 were built and saw service throughout the Mediterranean theater and on the Russian front. This example is seen with RAF roundels after the fall of Mussolini in 1943.

In April, measures were taken to sever the Axis lifeline across the straits between Sicily and Tunisia. Some 500 enemy transports (Ju 52/3ms, S.M.82s and Me 323s) were supplying the Axis armies in North Africa. Offensive sweeps against Sicilian airfields destroyed dozens of transports on their bases, and strong fighter patrols made the straits a killing ground. Among a number of big days for the Allied fighters was April 18, the day of the "Palm Sunday Massacre." A huge formation of some one hundred Ju 52/3ms, escorted by MC.202s, Bf 109s and Bf 110s, was intercepted by four squadrons of P-40s (the 57th and 324th Fighter Groups) with a top cover of RAF Spitfires. Fifty-one transports and sixteen of their escorts were shot down for the loss of six P-40s and one Spitfire. Four days later, a formation of twenty-one giant Me 323s, each carrying 10 tons of fuel, was caught and obliterated by Allied fighters, effectively ending the Axis airlift. Over a period of only seventeen days, the Axis transport losses in the North African campaign totaled 435 aircraft. The back of the Luftwaffe's airlift capability was broken.

Under incessant pressure, Axis resistance crumbled, and by May 7 the German air commander in Tunisia was ordering his squadrons to safety. Serviceable aircraft left for Sicily immediately, but the effectiveness of the Allied campaign was revealed in the more than 600 aircraft left behind as unfit to fly. Final surrender of all Axis units in North Africa came on May 13, when over a quarter of a million Axis troops capitulated and became prisoners of war. The Allied rejoicing was nowhere more enthusiastic than on Malta. The island's courageous survival, secured at great cost over many agonizing months of siege, now gained its reward as the once-enveloping power of the enemy withdrew into Europe.

The USAAF had not been enthusiastic about Operation Torch. The need to provide the air power for the operation was seen as an unwelcome diversion from the principal objective — the development of a bombing offensive against Germany. Nevertheless, the North African adventure had proved invaluable. Combat experience had been gained at relatively little cost, and the basic principles of air and ground cooperation had been absorbed. The lessons were quickly incorporated into *Field Manual 100-20*, which was forthright in declaring: "Land power and air power are co-equal and interdependent forces.... The gaining of air superiority is the first requirement for the success of any major land operation.... The inherent flexibility of air power is its greatest asset.... Control of available air power must be centralized and command must be exercised through the air force commander if this inherent flexibility and ability to deliver a decisive blow are to be fully exploited." These principles, established in North Africa, would give rise to the overwhelming tactical air power which proved so vital to the overthrow of Hitler's "Fortress Europe."

East African Sideshow

While the Middle East main event was contested in the deserts of North Africa, confrontations occurred elsewhere in the region that drew fewer headlines but were still important. Indeed, at a time when British military successes were few and far between, the campaign in East Africa stood out as the exception. Fought as it was between relatively minor forces equipped for an earlier age of warfare, it was nonetheless significant.

Italian dominance in East Africa threatened to close the Red Sea route to Egypt, starving the British forces fighting in the desert of essential supplies. The Italians made the first bellicose move from Ethiopia, pushing the small British garrison out of Somaliland in August 1940. This was followed by slight penetrations into the Sudan and Kenya. Given the Italian's vast superiority in ground forces (200,000 to 19,000), the most effective ready response was the aggressive use of air power, even though the available aircraft of the RAF and the South African Air Force were limited in quantity and quality. Bombing raids began against the Eritrean port of Massawa as early as June 11, when Vickers Wellesleys succeeded in sending 780 tons of fuel up in smoke. At first, the Regia Aeronautica reacted with determination and enterprise, destroying fuel supplies on an airfield in Kenya and ten aircraft on the ground in the Sudan. C.R.42 biplane fighters, flown with dash by Italian pilots blooded in the Spanish Civil War, established local air superiority for a time on the border between Sudan and Ethiopia, shooting down a number of Gladiators. However, with the arrival of additional South African units, including a Hurricane squadron, the tide turned. During the early months of 1941, the Regia Aeronautica's operations in East Africa were severely curtailed, and by April, British, Indian and South African troops, advancing with strong air support, had recovered Somaliland and occupied Ethiopia.

At this early stage of the war, when the system of army/air force cooperation in the North African desert had still to be developed, it is worth noting that the idea was already flowering in East Africa. In his report, the victorious army commander made special mention of how soldiers and airmen had worked together, saying that the "Air force commander with his own communications advanced with the commander of the leading troops. The value of this arrangement from the Army point of view cannot be over stressed. [The air support] engendered the greatest confidence amongst both commanders and men."

Iraq and Syria

During the years between the wars, the RAF's principal reason for being in Iraq had been to keep the peace. By 1940, the main RAF base at Habbaniya, near Baghdad, had no operational squadrons but was the home of a large flying training school, equipped with ageing biplanes such as the Hawker Audax and Fairey Gordon, and with twin-engined Airspeed Oxfords, all of which were normally flown unarmed. Remarkably, in view of the importance of the region's oilfields and the fragile nature of political relationships with the Arab world, there had been little attempt to strengthen the British presence.

In April 1941, an anti-British faction led by Raschid Ali assumed power in Iraq and began promoting the Axis cause in the Middle East. On the morning of April 30, his intentions took dramatic form when some 9,000 troops and twenty-eight pieces of artillery dug themselves in on a shallow plateau overlooking the Habbaniya base. Formal notes were then delivered by Iraqi envoys, insisting that no RAF personnel could leave the base, nor could any aircraft fly. The RAF men had not been idle, however. Raschid Ali's rise had inspired them to devise ways of fitting bomb racks to their venerable trainers, and they went into action at first light on May 2, supported by the occasional long-range strike by Wellington bombers. In the days that followed, the flying school aircraft, operating under continual shellfire, maintained an incessant attack on the Iraqi positions, while the Wellingtons and a detachment of Blenheim fighters contrived to keep the Iraqi Air Force on the ground. A few Luftwaffe Heinkel He 111s and Messerschmitt Bf 110s arrived from Greece, but they were too little and too late. Their morale shattered by persistent hounding from the air,

The A-36 was an Allison-engined Mustang that was used mainly at low level and was heavily involved in both the North African and Italian campaigns. Prominently featured in the A-36 were the dive brakes, much needed on an aircraft that accelerated eagerly in dive-bombing attacks. The restored A-36A at the USAF Museum is painted as Margie H, *flown by Captain Lawrence Dye of the 27th Fighter Bomber Group in Tunisia, Sicily and Italy.*

the Iraqi soldiers melted away after dark on May 5. A relief column of motorized infantry and artillery, sent to restore the position, was caught in the open by forty of the RAF trainers and effectively destroyed. To complete Raschid Ali's discomfiture, efforts were made to isolate him by severing his communications. His radio station was destroyed by bombing, and many of the telephone lines radiating from Baghdad were cut by the simple method of flying through them with an Audax. With the threat removed, Habbaniya became a base for offensive action, and by the end of May, British Army units, brought up from Basra, had entered Baghdad, forcing Raschid Ali to flee.

It may have been a sideshow to the main event, but without the pugnacious defiance of a few RAF pilots in obsolete training aircraft, Iraq might have become a German satellite in 1941. Winston Churchill later wrote: "The spirited defense of Habbaniya by the Training School was a prime factor in our success. The Germans had at their disposal an airborne force which would have given them Syria, Iraq and Persia, with their precious oil fields." The repercussions of such an event would surely have had untold effects on the rest of the war.

One threat in the Middle East having been disposed of, there remained the problem of Syria, where there were forces loyal to Vichy France, including a substantial air force. German aircraft, too, had been observed using Syrian bases, from where it would have been possible for them to attack targets in Iraq, Persia and the Suez Canal.

Distasteful though it was to consider attacking French forces, the decision was taken to invade Syria. The assault began on June 8, 1941, supported by about sixty bombers and fighters. The French reaction was fierce, and aerial combat with Morane 406s and the excellent Dewoitine 520s frequent. The Fleet Air Arm's Fairey Fulmars, protecting British ships offshore, were outclassed, and a number were shot down. French bombing of British troops was effective until June 28, when all six Martin Marylands attacking an advancing British column were shot down by a Tomahawk squadron. Taken together with the loss of many aircraft on the ground during attacks on their airfields, this marked the end of serious resistance by the Armée de l'Air. An armistice was signed on July 14, 1942, and the majority of French airmen moved to join their colleagues already fighting on the Allied side.

Advance into Italy

At the Casablanca conference in January 1943, it had been agreed that the defeat of the Axis forces in North Africa would be followed by an invasion of Sicily and then of Italy. As a preliminary step, the Allied air forces began to pound Pantellaria during the latter part of May and early June 1943. This heavily defended island in the middle of the Sicilian Straits boasted an airfield that could be used as a forward base from which to provide air cover for the Allied landings on Sicily. It was on the receiving end of five thousand bombing sorties; as assault forces approached the island on June 11, the defenders ran up a white flag. Pantellaria had been conquered by air power alone.

A continuous air campaign had also been carried out against Axis airfields and ports in Sicily and southern Italy, and the tempo of this rose as D-Day for the Sicilian invasion drew nearer. During June and the first ten days of July, about 1,000 Axis combat aircraft were destroyed by the Allied air campaign. The few airfields left untouched became killing grounds where Allied fighter-bombers took full advantage of a generous selection of targets for their strafing and bombing attacks. In effect, the Luftwaffe in the region was defeated before the invasion began.

The invasion of Sicily began on the night of July 9–10, 1943. The operation was massively supported by Allied air forces, and opposition from enemy aircraft was negligible. Allied air supremacy was complete, but there were still aspects of the air operation that went sadly awry, notably those

> *"The Kitty had 124 bullet holes in it. All the perspex down the left side had gone; instruments were shattered; there were no flaps and a flat tyre… one earpiece was missing from my helmet; there was a large hole through my flying suit under the arm and another behind my knee. I was unscratched but my ego had been badly dented."*
>
> JOHN WADDY (LATER AN AUSTRALIAN MEMBER OF PARLIAMENT), DESCRIBING THE RESULT OF A RUNNING BATTLE WITH TWO BF 109S, JUNE 1942.

concerned with paratroop operations and air-naval cooperation. Friendly fire incidents were numerous; naval gunfire forced covering Allied fighter patrols up to higher altitudes, and shot down some of the twenty-three C-47s lost during paratroop operations. Alarmed by the gunfire and dispersed by bad weather, the C-47s scattered their paratroops over a wide area. Sixty-nine out of 137 Horsa and Hadrian gliders released fell into the sea, and another fifty-six were scattered far from their planned landing places. To make things worse, similar errors occurred again on July 11 and 13, when Allied transports once more flew through friendly fire and were shot down in numbers. Investigations after these bungled affairs led to specific recommendations that benefited later airborne operations. In particular, it was emphasized that planning for such operations should be done in one nominated headquarters and that every effort should be made to ensure that associated ground and naval forces were informed of the plan well ahead of time.

By mid-August 1943, all enemy resistance in Sicily had been overcome. The Axis forces had been deprived of air cover and slowly strangled by incessant attacks on their supply lines from the north. Fewer than 400 Allied aircraft had been lost, but the campaign had cost the Axis air forces at least 1,850 machines. The defeat and the constant pressure of air bombardment against targets as far away as Rome and Milan helped to bring down dictator Benito Mussolini and drive Italy out of the war. On September 8, all Italian forces laid down their arms and surrendered to the Allies.

U.S. commanders had not been enthusiastic about a campaign against the "soft underbelly of Europe" after North Africa had been secured. They feared that involvement in southern Europe might detract from preparations for an invasion of France in 1944. Now, with the fall of Mussolini, General Eisenhower pressed for immediate landings on the Italian mainland in the hope of completing a rapid occupation of Italy and acquiring bases from which to attack Germany from the south. In this, the Allies were

This Macchi MC. 205 Veltro is exhibited at the Italian Air Force Museum, Vigna di Valle, Italy. The Veltro (Greyhound), an exceptional fighter, arrived too late to have any significant effect on the outcome of the Italian campaign. Flown against the Allies until the Italian Armistice, a number of Veltros then changed sides and were used by the Co-Belligerent Air Force on the Jugoslav front until the end of the war.

only partially successful. Troops landed in the toe of Italy and at Salerno, near Naples, early in September fought their way north to occupy Naples on October 1, but only after a bitter struggle. The Luftwaffe did its best to interfere with the landings at Salerno, and had some initial success while Allied fighters were operating from bases in Sicily and therefore spending only a limited time over the beaches. Ferocious German Army counterattacks did occur and, at one stage, threatened to push the invaders back into the sea, but eventually Allied air power prevailed, establishing local air superiority and disrupting the flow of supplies to the front. From September 12, P-38s and Spitfires were operating from inside the beachhead, together with Fleet Air Arm Seafires, and from then on, the Luftwaffe's power to intervene diminished significantly. The Salerno battles cost the Luftwaffe 221 aircraft, more than twice the Allied loss of eighty-nine. This was compounded by heavy attacks on airfields around Foggia on September 17 and 18, in which some 300 Luftwaffe aircraft were destroyed on the ground.

General Giorgio Bertolaso standing alongside a Macchi MC.205 Veltro, a type he flew both against and with the Allies in 1943.

Nevertheless, German airmen did record some considerable achievements at sea with weapons that foreshadowed the future. Among them were the sinking of the Italian battleship *Roma*, on its way to surrender in Malta, and the disabling of the British battleship *Warspite*. Both were hit by guided bombs launched from Dornier Do 217K-2s.

Soon after the Allies began moving north from Naples, worsening weather and determined German resistance stabilized the front on the prepared defenses of the Gustav Line, halfway between Naples and Rome. For more than six months, their movement hampered by mountainous terrain and severe winter weather, the Allied armies battered themselves against this line and were denied. In the air, results were more positive. The Allied air assault drew Luftwaffe squadrons south and so had a beneficial effect on

the Eighth Air Force's bomber offensive from England. Without the substantial Luftwaffe combat losses in Sicily and Italy, the near defeat of the Eighth over Germany in 1943 might have developed into disaster.

Equally significant was the capture of a number of Italian airfields around Foggia on the Adriatic coast. From there, after the end of 1943, the heavies of the newly formed Fifteenth Air Force, commanded by Major General Nathan Twining, could cover strategic targets all over northern Italy, southern Germany, Austria and Rumania. Ploesti's oil complex came within easy reach and was visited regularly by USAAF bombers operating at high level. Before Ploesti was overrun by the Red Army in August 1944, it had been attacked by some 7,500 heavy bomber sorties, and oil production had almost dried up. About 350 Allied aircraft were lost in attacking Ploesti, but it was judged a small price to pay for achieving a serious reduction in Germany's capacity to fuel its forces during the final year of the war. Heavies from Foggia also delivered telling blows on the German aircraft industry, particularly the Messerschmitt factory at Wiener Neustadt.

Important though strategic operations were, in Italy the emphasis was on supporting the ground war. Priority was given to maintaining air supremacy; then came interdiction of enemy supply lines and direct support of ground forces. At the heart of these operations were the fighters and medium bombers (A-36s, P-38s, P-39s, P-40s, Spitfires, Beaufighters, A-20s, B-25s and B-26s), although heavy bombers were also called on to fly tactical missions as necessary. The introduction of a forward air control system and improvements in air-ground communications allowed precise strikes to be made on enemy positions immediately in front of friendly troops, within the area between the front line and the normal bomb-line, even when bombs were dropped from medium altitudes. The air control idea, originated by the British, was known as the Rover system: an RAF controller (usually a pilot) and an army liaison officer "rover" as needed from brigade to brigade along the front, directing strikes against engaged enemy forces by VHF radio. Rover Davids were British and Rover Joes were American.

In an effort to break the impasse in central Italy, Allied troops landed at Anzio, north of the Gustav Line, on January 22, 1944. Despite the tactical surprise, largely because the Luftwaffe was prevented from operating in the battle area, the landings were not a success. Thousands of sorties were flown against enemy airfields and surface communications before the assault, and the Anzio landings were almost unopposed, but the German Army reacted swiftly to seal off the beachhead. At the same time, a major Allied offensive stalled on the Gustav Line, and as the German position there consolidated, more German troops were moved to Anzio. A series of heavy attacks on the bridgehead might well have succeeded in bringing about its collapse had not the Allied air forces held such marked air superiority. During this critical period, the Luftwaffe was able to fly about 150 sorties per day over the front lines, whereas the Allies consistently managed to put up almost ten times that many.

A-36s were among the aircraft harassing the German troops. The A-36 was the ground-attack, dive-bomber version of the P-51, and it had the advantages of the Mustang's clean design. Although fitted with dive brakes, it was seldom used as a dive-bomber, shallow dives and strafing runs being its usual attack profiles. Unlike most other aircraft considered for dive-bombing, it was fast and maneuverable. Having got rid of its bombs, it could engage enemy fighters on equal terms at low level. Unfortunately for the aircraft's reputation, A-36s seemed to be involved in more than their share of friendly fire incidents. General Omar Bradley

A Macchi MC.200 Saetta was the front-line fighter of the Regia Aeronautica at the outset of WWII. Apparently wishing to surrender and anxious to reduce the chance of being shot down by trigger-happy gunners, this one is seen arriving over an RAF base in Italy at very low level after the fall of Mussolini.

recorded his own experience when A-36s attacked a column of American tanks: "The tankers lighted their yellow smoke bombs in a prearranged recognition signal. But the smoke only caused the dive-bombers to press their attacks. Finally in self defense the tanks turned their guns on the aircraft. A ship was winged and as it rolled over, the pilot tumbled out in a chute. When he landed nearby to learn that he had been shot down by American tanks, he bellowed in dismay. 'Why you silly sonuvabitch,' the tank commander said, 'didn't you see our yellow recognition signal?' 'Oh, ——!' said the pilot. 'Is that what it was?'" (Several other instances of A-36s attacking their own troops are given in Dr. Richard Hallion's book, *Strike from the Sky.*)

At the heart of the Gustav Line was the town of Monte Cassino, dominated by the abbey of St. Benedict. Convinced that the enemy were using the abbey to direct their defensive operations, the Allied commanders ordered it bombed. On February 15, 1944, the abbey was destroyed by B-17s, B-25s and B-26s, which dropped nearly 600 tons of bombs during the day. One month later, with the stalemate still unbroken, the town itself was flattened by over 1,000 tons of bombs. The record of the B-26 squadrons in this attack was remarkable, with close to 90 percent of their bombs falling within the target area of 1,400 by 400 yards. (Air Marshal Sir John Slessor was General Ira Eaker's deputy in Mediterranean Air Forces. In a letter to the RAF's Chief of Air Staff in April 1944 he commented on "the astonishing accuracy of the medium bomber groups — particularly the Marauders (B-26s); I think that the 42nd Bombardment Group…is probably the best day-bomber unit in the world.") The B-17s were not so impressive, and several of their bombs fell among Allied troops, who were positioned only 1,000 yards from the edge of the town.

The tremendous attack was effective in destroying Monte Cassino, but it was found that the use of bombers for close-support operations was a two-edged sword. Apart from friendly fire hazards, the problem with wielding a bomber force as a club with which to crush dug-in enemy troops was that the concentrated bombing created obstacles in the form of craters and masses of rubble that impeded advancing infantry and made it almost impossible to maneuver tanks. The tremendous destruction also deluded ground commanders into believing that enemy resistance after such an air attack would be negligible, but that was seldom the case.

Denied by the tenacity of the Germans both on the Gustav Line and at Anzio, the Allied commanders launched Strangle, an operation aimed at severing supply lines in northern Italy, so starving the German war machine and forcing a withdrawal. Between March 19 and May 11, 1944, Allied aircraft flew over 50,000 sorties against railway lines, tunnels, bridges and ports. It was a massive effort, but Strangle did not achieve the results its proponents predicted. The Germans were not forced to withdraw by the use of air power alone. However, their capacity to maintain their stocks of ammunition and food (or to move at all behind the front) was seriously diminished. When Strangle gave way to Diadem, a combined Allied air-ground offensive begun in May, the Germans were unable to maintain their resistance. The Gustav Line crumbled and the Allied forces swept forward, entering Rome on June 4, 1944, to join up with troops at last breaking out of the Anzio beachhead.

It had been almost a year since the invasion of Sicily. The quick Allied occupation of Italy originally hoped for had not materialized, and the Italian campaign was far from over. German resistance in Italy would persist until the last days of the war, while the Allies concentrated more of their efforts on other fronts. By the time Rome was taken by General Mark Clark's Fifth Army, the Allied forces in Italy had already had to accept the diversion of many units needed for the buildup of the Normandy invasion force in England (Overlord). Others would follow for an invasion of southern France (Anvil). France now featured at center stage, while Italy rumbled on, almost forgotten, in the background.

The reassuring presence of their own air cover little more than a distant memory, the German army retreated northward to form another defensive line, the Gothic, in the mountains south of the River Po valley. There the

> "I had observed the famous Flight Lieutenant Pattle in the mess tent several times. He was a very small man and very soft-spoken, and he possessed the deeply wrinkled doleful face of a cat who knew that all nine of its lives had already been used up."
>
> ROALD DAHL, *GOING SOLO*

These men flew and fought with the 332nd Fighter Group out of Northern Italy, to become known later as "The Tuskegee Airmen." This unit developed a reputation for getting the job done, never losing an escorted bomber to enemy action. From left, Bertram A. Levy, Henry L. Moore, Eugene J. Richardson Jr. and John L. Harrison Jr.

opposing armies faced each other through the miseries of a second Italian winter. Whenever the weather allowed, the Allied air forces kept up the pressure of their interdiction campaign, pounding transport routes until rail networks were a shambles and daylight travel of any kind, even by bicycle or mule, was unsafe. In the spring of 1945, when the Allied armies resumed their offensive, the Germans in Italy were no longer capable of effective resistance. They fell back across the Po, harassed unremittingly from the air, and finally surrendered on May 2, 1945.

The lessons learned by the Allies in the Mediterranean theater were not forgotten. Allied air superiority had allowed the ground forces the maximum possible flexibility in their operations. Strong medium bomber forces, notably

of B-25s and B-26s, had been at the heart of an interdiction campaign that had subjected enemy supply lines and airfields to an incessant pounding, seriously limiting freedom of action for the German Army and the Luftwaffe. The dramatic impact of the fighter-bomber had been repeatedly demonstrated, both in direct support of troops in contact with the enemy and in harassing movement of any kind behind the front. As General Ira Eaker wrote in February 1945: "The Mediterranean theater has been the primary crucible for the development of tactical air power and the evolution of joint command between Allies." At least some of these hard-learned lessons were to be carried forward and applied in WWII's climactic year, a year that began with the Allied invasion of Normandy.

CHAPTER 3

The Eastern Front

Before dawn on June 22, 1941, Hitler took his biggest gamble of the war, unleashing Operation Barbarossa against the Soviet Union while undefeated enemies fought on against him to Germany's west and south. He had always held that Germany should never fight on more than one front, but, frustrated by Britain's recalcitrance in the west and enmeshed in Mediterranean battles because of Mussolini's failures, he still felt compelled to pursue Germany's Lebensraum ("living space") in the vast territories of the Soviet Union without delay. It was his hope that a swift victory would persuade Britain to come to terms and deter the United States from entering the war. He also feared that time was working in favor of the Soviets, who, left in peace, would build their military strength and begin their own expansion westward when ready.

Operation Barbarossa

The German host facing the Soviet Union, including reserve formations in the rear, was the largest so far assembled in the history of warfare — almost 4 million men in 180 divisions, with 3,350 tanks and 7,200 guns. In addition, there were units from Italy and Rumania, and more were in the offing from Finland, Hungary and Czechoslovakia. There was even a volunteer division from Spain. Supporting this massive assembly were four Luftflotten controlling well over 2,000 aircraft, including 600 single-engine fighters, 850 medium bombers, over 200 dive-bombers, and strong transport and reconnaissance forces. On paper, it seemed that the Soviets should be capable of meeting even this huge challenge in the air. The Soviet Army's Military Aviation Forces (Voenno Vozdushnye Sily, or VVS) were numerically superior, with at least 12,000 aircraft on strength, some 10,000 of which were based in the west. However, the quality of the VVS was poor, with aircraft generally a generation older than those of the Luftwaffe, a disadvantage exacerbated when, despite a barrage of warning signs, the Soviets allowed themselves to be surprised by the German assault.

As the Luftwaffe swept down on the western Soviet airfields, the VVS aircraft stood in orderly rows, as if for peacetime inspection. The few I-16 fighters that did get airborne were generally brushed aside by battle-hardened German pilots. By the end of the day, some 1,489 VVS aircraft had been destroyed on the ground, and another 322 shot down. Soviet bombers tried to respond by attacking Luftwaffe airfields and German troop concentrations, but the formations of SB-2s and DB-3s did so unescorted and were massacred by defending fighters. At the end of

Opposite Page
A memorial to Soviet airmen stands in front of an Ilyushin Il-2 in Warsaw.

The Brewster Buffalo was regarded by most fighter pilots (including those of the RAF, seen here) as an inferior aircraft. This view was not shared by the Finns, many of whom used the Buffalo to great effect against the Soviet Air Force.

the first week, VVS losses had risen to 4,017, at a cost to the Luftwaffe of a mere 150 machines. At the same time, the German fighter units demonstrated their mobility, advancing behind their army at an unprecedented rate. Seven days after the start of the offensive, they were 150 miles from their starting points, and by July 21, they were another 200 miles further on, operating from fields just to the west of Smolensk. From there, Heinkel He 111s and Junkers Ju 88s were able to strike at Moscow. Stalin's prewar claims that the Soviet Union had the world's strongest air force were shown to be hollow, and it seemed that the effects of his purge of the military command structure in the late 1930s, which included the execution of numerous senior air force officers, were now being exposed in the evident inability of the VVS to defend the Soviet Union.

Far to the north, the Finns joined in on the German side and rapidly recovered the territory lost to the Soviets in the previous year. The Finnish Air Force fought with a rejuvenated front line, including American aircraft such as the Curtiss Hawk and the Brewster 239, a modified version of the Buffalo, an aircraft regarded with disdain in other air forces but admired by the Finns. Many of the Finnish Air Force aces scored heavily while flying Brewster's much-maligned fighter, including the two most successful, Eino Juutilainen and Hans Wind. Thirty-three of Juutilainen's ninety-four victories (the highest total recorded by a non-German) came while flying the

Brewster 239. In his opinion, it was "clearly the best fighter arriving during the temporary peace." He compared them to "fat hustlers, just like bees. They had speed, agility and good weaponry, too. We were happy to take them anywhere to take on any opponent." This high regard is reflected in the aircraft's Finnish nickname, "Taivaan Helmi" (Pearl of the Skies).

With the VVS units ahead of them either destroyed or rendered largely ineffective, the invading German forces were able to concentrate on practicing the blitzkrieg tactics that had served them so well on other fronts. Junkers Ju 87 Stukas came into their own once more, blasting strong-points resisting the German panzers and, together with the medium bombers, cutting off Soviet supply lines and making it impossible for their opponents to mount counter-attacks. As before, the system worked well. In a series of encirclement battles at Minsk, Smolensk, Gomel, Kiev and Vyazma, the Soviets were overwhelmed, the Germans capturing over two and a half million prisoners, nearly 10,000 tanks and more than 16,000 artillery pieces. At least 7,500 VVS aircraft had been destroyed by October. In the process, the Germans had reached a line stretching from Lake Ladoga in the north to the Sea of Azov; their troops in the center had reached a point only 120 miles from Moscow. They could hardly believe what they had accomplished.

For Luftwaffe pilots, these were heady days. The Bf 109s of Jagdgeschwader 51, led by Werner Mölders, were at the forefront of the battle. On June 30, 1941, they annihilated a large force of Soviet bombers, shooting down 114. Mölders accounted for five that day to raise his score to eighty-two, so becoming the first pilot to exceed Richthofen's WWI total. JG 51 as a whole gained the distinction of being the first fighter unit to record the destruction of 1,000 enemy aircraft, counting all conflicts. Two weeks later, Mölders gained his hundreth victory, and by mid-August three more fighter units (JGs 3, 53 and 54) had passed the 1,000 mark. JG 51 went on to reach 2,000 in mid-September, with some 1,350 of those claimed since the start of Barbarossa. Many other remarkable aviators laid the foundations for their combat careers during this period, among them Bf 109 pilots Gerhard Barkhorn (301 victories) and Günther Rall (275), and Ju 87 pilot Hans-Ulrich Rudel, who eventually flew 2,530 combat missions, more than any other airman anywhere. Rudel began with the spectacular sinking of the Soviet battleship *Marat* at Kronstadt on September 23, 1941, and finished the war having destroyed three ships, seventy landing craft, and 519 tanks. (Rudel was the only person to achieve the fourth additional grade of award to the Knight's Cross — oak leaves, swords, diamonds and golden oak leaves.) The remarkable figures achieved by some Luftwaffe pilots were the product of much more than skill, although they had that in abundance. They were also a reflection of their serving continuously in front-line units, never being rested in noncombat jobs as were most of their opponents. Flying in combat throughout the war, and more often than not in a target-rich environment, they had ample opportunities to build their scores. Perhaps most significantly, they were survivors.

Good though the news was for the Germans on the Soviet front in the autumn of 1941, all was not quite as it seemed. It

was now that the first signs of trouble appeared for the Germans as some unforeseen factors began to influence the struggle. The huge VVS losses, for example, had been mainly of obsolete aircraft. Barbarossa was launched when the Soviets were beginning a much-needed program of reorganization and reequipment, and newer aircraft of much better performance were already being manufactured at a faster rate than were their German counterparts. It was also true that most of the VVS losses had been suffered on the ground, which meant that the number of aircrew casualties had been relatively small, so there was no shortage of airmen to fly the new aircraft. On the other hand, whereas the Luftwaffe losses had been only one-fifth of their opponent's, they had been taken from a far smaller base and were all of modern aircraft and experienced crews. Luftwaffe replacements were hard to come by, since demands in the west and in the Mediterranean theater had to be met, too. Even the German success had itself complicated the situation. As the advance into the vast areas of the Soviet Union continued, the facts of geography confronted the Luftwaffe with the need to cover an ever-expanding front with a reducing force. To confound things still further, the Soviet's great winter allies now entered the picture: rain, snow and ice made flying hazardous,

Feared by the German army as flying tanks, the heavily armored Ilyushin ground attack aircraft were essential elements of the great Soviet offensives from Stalingrad on. More than 35,000 Il-2 and Il-10 Shturmoviks were produced.

airfields unusable, roads impassable, resupply difficult, and machines intractable.

Taking advantage of the severe conditions, the Soviets mounted several counterattacks, including one to the northwest of Moscow. They made limited progress but, around the town of Demyansk, they surrounded 100,000 German soldiers. It seemed that the Wehrmacht was about to suffer its first major defeat in the Soviet Union, but it was decided that the Luftwaffe should try to save the situation, sustaining the isolated units by air. The curtain rose on the first major airlift in history on February 20, 1942, when Ju 52/3ms began flying into Demyansk in an endless stream. Day after day, in all weathers and in the face of heavy anti-aircraft fire and VVS fighters, the Ju 52/3ms kept coming. By the time the siege was broken on May 18, the transports had flown more than 33,000 sorties, delivering 64,844 tons of supplies. There were 30,500 reinforcements taken in and 25,400 casualties brought out. It was a staggering performance, but it had a dark side. It had cost 265 transport aircraft, which the Luftwaffe could ill afford to lose, and it had given the German High Command the false impression that a surrounded force could always rely on being supplied by air.

After the relative stalemate during the winter of 1941/42, the Germans planned to resume the exhilarating progress of Barbarossa's early days, but with the emphasis shifted to the southern front. Hitler reasoned that the loss of the principal grain and oil-producing regions in the south would cripple the Soviet war machine. He therefore directed that the main German spring offensive should be launched through the Ukraine toward the Crimea and the Caucasus. The Soviets, expecting the main effort to be directed at Moscow, were surprised once again, and the Germans were able to make rapid progress, capturing the Crimea and penetrating to the foothills of the Caucasus and the River Volga at Stalingrad by the summer of 1942. Impressive though these advances were, they served only to exaggerate German problems, greatly extending supply lines and dangerously expanding the front.

The Luftwaffe's lack of a strategic bombing force now had serious consequences. In a monumental achievement, the Soviets had uprooted the major elements of their war industry and carried it east of the Urals, beyond the range of German bombers. From there an increasing flood of war material flowed, the VVS making good its losses with new

MiG-3, Yak-1 and LaGG-3 fighters, Il-2 attack aircraft, and Pe-2 light bombers. In 1942, the relocated factories produced some 25,000 aircraft, 10,000 more than were built that year by German industry. (Military aircraft production figures demonstrate the Allied material advantage in WWII. In 1942, the Allies [the U.S.A., U.K., British Commonwealth, U.S.S.R.] built 101,519 aircraft, four times the Axis [Germany, Italy, Japan] total of 26,670. In 1943, the figures were 151,761 to 43,100, and in 1944, 167,654 to 67,987.) While none of the fighters produced in 1942 was yet a

It would be difficult to imagine a more unlikely WWII combat aircraft than the little Polikarpov Po-2. First introduced in 1928, the Po-2 remained in production until 1952, by which time more than 20,000 had been built. Slow, stable and reliable, this simple aircraft was adapted to fill many roles — trainer, light transport, reconnaissance, and ambulance among them. Surprisingly, the Po-2 also proved to be effective as a light bomber, and was flown by the "Night Witches," Soviet women combat pilots who operated at night over the German lines, perpetually harassing German forward units. The Po-2s on these pages can be seen at the Muzeum Lotnictwa Polskiego in Krakow, Poland (opposite), and at La Ferte Alais near Paris.

One of the versatile Po-2's many roles was that of air ambulance. The rear cockpit makes way for a stretcher compartment.

match for the Bf 109F, they were all great improvements on their predecessors and they were produced in quantities that more than made good the continuing attrition. The Luftwaffe could still impose local air superiority where needed, but its losses were increasing and were harder to replace.

German pilots were also finding that the Soviet defenders were gaining in experience and determination. They already knew that many Soviets flew with desperate courage, as was evidenced by the deliberate adoption by the VVS of ramming *(taran)* as a combat technique. Especially in the early days, when they were flying considerably inferior machines, the *taran* was frequently seen as the only way to guarantee the destruction of the enemy. Nine rammings took place on the first day of Barbarossa, usually when a pilot had exhausted his ammunition. By the end of the war, the *taran* had been used against the Luftwaffe more than 200 times. Lieutenant Boris Kobzan survived the highest number of ramming attacks with a total of four, and Alexander Khlobystov made three. Seventeen other VVS pilots were credited with ramming success twice.

Soviet Phoenix

In 1942, air battles continued to be fought all along the 2,000 mile front stretching between the White and the Black Seas, but the confrontation that took place in the skies around Stalingrad was pivotal. It was there that the VVS began to steal the initiative from the Luftwaffe, establishing a pattern that would be fully developed in two crucial battles in 1943 — the Kuban and Kursk. Drastically reformed by General Alexander Novikov and increasingly equipped with modern machines, including British and American aircraft besides improved versions of their own, the VVS grew increasingly assertive during the long, grinding struggle for Stalingrad. The German Sixth Army commanded by General Paulus, accustomed to the classic blitzkrieg tactics of moving swiftly over the open steppe with the close support of the Luftwaffe, became enmeshed in a murderous close-encounter street fight with the Soviet Army, with advances measured in yards rather than miles. German close-air support, in the absence of obvious targets in a city reduced to piles of rubble, could do little to affect the issue on the ground.

As the Sixth Army was drawn more and more deeply into Stalingrad's streets, Marshal Georgi Zhukov was given command of the Soviet forces. He believed that the Axis forces were overextended and that an opportunity existed for them to be decisively defeated. Keeping just enough troops in Stalingrad to maintain a precarious foothold, Zhukov built up massive forces far back on the flanks of the Axis salient. The flanks were held by Rumanian and Italian armies, less well equipped and not so committed to the destruction of the Soviet Union as their German allies. On the morning of November 19, 1942, the Soviet counter-offensive was unleashed, and five days later, the jaws of a giant pincer movement closed, trapping the German Sixth Army and part of the Fourth Panzer Army, more than quarter of a million men, in a pocket about 30 miles long by 25 miles wide.

The experience of the successful airlift operation at Demyansk now reinforced Hitler's determination to order Paulus to stand fast, and Göring foolishly assured the Führer that the job could be done, thereby committing the Luftwaffe to a hopeless task. To maintain his position and continue to fight, Paulus had to have about 750 tons of supplies per day. To deliver that amount, 375 Ju 52/3ms needed to land in the pocket every 24 hours. Even in good weather, this was far beyond the Luftwaffe's capabilities. Given the low normal availability rate of 35 percent, a huge force of over 1,000 transport aircraft would have had to be assembled. Even though other fronts were denuded of Ju 52/3ms to cope with the emergency, and aircraft such as He 111s, He 177s, and Fw 200s were added to the fleet, the task was beyond them. The winter, too, affected the number of delivery flights that could be made, heavy snow and severe cold seriously reducing the sorties flown. Transports braving the winter storms to reach the pocket had to run the gauntlet of VVS fighters and cross an increasingly dense belt of antiaircraft guns. Accidents

Among the many Allied types to operate with the Soviet Air Force was the Hawker Hurricane. This Hurricane IIA operated from Vaenga, near Murmansk.

were frequent, brought on by the appalling conditions or by aircrew fatigue, and VVS ground-attack aircraft deepened German misery with frequent strikes at heavily congested airfields. Throughout December 1942 and January 1943, the best efforts of the Luftwaffe averaged a daily delivery of less than 100 tons to the besieged Germans. At the end of January, with the last of his airstrips overrun and unable to resist the crushing pressure of the encircling Soviets any longer, the recently promoted Field Marshal Paulus surrendered. Only 90,000 of his men survived the siege to be taken prisoner and not more than 5,000 of those ever returned to Germany.

The defeat suffered by the Wehrmacht at Stalingrad was grievous, but the impact of the struggle on the Luftwaffe was no less devastating. Losses included almost 200 fighters and 495 transports: 269 Ju 52/3ms, 169 He 111s, forty-two Ju 86s, nine Fw 200s, five He 177s, and one Ju 290. As important as the material loss was the effect that crew losses had on other parts of the Luftwaffe. Many of the airmen who flew into Stalingrad were on temporary detachment from their normal duties, notably as instructors, and their loss caused crew shortages and disruption in training programs that were not easily overcome.

To the Luftwaffe men who faced the VVS during the battle for Stalingrad, it was evident that their Soviet opponents were no longer the disorganized, poorly equipped enemies of Barbarossa. They were aggressive, persistent and courageous, and there were new aircraft for them to fly, La-5s and Yak-9s, which at the low altitudes where most combat took place were a match for the Bf 109 and Fw 190. The Soviet squadrons were now led by battle-hardened veterans, many of them, such as Aleksandr Pokryshkin

OPPOSITE *Dr. Galina Brok-Beltsova, a Russian combat aviator, flew and fought in the battle of Konigsberg. She was decorated by Stalin; her awards include three orders of the Soviet Union as well as thirteen other ribbons. A navigator in the 125th Regiment, flying in Pe-2 bombers, she participated in forcing the retreat of the German occupiers from the Soviet Union. After the war, Galina completed a doctorate in history and became head of the History Department at the Moscow Engineering Institute.*

ABOVE *On display at the Polish Military Museum in Warsaw, one of the world's few remaining Petlyakov Pe-2 twin-engined light bombers used extensively by the Soviets in their war against Hitler.*

RIGHT *A document from one of Dr. Beltsova's decorations and a wartime photograph of her and her unit comrades in front of a Pe-2. The X marked in ink on the photograph is Dr. Beltsova.*

BELOW *The header from a World War II Soviet government publication.*

(59 victories) and Vitali Popkov (41), on their way to becoming aces of some stature. The ground-attack squadrons were making themselves felt, too. Flying the heavily armored Il-2 Shturmovik, they attacked airfields, vehicles and troop concentrations relentlessly, and they joined in against the Ju 52/3ms when the opportunity arose. On January 9, 1943, seven Il-2s gave a powerful demonstration of their effectiveness. They flew low-level to the German airfield of Sal'sk, 250 miles from Stalingrad, where more than 300 German aircraft were concentrated. In a series of strafing runs over the congested aircraft parking area, the Soviet airmen destroyed seventy-two Luftwaffe machines.

At the other end of the offensive scale for the VVS were the U-2 units. Polikarpov's little open-cockpit biplane, designed as a primary trainer in 1927, became a thorn in the side of the invading Wehrmacht. (The Polikarpov U-2 was redesignated Po-2 in honor of its designer after his death in 1944.) Dozens of night-bomber regiments were formed to fly the U-2VS version which was fitted with racks capable of carrying up to 500 pounds of bombs. At Stalingrad and in all the other Soviet offensives, they were used in large numbers against German troop positions after dark. Their harassing attacks, flying slowly at low level (maximum speed was 90 mph), were remarkably effective. Neither Luftwaffe night fighters nor antiaircraft guns were very successful in discouraging their operations, the slow speed and relative quietness of the U-2s serving to make them difficult targets. (The success of the VVS night harassment tactics inspired their adoption by the Luftwaffe. Units were formed to fly small biplanes such as the Arado 66 or Gotha 145 in low-level night missions dropping antipersonnel bombs on enemy troop concentrations.) Among the most celebrated of the U-2 units was the 588th Night Bomber Regiment, which was staffed entirely by women, from pilots to mechanics. The "Night Witches" of the 588th flew 24,000 combat sorties during the war, and twenty-three of its pilots were made Heroes of the Soviet Union. Nor were they the only female units involved in aerial combat. Other women went into combat flying Yak-7 fighters, Pe-2 bombers or Il-2 Shturmoviks.

The Battle of Kursk, *by Nicolas Trudgian. Hans-Ulrich Rudel's Ju 87 Stukas attacking Soviet tanks during the Battle of Kursk in July 1943.*

The Kuban

In the spring of 1943, the German 17th Army was dug in on either side of the Kuban River, clinging to the last Axis foothold in the Caucasus, a peninsula separating the Sea of Azov from the Black Sea. The clash between armies here, though fierce, was not at center stage and was overshadowed by events further north. However, the aerial battles escalated into a major confrontation that confirmed the growing strength and capability of the VVS. In February, Soviet ground forces had established a beachhead at Myskhako, on the right flank of the Seventeenth Army, which threatened to destabilize the German position. An offensive to drive the Soviets out began on April 17, and for the first two days the Luftwaffe was able to operate in support of the Wehrmacht with almost no interference, but their attacks failed to loosen the Soviet grip on the beachhead and German troops made little progress on the ground. On April 19, the situation began to change. The

VVS appeared in strength to challenge the Luftwaffe aggressively. Large bomber formations struck at German troop positions, and the intensity of the aerial fight increased sharply. By April 29, the focus of the struggle had shifted some 20 miles north to Krymskya, as the Soviets mounted their own combined offensive against the center of the German line. After a night of preparation during which the "Night Witches" of the 46th Bomber Regiment harassed the enemy in their U-2s, the main assault began with a VVS onslaught of 144 bombers, 82 attack aircraft and 265 fighters. The Luftwaffe responded in kind, and the ensuing air battles became swirling dogfights, with up to a hundred aircraft from each side contesting the air space over the front again and again every day for weeks on end.

The Kuban campaign boiled on until the first week in June, ending in stalemate. The VVS, however, emerged from this aerial cauldron with an increased sense of its own worth. As the official Soviet history says: "[The Kuban air operations] provided a school for the Soviet Air Force to perfect its skills." Throughout the battle, the Luftwaffe remained a dangerous foe, and the VVS was able to claim air superiority over the front only occasionally, but it was apparent to both sides that the confrontation in the air was now a more equal contest, with the alarming prospect for the Luftwaffe that, no matter how many of their opponents they shot down, the strength and competence of the VVS went on rising inexorably.

At the same time, there was less disparity of abilities at an individual level, and a number of Soviet pilots enhanced their reputations considerably in the skies of the Kuban. Aleksandr Pokryshkin continued to grow in stature and lead by example, deriving and teaching air-combat tactics as he observed his enemy and learned from combat experience. Flying his Bell P-39 Airacobra over the Kuban, Pokryshkin added twenty victories to his personal total. There were many others who emerged under his tutelage and went on to become leading VVS aces, among them the Glinka brothers, Dmitriy and Boris (21 and 10 during the Kuban campaign; 50 and 30 at the war's end), and Grigory Rechkalov (11 and 58). At least seven other VVS pilots shot down ten or more over the Kuban. Exact figures of total aircraft losses by both sides are hard to come by, but it seems likely that the Luftwaffe lost some 800 while claiming more than 2,000 VVS aircraft destroyed in combat. This apparent victory for the Luftwaffe was not what it seemed, however. By this stage of the war, the irresistible mathematics of supply and demand were moving inexorably in the Soviet Union's long-term favor.

In the Battle of Kursk, the Ilyushin Il-2s destroyed hundreds of German tanks with their 37 mm cannon and hollow-charge bombs. In Stalin's opinion, the Il-2s were "as essential to the Red Army as air and bread."

The Greatest Battle

For a short while in the spring of 1943, the German forces in the Ukraine relived their success of the previous year. Soviet units, racing west from their victory at Stalingrad, outran their logistic support and were pushed back by General von Manstein in the last successful German offensive of the war. In this he had the able support of General Wolfram von Richthofen's Luftflotte 4, which, released from the demands of Stalingrad, managed to average 1,000 sorties per day. By the time the German advance was brought to a halt, it had recovered the city of Kharkov and driven a wedge into the Soviet front that formed the southern boundary of a huge salient, 100 miles across, centered on the small town of Kursk. Studying his maps, Hitler decided that an operation should be launched to straighten out the front while destroying the Soviet forces in the huge bulge. Massive forces would be hurled at the shoulders of the salient, driving forward in blitzkrieg fashion to meet each other behind trapped Soviet troops.

Preparation for Operation Citadel drew in German forces from other fronts to provide sufficient strength for the assault. The Luftwaffe managed to assemble over 2,000 aircraft, but the demands of the Mediterranean and the West meant that only 600 of these could be fighters.

ILYUSHIN IL-2

The National Air & Space Museum in Washington, D.C., has restored an Ilyushin Il-2. Notable is the fact that most of the aircraft's heavy armor is fitted to cover the engine and fuel tanks. From the cockpit rearward, the Il-2 is made of wood. The gunner's cockpit contains a webbing strap to serve as a seat. The engine (a 1,770-horsepower Mikulin) was photographed in Krakow, Poland.

German ground forces learned to fear the Il-2 Shturmovik, which played a decisive role in the Soviet campaigns from Stalingrad to Berlin.

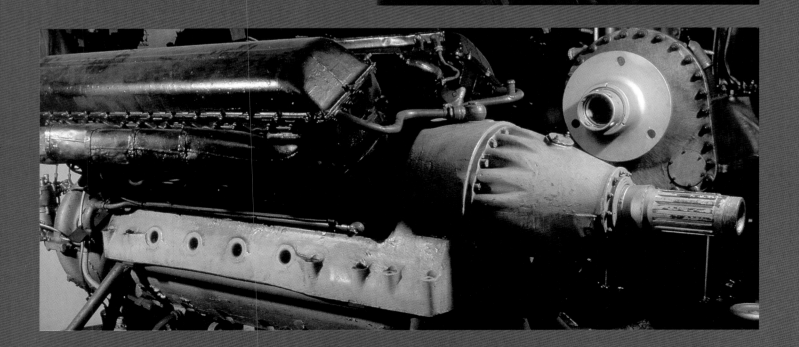

The Tupolev SB-2 had its operational debut during the Spanish Civil War. Later SB-2s saw combat against the Japanese and the Finns. By 1941, they were becoming obsolescent and were transferred to less demanding roles.

There were 1,200 bombers and 100 of the new Henschel Hs 129 attack aircraft, the German equivalent of the Shturmovik. It would have been difficult to keep the preparations for such a massive operation secret in any event, but the Soviets were well aware of what Hitler intended, well-placed intelligence sources combined with thorough aerial reconnaissance providing them with all the necessary information. They planned to meet the challenge, packing the bulge with combat units and building a series of formidable defensive barriers. By the time the Germans were ready, the Soviet forces waiting to meet them included 1.3 million troops, 20,000 guns and mortars, and 3,600 tanks and self-propelled guns. The strength of the VVS for the initial phase of the battle comprised the 2nd and 16th Air Armies, backed by the 5th and the 17th, which together provided 1,060 fighters, 940 ground-attack aircraft and 900 bombers. Taking into account other Air Armies held in reserve, the VVS could call on over 5,400 combat aircraft for the Kursk campaign, almost all of them modern types quite capable of holding

> *"Once committed to an attack, fly in at full speed. After scoring crippling or disabling hits, I would clear myself and then repeat the process. I never pursued the enemy once they had eluded me. Better to break off and set up again for a new assault…. Combat flying is based on the slashing attack and rough maneuvering…fancy precision aerobatic work is really not of much use."*
>
> ERICH "BUBI" HARTMANN, JG 52, WORLD'S LEADING ACE, WITH 352 AERIAL VICTORIES IN WWII.

their own with the Luftwaffe. There had also been changes in the way the VVS operated. Inter-unit communications had been improved, radar was more commonly available, and radio sets had become standard equipment in front-line aircraft. And 154 new airstrips, stocked with fuel and ammunition, were provided for the use of the 2nd and 16th Air Armies alone.

Aware on the morning of July 5 that the German assault was imminent, the VVS launched more than 400 aircraft in a predawn raid against five airfields near Kharkov, aiming to catch the Luftwaffe as it formed up on the ground for its opening sorties. The plan backfired. German radar gave ample warning of the raid, and fighters from JG 3 and JG 52 were scrambled in good time to intercept. The ensuing air battle was a disaster for the VVS, with the Bf 109Gs shooting down 120 Soviet aircraft at minimal cost to themselves. By the end of the day, the Luftwaffe claimed 432 victories, and 24 hours later the total had risen to 637. Such carnage in the air had a powerful effect on the ground battle. For the first two days, the VVS fighter force was in disarray, unable to counter German air operations effectively. Two Soviet major generals commanding Fighter Corps were replaced because it was judged that their fighters were failing to meet their commitments. Nor were the formidable Shturmoviks at first successful in blunting the advance of the panzers. Lacking strong fighter cover at this point, few of the small Il-2 formations got through to bring their

37 mm cannon to bear on the German tanks. On subsequent days, they were ordered to fly in much larger groups and to attack with cannon and hollow-charge antitank bombs using the "circle of death" tactic. This involved the Il-2s passing the oncoming panzers to one side before turning in to attack them from behind in a 30-degree dive, releasing their bombs at 200 to 300 yards from the target. As Shturmovik pilot Alexander Yefimov described it: "We usually tried to attack from the rear where the armor was thinner and where the most vulnerable components were located — the engines and the fuel tanks…the effect was staggering." In one such attack, the 9th Panzer Division lost seventy tanks in twenty minutes. Yefimov felt that his aircraft was a willing partner in battle: "The Il-2 was well disposed to combat. It invited you to attack." Stalin needed no convincing, his belief in his Shturmoviks reflected in his remark that "They are as essential to the Red Army as air and bread."

The antitank operations mounted by the Luftwaffe were almost equally impressive. Operating under heavy fighter cover, the small numbers of heavily armored Hs 129s proved their worth, on one occasion destroying fifty Soviet tanks in one hour. A modification of the ubiquitous Ju 87 Stuka also showed its promise. Armed with two 37 mm cannon slung under the wings in detachable pods, the sluggish Ju 87 was even slower and less maneuverable, but in the hands of Hans-Ulrich Rudel, it was an armored soldier's nightmare. On July 5, Rudel personally destroyed twelve Soviet tanks. While he hunted at low level, many of the fighter pilots flying above him also had good days. Hubert Strassl of JG 51 flew four sorties of intense combat and claimed fifteen shot down, and he was not the only pilot to get into double figures — Johannes Weise and Walter Krupinski of JG 52 claimed twelve and eleven respectively.

The Petlyakov Pe-8 was a Soviet attempt to produce a four-engined strategic bomber to match those of the U.S. and Britain. It began reaching Soviet squadrons in 1940, but was never successful, being plagued by technical problems throughout its service life. Production ceased in 1944 after relatively few had been built.

The VVS, too, had its share of heroes. During the whole of the Kursk battle, Arsenii Vorozheikin achieved nineteen victories (fifty-two by the end of the war), and a young man named Ivan Kozhedub survived a near fatal encounter with Bf 109Gs on his first combat mission to shoot down eight. He would go on scoring consistently until the end of the war, raising his total to sixty-two, so becoming the highest-scoring Allied ace of WWII. However, perhaps the most remarkable fighter pilot at Kursk was Alexei Maras'yev. In April 1942 he had been shot down and had crashed in German-held territory, severely injuring both legs in the process. For nineteen days he crawled to the Soviet lines, subsisting on berries and insects. Both legs had to be amputated below the knee, but Maras'yev was not to be discouraged. Fitted with artificial limbs, he rejoined his unit in time to fight at Kursk, where he claimed ten aerial victories. He survived the war with a final score of nineteen, and the Gold Star of a Hero of the Soviet Union.

As long as the Luftwaffe had the upper hand, the Wehrmacht seemed to be making progress on the ground. On the southern edge of the salient, in particular, Manstein's troops initially tore a huge gap in the first Soviet line of defense. The fighting between the opposing armored forces was fierce, with punishing losses being suffered by both sides. Even as early as the second day of the struggle, however, it was apparent that the Luftwaffe would be unable to maintain the pace of its operations. Having flown 4,298 sorties on the first day, it could manage only 2,100 the next, and the total continued to fall as each day went by. At the same time, the VVS began to improve, fortified by rapid replacements and generous reinforcement. By July 10, the

In the Lavochkin La-7, the Soviets had a fighter that could take on the best of the Luftwaffe. Powered by a 1,850-horsepower Shvetsov radial, the La-7 was fast and ideally suited to the low-level combat of the Eastern Front. Among the units to fly the La-7 was the Normandy Nieman Regiment, which had a lion badge and was manned by French pilots.

German offensive had ground to a halt, having gained 20 miles on the southern edge of the salient, and only 8 miles to the north. On July 12, in a desperate attempt to break through the impasse, the Germans hurled two groups of 600 and 300 tanks forward from the south. They were met by an equal number of Soviet tanks in the largest armored battle ever fought, with each side calling on its air force for strong antitank support. At the end of the day, the German thrust had been repulsed. Both sides had suffered grievous losses, both in the air and on the ground, but the Soviets had replacements in the wings and the Germans had not.

At this point, Hitler lost his nerve. News of the Allied landings in Sicily and of a building Soviet offensive toward Orel, on the northern flank of the Kursk salient, convinced him that Operation Citadel should be abandoned. It was formally canceled on July 17, and a number of German formations were transferred to Italy. German hopes of regaining the initiative against the Soviet Union had been dashed at Kursk, and were never to be restored. From July 1943 onward, it would be the fate of the German forces to beat a fighting retreat all the way to Berlin, as the Soviets, in ever-increasing strength, engaged in relentless pursuit. The respective aircraft losses at Kursk probably favored the Luftwaffe by at least two to one, but the VVS held the upper hand in the air when the battle was over. The diminished Luftwaffe would later show that it was still capable of achieving local air superiority for a while, but the general trend was irreversible. The VVS was now markedly superior to the

Luftwaffe numerically, flew aircraft that were roughly equal in capability, and was catching up fast in the fields of tactics and training. The Soviets were also fighting on one front, whereas the Luftwaffe was spread ever more thinly over three, its strength being whittled away in endless battles at the edges of Hitler's crumbling empire with little thought for the forthcoming need to give priority to the defense of the Reich.

Ace of Aces

It remained true, right to the end of the war, that there were Luftwaffe pilots whose outstanding capabilities enabled them to survive against the odds and to excel in individual combat. The supreme exponent of the fighter pilot's skills was Erich "Bubi" Hartmann, a late starter who did not reach a fighter squadron until October 1942, when he was posted to JG 52 in the Caucasus. His first victory on November 5 was over an Il-2, but pieces of his victim's aircraft struck Hartmann's Bf 109, evening the score by forcing him to crash-land. Six months later, he had flown over 100 missions but had raised his score to just seven. Success began to come more quickly during the Kursk battle, when he shot down seven enemy aircraft on July 7, but it seemed as though his combat career had come to an end on August 19, when he was brought down by ground fire and captured by Soviet troops. He feigned injury and was put aboard a truck to be taken to the rear. Some time later, the truck ran off the road when attacked by a Ju 87. The driver and the guards ran for cover and Hartmann ran in the opposite direction, reaching the German lines many hours

Marcel Albert became one of the leading French aces of WWII flying on the Eastern Front with the Soviet Air Force as a member of the Normandie Niemen Regiment. He finished the war with 23 aerial victories and was awarded the singular honor, for a non-Soviet, of being named "Hero of the Soviet Union" by Stalin.

later. By September 18, 1943, he had flown 300 missions and had 95 victories to his credit, but only six weeks later he had 148 and was awarded the Knight's Cross.

Hartmann's personal combat doctrine was by now established. He had concluded that dogfighting was a waste of time and effort, to be avoided if at all possible. It was his job, he believed, to be the hired assassin, shooting down as many enemy aircraft as he could while living to fight another day. To do that he took the trouble to ensure that the tactical situation was in his favor before committing himself to battle; then it was a case of getting in quickly, going very close and firing one solid burst, before using his excess speed to zoom away. He later speculated that perhaps as many as 90 percent of his victims never even saw him. The Oak Leaves followed his 200th kill

on March 2, 1944, and the Swords came on July 4 with his 239th. Now fully into his stride, he claimed another 78 in four weeks of intense air fighting, passing 301 with eight and eleven on successive days. He was awarded the Diamonds to the Knight's Cross on August 25. Over Rumania he had his first combat with aircraft of the Western Allies, and in the course of several clashes, shot down seven USAAF P-51s. Hartmann continued to fight to the end, scoring his final kill over Brno, Czechoslovakia, on the last day of the war. His total number of aerial victories was 352, scored in 1,425 missions, over 800 of which included combat. (It was Hartmann's misfortune that he was well known to both sides. Although taken into custody by American troops at the war's end, he was handed over to the Soviets, who held him in prison camps for ten and a half years before sending him home. When he had recovered his health, Hartmann joined the new West German Air Force in 1959 to command JG 71 [Richthofen] flying jet fighters, North American F-86s.)

Operating Hurricanes in the winter of Russia's far, frozen north was not easy. Ice, snow and freezing temperatures made the Merlin engines temperamental and played havoc with the wood and fabric in the airframe. Ground crews performing maintenance in the open had to be bundled up with bulky clothing and thick gloves.

On to Berlin

By the end of 1943, the gathering momentum of the Soviet offensives had liberated Kiev and sealed off the German forces in the Crimea. The character of the Soviet advance had become well established. It involved a high degree of coordination between land and air forces. As the advance progressed, the VVS operated in strength, attacking enemy vehicles and positions immediately ahead of the troops. At the same time, bombers and attack aircraft carried out interdiction missions against airfields and communications behind the enemy front lines, and fighters provided a protective screen, challenging the Luftwaffe aggressively for local air superiority. These operations, undertaken boldly and with determination, were costly in men and machines, but their relentless application kept the Luftwaffe on the defensive. Once the Soviet forces renewed their offensive after Kursk, it became evident that the Luftwaffe no longer had the power to win a sustained confrontation with the VVS. By the beginning of 1944, the Luftwaffe could put some 2,000 operational aircraft into the front line in the east, but the VVS faced them with over 8,000, with more arriving every day. In a desperate bid to redress the balance, proposals were made at the highest levels and plans drawn up for the Luftwaffe to turn belatedly in the direction of strategic bombing, meant to strike at the roots of Soviet military power, the factories and power plants buried deep within the Soviet Union. It was a task far beyond the Luftwaffe's capabilities and came to nothing. The means available to attempt such a mission were too little, and it was very much too late.

The Soviet forces stormed forward irresistibly during the early months of 1944. Leningrad was relieved after a 900-day siege; the Ukraine and the Crimea were cleared of the enemy; and by June, the Soviets were poised to launch Operation Bagration, a massive assault aimed at recovering Byelorussia. With considerable sense of theater, it was timed for June 22, three years to the day since the start of Hitler's Operation Barbarossa. The Luftwaffe, with some 2,000 aircraft covering the whole Eastern Front from the Baltic to the Black Sea (fewer than 400 of them single-engine fighters), braced for the onslaught of the VVS, which now had 13,500 aircraft in its front line, 6,000 of them deployed to support Bagration. When it came, the impact of Bagration was devastating. As the German ground forces were swept aside, the Luftwaffe redeployed some 270 fighters and ground-attack aircraft from other fronts to stem the rout. Aircraft until then thought essential to cope with the demands of the Allied bridgehead in Normandy and the fronts in Italy and the Balkans were thrown into the maelstrom of Byelorussia. They proved inadequate and did little to ease the situation. By the end of July, the Luftwaffe in the east was down to no more than 1,750 aircraft all told (only 315 single-engine fighters) and was suffering from the inevitable dislocation brought on by being continually uprooted as the headlong German retreat continued.

Just before launching Bagration, the Soviets attacked along the Finnish frontier, forcing a general retreat that led to a truce with Finland on September 4. Rumania had already capitulated following a coup d'état, and within days the Bulgarians defected from the Axis. The loss of the Ploesti oil-fields exacerbated an already severe German fuel shortage, limiting the amount of flying even the depleted Luftwaffe could undertake. (On September 11, 1944, the Luftwaffe managed to fly only 250 sorties over the whole of the Eastern Front in response to some 2,500 by the VVS.) In these circumstances, the Luftwaffe was unable to have much effect on the overall military position. By the end of the year, it was apparent that the situation was past saving and that the once powerful Luftwaffe was no longer a factor to be seriously reckoned with in countering the awesome might of the VVS.

As more and more of Eastern Europe fell under Soviet influence, a conscious effort was made to "internationalize" VVS operations by forming foreign volunteer air regiments. The most celebrated of these had existed since 1942, when Free French volunteers traveled to the Soviet Union to organize the "Normandie Regiment." From October 1944, it was renamed "Normandie-Nieman" in recognition of its outstanding contributions during the crossing of the Nieman River. Several of its pilots were awarded the Gold Star of Hero of the Soviet Union, including Marcel Albert, who became the Armée de l'Air's top

scorer with twenty-three victories. Fourteen French pilots serving with the "Normandie-Niemans" were credited with ten victories or more. In the latter stages of the war, the French were joined in the VVS by regiments of Poles, Czechs, Rumanians and Bulgarians. From the Soviet point of view, there were political advantages to be had from the inclusion of nationals from eastern Europe, in regions where it was hoped that the Soviet Union's writ would loom large in the postwar years.

In 1945, with Soviet armies sweeping into the Baltic states, Poland, Yugoslavia, Hungary, Austria and Czechoslovakia, the Luftwaffe continued to attempt the impossible, shuffling units around from one crisis to the next in futile attempts to check the German collapse. As the end grew near, the decision was made to concentrate much of the Luftwaffe's remaining power on the Eastern Front, consciously reducing the reaction to Anglo-American progress while resisting as far as possible any further Soviet advance into Prussia. The shrinking perimeters of the Reich may have served to ease the Luftwaffe's problems by shortening the fronts to be covered, but this was more than offset by the fuel crisis and the severe shortage of spares, brought about by the loss of access to factories overrun by the Soviet forces.

Nevertheless, the final Soviet offensive, launched across the River Oder in the middle of April, was met by a last convulsive effort on the part of the Luftwaffe, which flew some 1,000 sorties per day from airfields near Berlin in a desperate effort to slow the enemy down. Among the attacks made on Soviet communications were some directed against bridges using Mistel composite weapons systems. Fw 190s or Bf 109s were combined with pilotless Ju 88 airframes packed with explosive. Fighter pilots flew the cumbersome Mistels to arrive at a point about 1,000 yards from their targets, releasing the Ju 88 guided missiles in dives at about 400 mph. Successes were achieved against bridges over the Oder, Neisse and Vistula Rivers, but the casualty rate was high and the attacks had little effect on Soviet progress. By May 2, 1945, the Soviet flag was flying over the Reichstag in Berlin.

> "German air personnel learned the grim truth that the VVS in 1943 had acquired new competence born of battle experience and upgraded air tactics. After Kursk, the Luftwaffe no longer possessed the means to win any sustained air battle with the Soviets."
>
> VON HARDESTY, RED PHOENIX

CHAPTER 4

Strategic Bombing Offensive

Dᴜʀɪɴɢ ᴛʜᴇ ᴡɪɴᴛᴇʀ ᴏꜰ 1941/42, as the shocking implications of the Butt Report were being digested and the first of Bomber Command's new aircraft were becoming operational, there was something of a pause for breath in the bombing offensive. The lull was broken in February 1942, following the arrival of yet another directive and a new Commander-in-Chief, Air Marshal Sir Arthur Harris.

Night Assault on Germany

"Cometh the hour, cometh the man." Air Marshal Harris was an old-fashioned warrior and a devotee of Trenchard's strategic air power doctrine. He had no doubts about what had to be done, and he was gratified to find that the tools for him to do it were at last coming to hand. His directive was unequivocal. It said that he could "employ his forces without restriction" and was specific about concentrating the assault on "the morale of the enemy civil population." Reinforcing the directive's intention, Sir Charles Portal, the Chief of the Air Staff, spelled it out with the utmost clarity in a follow-up letter. "I suppose it is clear," he said "that the aiming points are to be built-up areas and not, for instance, dockyards or aircraft factories."

Given a green light for a campaign of area bombing against German cities, it was a pity from the C-in-C's point of view that more of the new heavy bombers were not immediately available. The Stirling, Halifax and Manchester, conceived as early as 1936, had all suffered teething troubles and were late coming into service. Although their numbers rose steadily during 1942, the Stirling remained a disappointment and the Manchester was an outright failure. However, the first few examples of a fourth "heavy," the Lancaster (originally the Manchester III), had just arrived in the Command, and these promised to be ideal for Harris's purpose. Indeed, before 1942 was out, it became obvious that the Lancaster was a truly outstanding aircraft, and by war's end, it equipped no fewer than fifty-six front-line squadrons.

Besides being the beneficiary of improvements in the range, speed, ceiling and weight-lifting capacity of his aircraft, Harris also presided over a period of technological development that was, in many ways, even more significant. The Butt

Oᴘᴘᴏsɪᴛᴇ Pᴀɢᴇ
Artifacts of the USAAF's Eighth Air Force — flying clothing, badges of rank, ammunition and navigational instruments lie among pictures showing the harsh reality of combat and visions of girls back home. In the background are maps of target areas in Germany.

Air Chief Marshal Sir Arthur Harris, Commander-in-Chief, RAF Bomber Command, at his desk. His SASO (Senior Air Staff Officer), Air Vice-Marshal Robert Saundby, is by his right shoulder.

argued that Germany could be bludgeoned to defeat in six months if a force of 4,000 heavy bombers were assembled. Air Marshal Harris sensed that Bomber Command stood at a crossroads. He determined to stage a demonstration of strategic air power that would disarm the critics and ensure the future of the bombing offensive. He began with raids on the Baltic cities of Lubeck and Rostock. Although they were out of its range, Gee was used to its limit to reduce navigational errors, and the inclusion of a high percentage of incendiaries in the bomb loads resulted in fires that destroyed huge areas of both cities. From then on, the fact that fire is usually more destructive in a built-up area than high explosive was recognized by Bomber Command, and incendiaries always figured as major weapons.

Report had identified the Command's principal problem as being one of navigation. If aircraft could not get within 5 miles of a target, accurate bomb-aiming was irrelevant. In 1942 came Gee, the first of a series of aids that would largely resolve the navigation problem. Gee had its limitations. Its "line-of-sight" transmissions from the United Kingdom meant that it could not be used beyond the western areas of Germany, and it was not sufficiently accurate to be successful as a bombing aid. However, within its limits, it did enable the bomber force to concentrate more effectively while navigating individually to the correct target area. It was followed some months later by Oboe, which was used for bombing, and H2S, an airborne radar that gave navigators a rough picture of the earth beneath the aircraft.

In the early days of his command, with these advances in prospect, the C-in-C was sure that in a year or so he would be supervising a bomber force with the potential to achieve all that was asked of it. He was also aware that, in light of the disappointing results so far, there were many who opposed the creation of such a force. Churchill still supported the bomber offensive, but even he had expressed his concern over the results being achieved by the campaign and he had rejected a plan put to him by the CAS that

Encouraged by these successes in the Baltic, Harris revealed his master stroke. Even though Bomber Command's front-line strength was apparently little more than 400 aircraft, he proposed sending a force of 1,000 bombers against a single German target. The CAS and the Prime Minister liked the idea and, by pressing into service every available aircraft, including those held as reserves and at training units, the C-in-C was able to assemble a total of 1,047 for the great raid. The force was launched against Cologne on May 30, 1942, and Germany's third largest city suffered severely in the ensuing onslaught. It was a remarkable performance. Forty-one bombers were lost, a record number, but that represented just 3.9 percent of the total and so was deemed acceptable in view of the grievous damage inflicted on Cologne. Harris had made his point, and had also established broad tactical guidelines for Bomber Command that would be followed and improved on for the rest of the war.

First, accurate navigation to the target was assured by arranging that the leading aircraft would be Gee equipped. That done, the center of the city's built-up area was used as the primary aiming point, and heavy loads of incendiaries were dropped early to start fires on which succeeding aircraft could bomb. Then the force was concentrated in time and space; bombers approached the target in a stream and the whole raid lasted only ninety minutes, saturating the defenses. Finally, an aircraft was introduced that would feature in Bomber Command's operations for the rest of the war. On the morning after the raid, four Mosquitos cruised high over Cologne to take pictures and add their bombs to the confusion below.

Before the "1000 force" was dispersed, it was used twice more, against Essen and Bremen, albeit with less success than against Cologne. Given the established front-line strength, it was impracticable to continue raiding on this scale, although the British public was eager for more. Despite the encouragement of now having the United States as an ally, the war news remained almost universally depressing, and Bomber Command's massive efforts were cheered enthusiastically as the one bright spot on the national horizon.

As 1942 progressed, arguments intensified over whether or not a specialized target-finding force was needed to spearhead attacks. Opponents resisted on the grounds that it would become an elite, drawing the most experienced crews away from squadrons where their influence was sorely needed. This view, held by Harris himself, was opposed by the CAS, but a compromise was agreed upon in which several ordinary squadrons were nominated as the founding members of what would become known as the Pathfinder Force.

The Vickers Wellington was the best of the prewar twin-engined bombers. It served in many roles with RAF front-line squadrons throughout WWII, but was withdrawn from operations with Bomber Command in October 1943. Wellingtons took part in one of the first RAF raids of the war, against German warships near Brunsbuttel on September 4, 1939, and 599 Wellingtons were the backbone of the first 1,000 bomber raid on Cologne during the night of May 30, 1942. Such raids were devastating to German cities, as is shown by this photograph of the Ruhr taken late in the war.

WELLINGTON

The Wellington first flew on June 15, 1936, and survived in the training role in the RAF until 1953. A total of 11,461 of all versions was built. It was a fabric-covered mid-wing monoplane with turreted defensive armament and an internal bomb-bay. It was first powered by two Bristol Pegasus radials; later variants were fitted with Bristol Hercules or Rolls-Royce Merlins. The Wellington's unique geodetic construction was designed by Barnes Wallis. This built up the fuselage from a tremendously strong network of steel channel-beams, some of which can be seen in the photograph at top right. In common with other RAF bombers, the Wellington was a single-pilot aircraft: see the cockpit at lower right.

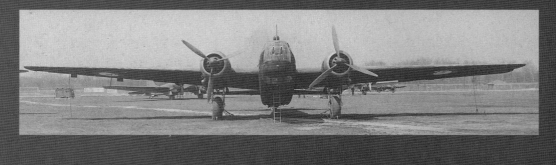

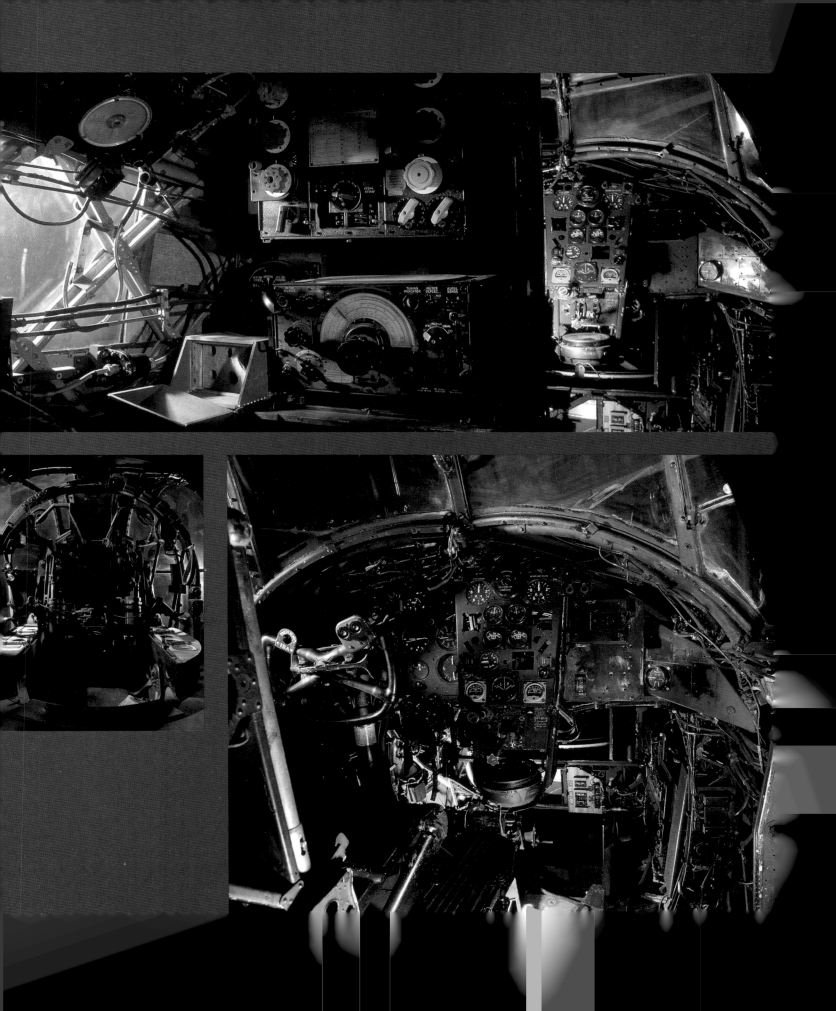

Early in 1943, after more than three years of unrelenting struggle, it seemed that all the efforts to build Bomber Command into a weapon that could significantly influence the outcome of the war had been rewarded. Four-engined bombers and the new Mosquitos were flowing from the factories, and there were bigger and better bombs for them to carry, besides a cornucopia of technological improvements. Gee, Oboe and H2S were joined by devices that gave early warning of gun, searchlight and night-fighter radars, and others that jammed German control frequencies. Hooded flares lit the targets without dazzling the crews, and the Pathfinders had target indicator bombs in a variety of colors. Intruders and diversionary raids helped to harass and stretch the German defenses. Added to all this was the fact that there was no longer any shortage of aircrew. New crews were pouring out of training schools all over Britain, the Empire and the United States. Over a third of them were not British; Bomber Command was becoming an increasingly cosmopolitan organization including men from Canada, Australia, New Zealand, South Africa, Poland, France, Czechoslovakia, Norway and a host of other countries. The scale of Canada's effort in particular was recognized in January 1943 when No. 6 (Canadian) Group was added to the Command's operational strength.

Bomber Command benefited in another way, too. It was no longer to be alone in its assault on Germany. At the Casablanca Conference in January 1943, a directive was issued by the Allied Combined Chiefs of Staff that laid the foundations for a combined bomber offensive involving Bomber Command by night and the U.S. Eighth Air Force by day. This was followed six months later by yet another directive code-named Pointblank, which, in its final form, was imprecise in its definition of a "combined offensive." In effect, it was interpreted by each of the respective commanders as authorizing him to fight as he saw fit. Cases of coordination on specific targets did occur, but Pointblank was more honored in the breach than in the observance.

The U.S. Eighth Air Force set out to attempt a precision bombing campaign that would, in the first instance, "seek the destruction of enemy fighters in the air and on the ground,"

> *"I suppose it is clear that the aiming points are to be the built-up areas and not, for instance, dockyards or aircraft factories."*
>
> AIR CHIEF MARSHAL SIR CHARLES PORTAL, CHIEF OF THE AIR STAFF, IN A LETTER TO C-IN-C BOMBER COMMAND, 1942

not least by attacking the component parts of the German aircraft industry. Air Marshal Harris, who described such things as "panacea targets," chose to continue his campaign against German cities, emphasizing the phrases in Pointblank that repeated those of earlier directives about "the morale of the German people." If the combined bomber offensive lived up to its name, it was primarily in the determination of the two air forces to strive for the defeat of their common enemy, and to do so by complementing each other's methods. Accordingly, from 1943 onward, Germany suffered the relentless pressure of round-the-clock bombing. Air Marshal Harris himself defined RAF Bomber Command's "main offensive" as lasting from March 1943 until the spring of 1944. Although targets were struck in all parts of Germany throughout that period, the year's principal endeavors were roughly concentrated into three main battles.

The Ruhr

The Battle of the Ruhr opened on March 5, 1943 with a raid by 442 aircraft on Essen, and lasted until July. At its peak, in May, 826 bombers were sent against Dortmund. In all, some forty-three major attacks were made against the most heavily defended targets in Germany, and the battle was marked by rising losses in the bomber squadrons. One raid on Pilsen was memorable for costing 11 percent of the force. Bomber Command lost a total of more than 1,000 aircraft from all the raids undertaken during this period.

The most ambitious attempt to bring the Ruhr's industries to a halt was a raid on the dams that controlled their water supply. This was an operation of high risk and low probability of success. When the raid was first proposed to Air Marshal Harris, he ridiculed it: "This is tripe of the wildest description. There are so many ifs and buts that there is not the smallest chance of it working." In time, however, Harris was persuaded. A special duties squadron, No. 617, was formed under the command of Wing Commander Guy Gibson for the specific purpose of attacking the dams. RAF Bomber Command's most experienced crews were gathered together and equipped with

The Dambusters. Breaching the Mohne, *by Gerald Coulson. Mick Martin's 617 Squadron Lancaster climbs away after releasing his bomb at the Mohne Dam on the night of May 16/17, 1943. Guy Gibson's aircraft, lights on, draws enemy fire to Martin's right.*

Lancasters modified to carry a cylindrical "bouncing bomb" weighing almost 10,000 pounds. The mission demanded an extraordinary level of flying skill. The crews had to be able to fly their heavily laden Lancasters for long distances at 150 feet or less to find a pinpoint target at night. They then had to achieve a bombing error of no more than 25 feet by releasing their weapons from exactly 60 feet above the surface of the lake, 450 yards from the dam, at a speed of 240 mph — all of this in darkness and under fire. If delivered correctly, the bomb would bounce across the water, strike the dam wall and roll down to explode deep below the surface, the shock cracking open the dam. On the night of May 16, 1943, nineteen Lancasters took off in three waves to attack the Möhne, Eder and Sorpe Dams. Three had to turn back and eight were lost during the raid. The attacks were carried out with great precision, and both the Möhne and Eder Dams

were breached, releasing tidal waves of water that devastated the local areas. However, though the damage was great, it did not prove decisive. It brought inconvenience to the Ruhr industries rather than disaster. Spectacular achievement though the raid certainly was, but the cost of the mission was great — eight of Bomber Command's best crews out of nineteen, a crippling loss rate of 42 percent. No. 617's performance was recognized with gallantry awards for thirty-three of the aircrew, and Guy Gibson received the Victoria Cross and the American Legion of Merit.

The Dams raid had profound effects far beyond its original intention. The tactics devised for the raid evolved into the low-level and master bomber techniques that so dramatically improved the performance of Bomber Command as a whole in 1944. Toward the end of the war, these techniques enabled targets to be attacked with a precision unknown in

AVRO LANCASTER

The Avro Lancaster was the RAF's principal weapon in the bomber offensive against Germany. Between the date of the first Lancaster operations in April 1942 and the end of the war, Lancasters flew 156,000 sorties in Europe and dropped 608,612 tons of bombs. The normal bomb load of the Lancaster was around 12,000 pounds, usually including a single 4,000-pound Blockbuster and combinations of 1,000-pound, 500-pound, or 250-pound bombs, or 250-pound small bomb containers (carrying incendiary bombs). Other combinations included fourteen 1,000-pound bombs (GP short-tail type), six 1,500 mines, six 2,000-pound high-capacity bombs, or a single 8,000-pound and six 250-pound bombs. Lancasters with bulged bomb doors were able to accommodate the 12,000-pound Tallboy deep penetration bomb, and the 22,000-pound Grand Slam was lifted by specially modified aircraft. Lancasters dropped 132 tons of bombs for each aircraft lost, compared with 86 for the Halifax and 41 for the Stirling. Total Lancaster production was 7,377, of which 3,345 were lost on operations.

Avro Lancaster Bomber NX611 *Just Jane*, seen here, is on display at Lincolnshire Aviation Heritage Centre in the United Kingdom. OPPOSITE BOTTOM Merlin engines three and four snarling purposefully on the wing of the RAF Battle of Britain Memorial Flight's Lancaster. Dan Patterson took the photograph while flying over Lincolnshire in August 1995. He describes the sound of flying with four Merlins as "Awesome — like being inside a formation of four Spitfires."

Flight Lieutenant Bill Reid flew Lancasters with 61 and 617 Squadrons on thirty-four missions over Germany. On his tenth, his aircraft was attacked twice by night fighters near the Dutch coast. Two of the crew were killed and the aircraft severely damaged. Bill Reid was seriously wounded, but he said nothing about his injuries and continued to the target to drop his bombs. He managed to return the aircraft to England and later received the Victoria Cross, Britain's highest award for gallantry. On his last operation, Reid's aircraft was struck by bombs from another Lancaster. He survived the breakup of his aircraft and ended the war as a POW.

The Lancaster was flown by a single pilot, in keeping with an RAF policy initiated by concern over the limited capacity of the pilot training organization. The views on the right show the single-pilot cockpit and the navigator's position, dominated by the screen of the H2S radar.

The leading figures at the Lincolnshire Aviation Heritage Centre are brothers Fred and Harold Panton. Their Avro Lancaster, *Just Jane*, stands behind them. *Just Jane* does not fly, but on select occasions aircraft taxis around the site, the four Rolls-Royce Merlins thrilling the crowds with their unique rasping snarl. Engineers Ian Hickling and Roy Jarman maintain the Lancaster in superbly original condition, confident that *Just Jane* could fly if the Pantons wished it.

In 1997, Dan Patterson spent a few days with the Battle of Britain Memorial Flight at RAF Coningsby. While there he was privileged to photograph the BBMF Lancaster (at the time finished in the markings of a famous IX Squadron aircraft, *Johnny Walker*) from inside during flight. BOTTOM LEFT, the flat Lincolnshire countryside stretched away in front of the nose. The bomber's shadow races ahead on the approach to landing BOTTOM RIGHT, and ABOVE *Johnny Walker* just before touchdown at Coningsby.

Near RAF Coningsby is the old Blue Bell Pub. Covering the ancient walls are photographs of the bomber squadrons that were based in the area during WWII. Silver models of the Lancaster and Mosquito are in the bar, and signatures of airmen are written on the ceiling between the great beams.

The Assault's Final Phase

During the final nine months of the war, Germany again suffered the persistently destructive scourge of bomber attack, but now the tide of battle flowed increasingly strongly in favor of the attackers. Bomber Command and the Eighth Air Force penetrated enemy airspace in ever greater numbers as the German defensive perimeter shrank and the Luftwaffe's capacity to resist the onslaught weakened. Denied the benefit of early warning, starved of fuel and short of pilots, the Luftwaffe fought on, but faced the inevitability of defeat. RAF losses fell to an average of less than one percent. At the same time, Bomber

Command's ability to find, mark and destroy targets reached a level of competence that would have been thought unobtainable at the time of the Butt Report. Cities such as Nuremberg and Dresden, which had resisted or avoided all of Bomber Command's earlier efforts, were struck with crushing efficiency. The German transportation system, radiating from the cities, was effectively brought to a standstill, and flow from the oil industry fell to a trickle as the daylight precision attacks of the Eighth Air Force, now shielded by Mustang escort fighters, remorselessly eliminated its production capacity. In these closing months of the war, the strategic bombing forces of the Allies were irresistibly powerful and were indeed capable of delivering the "devastating, exterminating attack" spoken of by Churchill in the dark days of 1940.

With the benefit of hindsight, it is not difficult to find fault with those who were responsible for the policies that first shaped and then directed the activities of Bomber Command in WWII. It is hard to excuse the inadequate preparation of the bomber force in 1939, and there will always be those who are vehement in their criticism of the apparently unbridled use of Bomber Command's hard-won power in 1945. Such commentaries often fail to heed the discipline of viewing events through the eyes of those who were involved at the time. It must be remembered that the limits of strategic air power were not understood in 1939, that the realities

Fewer than forty Lancasters survived to record more than 100 missions over Germany. The most famous of these is S for Sugar, *which returned safely from 136 operations.* S for Sugar *is seen here being refueled during the war and, more recently, in the RAF Museum, Hendon, bearing 136 bomb symbols and Göring's boast "No Enemy Plane Will Fly Over The Reich Territory."*

of a bombing offensive had to be learned the hard way, that throughout the war most British people reacted to news of bombing raids on Germany with deep satisfaction, and that political and personal convictions continually influenced the use of the bomber weapon.

The rights and wrongs of the bombing campaign against Germany will likely always be a subject for debate among historians and air power strategists. There are some things, however, that are beyond dispute. Astonishing levels of courage and resourcefulness were evident on both sides of the conflict. Contrary to all predictions, the German people showed that they could absorb the most appalling punishment without breaking. For their part, the bomber

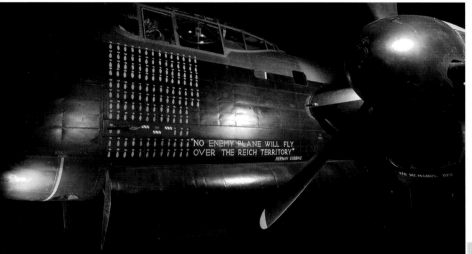

The personal logbook and scrapbook of Captain David Tyler of the 305th Bomb Group, based at Chelveston, England. Note that his 25th and last mission was to Schweinfurt on August 17, 1943.

crews maintained their spirit and resolution while facing the unparalleled dangers of aerial combat by night and in the knowledge that the odds for their survival were not favorable. The awful truth is that almost 60 percent of the 125,000 aircrew who served in Bomber Command between 1939 and 1945 became casualties of one sort or another, and over 55,000 of them died. Flying in bomber aircraft was one of the most hazardous occupations of the war. Among the combatants of both sides, only German U-boat service proved more lethal to its practitioners.

Finally, there is the question of the contribution made by the bombing campaign to the defeat of Nazi Germany. It may be true that strategic bombing did not live up to the promise held out by air power strategists that the war could be won by air assault alone. It has been suggested that the vast resources devoted to the bomber force could have been better used elsewhere. These judgments seem to pay little regard to the long years when Bomber Command was the only offensive instrument available for striking back at a rampant Germany. Wars are not won by being defensive, and, for the British people in their darkest days, it was the aircrew of Bomber Command who kept the offensive flame burning and lit the way to eventual victory.

Daylight Offensive

The first Eighth Air Force airmen to see European action were Captain Charles Kegelman and his crew from the 15th Bombardment Squadron. Flying a

> *"[The Eighth Air Force] flew, in broad daylight, escorted bomber missions into every sector of Germany. There wasn't a target in the Third Reich…which was safe from their attentions…this was accomplished in the teeth of the strongest and most lethally-equipped defensive fighter force which had ever been assembled ….[The achievement] stands as a paragon of America's belief in the art of the possible. And of her refreshing conviction that if convention says no, the answer most probably is yes."*
>
> LADDIE LUCAS, *FIVE UP: A CHRONICLE OF FIVE LIVES*

Douglas Boston (A-20) borrowed from the RAF, they were quietly added to a force striking the Hazebrouck marshaling yards in France on June 29, 1942. USAAF crews entered the fray more formally a few days later, marking July 4 by joining a British squadron in attacking German airfields in Holland from low level. It was not an auspicious start. The enemy flak was as fierce as any the RAF veterans could remember, and two American crews were shot down. A third, Kegelman's, survived through a display of gritty determination and superb airmanship. On the run in to De Koog airfield, Kegelman's aircraft was hit in the right engine. The propeller flew off and flames erupted beneath the cowling. As the low-flying Boston slewed to the right, the right wingtip and rear fuselage scraped the airfield surface. Dragging his crippled aircraft back into the air, Kegelman got rid of his bombs and blasted a flak tower with gunfire. The engine fire went out, and Kegelman succeeded in staggering back across the North Sea. His thoroughly deserved Distinguished Service Cross was the first of many gallantry awards won by the Eighth Air Force.

As the year wore on into August, the impatience of American leaders for the main Eighth Air Force bombing campaign to begin became more obvious. The laborious business of creating a new air force in another country seemed unending, and even with the first bombers in place, further delays were imposed by the minimal level of training of some arriving aircrews, and by an enemy that was soon recognized as a frustratingly ever-present threat — the fickle weather of northwest Europe. At last, on August 17, the skies cleared sufficiently to allow twelve B-17Es of the 97th Bomb Group to fly their first operational mission. Escorted by RAF Spitfires, they attacked the marshaling yards at Rouen in France. Opposition was light,

LEFT Rosie's Crew/Thorpe Abbotts 1943, *by Gil Cohen. Robert "Rosie" Rosenthal briefs his 100th Bomb Group crew before boarding the B-17F* Rosie's Riveters *at Thorpe Abbotts, England, in 1943.*
OPPOSITE Coming Home — England 1943, *by Gil Cohen. A typical scene on an Eighth Air Force airfield in eastern England after a mission.*

the visibility was good, and the bombing from 23,000 feet was reasonably accurate. The 97th's aircraft returned to base almost untouched to find that British monitors had heard a German voice reporting "twelve Lancasters heading inland." The error was perhaps understandable at this stage, but the German controllers were to have every opportunity to grow familiar with the shape of the B-17 as time went by.

The first B-17 raid raised American morale considerably. The Eighth was in action, even if on a small scale, and the smoothness of the operation hinted at great things for the future. It was notable, too, for some of the prominent air force figures involved. The mission was led by Colonel Frank Armstrong, with Major Paul Tibbetts in the copilot's seat. General Ira Eaker was in the leading aircraft of the second flight, a B-17 bearing the name *Yankee Doodle.* Congratulations to Eaker came immediately from the Commander-in-Chief of RAF Bomber Command, Air Marshal Sir Arthur Harris, in a message that said: "Yankee Doodle certainly went to town and can stick another well-deserved feather in his cap!"

The early promise of the Rouen raid seemed to be confirmed by eight more missions flown against other targets in France or the Netherlands between August 19 and September 5. None was large nor represented a deep penetration of enemy

territory, and all were heavily escorted by fighters. Nevertheless, the bombing was generally quite accurate and no B-17s were lost. The growing confidence of the bomber crews and their commanders received its first check on September 6 during a raid on aircraft factories at Meaulte in France. For the first time, Luftwaffe fighters pressed home their attacks on the bomber formation, and two B-17s were shot down. Several others were damaged and came back with casualties.

Weather restricted operations in the following weeks, but on October 9 the bombers of the Eighth again faced serious opposition. On that day, General Eaker issued his first mission tasking for over 100 bombers, eighty-four B-17s and twenty-four B-24s. Accompanied by fighter escort, they were to attack targets near Lille. Mechanical failures forced fifteen B-17s and fourteen B-24s to turn back, reducing the force to seventy-nine. The Luftwaffe harried the bombers continually over northern France, shooting down four and damaging most of the rest. The bombing results were poor, but concern over the negative aspects of the mission was overridden by claims that fifty-six fighters had been destroyed, twenty-six more probably destroyed, and another twenty damaged (in intelligence officer's shorthand, 56-26-20). Since this almost equaled the total number of Luftwaffe fighters then thought to have

128   AVIATION CENTURY

been in the area, the news was welcomed, but with some skepticism. The figures were eventually reduced to 21-21-15, but even that was probably excessive. It had to be accepted that in the confusion of battle, with many gunners firing at the same fighter, claims were going to be exaggerated. While this added to the problems of assessing the enemy's losses, it at least had the positive effect of boosting the morale of the bomber crews. (Postwar researches showed that gunners' claims averaged about three times Luftwaffe losses. The battle of October 9, 1942, is perplexing because only two Luftwaffe losses can be traced. Equally baffling was a running fight in which "Wild Bill" Casey's crew defied a succession of fighter attacks on November 23, 1942. Casey's gunners described shooting down seven Fw 190s in twelve minutes. They "disintegrated" or "hit the sea," and more than one pilot was seen to "bale out." German records for that day indicate that one Fw 190 was lost. None of this suggests that the gunners' claims were not genuinely made, but it does reveal the difficulty of remaining precise and dispassionate while under the stress of combat.)

Another problem that was to bedevil the Eighth Air Force throughout its time in England showed itself on the Lille mission. Operating large aircraft in close proximity introduced an obvious collision hazard that had to be accepted. In 1942, the problem was relatively minor since the number of USAAF aircraft in the United Kingdom was still quite small. Even so, two B-17s of the 92nd Bomb Group on their way to Lille collided over the Channel, one being stripped of its rudder and part of the fin, and the other losing two engines and rupturing a fuel tank. On this occasion, both aircraft managed to get back for emergency landings, but later incidents did not often have such happy endings. As the Eighth grew in strength, the challenge of operating thousands of aircraft in the uncertain weather and restricted airspace of eastern England sometimes proved too great, with disastrous results for the aircrews involved. (The collision on the Lille raid was the first of more than 100 between heavy bombers of the Eighth Air Force during the war, and the vast majority of them were fatal to the crews.)

With four B-17 and two B-24 groups available, and the force blooded in combat, Eaker was looking forward to further growth and to planning operations in which his bombers could penetrate the German heartland and strike the enemy with real power. So far, his crews had been gaining valuable experience but had been limited to attacks that were little more than pinpricks. Unfortunately for Eaker, higher authorities were about to make it impossible for him to develop the bomber offensive as he would have wished.

B-17 FLYING FORTRESS

OPPOSITE TOP Through the plexiglass nose of a B-17 flying into the sunset, the bombardier's view over the Norden bombsight.

OPPOSITE BOTTOM The United States Air Force Museum's B-17G , *Shoo Shoo Baby*. Based with the 91st Bomb Group at Bassingborn, England, this bomber and her crew flew twenty-two missions over occupied Europe. On the twenty-third mission to Poznan, Poland, the B-17G suffered combat damage and was flown to Sweden, where it survived the war and had a long flying history. It was finally returned to the U.S. for a long restoration returning it to the form of an operational Eighth Air Force bomber. *Shoo Shoo Baby*'s last flight was to the USAFM in October of 1988.

RIGHT Engines number 3 and 4, from the starboard-side navigator's window. The reliable Wright Cyclone engines developed 1200 horsepower and often returned bomber and crew to base even after suffering serious combat damage.

BELOW Wartime photograph of a B-17 from the 390th Bomb Group at strike altitude over Europe.

OPPOSITE TOP The cockpit of B-17G *Shoo Shoo Baby*. It has a remarkably simple display of instruments: the pilot's essential flying information is centered on the panel so that both the command pilot and the copilot could safely fly the bomber. One of the differences between RAF and American bomber crews was the two-pilot crew on the flight deck. On the right side of the panel are the gauges that tell the flight crew the crucial temperatures and pressures for the four engines. Legend has it that the notches carved into the control wheels denoted missions completed. OPPOSITE BOTTOM LEFT The engine pedestal between the pilots of the Flying Fortress contains the throttle controls for the bomber. Flying a B-17 required an unusual palm-up grasp of the four throttles. Formation flying of this heavy and often overloaded bomber was very taxing and required constant adjustment of the power settings. Below the throttles are the electronic controls for the autopilot. On a bomb run, the pilot would engage this unit, and the Norden computing bombsight, operated by the bombardier, controlled the bomber. The red handles are control and tailwheel locks. OPPOSITE BOTTOM RIGHT The view toward the tail of a B-17 in flight, through the radio room hatch. B-17s carried a single .50-caliber machine gun in this position; in flight the plexiglass hatch was often stowed so that this man had an uncluttered view of the aerial combat going on around him.

ABOVE The view of the tail gunner in the "Purple Heart" corner. The gunner in the last bomber of the low squadron in the formation would have this unimpeded view of the landscape rolling away as he flew backward into combat.

RIGHT The tailgun position on B-17G *Shoo Shoo Baby*.

100TH BOMB GROUP

Men of the 100th Bomb Group. Stationed at Thorpe Abbots in East Anglia (ABOVE AND BELOW), the 100th participated in nearly all of the crucial missions the Eighth Air Force flew, including Bremen, Munster, Schweinfurt and Regensburg, as well as later war missions deep into Germany and support of the D-Day invasion. Theirs is one of the most active veterans groups from the aerial conflict; these portraits were made during their reunion in Ohio in 1999 at the United States Air Force Museum.

ABOVE Don Atkinson, top turret/flight engineer; James Musser, pilot of *Moose,* 418th Squadron. BELOW Owen. D. "Cowboy" Roane, colorful pilot of *Bigassbird.* According to the 100th's history, every veteran has a "Cowboy" story to tell.

TOP LEFT General Thomas Jeffrey , Commander of the 100th Bomb Group, appointed by General Curtiss LeMay in May of 1944. General Jeffrey commented how pleased he was to still be wearing his original A-2 leather flight jacket.
TOP RIGHT Four of the ten-man crew from the *Boeing Belle,* 351st Squadron: William J. Howard, "Pop," right waist gunner;

Robert Stachel, tail gunner; Everett Kennedy, copilot; and Don Thompson, navigator.
BOTTOM LEFT John Peters and Robert Dell, 349th Squadron.
BOTTOM RIGHT General Jack Wallace, Commander of 100th Bomb Group; Chuck Gutenkust, 350th Squadron.

Mission Regensburg, *by Gil Cohen. Inside* Just a-Snappin', *a B-17 of the 100th Bomb Group over Regensburg, on August 17, 1943. From his position in the nose, bombardier Jim Douglass indicates bomb release with a thumbs-up to navigator Harry Crosby, who notes down the exact time. Crosby was a lead navigator for the 100th BG, and later the author of a classic book about the Eighth Air Force experience,* A Wing and a Prayer.

Harry Crosby in 1999. Crosby went on to earn his PhD from Stanford University, was supervisor of the Rhetoric Program at the University of Iowa, chairman of the Department of Rhetoric at Boston University and director of the Writing Center at Harvard University.

Americans Over the Reich

In January 1943, Roosevelt, Churchill and their Combined Chiefs of Staff met in Casablanca to discuss the future direction of the war. Daylight strategic bombing was among the operations subjected to their scrutiny. The claims of its USAAF advocates were still unproven, and not a single Eighth Air Force bomb had yet fallen on Germany. The British remained of the opinion that the Eighth should become part of the night-bombing offensive, and the U.S. Navy was saying that the resources needed to build up a bomber force in the United Kingdom would be better expended in the Pacific.

At this stage of the war, there was very little supporting evidence to defend the USAAF's position. Since being ordered to give priority to Operation Torch in North Africa, the Eighth had accomplished nothing of great significance. The shortage of aircraft and crews, and the appalling winter weather in northwest Europe had placed tight limits on both the strength and frequency of operations. Worse still, most of the operations flown were in response to a directive to concentrate on the U-boat pens in France, targets that were nearly impervious to attack and were well defended. From almost every point of view, the results achieved by the Eighth were discouraging. Between mid-October 1942 and mid-January 1943, a total of just over 1,000 bomber sorties had been dispatched, but more than 400 of these had failed to attack. In September 1942, the number of aircraft returning from raids with repairable battle damage was 13.3 percent of the attacking force; by December, it was up to 42.1 percent. Total losses had risen from 3.7 percent in November to a disturbing 8.7 percent in January.

One of the factors affecting these worrying figures was a change in the tactics of Luftwaffe fighters. On November 23, 1942, during a mission against Saint-Nazaire, fighters led by Oberleutnant Egon Mayer began to attack the bomber formations from the front. At that time, neither the B-17 nor the B-24 was heavily armed in the nose, and there were blind spots that the guns of the upper and lower turrets could not cover. The rapid closing-rates of frontal attacks demanded considerable skill and determination from fighter pilots, but they also made the fighters more difficult targets for the gunners, presenting them with small frontal-area targets and high crossing-speeds. With the introduction of frontal attacks, Luftwaffe pilots began to score consistently against the bombers of the Eighth, and this tactic became a feature of the struggle throughout the air war in Europe. Almost immediately, countermeasures were sought. More forward-facing guns were added to the B-17s and B-24s, and new formations were devised to ensure that all the bombers made the most of mutual protection. At first, the bomber formations flew in elements of no more than three aircraft, loosely coordinating their mutual support. By 1943, the Eighth's bombers were going to war in combat boxes of eighteen to twenty-one aircraft, with two or three boxes flying together in a defensive formation.

Only too well aware of the problems confronting the Eighth, "Hap" Arnold summoned Ira Eaker to the Casablanca conference to present the case for strategic daylight bombing. Eaker brushed aside past and present difficulties and concentrated on the prospects for the future, winning over Churchill by describing an offensive in which the USAAF by day and the RAF by night subjected Germany to a relentless pounding, to "soften the Hun for land invasion and the kill." Churchill's imagination was caught by Eaker's arguments, particularly one that became a slogan, a pledge to bomb the Third Reich "round the clock."

Looking out the navigator's window, above his table in the nose of the B-17. The tools of his trade were charts, flight computers and sharpened pencils. The navigator's job was to inform the pilot of position and upcoming course alterations, and to know how to direct the bomber back to base from any point on the mission.

"DUTCH" BIEL
390TH BOMB GROUP PHOTOGRAPHER

OPPOSITE PAGE
TOP "Dutch" and a German Junkers Ju 88.
RIGHT Gunther "Dutch" Biel of the 390th
Bomb Group. The images he recorded have left
us with a rich historic record of the air war
over Europe.
FAR LEFT Dutch on one of his missions as a
Bomb Group photographer, a 390th Bomb
Group B-17G in formation off the right wing.
THIS PAGE
Combat images from the collection of
"Dutch" Biel, showing contrails, bombers
and fighter escorts.

THE PLOESTI RAID

Ploesti: The Odyssey of Utah Man, by Gil Cohen. The exhausted crew of B-24 *Utah Man* back at base near Benghazi, Libya, after bombing the oil refineries at Ploesti on August 1, 1943. Aircraft captain 1st Lieutenant Walt Stewart describes an incident to Major Ramsay Potts, operations officer of the 93rd Bomb Group. Dan Patterson took this portrait of Colonel Walt Stewart at his home in Utah. Walt's cat supervised the proceedings.

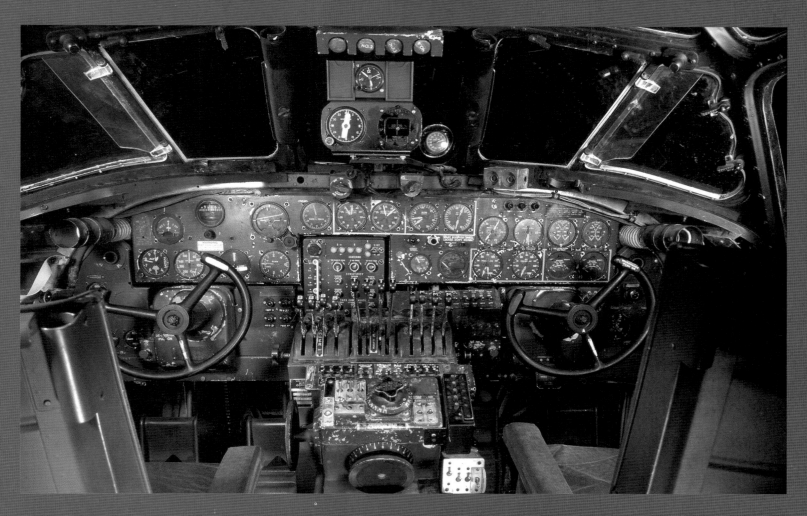

Ramsay Potts was a twenty-six-year-old major when he flew a B-24 named *The Duchess* on the USAAF's low-level attack against the Rumanian oilfields at Ploesti on August 1, 1943. More than fifty years later, Major General Potts renewed his acquaintance with the B-24's spacious cockpit at the USAF Museum, Dayton, Ohio.

STRAWBERRY BITCH

Strawberry Bitch, the B-24D Liberator on display at the USAF Museum, Dayton, Ohio, flew missions from North Africa in 1943–44. The B-24's tail turret was roomier than that of the B-17, but the tail gunner was still the loneliest man in the crew, physically separated from his colleagues and unable to see the hazards into which the aircraft was heading. The deep greenhouse nose of the B-24D was modified in later variants to take a turret with twin .50-caliber machine guns.

As a result of Eaker's persuasions, the Allied leaders were able to agree that a coordinated bombing offensive, by day and night, was the only way immediately available to carry the war to Germany, and that it was indispensable preparation for the eventual Allied invasion of Europe. A directive was issued which called for a combined bomber offensive aimed at "the progressive destruction and dislocation of the German military, industrial and economic system, and the undermining of the morale of the German people to a point where their capacity for armed resistance is fatally weakened."

Less than a week after the end of the Casablanca conference, on January 27, 1943, the Eighth Air Force opened its long campaign against Germany with a raid on Wilhelmshaven. Fifty-five aircraft out of the ninety-one launched bombed their targets, but cloud and fighters spoiled their aim and the bombing was not very effective. One B-17 and two B-24s were lost, but the gunners had a good day, claiming twenty-two fighters shot down. (The actual score was seven.) The first step having been taken, the offensive against German targets did not build up as had been hoped. Between the first Wilhelmshaven raid and mid-August 1943, more than six months later, there were fewer than twenty days when the Eighth was able to

BELOW *Late-evening low pass of a restored B-24 flown by Dave Tallichet.*
RIGHT *From the collection of the Museum of Flight, Seattle, a captured German photograph showing a shot-down B-24 from the Ploesti mission, being inspected by German officers.*

penetrate German airspace, although other raids were carried out in France and Holland. Eaker's masters in Washington had difficulty grasping the reasons for such slow progress, although their policies were in large part responsible for the problem. Eaker had to withstand a continual stream of criticism as the Eighth battled the enemy, the European weather, the diversion of assets to other theaters, shortages of spares, and the problems of aircrew arriving inadequately trained. There were times when half of Eaker's meager force was grounded because neither spares nor qualified aircrew were available.

Those missions that were flown into Germany included the Eighth's first attacks on Kiel, Hamburg and the Ruhr, and with them came an inkling that unescorted daylight bombing might not be so feasible after all. Notable losses were suffered on June 13 (twenty-two B-17s of sixty attacking Kiel), July 25 (fifteen B-17s of 100 against Hamburg), and August 12 (twenty-three B-17s of 133 over the Ruhr).

BELOW *The top turret gunner's view from inside his plexiglass dome, which places him outside of the airplane, looking aft toward the distinctive twin rudders of the B-24.*
RIGHT *Lieutenant Stan Staples, 461st Bomb Group, remembered, "We used to synchronize the props by leaning our heads back so that we could watch the shadow pattern of the blades. If the shadow moved toward or away from you, the engines were not on the same rpm, but when the shadow stood still, the rpm were synchronized and the engines would purr."*

On these days, and a number of others, the absence of escorting fighters was severely felt. The P-47 Thunderbolts tasked for escort duty could not accompany the bombers past Aachen on the German border, after which the Luftwaffe took over. Not content with swarming in on the bombers from head-on (at least one head-on collision was reported between a B-17 and a Focke-Wulf Fw 190 in this period), the German fighter units tried several new tactics, including aiming bombs and salvoes of rockets at the formations. (On July 28, 1943, a B-17 of the 385th Bomb Group was struck by a rocket and broke up, the pieces crashing into two other B-17s that were also destroyed.) The determination of the Luftwaffe to oppose the USAAF was obvious, and was to become even more apparent in the latter half of 1943.

The significance of high loss rates was not lost on the bomber crews. In 1943, twenty-five missions were needed to complete a tour of combat duty. Statistically, the four-percent loss rate — four in every hundred aircraft sent on operations would be lost — would result in no crew finishing a tour. Double-figure percentages suggested that all bomber aircrew would quickly reach a point where they were living on borrowed time. As the months went by, the slow pace of the bomber offensive stretched out the accu-

mulation of combat missions into an agony of waiting, and the number of crews who reached the end of their tours seemed frighteningly small. It was June 1943 before a crew of the 91st Bomb Group, together with their B-17F, became the first in the Eighth Air Force to complete a combat tour and fly back to the United States. It was a sufficiently notable event for Captain Bob Morgan's crew and their B-17, *Memphis Belle*, to be sent on a publicity tour of the U.S. to promote the sale of war bonds. (*Memphis Belle* survived the war to be preserved in Memphis, Tennessee.)

Ploesti

Among the primary objectives listed in the directive governing the Combined Bomber Offensive were ball bearings and oil. In August 1943, the USAAF turned its attention to both of these vital products and launched two daylight raids that penetrated more deeply into Europe than bombers had before. The first, against the Ploesti oil refineries in Rumania, which produced almost two-thirds of the oil used by the Axis powers, was carried out by B-24s operating from North Africa. Two groups from the resident

A rare P-47D Thunderbolt "razorback" on display at the United States Air Force Museum. This early version of the large Republic-built American fighter saw action in the skies over occupied Europe. The shape and size of the P-47 earned it the nickname "Jug." It was powered by the very reliable Pratt & Whitney R-2800 radial engine, which developed 2,000 horsepower.

Ninth Air Force (98th and 376th) joined two groups deployed from the Eighth in the U.K. (44th and 93rd) and a new group flown from the U.S. (389th) in sending 177 B-24s across the Mediterranean on August 1, 1943. To achieve maximum impact, the plan was to fly the raid at extremely low level, with waves of B-24s going through the target area almost nose to tail.

On the face of it, the B-24 was not the ideal aircraft to fly at low level and in close proximity to lots of others. It was 110 feet across the wing and weighed 60,000 pounds, so was often described as looking and flying like a truck. Pilot Carl Fritsche says: "To fly formation for several hours in a B-24 required endurance. The controls took so much strength to move that you didn't have to worry about getting to sleep after a long mission." The B-24's great advantage was its range. It was selected for the Ploesti mission because in 1943 it was the only bomber capable of getting there and back. The round-trip to the refinery from Libya was about 2,700 miles, and some aircraft were in the air for more than sixteen hours.

For the Ploesti raid to be an unqualified success, the attack needed to be led by the best navigators, to be undisturbed by bad weather en route, to face light defenses, and to catch those defenses by surprise. Unfortunately, none of these conditions was met. As the leaders approached the

coast of Greece on the outbound leg, the B-24 *Wongo Wongo*, carrying the mission's lead navigator, suddenly dived steeply into the sea. A second aircraft, this one with the deputy lead navigator, circled to investigate and was left far behind. Over Albania, severe weather disrupted the B-24 formations, splitting them into two main groups. Approaching the target area, the aircraft carrying the mission commander, Brigadier General Ent, turned too early and took the leading groups (376th and 93rd) toward Bucharest instead of Ploesti. Major Ramsay Potts of the 93rd and Major Norman Appold of the 376th both broke radio silence to warn of the mistake, but by this time the cohesion of the raid had been lost forever. These two groups finally turned to approach Ploesti from the south instead of the northwest. Crews were told to attack targets of opportunity. To add to their problems, the Ploesti raiders had been misled about the strength of the defenses. By August 1943, Ploesti was one of the most heavily defended areas in Europe, bristling with antiaircraft guns and with fighters based nearby. Nor were the B-24s blessed with the advantage of surprise, as they were seen by German radar before they crossed the Greek coast.

Their ordered ranks gone, the raiders attacked Ploesti in ragged flocks from several directions, few finding their allocated targets and all of them heavily engaged in a running battle with German gunners in flak towers, on freight trains or hidden in haystacks. Within minutes, Ploesti was covered in flame and smoke as bombs found oil-storage tanks and aircraft fell to the defenders' guns. B-24s hurtled between refinery chimneys and dodged other bombers coming at tthem head on. Aircraft attacked whatever targets presented themselves among the dense clouds of oily smoke, and others flew through the blast of the resulting explosions. Colonel Leon Johnson, leader of the 44th Bomb Group, said it was "indescribable to anyone who was not there. We flew through sheets of flame, and airplanes were everywhere, some of them on fire and some of them exploding." Countless acts of heroism and grim determination marked the battle. One of the more memorable was that of Lieutenant Lloyd Hughes. The tanks of his B-24 punctured and streaming fuel, Hughes pressed home his attack at the Campina refinery through a wall of flame. His aircraft's liquid fuse of leaking fuel ignited and fire enveloped the aircraft, but Hughes held it level and delivered his bombs before attempting a crash landing. Two gunners survived the impact. Lloyd Hughes died and was one of five airmen to be awarded the Medal of Honor for the Ploesti raid. Other posthumous Medals of Honor were awarded to Lieutenant Colonel Addison Baker and Major John Jerstad (93rd BG). Surviving recipients were Colonel Leon Johnson (44th BG) and Colonel John "Killer" Kane (98th BG).

Escaping the fires of Ploesti, the surviving B-24s were harassed by fighters all the way to the Ionian Sea. Several diverted into Malta and Cyprus,

and others struggled into Turkey, where the crews were interned. Still others crashed into the Mediterranean, leaving just eighty-eight to reach their home base in Libya. In all, fifty-four B-24s were lost, forty-one of them in combat. There were 532 men did not return from the raid, including more than 100 taken prisoner or interned. The damage sustained by the surviving aircraft was such that only thirty or so of the original 177 were fit for combat on the following day. The aircrews having made so valiant an effort and paid such a high price, their commanders hoped that the rewards would be equally great, but they were to be disappointed. Severe damage had indeed been inflicted on Ploesti, and total refining capacity had been reduced by 40 percent. However, the refinery had been running at less than full capacity. Within days, idle plant was brought on line to replace lost production, and the Allies thought it would be impractical to try repeating such a costly mission. Total loss rates of over 30 percent could not be borne. Unescorted long-range, low-level attacks by heavy bombers against defended targets disappeared from the options open to the USAAF, never to return.

A P-47 fighter pilot's flight gear. At top left is a Twelfth Air Force silk scarf, to its right a propeller manual from Curtiss Electric. At center right, inside the webbing from an American-style parachute, is a Royal Air Force lifejacket with survival items in the right pocket. The green B-10 flight jacket at left replaced the famous leather A-2 late in the war. On top of the blue pilot's manual is a Ninth Air Force patch; the airmen of the Ninth revolutionized tactical air support after D-Day.

Bf 109

In 1997, Dan Patterson was at Duxford, the Imperial War Museum's airfield near Cambridge, England, and was able to photograph two restored Messerschmitt Bf 109Gs both on the ground and, from the cockpit of a North American T-6, in the air. OPPOSITE TOP Bf 109G-2 *Black Six* warms up before takeoff. *Black Six* was captured in Libya during WWII, so the air intake on the left of the engine has a tropical filter to protect against sand. Later, *Black Six* cruised over the south coast of England, in skies familiar to the Luftwaffe's Bf 109E pilots in 1940. The Bf 109G-10 (right) was a later production version with a taller fin, fitted to give the pilot more control authority on takeoff and landing. Note also the clear canopy, introduced to improve all-round visibility. The spiraling spinner fronts a 2,000-horsepower Daimler-Benz engine, impressive power for such a small airframe.

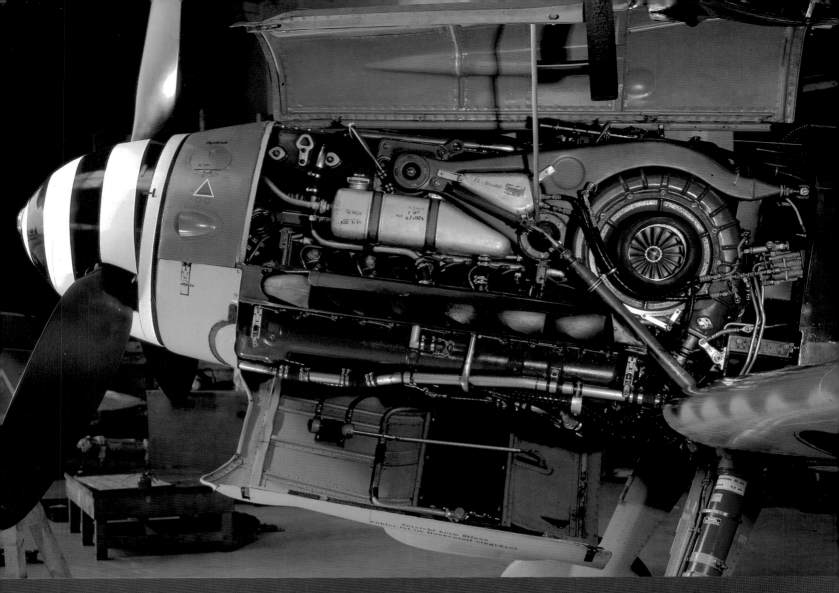

ABOVE With the cowling open, the size of the Daimler-Benz 605D is readily apparent. The silver container is the coolant header tank, and below it are the inverted-V exhaust stubs. The nautilus-like blower spins at extremely high rpm, its whine giving the Daimler-Benz a distinctive sound.

RIGHT Luftwaffe ace Gunther Rall in the cockpit of the Bf 109 at the Smithsonian's National Air & Space Museum in 1997. All of his 275 aerial victories were gained in Bf 109s.

RIGHT The cockpit of the Bf 109G was a snug fit for the average pilot. The standard instrument panel was neatly arranged straight ahead, with the fuel and oil gauges down and to the right. Next to them is a small silver handle for emergency undercarriage lowering. The stick has a trigger for the guns in the front and a bomb-release button on top. Bulging out of the floor ahead of the stick is the cover for the breech of the 20 mm cannon.

BELOW Luftwaffe artifacts. A bearskin-lined high-altitude flight jacket is at top left. Inside it is a uniform shirt dating from the Battle of Britain. A life-preserver and parachute are at top right, with flight boots (also from the Battle of Britain) at bottom right. A helmet and lightweight flight suit are on the left. The rings at top center have purple stones that identify the wearer as a veteran of the Eastern Front. The ring with gold trim is that of a senior officer.

P-47D

A restored P-47D owned and flown by Butch Schroeder of Danville, Illinois. Painted in the invasion markings of Colonel David Schilling, Commander of the 56th Fighter Group, based in England at Halesworth from July 8, 1943, through April 18, 1944, and then at Boxted from April 18, 1944, through September 9, 1945.
RIGHT The mighty Pratt & Whitney R-2800 warming up on the ramp.
OPPOSITE TOP The side view of the P-47 makes instantly apparent the reasons for the nickname, "Jug." The designers at Republic placed the turbo-supercharger, necessary for high-altitude combat, behind the cockpit. The associated plumbing and ductwork created the need for the deep and round fuselage. The Seversky P-35 is a direct predecessor to the Thunderbolt, and can be seen in *Aviation Century The Early Years*, Chapter 3.
OPPOSITE BOTTOM Straight at the camera, the Thunderbolt takes off. The landing gear for this fighter was unique: as it retracted it also contracted 9 inches. The gear needed to be longer on the ground for propeller clearance, and shorter in flight to allow for the gun bays.

RESTORED WARBIRDS

The flying results of the work of Mike Vadeboncoeur, aircraft restoration expert. Mike owns Midwest Restorations in Danville, Illinois, where he flys and restores warbirds. Since 1993, Mike has won the EAA Grand Champion Restoration Award for World War II warbirds twice and Reserve Champion twice as well as Four Golden Wrench awards from Snap-on Tools. He is one of the world's experts in the restoration of P-51 Mustangs.

ABOVE Butch Schroeder's P-51, *Lil Margaret*, restored in the markings of Clyde East, a photoreconnaissance pilot as well as an ace. 1993 Grand Champion at Oshkosh.
BELOW LEFT Mike in front of his 2002 Grand Champion winner, P-51 *Cripes a Mighty*.
BELOW RIGHT The front end of Butch Schroeder's P-47 Thunderbolt, restored by Mike Vadeboncoeur and Midwest.

ABOVE AND RIGHT The P-51 owned by Ken Wagnon of Wichita, Kansas. Restored in the markings of George Preddy, *Cripes a Mighty* was a 352nd Fighter Group airplane. Preddy, one of the great fighter pilots of the Eighth Air Force, was shot down and killed on Christmas Day 1944. Leaning on the wing of the restored Mustang is Art Snyder, who was Preddy's crew chief late in 1944. The original photo of Art Snyder from 1944 was recreated at the dedication of this restored fighter.

BOTTOM RIGHT In addition to his duties as crew chief, Art Snyder also provided haircutting services and Major Preddy allowed him to advertise on the nose of *Cripes a Mighty*. Here Snyder repaints the cost of a haircut onto the nose of the restored fighter.

BELOW Arthur "Snoot" Snyder.

Designed in response to a request from the British Purchasing Commission in 1940, the P-51A Mustang was powered by a 1,150 horsepower Allison V-1710, closely cowled and with the ducted radiator situated well aft to reduce drag. The result was a very fast aircraft with long range, but it lacked high-altitude power and so was used principally at low level. One section of the cockpit canopy on the P-51A was hinged on the left to the fuselage, and another at the top was raised to allow pilot entry. Two latches held the narrow canopy closed in flight. The razorback fuselage and narrow canopy of the P-51A helped to reduce drag, but left a large blind spot behind the pilot. These reenactments of a WWII scene took place in October 1994.

Schweinfurt

On August 17, 1943, it was the turn of Germany's ball-bearing industry. At that time, Schweinfurt's factories produced half the bearings needed by the Nazi war machine. It was decided to fly a maximum effort by B-17s of the Eighth Air Force against both Schweinfurt and Regensburg, site of a Messerschmitt aircraft factory. Regensburg was the deeper of the two into Germany, and it was planned for the 4th Bomb Wing groups allocated to that target to lead the way for the whole force and continue to North Africa after bombing. The idea was to time the 1st Bomb Wing's raid on Schweinfurt so that Luftwaffe fighters opposing the Regensburg mission would be on the ground refueling when the second force arrived. It was unfortunate that the English weather disrupted the plan. On the morning of August 17, fog blanketed the airfields of the Eighth and prevented the intended dawn start to the operation. The 4th Bomb Wing airfields began to clear first, and the Regensburg mission got airborne, but thick fog persisted over the 1st Bomb Wing, and the Schweinfurt force was delayed for more than three hours.

Fog also disrupted operations for the 4th Bomb Wing's fighter escort of P-47s. Only one group made contact with the bombers, and even they had to turn back near the German border. Colonel Curt LeMay, leading the Regensburg attack with the 96th Bomb Group, later remarked that the only escorts he saw "had black crosses on their wings." The 4th Bomb Wing began its journey across Europe with 139 B-17s, but that number began falling before they reached German airspace. Both Luftwaffe fighters and flak left their mark while the B-17s were still over Belgium. By the time they reached Regensburg, fourteen bombers had been shot down, and three others had been forced to jettison their bomb loads. There were 122 B-17s left to strike the Messerschmitt factory.

Elements of a B-17 group seen through the eyes of a B-17 ball-turret gunner.

The two leading groups had never come under serious attack and were intact, but some of those further back had taken a severe beating, particularly the 100th Bomb Group, which had lost six of its original twenty-one aircraft and had several others damaged.

Looking back from near the front of the aerial armada, Staff Sergeant Earl Spann (390th Bomb Group) had a grandstand view: "The trip into Germany was a bloody battle all the way. It was mostly fighter planes but also heavy flak at times…. From our position, I could see behind us and there were planes falling everywhere, a lot of ours and a lot of theirs. Many trails of smoke could be seen coming up from crashed planes. A lot of brave men had died…."

Lieutenant Colonel Beirne Lay (100th BG) encapsulated the intensity of the struggle in the phrase: "Each second of time had a cannon shell in it." (Beirne Lay subsequently wrote the screenplay for *Twelve O'Clock High*, the epic film about Eighth Air Force operations.)

On the final approach to Regensburg there were few fighters and little flak. Visibility was generally excellent and the bombing was accurate. No B-17s were lost in the target area (although three were badly damaged and did not reach Africa) and the Messerschmitt factory was heavily hit. LeMay's Wing could hardly have done a better job. At the time it was thought that Messerschmitt production must be severely curtailed, and there is no doubt that several weeks of production were lost, later estimated at perhaps the equivalent of 1,000 fighters. What was not then realized was that the bombs being used (500 pounds high explosive, plus incendiaries) were powerful enough to knock down buildings but not to destroy machine tools. Within weeks, the Germans had dispersed their production facilities and were on their way to being back in business. Nevertheless, the raid did achieve one great success that was concealed from the Allies at the time. Among the items destroyed were jigs

Long-range escort for USAAF bomber formations meant extra fuel tanks had to be added to single-seat fighters. The additional fuel was contained in disposable "drop tanks" that were carried under the fighter's wings or under the fuselage. The metal teardrop-shaped tanks (above) were a later replacement for the innovative earlier British design (right), which used tanks made of paper, laminated and treated to be leakproof. Standard procedure was to use the fuel in these tanks on the first legs of a long mission so they could be discarded before entering aerial combat.

for a revolutionary new fighter — the jet-propelled Messerschmitt Me 262.

The 4th Bomb Wing landed in North Africa some five hours later, having faced little further opposition. By not turning back from Regensburg, they appeared to have taken the Germans by surprise. Attrition took its toll, however, as damaged aircraft continued to fall out of formation. On landing, twenty-four B-17s were missing from the 139 that had crossed into Europe. Of those, nine had come from the 100th Bomb Group, a crippling unit loss rate of over 40 percent.

Shortly before midday, the 1st Bomb Wing was finally ordered into the air. The original plan of mutual support with the 4th Bomb Wing long since abandoned, it was clear that the long flight to Schweinfurt and back would be a hazardous operation, but the decision was taken to go ahead. In all, 222 B-17s crossed the Dutch coast and faced a Luftwaffe fighter force that had been reinforced and prepared to meet what they believed would be the Regensburg force on its way back to England. Almost 300 Luftwaffe fighters were ready and waiting for the fight along the route into southern Germany.

The wide undercarriage of the P-51 Mustang gave this remarkable American fighter solid ground-handling capabilities. Many fighter airbases used grass runways, and after the invasion, fighter units often operated out of forward bases and the runways could be dirt or the rough PSP, or pierced steel planking. ABOVE *Butch Schroeder's award-winning Mustang warms up on the ramp, the 11-foot propeller etching a golden circle.* LEFT *The Merlin at full song, the Mustang roars into the skies.*

THE ROLLS-ROYCE MERLIN ENGINE

LEFT The engine that was at the forefront of the Allied victory in the air war over Europe — the Rolls-Royce Merlin. It was a direct descendant of the engines developed for the Supermarine Schneider Trophy racers of the 1920s and 1930s (see *Aviation Century The Golden Age*, Chapter 3). The Merlin powered such successful aircraft as the Spitfire, Hurricane, Lancaster and Mosquito before being tried in an early model of the P-51 Mustang. The mating of this powerful and reliable engine and North American's superb airframe produced a fighter with extraordinary range and high-altitude performance, transforming the Mustang into the aerial weapon needed to defeat the Luftwaffe.

BELOW The often unsung heroes of the aerial battles were the mechanics and technicians who kept these high-powered flying weapons in the air. They would work all night in appalling weather to keep their units up to strength.

ABOVE Wartime image of a P-47 receiving field maintenance on the radial engine.

LEFT The toolbox and personal tidbits that a line mechanic used while "turning wrenches" on a units P-47. In addition to the tools of the trade, and the special tools of an armourer, essential equipment included the ever-present Thermos bottle for a quick warm-up, a pack of "Luckys," and a baseball glove for the long stretches of boredom while "their" fighter was being used by the pilot.

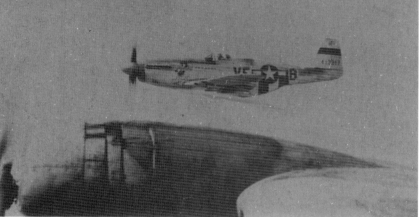

LEFT *A P-51D piloted by USAAF ace James Goodson escorts a B-17.* ABOVE *P-51D pilots were confident that their sleek machines were the best all-round fighters of the war.*

Up to the German border, first Spitfires and then P-47s did a good job of holding the Luftwaffe at bay. Things changed dramatically as the last Allied fighters left. Lieutenant William Wheeler (91st BG) recalled the scene: "The thing I remember most vividly is that the Germans started making their initial attack almost exactly at the same time as the P-47s above us made their 180 degree turn to return to base…. Looking back at it now, I think that very moment…was the major turning point when the Air Force had it proved to them that their idea of sending B-17s unescorted on a deep penetration was not valid. It broke the back of the theories of those who were convinced that the Flying Fortress could protect itself if you had good formation discipline and that excellent fifty caliber gun…."

This time it was the leading groups of the 1st Bomb Wing that bore the brunt of the Luftwaffe's assault. The German fighter leaders deployed their Staffeln well ahead of the B-17s in line abreast, as many as fifteen fighters at a time, for waves of head-on attacks that followed relentlessly one after another. The B-17 aircrew who experienced it testified to the ferocity and determination with which the German airmen pressed home their attacks. Staff Sergeant John Thompson (waist gunner, 384th BG) spoke for many of his comrades when he recalled the battle: "I witnessed something that mankind will never see again. It was rare to see hundreds and hundreds of aircraft in the sky at once. On one occasion our formation made a small turn and I was able to look back. It looked like a parachute invasion of Germany…. Planes were going down so often that it became useless to report them."

Lieutenant Donald Rutan (copilot, 381st BG) was mesmerized by what was going on in front of him: "There wasn't much sense in calling out fighters that day; everything was at twelve o'clock level for what seemed like an eternity. Each time they came in you thought that it would be our turn to get it. So many of our planes had gone. This was the fiercest we ever had."

Combat losses and battle damage took a savage toll of the 1st Bomb Wing on the long flight across Germany, but 184 B-17s reached and bombed Schweinfurt. Shaken and somewhat scattered by the ferocity of the running fight, many crews were then confused by the dust and smoke that soon covered the target area. The later groups, unable to identify the ball-bearing factories, followed their briefing instruction to aim at the center of the city. As a result, the bombing was not well concentrated, and although the factories were damaged, they were not destroyed. Some of the aircrew were only too well aware of their limited success, one navigator in particular complaining that they had suffered so much "only to come this far and miss the damned target."

Messerschmitt Bf 109G-2 Black Six *peels away from the T-6 camera aircraft over southern England in 1997.*

By the time the 1st Bombardment Wing fought its way back across Germany and reached the haven of its English bases, thirty-six of its B-17s had gone down. From the combined force of 361 heavy bombers that had crossed into Europe during the day, sixty had been lost. At least eleven

ABOVE *The Focke-Wulf Fw 190D-9 in the collection of the USAF Museum, Dayton, Ohio. The 190D-9 was one of WWII's outstanding fighters, able to hold its own with the P-51D or the later variants of the Spitfire.* LEFT *A secret WWII British technical report on the Fw 190D-9 commented that the cockpit was "roomy and well laid out" and that it was "comfortable except for a lack of head and shoulder room."*

escorts over Belgium, and five to accidents. Given the disappointing results achieved at Schweinfurt, it is apparent that the laurels of the day belonged to Germany's defenses. However, the Germans took the hint about the importance of Schweinfurt. Thought was given to dispersing ball-bearing production; the number of antiaircraft gun batteries around the Schweinfurt factories was more than doubled; and fighter units were withdrawn from duties elsewhere to cover the approaches to southern Germany. Despite their defensive successes, there were signs that the Germans were beginning to worry that they could be badly hurt by the persistence and growing strength of the Eighth Air Force.

In the remaining months of 1943, the hard lessons of Schweinfurt and Regensburg were driven home whenever the Eighth Air Force struck at targets within Germany. On September 6, in a depressing fiasco, 262 B-17s scattered bombs in the Stuttgart area through cloud, doing little damage and losing forty-five aircraft. Between October 8 and 10, there were 1,074 B-17s launched at various German targets, 855 of them bombed, and eighty-eight were lost. As always, these figures did not tell the whole story. On these raids, well over 600 aircraft were damaged, many never to fly again. (Curiously, one of the most celebrated examples of daylight

more were so badly damaged that they never flew again, and 162 others had lesser damage. Over 550 men had been killed or were missing. In one day, the Eighth Air Force had suffered losses equal to those of its first six months of operations.

Such alarming figures were thought at the time to have been offset by the success of the B-17 gunners. There were 288 Luftwaffe fighters claimed destroyed. Postwar research revealed that the Luftwaffe lost forty-seven fighters on August 17, 1943 — twenty-one to B-17s, twenty-one to precision bombing took place during this period, and with minimal loss. The Focke Wulf factory at Marienburg was attacked on October 9, 1943, by a force of 96 B-17s from the 94th, 95th, 100th, 385th and 390th BGs. Of the bombs dropped, 83 percent fell within 2,000 feet of the aiming point. Only two B-17s failed to return.)

Grimly determined that the Eighth Air Force should continue the battle of attrition and defeat the Luftwaffe, General Eaker gritted his teeth and sent his bombers back to Schweinfurt on October 14. A total of 291 B-17s set out and were confronted with a Luftwaffe performance described by the official USAAF history as "unprecedented in its magnitude, in the cleverness with which it was planned, and in the severity with which it was executed." In the face of such powerfully determined opposition, the attack on Schweinfurt was remarkable. This time the bombing was accurate and the ball-bearing factories were severely damaged, but the price was unbearably high — another sixty B-17s shot down, with seven more destroyed on return to England, and a further 138 damaged to some degree. Although 288 Luftwaffe fighters were claimed as destroyed (German records suggest only thirty-five, although many more were damaged), even that exaggerated figure could not obscure the fact that the Eighth Air Force was taking a beating. Over Germany, the Luftwaffe

was consistently imposing losses of well above 10 percent on the bombing force, and that was a rate that would lead inexorably to its destruction. It was ever more apparent that the daylight bombing offensive could not be continued, not in the absence of escort fighters with the range to accompany the bombers over Germany.

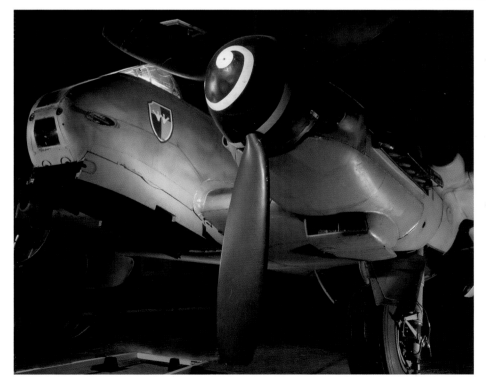

The Messerschmitt Me 410 Hornisse was a development of the disastrous Me 210, fitted with more powerful engines and a redesigned wing with automatic wing slots. Variants of the Me 410 included light bombers, heavy fighters, and reconnaissance aircraft. Introduced in 1943, the Hornisse was heavily armed and fast. It had some success as an intruder over the U.K. and was effective when it engaged USAAF bomber formations, but was no match for the more nimble escorting P-51s. This example is on display at Cosford in England.

TOP The cockpit of the Me 410 placed the pilot well forward, with the main armament below the cockpit floor. The basic flight instruments are offset to the left so that they are not blanked by the stick, but the engine instruments are hidden away low down between the pilot's legs.

This Messerschmitt Bf 110 is a G-4d/R3, on display at the RAF Museum, Hendon. It is equipped for night fighting with a FuG 220b Lichtenstein radar and an underbelly cannon pack. A failure in its original role of day escort fighter, the Bf 110 was very successful as a night fighter, even though the large radar antennae caused considerable drag.

Changes at the Top

The year 1943 had been a testing time for the Eighth Air Force, and as it drew to a close, the daylight offensive was in the balance. There were even experiments carried out in which some B-17 units joined the RAF's night offensive to gain experience in case daylight bombing had to be abandoned altogether. Unpromising as things looked, however, the persistence of the Eighth was about to be rewarded. The year 1944 would bring great changes and see the scale and intensity of the air war over Europe raised to levels unimagined in prewar years.

Among the changes was the replacement of General Ira Eaker as the commander of the Eighth Air Force. "Hap" Arnold's impatience with what he perceived as the slow pace of the air assault on Germany led him to initiate a

shakeup among his senior commanders. With Eisenhower and Tedder moving to the United Kingdom to prepare plans for the invasion of northwest Europe, Eaker was to take over from Tedder as commander of the Allied Air Forces in the Mediterranean. Spaatz would command the U.S. strategic air forces in Europe (coordinating the operations of the Eighth and Fifteenth Air Forces), and Doolittle would be the new commander of the Eighth Air Force.

The Tide Turns

As 1944 dawned, the Eighth Air Force began to feel that there was light at the end of the tunnel. The dark days of 1943 were over, and the pieces were coming together that would make the Eighth the mightiest instrument of air power ever assembled. U.S. industry and the air force training system were both now in high gear, and new aircraft and crews were pouring across the Atlantic in an ever-increasing flood. At the same time, new command structures were in place, designed to make the most of the lessons learned about the use of air power and to take advantage of the experience gained by senior commanders. Tactical procedures and combat techniques had been honed to a fine edge in the heat of battle, and changed policies aimed to ensure that these were used to the best possible effect. New equipments were on their way to add to the effectiveness of the force, among them H2X, an airborne bombing radar that would allow certain targets to be attacked through cloud, and — at long last — fighter aircraft capable of escorting the bombers to their targets and taking on the Luftwaffe on equal terms when they got there.

In the closing months of 1943, the burden of escorting the bomber forces over enemy territory had been borne principally by P-38s and P-47s. Extra fuel in drop tanks had made a difference, but the shorter range P-47s were still able to cover only parts of the bomber missions, while the P-38s had managed to reach out as far as such German cities as Bremen and Ludwigshaven. For all their advantages in range, however, the P-38s had other problems. Below 18,000 feet they were a match for the Luftwaffe's fighters, but at the heights they needed to operate as escorts, they were outclassed by the Bf 109s and Fw 190s. The extreme cold of high altitudes induced frequent failures in the P-38's Allison engines and challenged pilot endurance in cockpits almost devoid of heating. Even so, a P-38 was the first USAAF combat aircraft to fly over Berlin.

ABOVE *Overshadowed in Europe by the legendary reputation of the B-17, the Consolidated B-24 Liberator nevertheless made a significant contribution to the bomber offensive against Germany.* LEFT *By the end of the war, many German cities were reduced to rubble, with few buildings left intact.*

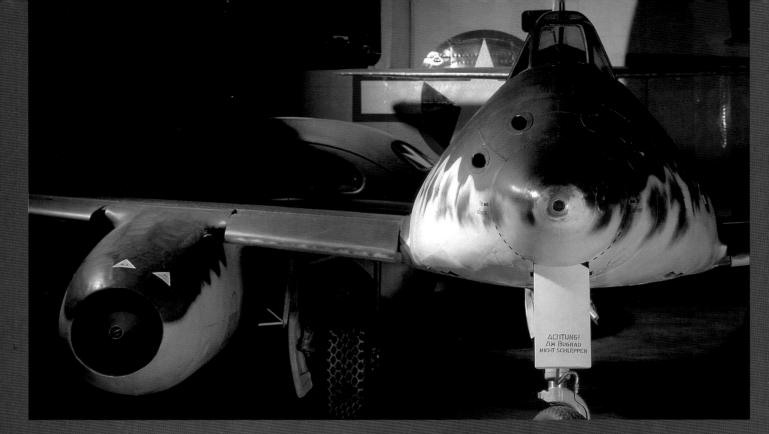

MESSERSCHMITT
ME 262 SCHWALBE

ABOVE The Messerschmitt Me 262 Schwalbe was a huge leap
forward in military aircraft design. Powered by two Junkers Jumo
axial-flow turbojets, the Me 262 was much faster and had more
firepower than any Allied fighter. Its principal weakness was the
unreliability of the engines, which needed a major inspection after
ten hours flying and had to be replaced after twenty-five hours.

ABOVE The cockpit layout of the Me 262 was simple,
with the flying instruments on the left and the engine
instruments on the right. At this early stage of jet
fighter development, there was no ejection seat and the
cockpit was not pressurized. LEFT Walter Schuck, seen
here in the cockpit of the Smithsonian's Bf 109, was a
leading Luftwaffe ace, with 206 aerial victories, eight of
them gained in the Me 262.

MESSERSCHMITT ME 163 KOMET

The Messerschmitt Me 163 Komet was a dramatic attempt to produce an effective fighter for point-defense against the USAAF's bomber formations. Its rocket engine gave it great speed and an unprecedented rate of climb, but it could provide power for no more than eight minutes, after which the Me 163 became a vulnerable glider. Operationally the Komet was a failure. Bringing the 30 mm cannons to bear on a target in one very high speed pass was difficult, and accidents (mostly fatal) were frequent.

TOP RIGHT With the Komet at the USAF Museum is Rudi Opitz, who was assigned to the Me 163 program in 1940 as the official Luftwaffe test pilot. He was responsible for the flight tests and pilot training program of the Me 163B, the military version of the rocket powered interceptor. Rudi Opitz has described the cockpit of the Me 163 as "quite good. It was comfortable and convenient, with great visibility."

BOTTOM RIGHT The rudimentary nature of the layout of instruments and controls are evident in this view of the Komet cockpit at the Canada Aviation Museum, Ottawa.

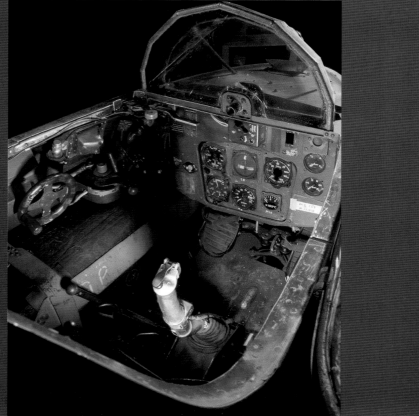

HAWKER TYPHOON

Originally intended as interceptor, the Hawker Typhoon survived severe teething troubles to become one of the most formidable weapons of WWII, a close-support fighter that turned the scales in many land battles after D-Day. The Typhoon's massive Napier Sabre engine, a 24-cylinder flat-H sleeve-valve, delivered 2,180 horsepower.

LEFT Pierre Clostermann, seen here in 2000 at the Musée de l'Air et de l'Espace, Le Bourget, is a celebrated French WWII fighter pilot and the author of several books, including a classic account of his wartime exploits, *The Big Show*. He flew Spitfires, Typhoons and Tempests with the RAF.

BELOW The cockpit of the Typhoon at the RAF Museum, Hendon, England, is reasonably complete, and holds most of the eighty-nine controls and instruments listed in the pilot's notes.

MARTIN B-26 MARAUDER

With its high wing-loading and fast landing speed, the Martin B-26 Marauder gained an early reputation as a widow-maker. Once crews became familiar with the aircraft's characteristics, this perception was shown to be undeserved, and the B-26 ended the war with the lowest loss rate per sortie of any bomber in Europe. The functional layout of the B-26 cockpit was popular with pilots. In photographs taken by Dan Patterson at the USAF Museum in 1996, the cylindrical fuselage of the Marauder and the dihedral of its tailplane are strikingly evident. The historic photograph shows B-26s on the airfield at Watton, England, during WWII.

DE HAVILLAND MOSQUITO

Known to the press as "the wooden wonder" because of its plywood construction, the de Havilland Mosquito was one of the most versatile and effective aircraft of WWII. Powered by two Rolls-Royce Merlins, it could achieve speeds above 400 mph and reach altitudes above 40,000 feet. The USAAF's need for a fast reconnaissance aircraft was met by acquiring Mosquitos under reverse lend-lease arrangements. The USAF Museum's Mosquito, seen here, is restored as a PR XVI used for weather reconnaissance by the 25th Bomb Group, Eighth Air Force.

GLOSTER METEOR

The first jet aircraft to be used by a front-line squadron was the Gloster Meteor, which became operational with the RAF's No. 616 Squadron in July 1944. (The experimental unit Erprobungskommando 262 flew the Me 262 in operational trials starting in April 1944 and scored its first victory over a Mosquito on July 26, 1944. The first front-line unit to get the Me 262 was Kommando Nowotny, which became operational on October 3, 1944.)

The first Meteor prototype is seen here at Cosford, England. However, it was the fifth prototype that was the first to fly on March 5, 1943. The prototype's cockpit added some unfamiliar instruments to the standard panel — gauges that read jet pipe temperatures and could register engine rpm up to 15,000. The Whittle W.2B engines used bore little resemblance to modern jet engines. At first they produced just 1,200 pounds of thrust each — not very generous for an aircraft weighing over four tons when empty.

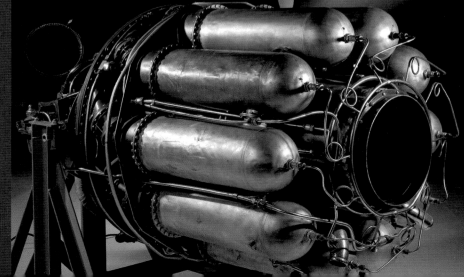

The Martin B-26 Marauder was a very effective medium bomber, well used by the USAAF's Ninth Air Force in Europe after D-Day.

home, descending to ground level and strafing enemy airfields as they presented themselves.

Doolittle regarded the freeing of the fighters as "the most important and far-reaching military decision I made during the war." In effect, the new fighter tactics gave another role to the bombers besides that of dropping high-explosives on German targets. They were now the bait that lured the Luftwaffe into a life or death struggle with the USAAF's long-range fighters. The Luftwaffe's General Adolf Galland has acknowledged the dramatic effect of the change: "Only now did the superiority of the American fighters come into its own. They were no longer glued to the slow-moving bomber formation, but took action into their own hands. Wherever our fighters appeared, the Americans hurled themselves at them. They went over to low-level attacks on our airfields. Nowhere were we safe from them, and we had to skulk on our own bases. During take-off, assembling, climb and approach to the bombers, when we were in contact with them, on our way back, during landing, and even after that, the American fighters attacked with overwhelming superiority."

Big Week

In concert with the new escort fighter policy, the Allies, intent on ensuring air supremacy for the invasion of France, hatched a plan to cripple the German aircraft industry. Known as Operation Argument, its objectives were factories for manufacturing aircraft components and ball-bearings, and for aircraft assembly. Bad weather prevented Argument from being launched during the early weeks of 1944, but the skies over Europe began to clear in mid-February. Between February 20 and 25 ("Big Week"), over 3,300 Eighth Air Force bomber sorties pounded Germany's aviation industry. They were joined by some 500 more from the Fifteenth Air Force in Italy, and RAF Bomber Command added another 2,750 at night. Nearly 4,000 fighter sorties accompanied the daylight raids. By the time weather closed in to bring "Big Week" to an end, the USAAF had lost 226 bombers (6.8 percent) and forty-one fighters; the RAF's losses from four major raids totaled 141 aircraft (5.1 percent).

To add to the Luftwaffe's problems, the long-range fighters had been let off the leash. Soon after General Doolittle took over the Eighth Air Force, he visited General Kepner, his fighter commander, who had been pressing for a more aggressive fighter policy. Fresh in Doolittle's mind was General Arnold's New Year message to him: "Destroy the enemy air forces wherever you find them, in the air, on the ground, and in the factories." On Kepner's office wall was a sign that reflected the concerns of previous commanders. It read: "The first duty of the Eighth Air Force fighters is to bring the bombers back alive." Doolittle ordered the closing phrase changed to read "is to destroy German fighters." Close escort, in which the fighters were not allowed to leave the vicinity of the bomber stream, was a thing of the past. Strong fighter forces would now range ahead of the bombers as hunters, and escorts would pursue enemy fighters aggressively, seeking their destruction rather than merely chasing them away. Released from close escort duty, fighters would be encouraged to look for targets of opportunity on the way

The Ninth Air Force under the command of General Quesada, using P-47s in a tactical role, changed the close air/ground support method of waging war. The armored columns of General Patton's Third Army were provided wth Air Force radios, and fighter pilots were rotated forward to work with the tanks and speak directly to the airborne fighter cover.

Bill Manos, a Ninth Air Force P-47 pilot, 513th Fighter Squadron, 406th Fighter Group, photographed in 2001. The restored Thunderbolt in the photo below is painted in the markings of the fighter that he flew over Europe after the invasion. He had two other Thunderbolts shot out from underneath him. Before the invasion, his group flew from Ashford in Kent close to the English Channel. Bill tells us, "We flew a lot of missions before D-Day, so we all knew that something big was about to happen. And it did. The morning of the invasion we took off at 4 A.M. and covered our sector of the beachhead. Each mission took about three hours — we flew fifteen hours that day."

After the invasion, his group moved to Normandy and was based near Sainte Mère Eglise (see Chapter 6) and was only 20 miles from the front. During that period, while attacking a German airfield at Rennes, his P-47 was shot down by flak: "We stayed on the deck for about 5 miles…. I never saw so much flak. I got hit by an 88 mm antiaircraft gun...it took 4 feet off my left wing." Bill was wounded in the shoulder and bailed out over German-held territory. Picked up by local French people, he was eventually returned to his unit.

In late 1944, Bill was one of the pilots assigned to the armored columns and was in Bastogne during the Battle of the Bulge.

In the fierce fighting of the first day of Big Week, three Medals of Honor were awarded to B-17 crew members, two of them posthumously. First Lieutenant Walter Truemper and Staff Sergeant Archie Mathies, navigator and flight engineer in a B-17 of the 351st Bomb Group, were killed trying to land their damaged aircraft at base. Their copilot already dead, they refused to bail out and abandon their badly wounded pilot, who survived the crash but died soon after. In a second incident highlighting the hazards of head-on attacks, a B-17 of the 305th Bomb Group became a straggler when its bomb load failed to release over the target and it was heavily hit by fighters. Cannon shells set an engine on fire and shattered the cockpit, killing the copilot and wounding eight other crew members. The pilot, 1st Lieutenant Bill Lawley, seriously hurt and bleeding profusely, held the dead copilot off the controls with one hand and recovered from a steep dive with the other. Electing not to bail out because of the serious injuries to his crew, Lawley made for the English Channel, surviving another fighter attack en route that set fire to a second engine. Shock and loss of blood caused Lawley to suffer a temporary collapse on the way home, but by the time the French coast was crossed, both engine fires had been extinguished and the bombs jettisoned. Over southern England a third engine died and Lawley, by now at very low altitude, managed to belly-land the B-17 on the grass airfield at Redhill, south of London, without further injury to his crew.

The cost of Big Week to the bombers had been relatively high, but far from fatal. The Luftwaffe, however, staggered under the repeated blows. The material injury to the aircraft industry and the losses of fighter aircraft — 355 fighters destroyed and 155 damaged — were undoubtedly serious but not disastrous in themselves. Under the organizational leadership of Albert Speer, German industry proved wonderfully resilient, dispersing its assets and actually increasing aircraft production in the months after Big Week. The real problem was that the lifeblood of the Luftwaffe was being drained away. In fighting to protect the Reich, well over 400 German fighter pilots were lost in February 1944. In March, the month of the attacks on

> *"What spies, what researchers burrowing in what libraries unearthed the statistics that sent us off to scatter burning planes and bodies all over Europe? And did we win or lose?"*
>
> ELMER BENDINER,
> THE FALL OF FORTRESSES

Berlin, the figure rose to nearly 500, among them a dozen of the greatest German aces, including Egon Mayer, the man who in November 1942 initiated the tactic of massed head-on attacks against B-17s. During the five months before the D-Day invasion, 2,262 German fighter pilots died. With losses like that, the Luftwaffe was irrevocably on the slippery slope to defeat. All the production in the world was of little use if there were not enough competent pilots to fly the aircraft.

During this period, when the Eighth Air Force began to impose its will on the Luftwaffe, the lion's share of fighter escort duty was still being borne by the P-47 Thunderbolt. Over 3,000 of the fighter sorties in support of Big Week were flown by P-47s. An unusually big fighter for its time, the P-47 was powered by the huge Pratt & Whitney R-2800 radial engine of over 2,000 horsepower. It was heavier than its rivals by several thousand pounds, and could not match them as a dogfighter. However, it was fast, ruggedly built, and heavily armed. It was almost impossible to run away from because it could outdive any of its likely opponents (until the appearance of the Me 262 jet), and a burst from its six .50-caliber machine guns was usually decisive.

The ruggedness of the P-47 was attested to by its capacity to withstand battle damage. Its combat loss rate was a remarkably low 0.7 percent, compared with the P-51's 1.2 percent. As a pilot in the 362nd Fighter Group said: "For the low-level job we had to do, where you couldn't keep out of the light flak and small arms fire, there wasn't a better plane than the P-47. It would keep going with damage with which other types would have fallen out of the sky." These characteristics endeared the Thunderbolt to its pilots, among them some of the great USAAF aces of WWII. The leading P-47 group was the 56th Fighter Group, commanded initially by Colonel "Hub" Zemke, one of the war's outstanding fighter leaders. By the end of the war, the 56th had destroyed 664.5 enemy aircraft in aerial combat, more than any other group in the Eighth Air Force, and many leading aces had scored their victories while on its roster, among them Christensen (21.5), Gabreski (28), Johnson (27), Mahurin (21), and Schilling (22.5).

The V-Weapons

The direct assault on the elements of German air power might have been even more intense if the Eighth Air Force had not occasionally been diverted from its primary task to add its weight to an Allied effort aimed at countering a new and initially puzzling enemy threat. Aerial reconnaissance

revealed that the Germans were building some very large concrete structures, including a number of ramps, in northern France. Photographs gave substance to other intelligence on the development of two German "vengeance" weapons — a small pilotless aircraft powered by a pulse-jet (the V-1), and a large ballistic missile (the V-2), both armed with warheads of about a ton. By December 1943, the Allied campaign against these weapons had been given the formal title of Operation Crossbow, and a chain of over seventy probable launching sites had been identified near the Channel coast of France, in an area some 10 to 20 miles deep and 300 miles long. Most of the ramps on these sites appeared to be aimed at London, but there was also concern that the new weapons might be capable of disrupting the planned invasion of Normandy.

During the first six months of Crossbow, the Allied air forces dropped over 36,000 tons of bombs on V-1 and V-2 installations, with the USAAF's Eighth and Ninth Air Forces delivering the lion's share. They succeeded in seriously

LEFT *A V-1 on its launch ramp can be seen at the Imperial War Museum's airfield at Duxford, near Cambridge, England.* BELOW *Targets that were heavily attacked by the Allied air forces both before and after D-Day were the V-1 flying bomb launch sites. The area near Calais still bears the scars of bomb craters made during these attacks.*

LEFT *The Smithsonian's Focke-Wulf Ta 152 awaiting restoration in 2001. Some surface paint had been removed to reveal traces of the aircraft's original markings.* BELOW *The cockpit was reasonably intact, but in need of the restoration team's care and attention.*

damaging all but a small number of the sites. General Doolittle and Air Marshal Harris grumbled about the repeated diversion of their heavy bombers from the assault on Germany, but the effort was not in vain. Operation Crossbow probably delayed the V-weapon program by three to four months. The first V-1 did not land in England until the night of June 12/13, 1944, and by then the Allied armies had secured their Normandy beachheads. Once under way, the V-weapon attacks increased rapidly in intensity, the V-2 joining the V-1 in the offensive against England on September 8. The V-1 (known as the "buzz-bomb" because of the distinctive note of its engine) was small and fast (400 mph), and was not easily intercepted. The V-2, approaching from the stratosphere at supersonic speed, was immune to interception. Both weapons were impressively destructive in built-up areas, but neither could be aimed accurately, and they were essentially indiscriminate. The scale of the German offensive was such that Crossbow had to be continued, but it did not overcome the threat completely. By the time the advance of the Allied armies brought the campaign to an end in March 1945, over 3,000 V-1s and 1,000 V-2s had fallen on British soil. Nearly 2,000 more V-weapons fell on Allied-held territory on the conti-

nent, mostly in and around Amsterdam. Destructive though they certainly were, the V-weapons ate up scarce German resources and achieved little of military value. They did, however, divert a considerable amount of Allied air power away from targets that had a more direct bearing on the outcome of the war.

By April 1944, it was apparent that the tide in the daylight bombing offensive had turned. The objectives of Pointblank and Argument had been largely achieved, and the Luftwaffe was no longer capable of holding back the flooding Allied air assault. German fighter-pilot loss rates were running at 25 percent per month, and replacements from the flying training schools had a life expectancy on a front-line squadron of no more than thirty days. As the Luftwaffe's effectiveness declined, so Allied air power grew until it was irresistible. By day, the USAAF air armadas operated over Europe at will, carving out an aerial victory that had seemed only a remote possibility in the dark days of 1943. To the surprise of most airmen, it was a victory being won because of an aircraft they had thought an impossible dream — an agile single-seat fighter with the range of a strategic bomber.

The Ninth Arrives

As the balance of the air war began to tip inexorably in favor of the Allies, an increasingly significant part was played by the newcomer to northern European skies — the Ninth Air Force. In drawing up the plans for the USAAF's role in the Allied invasion of France, the air force staffs had originally suggested that tactical air support would be provided by a greatly enhanced Air Support Command of the Eighth Air Force. By August 1943, General Arnold had decided that the tactical air commander should be Lieutenant General Lewis Brereton, who had proved himself in the Mediterranean theater, and also that the scale of air operations envisaged for the invasion warranted a separate tactical air force. Accordingly, when Brereton moved to the United Kingdom in October 1943, his Ninth Air Force headquarters staffs went with him, leaving their combat and support units behind to be absorbed by the Twelfth Air Force. The nucleus of the new Ninth was formed from tactical and support units transferred from the Eighth Air Force, which from then on concentrated on operating its burgeoning front line of heavy bombers and escorting fighters.

The primary mission of the Ninth was to support the Allied armies in their invasion of Normandy and their subsequent drive to defeat the enemy and occupy Germany. As its strength increased in late 1943 and the first months of 1944, the Ninth was blooded against Crossbow targets and in operations that supported the combined bomber offensive. By the date of the invasion, it was the most powerful

Major General "Pete" Quesada, IX TAC (right), and Major General Ralph Royce, Deputy Commander of the Allied Expeditionary Air Force, in France after D-Day.

tactical air force in the world, with three combat commands — IX Fighter Command with thirteen groups of P-47s, three of P-38s, and two of P-51s, led by the outstanding fighter leader Brigadier General Elwood "Pete" Quesada, who in 1929 had joined with Ira Eaker and "Tooey" Spaatz for the endurance flight of the *Question Mark*. Through IX Fighter Command, Quesada controlled two other commands, IX and XIX Tactical Air Commands. Both played significant parts in the Allied sweep through France and into Germany: IX Bomber Command with eleven groups of B-26 medium and A-20 light bombers, and IX Troop Carrier Command with another fourteen groups. In all, the Ninth could field some 4,500 combat aircraft plus about 2,700 gliders, and it had a personnel strength of 170,000. The Ninth was justified in claiming that it could, by itself, project more power than the entire Luftwaffe.

From the time of its formation in the United Kingdom until the end of the war in Europe, the Ninth Air Force was continually engaged in fierce combat. In little more than a year and a half, it flew almost 370,000 sorties and lost over 2,900 aircraft, 2,139 of them fighters. There were 240,000 tons of bombs dropped, 75 million rounds of ammunition expended, and 4,200 enemy aircraft claimed as destroyed. From these bald figures it can be seen that the contribution of the Ninth to the eventual Allied victory in Europe was immense.

CHAPTER 5

The Maritime War

THERE WERE CLOSE-FOUGHT struggles for survival at one time or another on every front in World War II, but none was more desperate nor more bitterly contested than the Battle of the Atlantic, which raged on over four long years. Churchill understood its vital nature from the start: "Amid the torrent of violent events one anxiety reigned supreme. Battles might be won or lost, enterprises might succeed or miscarry, territories might be gained or quitted, but dominating all our power to carry on the war, or even keep ourselves alive, lay our mastery of the ocean routes and the free approach and entry to our ports."

German submarines were at sea from the first day of the war, but the menace to Britain's maritime supply lines did not become severe until the fall of France in May 1940. From then on, U-boats had the use of Atlantic ports and could patrol more often and further out than before. They could also be assisted in their operations by long-range Focke-Wulf Fw 200 Condors operating from bases in France and Norway.

Despite the lessons learned about the usefulness of patrol aircraft during the latter stages of WWI, neither side had devoted much time to maritime aviation before 1939. Göring was not enthusiastic about allowing his Luftwaffe to squander its resources in supporting the German Navy, and it was a similar story in the RAF. Coastal Command was the RAF's "Cinderella," perpetually short of funds and largely equipped with obsolescent aircraft and inadequate weapons. Its very name said something about the limited view the service had of its intended role. In September 1939, the only reasonably modern aircraft in the Command were two squadrons of Short Sunderland flying boats and one of American Lockheed Hudsons. The Royal Navy shares the blame for the neglect, since it was supremely confident in the ability of its ships to defeat the underwater threat by use of Asdic (a device using sonic pulses to detect submerged objects) and saw little need for air support beyond watching for German surface ships in the North Sea.

Air power began to have an appreciable effect on the Battle of the Atlantic with the arrival of the Focke-Wulf Condor. An ingenious adaptation of the prewar airliner, the Condor quickly became what Churchill called "the scourge of the Atlantic." As modified, it could undertake fourteen-hour patrols with a load of four 550-pound bombs. Besides reporting Allied shipping to the U-boat fleet, Condors could be effective raiders in their own right. Between August 1940 and February 1941 they sank eighty-five ships totaling 363,000 tons. Such a serious threat had to be met with drastic action, and since aircraft carriers were not immediately available for

OPPOSITE PAGE *Swordfish Attack at Taranto, by Robert Taylor. Fairey Swordfish biplanes from HMS* Illustrious *carry out a night torpedo attack on units of the Italian Fleet in Taranto harbor, November 11, 1940.*

The Short Sunderland was a vital element of RAF Coastal Command's war against the German U-boats in WWII. Developed from the Empire class flying boats, the Sunderland was first used by the RAF in 1938 and gave outstanding service throughout the war, flying maritime reconnaissance, convoy escort and antisubmarine missions over the Atlantic and Indian Oceans, the North Sea and the Mediterranean. It had an endurance in excess of thirteen hours, and its defensive capabilities, fourteen machine guns in all, led Luftwaffe fighter crews to nickname it the "Flying Porcupine."

escort duty, the first step taken was to equip some merchant ships with aircraft catapults. CAM-ships (Catapult Aircraft Merchantman) each carried a single Hurricane (nicknamed Hurricat) that could be launched if a Condor threatened a convoy. As there were no means of recovering the fighter, the Hurricat pilot first engaged the enemy and then faced the unpleasant prospect of either bailing out or ditching near a ship in the hope of being picked up. Some 175 voyages were made with Hurricat protection, and on August 3, 1941, a Condor was finally shot down by an aircraft from a Fighter Catapult Ship, an expansion of the CAM-ship idea that carried several fighters. Hurricats were launched in anger only eight times. Six raiders were shot down for the loss of all the fighters and one RAF pilot. More important than the relative score was the effect of having CAM-ships in the convoys. Just by being there they forced the Condors to be more cautious and therefore less effective. Late in

1943, the Condor was joined in the long-range antishipping role by the Heinkel He 177 heavy bomber. Dogged by major development problems, the He 177 never exerted any serious influence on the war at sea.

A more satisfactory answer to the Condor problem than the CAM-ships eventually came with the introduction of small escort carriers, able to both launch and recover aircraft. Since they could carry additional aircraft such as the Fairey Swordfish for patrol duties, escort carriers also helped to foil the submarines, at least during the hours of daylight. It was evident that the mere presence of aircraft was enough to reduce the U-boat threat significantly by day. An aerial threat forced them to submerge, and that made it difficult for them to maintain contact with Allied convoys. It also put them down where there was more chance of their being detected by the Asdic of escorting destroyers and corvettes.

A better counter to the U-boat was the radar-equipped, maritime patrol landplane with a range to at least match that of the Condor, but neither radar nor suitable aircraft were available to the Allies in the critical first years of the war. The best of the RAF's patrol aircraft at that time were the Short Sunderland flying boat, which could operate for up to two hours 600 miles from base, and the Lockheed Hudson, which could reach out to 500 miles or so. Useful though these aircraft were inside their radius of action, without effective radar their usefulness was limited to daylight hours, and they still needed good fortune to make a visual sighting on a conning tower in the gray wastes of sea. Even with the development of bases in Iceland, Newfoundland and Nova Scotia, a large gap still remained in the mid-Atlantic that aircraft could not cover. That was the part of the ocean where the struggle between the Allied convoys and the German forces was at its most savage. To Churchill it was a battle that was "the dominating factor all

through the war." In 1942, when an alarming total of eight million tons of Allied and neutral shipping was sunk, the war at sea came close to determining the outcome of the war as a whole.

For a while, after the capture of a U-boat carrying an Enigma code machine in 1941, the British were able to read the German naval radio traffic and route convoys to avoid most of the submarines. Then, in February 1942, a more complex Enigma machine was introduced and the vital intelligence about U-boat dispositions was lost. During those dark days, Coastal Command remained the RAF's "Cinderella," priority being given invariably to building up a bomber force capable of striking massive blows at Germany. As the growing U-boat fleet enjoyed rich pickings off the east coast of the United States after the American entry into the war and the German stranglehold on the Atlantic lifeline tightened, Coastal Command had to fight on for most of time before 1943 with insufficient aircraft of

The "Hurricat" was a converted Hurricane carried by CAM-ships (Catapult Armed Merchantman) as an interim measure to provide air cover for Allied convoys in areas that land-based aircraft could not reach. The Hurricane was flown off, usually against the menace of the Focke-Wulf Fw 200 Condor, on a one-way flight; after defending the convoy the pilot had to bail out, or ditch his aircraft as near as possible to a ship, hoping to be picked up. The CAM-ship scheme was regarded as recklessly dangerous, but there was no other option available at the time, so it was adopted. The slogan was "Desperate times give rise to desperate measures."

To improve its capability for air defense at sea, the Royal Navy adopted the Sea Hurricane. Four Sea Hurricane IBs are seen here on the deck of an Illustrious-class aircraft carrier in 1942.

inadequate performance, hardly any suitable weapons, and a few early and unreliable sets of Anti-Surface Vessel (ASV) radar of limited range. For the RAF, it was a classic case of stretching limited resources to cover almost unlimited tasks, each one demanding priority. However, the enormous Allied losses at sea in 1942 threatened to solve the problem of priorities once and for all. Unless the menace of the U-boats could be curbed, there would be no oil for an Anglo-American bomber offensive, no buildup of forces to counter the Axis in North Africa, and no accumulation of men and material for an Allied invasion of Europe.

Events began to move against the U-boat fleet during late 1942 and early 1943 as a combination of improvements at last offered the hope that maritime patrol airmen might gain the advantage. Consolidated Catalinas equipped more squadrons, and Consolidated Liberators began operating from Iceland to close the mid-Atlantic gap; ASV III, a centimetric radar, proved able to detect a surfaced submarine clearly from 12 miles; reliable and lethal 250-pound depth charges were in use, soon to be joined by acoustic homing torpedoes; powerful airborne searchlights (Leigh lights)

were fitted on some aircraft to illuminate targets in the last stages of night attacks; and German naval transmissions were no longer secure, because the Allies had broken the Enigma coding system for the second time. By mid-1943, Admiral Karl Dönitz, Hitler's *Führer der U-Boote,* was admitting that things were not going well for his command. On May 24, 1943, he recorded in his diary that thirty-one U-boats had been lost already that month, and added: "Losses, even heavy losses, must be accepted if they are accompanied by proportional success in tonnage sunk. But in May one U-boat was lost for every 10,000 tons sunk, where not long ago one U-boat was lost for 100,000 tons sunk. Thus our losses in May have reached an intolerable level. The enemy air force played a decisive role in inflicting these high losses."

The Battle of the Atlantic was far from over, but the U-boat never recovered its dominant position. In 1944, the total tonnage of Allied shipping sunk was no more than an eighth of the 1942 amount, and less than a fifth of that figure was sunk in the North Atlantic. Shore-based aircraft had become the scourge of the U-boats, not only helping surface escorts to find and destroy them, but sinking large numbers unassisted. From sinking just one U-boat in the waters of the Atlantic, Arctic, and North Sea in 1940, and three in 1941, patrol aircraft accounted for 33 in 1942, 113 in 1943, 71 in 1944, and 81 in only four months of 1945. Many of the encounters were fierce, with some U-boat commanders electing to stay on the surface and fight it out. These brief, violent actions, erupting into the mind-numbing business of patrolling the endless sea, demanded matchless courage from those involved, as was shown on July 17, 1944.

At 1:45 that afternoon, Flight Lieutenant John Cruickshank and his crew began their twenty-fifth operational patrol in a Catalina of No. 210 Squadron. Eight monotonous hours into the sortie, the radar showed a contact in the Norwegian Sea, north of the Arctic Circle. It was a surfaced submarine, which confirmed itself as enemy by opening fire. Cruickshank immediately attacked, running in at 50 feet with the gunners doing their best to suppress the U-boat's flak. On the first pass, the Catalina's depth charges failed to release, so Cruickshank turned in again. This time the fire from the U-boat was devastating. Shells tore into aircraft, ripping holes in the hull and creating havoc among the crew. The navigator was killed instantly, one of the gunners was hit in the head, and the flight engineer was wounded in both legs. The windscreen was shattered, the radio destroyed and a fire started in the fuselage. Cruickshank was hit in the chest and legs, but ignored his injuries and continued his attack. Using the pilot's weapon release, he straddled the U-boat with six depth charges before pulling away into clouds. Behind him, the U-347 was sinking.

On the long flight back to base, loss of blood caused Cruickshank to lapse into unconsciousness several times, but the copilot, Flight Sergeant Jack Garnett, less seriously wounded, stayed at the controls. It was still dark when they reached their base at Sullom Voe in the Shetlands, five and a half hours after the action. Cruickshank, in great pain and breathing with difficulty, decided that they must wait for daylight before attempting to put the damaged aircraft down. An hour later, the Catalina settled onto the water and began to sink, but the throttles were kept wide open and the aircraft surged up onto the beach. A medical team was on

> "The aeroplane can no more eliminate the U-boat than a crow can fight a mole."
>
> ADMIRAL DOENITZ

the spot and Cruickshank was given an immediate blood transfusion in the aircraft. Later, in hospital, it was found that he had seventy-two wounds, the most serious being those to his chest and legs. For their courage in this successful action, Jack Garnett was awarded the Distinguished Flying Medal and John Cruickshank the Victoria Cross, his nation's highest military honor.

As long as submarines were forced to spend much of their time on the surface, they operated under the continual threat of detection, and probable destruction, from the air. By 1945, the Germans had taken the next step in the see-saw Atlantic struggle, introducing new submarines capable of high underwater speeds and equipped with the Schnorkel breathing device, which allowed the boats to remain submerged for long periods. Fortunately for the Allies, they came too late to affect the issue.

Northern Europe

From their bases in Norway, the Luftwaffe's flying boats and floatplanes covered the European waters inside the Arctic Circle. Others roamed the Baltic and ventured over the North Sea. The principal aircraft used were Heinkel He 115s, Dornier Do 18s and Blohm and Voss Bv 138s. By mid-1941 the ageing Dornier flying boats had been retired from front-line service, but the ubiquitous He 115 floatplanes soldiered on until well into 1944, mostly operating inside the Arctic Circle against the Allied convoys to the Soviet Union. The twin-boomed, three-engined Bv 138 was the He 115's northern partner. It had a shoe-shaped hull and was referred to by its crews as "The Flying Clog." Its long range and robust construction made it eminently suitable for convoy spotting and shadowing in northern waters, where it often broke a patrol to rendezvous with a U-boat for fuel. Bv 138s were even known to sit on the sea and wait on station for two or three days in the hope that a convoy would arrive.

Armed with torpedoes, He 115s were involved in the piecemeal destruction of Convoy PQ17 in July 1942. The British Admiralty, led to believe that an intervention by the battleship *Tirpitz* was imminent, withdrew the escort vessels and ordered the convoy to scatter. *Tirpitz,* far away in a Norwegian fiord, thereby brought about a German victory without raising

The Fairey Swordfish was an unlikely stalwart of the Royal Navy's offensive capabilities during WWII. With a performance and appearance that suggested a relic from WWI, it was generally known by the nickname "Stringbag." The Swordfish recorded some remarkable successes, including the sinking of Italian warships at Taranto and the fatal crippling of the Bismarck. *Its principal weapon was a single 18-inch, 1,600-pound torpedo slung beneath the fuselage.*

anchor. The Luftwaffe claimed thirteen of the merchantmen for the loss of five aircraft, and only eleven of thirty-five vessels that had sailed from Iceland survived to reach Archangel.

Two medium bombers adapted as torpedo aircraft were the He 111 and Ju 88. In September 1942, Convoy PQ18 set out from Iceland. It differed from its predecessors in having much stronger defenses against air attack, including an aircraft carrier. The Ju 88 torpedo-bomber formations adopted a tactic known as "Golden Zange," in which they opened out into line abreast some 12 miles from the convoy, with about 200 yards between aircraft. This allowed them to comb the convoy with multiple torpedoes and, at the same time, spread the defensive fire of the ships. The antiaircraft fire was described as "horrific" by the Ju 88 crews, who had to contend with naval fighters as well. A total of fourteen merchantmen of the forty in the convoy were sunk, together with a destroyer and a minesweeper. Four Fleet Air Arm fighters were shot down. On the debit side of the battle for the Germans, four U-boats were sunk and forty-one bombers were lost with their crews. In the icy waters of the Arctic there was no hope of survival. This was the last time the Luftwaffe used massed torpedo-bomber attacks.

An effective maritime operation of the Luftwaffe early in the war was the mining of British coastal waters. He 115s, Do 17s, He 111s, and Ju 88s laid mines in the approaches to the Clyde, the Firth of Forth, the Thames Estuary and the ports of Plymouth and Liverpool. On a black night in July 1940, Hajo Herrmann set out to lay mines in the harbor at Plymouth. During his steep gliding approach to the target, his Ju 88 collided with a barrage balloon. In the cockpit, confusion reigned as the aircraft quickly lost flying speed and fell off the balloon upside down. The aircraft tumbled earthward until the nose dropped and flying speed was regained. Herrmann recovered from the ensuing dive just in time to drop his mines in the harbor before escaping across the Channel. Mining operations continued sporadically for years, the last major efforts being made in the month after the Allied invasion of Normandy, when nearly 2,000 mines were laid off the invasion beaches during the hours of darkness.

Aircraft Versus Warship

It had long been recognized that naval aircraft could serve as much more than the eyes of the fleet. Torpedoes and bombs made it possible for them to undertake offensive roles. However, it was not until November 11, 1940, that an event took place that pushed back the traditional horizons of naval aviation, suggesting real strategic possibilities. On that day, a British naval force including the aircraft carrier HMS *Illustrious* reached a point 170 miles southeast of the Italian naval base at Taranto. Two waves of Fairey Swordfish biplanes, twenty-one in all, were launched to make a night attack on the Italian fleet in harbor. Eleven carried torpedoes and the others, bombs and flares. In the subsequent action, one battleship and two smaller warships were sunk and two more battleships were so damaged that they were ineffective for the rest of the war. At a stroke, the Italian fleet received a blow from which it never recovered and the balance of power in the Mediterranean swung sharply in the Royal Navy's favor. For the first time, aircraft operating alone had won a major victory against surface ships and achieved a result that changed the course of the war at sea. On the far side of the world, Japanese military planners took note.

Only two months later, HMS *Illustrious* was on the receiving end, subjected to concentrated attacks by Italian torpedo bombers and Luftwaffe dive-bombers when 60 miles west of Malta. Only the carrier's robust armored-steel box design prevented complete destruction. Six direct hits by armor-piercing bombs wrecked the flight deck and damaged below decks to such an extent that the ship had to be withdrawn from operations and sent to a U.S. shipyard for extensive repairs.

Five months after Taranto, the Royal Navy's aircraft struck again off the island of Crete's Cape Matapan. As Admiral Cunningham's Mediterranean Fleet sought to bring to battle an Italian naval force led by the battleship *Vittorio Veneto,* the new aircraft carrier HMS *Formidable* launched strikes by Fairey Albacore and Swordfish torpedo aircraft. The *Vittorio Veneto,* hit by three torpedoes, was severely damaged and the cruiser *Pola* stopped dead in the water. Unaware that the British fleet was only 70 miles away, the Italian admiral withdrew his battleship but sent two more cruisers with four destroyers to aid the stricken *Pola.* Without radar on a dark, moonless night, the Italian sailors knew nothing of the British ships' presence until the guns started firing. Within minutes, all three cruisers and two of the destroyers were sunk, victims of a situation created by air attack.

The defensive armament of the Swordfish was not impressive. It consisted of one .303 Vickers K machine gun in the rear cockpit.

In May 1941, the German Navy made a bid to create some havoc in the Atlantic with its surface ships. The battleship *Bismarck,* escorted by the cruiser *Prinz Eugen,* sailed from Norway under the command of Admiral Lütjens, aiming to enter the broad reaches of the Atlantic via the Denmark Strait between Greenland and Iceland. Intercepted west of Iceland on May 24, the *Bismarck* engaged the pursuing Royal Navy task force, sinking the battlecruiser HMS *Hood* and damaging the battleship HMS *Prince of Wales.* However, *Bismarck* did not come out of the encounter unscathed. Hit twice by shells from the *Prince of Wales,* the great battleship was taking on water and steaming at reduced speed. Admiral Lütjens initially headed south into mid-Atlantic but decided that he must take his ship to a French port for repairs. In the early hours of May 25, having detached the *Prinz Eugen,* he successfully evaded the shadowing British ships and turned east toward Brest. For more than twenty-four hours, as the Royal Navy diverted forces from all quarters to join in the chase, the *Bismarck* disappeared.

FAIREY SWORDFISH

Robert Spence of Muirkirk, Ontario, purchased deteriorating hulks of two Swordfish bombers in the early 1970s and restored this one to flying condition. The large biplane torpedo bombers flew throughout World War II.

LEFT The open cockpit of the Fairey Swordfish: the traditional large compass found in all British aircraft was here installed upside down, just under the windscreen. This naturally presented a problem for the pilots, so the compass was manufactured with the degree numbers printed in reverse and a movable mirror added under the compass so the pilot could determine his direction of flight.

The horizontal bar mounted forward of the windscreen is the torpedo aiming device. Imagine flying into the large-caliber fire coming from a German capital ship such as the Bismark in this open airplane and aiming your weapon with a "stick."

ABOVE The heart of the slow but steady Swordfish, the Bristol Pegasus engine. Earlier Pegasus engines developed 690 horsepower, but in later versions this rose to 750 horsepower. Robert Spence recounted that a veteran of Swordfish attacks on the German Navy told him that while they were attacking the Prinz Eugen, a large-caliber shell took the top cylinders right off his engine and it kept running.

The Supermarine Walrus was another British WWII aircraft that was antiquated in appearance and attracted an unusual nickname, "Shagbat." Its uncompromisingly naval hull hung below high-set biplane wings carrying a single Bristol Pegasus radial with a pusher propeller. One of the principal duties undertaken by this strange aircraft was air-sea rescue, and many pilots shot down in the seas around Britain owed their lives to the reliability of the Walrus and the dedication of its crews.

On the morning of May 26, a patrolling RAF Catalina, piloted by Flying Officer Dennis Briggs and Ensign "Tuck" Smith of the U.S. Navy, spotted the *Bismarck*. (Ensign Smith was one of the USN pilots helping RAF crews convert to their lend-lease Catalinas. Since the U.S. was not yet in the war, his presence on this flight was a secret from both the Germans and the American people.) The reported position seemed to show that Admiral Lütjens had escaped. None of the British battleships was close enough to make contact before the *Bismarck* was within range of protective Luftwaffe cover. With darkness closing in, only the Swordfish of the carrier HMS *Ark Royal* stood between the German sailors and their haven. Old, slow biplanes though they were, it was their eleventh-hour intervention that doomed the *Bismarck*. Operating in appalling weather just before nightfall, they pressed home their attacks. Two torpedoes struck the *Bismarck*, one of which damaged the steering

mechanism, locking the battleship into a continuous port turn. On the morning of May 27, the British capital ships HMS *King George V* and *Rodney* caught up with their out-of-control enemy and pounded *Bismarck* into a blazing hulk. When all of the German guns had been silenced, the cruiser HMS *Dorsetshire* delivered the final blow with torpedoes. The crew of the *Bismarck* had fought with courage and spirit, sinking a major British warship and outwitting all forms of surface pursuit. Escape was denied only because of sorties flown by a flying boat and a few ageing biplanes. Although they did not fire the final shots of the battle, it was effectively their efforts that sent the pride of the German Navy to the bottom of the Atlantic.

The next major confrontation between the German Navy and British aircraft saw a rare reversal for air power as the ships got the better of it. The battlecruisers *Scharnhorst* and *Gneisnau*, together with the cruiser *Prinz Eugen*, had been bottled up in the French port of Brest, under regular attack by RAF bombers, for many months. In a bold move to recover their warships to home waters, the Germans broke out of Brest on the night of February 11, 1942, and steamed northeast through the English Channel. Bad weather and radar failure in a patrolling Hudson combined to cover the escape, and the warships were in the Straits of Dover before any action was taken against them. Swordfish torpedo aircraft were again called on to intervene, but this time without success. Six Swordfish of No. 825 Squadron, led by Lieutenant Commander Eugene Esmonde, were committed to the attack. All six were shot down and not one torpedo hit a target. A second torpedo attack by Bristol Beauforts and some high-level bombing sorties were equally wide of the mark. If British air power could claim any credit, it came later when both the *Scharnhorst* and the *Gneisnau* were damaged by RAF-laid mines off the Dutch coast before they reached port. In every other way, the operation was one of the war's most humiliating events for British airmen.

After the loss of the *Bismarck*, Germany's only remaining first-line battleship was the *Tirpitz*. The anxiety promoted by the thought of this mighty vessel getting out of its Norwegian fiord to play havoc with the Atlantic and Arctic convoys forced the British to pay it considerable attention. Reconnaissance sorties were flown frequently to confirm the battleship's position, and several missions were carried out by naval dive-bombers and torpedo aircraft in attempts to inflict damage. Even though these operations and others succeeded in keeping the *Tirpitz* bottled up for most of the war, the threat remained, and not until November 1944 was it finally removed.

The cockpit of the Walrus has the feel of being part of a boat. It is large and sturdily built, and the cabin's windows are uncompromisingly angular. Even the control column suggests a ship's wheel.

In a rare example of a successful attack on a major warship by bombers flying level at high altitude, thirty Lancasters of Nos. IX and 617 Squadrons aimed 12,000-pound Tallboy bombs at the battleship while it lay tied up near Tromsö. Two direct hits caused considerable damage, but it is believed that the ship was destroyed by a near miss. The *Tirpitz* was moored above a shallow shelf at the edge of the fiord, and the explosion of a Tallboy alongside blew a huge hole in the water into which the ship rolled. It settled upside down with the keel visible, and was described as having been capsized rather than sunk. In any event, the *Tirpitz* was no longer a threat to Allied shipping.

CHAPTER 6

D-Day and Beyond

IN THE TASKING FOR the invasion of Normandy (Operation Overlord), the Allied air forces were given the primary responsibility of preventing the Luftwaffe from interfering with the amphibious assault. The strategic bombing offensive had been working toward this end for some time. The losses inflicted on the Luftwaffe by the Eighth Air Force in particular during the first half of 1944 had effectively broken the back of the German fighter force. Nevertheless, there was no room for complacency. The pressure had to be maintained so that there would be no possibility of the Luftwaffe making things difficult for the Allied armies, and there were a great many other tasks that needed doing by the USAAF and the RAF in preparation for an amphibious operation of unprecedented scale against a heavily defended coastline. These other tasks — reconnaissance, destruction of coastal defenses, and isolation of the invasion area — became increasingly important as D-Day drew nearer.

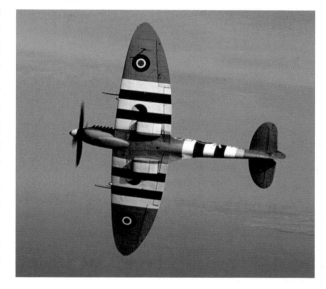

If there was one thing the Allied leaders agreed upon, it was that without overwhelming strength in the air, the invasion would not be a practical operation of war. In just a few short years, even the most critical of prewar skeptics had grown to realize that air power had become a dominant factor in modern warfare. While it might still be unproven that the defeat of an enemy nation could be accomplished by air power alone, few now believed that victory, either

LEFT *On the morning of June 6, 1999, the 55th anniversary of the invasion, looking toward Utah beach from Pointe du Hoc, where the U.S. Army Rangers scaled these cliffs using ropes, grappling hooks and ladders from the London Fire Department. The barbed wire still keeps visitors from areas that may contain unexploded ordnance from the battle.* ABOVE *Over the English Channel, a Spitfire IX banks away, displaying the invasion stripes applied to all combat aircraft seen over the beaches on June 6, 1944. The troops and sailors that made up the invasion forces were repeatedly briefed not to fire on any aircraft painted with these stripes.*

The German bunkers guarding the Normandy beaches were formidable, with guns protected by several feet of reinforced concrete. Counterfire directly into the embrasure was the only way of seriously affecting the German gunners. In a furious duel with the guns at Longues the cruiser HMS Ajax *did just that with a shell that struck the gun on its way into the bunker.*

on the battlefield or finally in war, could be won without it. If there were disagreements, they arose in deciding how best to apply air power in achieving victory.

As plans for the invasion were laid, the Allied commanders split into two camps, with the heavy bombers of the Eighth Air Force and the RAF among the principal bones of contention. The debate did not divide along national or service lines. The bomber men, led by General Spaatz and Air Marshal Harris, believed that the best way to weaken German opposition to the invasion was to keep pounding away at the industrial heart of Germany, Spaatz naming the oil industry as the most vulnerable target. Those ranged against them included Air Marshal Tedder (Eisenhower's deputy), Air Marshal Leigh Mallory (Commander of the Allied Expeditionary Air Forces), and General Brereton (Ninth Air Force). They believed that it was vital to paralyze the enemy's ability to move by destroying as much of the rail network as possible in Belgium and northern France, and that the participation of the heavy bombers in that effort was essential. After a protracted and

often passionate argument, General Eisenhower decided that the transportation plan was the one that would contribute most directly to the success of the invasion.

On April 14, 1944, to the discomfort of Spaatz and Harris, the Combined Chiefs of Staff placed the Eighth Air Force and RAF Bomber Command under Eisenhower's direction until after the Allied armies had successfully established themselves on the continent. From April 14, besides his responsibilities for huge naval and ground forces, Eisenhower commanded or directed the Allied Expeditionary Air Forces (Ninth Air Force, the RAF's 2nd Tactical Air Force and the Air Defence of Great Britain), the U.S. Strategic Air Forces (Eighth Air Force, Fifteenth Air Force), and RAF Bomber Command. On D-Day, this formidable combination had available for operations from the United Kingdom 3,467 heavy bombers, 1,645 medium and light bombers, 5,409 fighters, and 2,316 transports. The Luftwaffe then had a front line that included some 3,200 combat-ready fighters and bombers to cover demands on all fronts — east, west and south. From the numbers, it had been clear to the Supreme Commander for some time that his air forces should have no difficulty in providing the air supremacy so essential over the Normandy beaches. He was encouraged to find that they were equally effective in meeting their other challenges.

In the weeks leading up to D-Day, the Allied air forces concentrated their efforts on a wide variety of targets near the Channel coast, taking care to mislead the German commanders as far as possible by hitting two targets outside Normandy for every one in the invasion area. Airfields within 130 miles of the proposed beachhead were pounded and rendered almost untenable, while the Eighth Air Force persisted in mounting at least some raids against strategic targets in Germany, both to discourage the Luftwaffe from moving fighters forward into France and to continue the battle of attrition that had been so effective.

Since the enemy's coastal defenses were heavily fortified, attacks on them were generally not nearly so profitable, with the notable exception of the radar stations. By D-Day, more than 80 percent of the radar coverage along the Channel coast had been destroyed, some sites near Calais being deliberately left intact so that the ingenious spoofs devised to mislead observers as to the objective of the main Allied landings could be detected. In effect, the enemy defenders were blinded and left vulnerable to the confusion over Allied intentions that engulfed them on the morning of June 6, 1944.

Attrition of the enemy's rail network began with attacks on rail centers and repair facilities in the hope of crippling the entire system. An intense campaign involving every type of offensive aircraft, from heavy bombers to fighters, achieved impressive levels

Over 250 Airspeed A.S.51 Horsa gliders carried airborne troops into action in the initial assault on Normandy in the early hours of June 6, 1944.

of destruction. A German Transport Ministry report of May 15 admitted: "Large scale strategic movement of German troops by rail is practically impossible at the present time, and must remain so while attacks are maintained at their present intensity." Even so, the campaign was not producing the results expected by the Allied commanders. German ingenuity was countering the effects of much of the damage caused. On May 20, the campaign escalated when wide-scale fighter sweeps were authorized to attack the railways. The most spectacular of these were the "Chattanooga Choo-Choo" missions, which began on May 21 with a sweep involving 763 AEAF and 500 Eighth Air Force fighters. Locomotives, wagons, signal boxes and maintenance sheds were attacked wherever they were found, and moving trains, usually betrayed by a telltale stream of smoke, were hounded unmercifully. Similar missions were flown on several of the following days, bringing sharp reductions in the numbers of trains running in daylight.

The culminating blow in the campaign to deny the enemy freedom of movement was the destruction of the Seine River bridges. Until early May, it was thought that the bridges might prove unrewarding targets. One estimate suggested that heavy bombers would have to drop 1,200 tons of bombs against each bridge to ensure that it would be unusable. However, on May 7, 1944, a dramatic demonstration of fighter-bomber power offered a much cheaper solution. Eight of "Pete" Quesada's P-47s delivered two 1,000-pound

AIRBORNE INVASION

Looking at the invasion areas from the sea, the left and right flanks of the target area in Normandy were to be attacked from the air by glider-borne troops and by paratroopers. The left flank was attacked by the British Airborne forces and the right flank by American Airborne divisions. The element of surprise and swift actions by these units, followed by determined small unit combat actions held the flanks of the entire invasion until they could be relieved by the main invasion forces coming from the beaches. Often the individual accomplishments of small groups of well-trained men saved the day.

On June 5, 1999, the 55th anniversary of their action on D-Day, these men returned to the bridge now named for their unit insignia, Pegasus. With the British 6th Airborne, under the command of Major John Howard, Staff Sergeant Geoff Barkway, Army Air Command Glider Pilot, and Sergeant Peter Boyle, B Squadron, flew the Number 3 glider to a landing just where the flags are between their shoulders. They described their flight into combat in a Horsa glider: "We were towed by a Halifax and released at 12:15 A.M. at 6,000 feet, several miles offshore. We had a map, a flashlight and a stopwatch. With timed turns we landed [gesturing behind them] just over there, about 20 yards from the bridge." Sergeant Boyle lost his right arm that night in action once the airmen became infantry after the

landing. Air Chief Marshal Leigh-Mallory, Commander-in-Chief of the Allied Expeditionary Air Forces, called the feat the war's finest piece of airmanship.

BELOW The stone marker on the far side of the bridge where Sergeant Barkway landed his glider.

ABOVE Arlette Gondrée Pritchett, operates the Gondrée Café, a small restaurant on the other side of the river from where the gliders of the 6th Airborne landed on the night of June 5/6, 1944. The historic café is now considered the first building liberated in the invasion. Arlette was four years old that night. Each June 5, she hosts a reunion of the Airborne and welcomes the veterans who liberated her family's home and business.

RIGHT Arlette and one of the Pegasus veterans. She was telling us of her fondness for these men when a very elderly man with many medals on his chest walked into the café. They shared a look that words cannot describe — he had been ill — and he said to Arlette, "I never thought I would see you again." She left our table and embraced this veteran bringing everyone in the room to tears.

TOP RIGHT The Pegasus Bridge, the signs of combat during the night of June 5/6, 1944, still visible on the steel structure that was the left flank of the D-Day invasion.

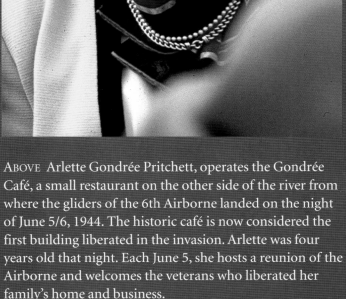

SAINTE MÈRE EGLISE

LEFT At the United States Air Force Museum, a C-47 in the markings of the D-Day airborne forces. The black and white stripes under the wings represent one of the more remarkable feats of organization during the war. Almost overnight, all of the aircraft that would be seen over the beaches were marked with these distinctive stripes, applied with whatever was available — mops, rags, brushes, brooms — making for a very unmilitary look to these essential markings.

OPPOSITE BOTTOM LEFT Jack Reames of Vandalia, Ohio, 82nd Airborne Division, 508th Parachute Infantry Regiment, C Company, made his first combat jump into Normandy at 3:17 A.M., June 6, 1944. Due to weather and enemy fire, the Airborne Divisions (82nd and 101st) were scattered across the attack areas, most landing many miles from their intended zones. He was just nineteen years old when he jumped into scattered opposition and landed several miles inland from his objective, the village of Sainte Mère Eglise. By dawn he had marched to the sound of the guns and shortly after entering the village became involved in the hard-fought battle to hold the right flank of the invasion, fighting in an alleyway in the shadow of the church in the town square.

OPPOSITE BOTTOM RIGHT Jack Reames, in a photo taken during the Market-Garden actions in Holland in autumn 1944; he also fought and was wounded in the Battle of the Bulge in December of that year.

BELOW LEFT The Norman church in the center of Sainte Mère Eglise, featured in the film *The Longest Day.* On D-Day, its distinctive spire was made memorable when Private John Steele's parachute caught on the steeple. To this day, the village keeps a chute there as a memorial.

BELOW RIGHT One of the stained-glass windows in the church celebrates the landings and the long road to the liberation of occupied Europe.

Cruising at 240 knots, a Mustang chases its shadow.

That was a question that German soldiers got tired of asking. By the close of D-Day, with the Allied armies tightening their grip on the beachheads, the awesome power of the Allied air forces had been clearly demonstrated, and the more perceptive Germans must have realized that the pattern of the war in the west had been set. Those 171 squadrons of Allied fighters had ensured that the Luftwaffe would be conspicuous by its absence, and that anything moving among the hedgerows of Normandy would be strafed. (Fifteen squadrons were allocated for shipping cover, fifty-four patrolled the beaches, thirty-three escorted the bombers and conducted offensive sweeps, thirty-three undertook interdiction of the areas inland from the beaches, and thirty-six were available for direct support of the assault forces.) German soldiers generally grew to accept that it was their grim lot to fight on while being harassed incessantly by the Allied air forces, without hope of significant help from the Luftwaffe. Even though over 1,000 additional fighters were moved forward from Germany by early July, they accomplished relatively little. Allied air supremacy was a reality that was made very apparent in the weeks and months following the Normandy invasion.

Tactical Air Rampant

The days following D-Day were critical for the Allies, and the immediate task for the air forces was plain. Although the assault forces were ashore, the beachheads were far from secure, and it was vital that the speed of any German reinforcement should be slower than the rate of the Allied buildup. The fighters of Ninth Air Force and the RAF's 2nd Tactical Air Force had to make it as difficult as possible for German units to move into the battle area. On D-Day itself, the Allies were greatly helped by the indecision of the German high command. Until late afternoon, poor flying weather prevented tactical aircraft from operating freely, and three Panzer divisions that might have intervened in the battle were prevented from doing so by the hesitancy of Hitler and his general staff. By the time the armored divisions were released, the skies had cleared and the opportunity was lost. Panzer Lehr division, needing to cover only 130 miles to the front, found it impossible to make progress at more than 6 or 7 miles per hour because of aerial attack. As Major General Fritz Bayerlein, commander of Panzer Lehr, has recalled: "By the end of the day [June 7] I had lost forty tank trucks carrying fuel and ninety others. Five of my tanks were knocked out, and eighty-four half-tracks, prime movers and self-propelled guns."

Interdiction of the German Army's rear areas intensified after D-Day. Attacks on bridges became more frequent, including the crossings of the Loire with those of the Seine now that there was no need to disguise the Allies' intentions. Attacks on rail centers continued, and German supply dumps were bombed systematically. Much of the Allies' target selection was driven by intelligence from Ultra, which often revealed the whereabouts of significant targets and indicated which attacks were being most effective. An Ultra-inspired air strike on June 10, 1944, destroyed Panzergruppe West HQ and killed many of its staff, thus removing the vital armored forces control center from the battle.) Equally rewarding was the massive campaign of armed reconnaissance conducted by the fighters of the Ninth Air Force and the 2nd Tactical Air Force over Normandy and the surrounding region. In daylight, it became almost impossible for anything to move anywhere in the area without attracting the attention of Allied fighters. One German officer observed that "the effect of Allied air superiority on the Normandy front and as far as Paris is so great that…even single vehicles are used by day only in the most extreme emergencies." As early as June 10, Field Marshal Erwin Rommel was reporting that "Every traffic defile in the rear areas is under continual attack and it is very difficult to get essential supplies of ammunition and petrol up to the troops." (On July 17, 1944, Rommel experienced the implacable ferocity of the Allied fighter sweeps at first hand when his staff car was strafed by two Spitfires. His driver was killed, and Rommel's skull was fractured when

the car plunged off the road, effectively ending his career.)

As the battle for Normandy dragged on, providing close air support to the troops became ever more important, and soldiers and airmen cooperated in developing methods of making that support increasingly effective. Radars originally designed for air defense were incorporated into a system for the control of air strikes, and at Quesada's instigation, IX TAC began flying "armored column cover" (ACC) missions. An air support party, in a tank equipped with VHF radio, was added to each tank column, over which IX TAC aircraft flew on call from dawn to dusk, looking for trouble. As the IX TAC operation order of the time put it: "Each of the rapidly advancing columns will be covered at all times by a four ship flight…They may attack any target which is identified as enemy, directing their attention to the terrain immediately in front of the advancing column."

The contrast in the behavior of the opposing armies brought about by the Allies' aggressive use of their dominant air power could not have been more marked. On the German side of the line, movement by day was almost impossible, and troops were forced to keep their vehicles hidden from the searching eyes of roving fighter pilots. On

At low level, the P-51 shadow flickering over the trees confirms the feeling of speed.

the Allied side, tanks and trucks often moved openly in tightly spaced columns, confident that the Luftwaffe was incapable of offering any threat worth bothering about. Later in the campaign, the Luftwaffe occasionally concentrated its forces and managed to strike back. Such leaks in the Allied air umbrella invariably drew strong protests from the ground troops, who had come to expect nothing less than complete protection. That soldiers could voice such complaints about the infrequent and generally ineffectual efforts of the Luftwaffe offered apt comment on the benefits of air supremacy. Allied soldiers had grown accustomed to the warmth of the air's security blanket. Their German counterparts could only shiver in their nakedness.

If tactical aircraft were considered an integral part of the Allied armies' daily operations, the use of heavy bombers in direct support of troops was more controversial. Effective though they had been during the pre-invasion campaign to seal off Normandy, they were less successful during the invasion itself, when much of the immense weight of their bombardment fell on empty fields. Subsequent efforts to use them to break the impasse on the Allies' left flank, in front of Caen, were also disappointing.

Short bombing caused casualties among some forward Allied troops, and the German defenses, although savagely pounded, were not broken. Nevertheless, plans were laid to use the Eighth Air Force heavies to launch Operation Cobra, a massive blow intended to break the U.S. First Army out of the miseries of Normandy's "bocage" country. (The "bocage" was Norman farming country made up of small fields bounded by thick hedgerows and sunken lanes. It was ideally suited for mounting a stubborn defense.)

Cobra got off to a false start on July 24 because of bad weather. Only part of the force attacked, and erratic bombing caused casualties on both sides of the line. Forceful reminders of the grave consequences of inaccuracy were given to all units before the USAAF committed its aircraft to a maximum effort on the following day. In all, 1,508 heavies, 380 mediums and 559 fighters struck at the German defenses immediately to the west of the little town of Saint-Lô. The very sight of such massive formations inspired awe in both friend and foe, and the three-hour bombardment they unleashed was terrifying in its concentrated ferocity. The organization of many German units was broken in an experience most frequently described by

P-47s gather for the camera. This is not a formation in which to give battle. Note that the P-47s at the top of the picture are older models without the clear vision canopy.

A P-47 over the trees.

survivors as "shattering." General Bayerlein of Panzer Lehr found that 70 percent of his personnel were "dead, wounded, crazed or dazed," and, under interrogation after the war, Field Marshal von Rundstedt said that the Saint-Lô bombing was "the most effective, as well as the most impressive, tactical use of air power in his experience." Unfortunately, as before, there were some gross bombing errors, and the U.S. 30th Infantry Division was the principal sufferer. Over 100 American soldiers died, among them Lieutenant General Lesley McNair, the highest-ranking U.S. officer killed in WWII. Distressing though the friendly-fire losses were, the U.S. ground forces were not discouraged for long. They surged forward, breaking through the crumbling barrier of German resistance to throw off the straitjacket of Normandy's "bocage."

Cobra confirmed the obvious truth that the heavy bomber force was more akin to an indiscriminate bludgeon than a precise rapier, especially when used tactically. Understandably, there were bitter reactions from the troops who had suffered from the waywardness of the "friendly" bombardment. Many of the Army's ground commanders began to believe, along with Spaatz and Harris, that heavy bombers were better left to their strategic tasks. Nevertheless, it was generally conceded that the Eighth Air Force heavy bombers had been the keys which unlocked the German defenses at Saint-Lô. The U.S. VII Corps gave its opinion that "Our losses would have been infinitely greater, and our success would perhaps never have materialized, if it had not been for the overall effectiveness of this heavy bombardment."

As the number of U.S. troops in France approached the million mark and control became too unwieldy for one headquarters, the ground forces split into two separate armies, the First (Lieutenant General Courtney Hodges) and the Third (Lieutenant General George Patton). Quesada's IX TAC continued its old association with First Army, and the newly activated Third Army was allocated an air force of its own, XIX TAC commanded by Major General O.P. Weyland. As the airmen of XIX TAC were to find out, they had a tiger by the tail. Swinging at the outer edge of the Allied armies' "opening door" offensive under Patton's forceful leadership, the Third Army moved across France against limited opposition at great speed. And so XIX TAC had to keep up, moving its headquarters and squadrons forward continually and operating from hastily repaired or improvised airfields to ensure that soldiers always had air cover when and where it was most needed. In the achievement of this remarkable feat, the labors of the Ninth's engineers and logistical units were nothing short of Herculean. As time went by, Patton came to rely increasingly on having such a responsive tactical air arm to call on. In a development that revealed the level of trust and cooperation reached between air and ground commanders, he asked XIX TAC to take on the responsibility of protecting Third Army's long, exposed southern flank during its headlong advance.

The U.S. Army had burst out of the Cotentin Peninsula at Avranches by the end of the first week of August 1944, and its spearheads swept forward both west across Brittany and east toward the Seine. In a desperate attempt to stem the hemorrhage, Hitler ordered a counterattack to be made through Mortain to the sea, aiming to sever the head of the American advance from its body of support. Built around five Panzer divisions, and backed by a rare concentration of Luftwaffe fighters, this was a formidable thrust. It was thrown back in one of the war's best demonstrations of interservice and inter-Allied cooperation. Slowed by stubborn resistance from American infantry, the German armored columns were savaged from the air. Rocket-firing Typhoons of the RAF's 2nd Tactical Air Force took on the Panzers while IX TAF's fighters kept the Luftwaffe from interfering. To the dismay of the Wehrmacht, not one

Luftwaffe fighter appeared over the battlefield and the Panzer spearhead was stopped in its tracks with heavy losses. When the German generals finally accepted that their counterattack had failed, they began a process of withdrawal that soon accelerated into the chaos of headlong rout. As a consequence of Hitler's reluctance to abandon Mortain, the orders for retreat were given too late, and the stage was set for one of the most destructive demonstrations of tactical air power ever seen.

With the British and Canadians driving south toward Falaise, and the U.S. Third Army racing to take Argentan from the south, the German Seventh Army and Fifth Panzer Army became almost completely encircled in an oval pocket, which by August 14 was less than 50 miles long and not more than 30 miles across at its widest point. The one remaining path of escape to the east was then only 10 miles wide and being squeezed shut under Allied pressure. The interior of the Falaise Pocket and the narrow neck of its exit became classic killing grounds for Typhoons, Mustangs, Spitfires and Thunderbolts as German troops struggled to find a way out. The RAF's rocket-firing Typhoon gained an especially lethal reputation, its mere appearance over the battlefield producing the same effect on troops that the Stuka had in the early days of the war.

At Falaise, as described by Typhoon pilot Desmond Scott, "The road was crammed with enemy vehicles — tanks, trucks, half-tracks, even horse-drawn wagons and ambulances, nose to tail, all pressing forward in a frantic bid to reach cover… hundreds of German troops began spilling out into the road to sprint for the open fields and hedgerows…there was no escape. Typhoons were already attacking and within seconds the whole stretch of road was bursting and

B-26s of the Mediterranean Allied Tactical Air Force had a big part to play in softening up the enemy defenses before Operation Anvil, the Allied invasion of southern France in August 1944.

A B-24 approaches its target at 20,000 feet.

blazing under streams of rocket and cannon fire…. It was an awesome sight…an army in retreat, trapped and without air protection. The once proud ranks of Hitler's Third Reich were being massacred from the Normandy skies by the relentless and devastating power of our rocket-firing Typhoons."

Tanks and guns were destroyed in their hundreds, soft-skinned vehicles by the thousand. Although as many as 40,000 German soldiers escaped the Falaise trap, they left most of their equipment behind, together with some 60,000 of their colleagues — 50,000 as prisoners, 10,000 of them dead.

Southern Intrusion

While these heady days were passing into history in the north, the Allies struck at Hitler's fortress from another direction. On August 15, 1944, Allied forces invaded the south of France and, profiting from lessons learned in previous amphibious operations, they were quickly ashore. It is true that the German forces facing the invasion were inferior to the invaders both in quality and quantity, but ground commanders were quick to acknowledge that Allied air supremacy saved many lives and a great deal of time. Commanded by Brigadier General Gordon Saville, XII Tactical Air Command operated with the bombers of the Mediterranean Allied Air Forces at the heart of the air campaign. Persistent interdiction before the landings disrupted enemy supply lines, and counter-air activity removed the Luftwaffe threat. Most of the coastal defenses were neutralized, and both the airborne assault and the landings went in under a powerful air umbrella. With all the benefits of effective air-ground cooperation, the Allied forces swept forward and in early September made contact with the right wing of Patton's Third Army west of the Swiss border. At that point, having proved its combat capabilities in the Italian campaign and during the drive through southern France, XII TAC left the operational control of the MAAF to add its strength to the already formidable power of the TACs controlled by Ninth Air Force.

In effect, by the end of 1944, each of the armies had its own air force: First Army had IX TAC (Quesada); Third Army, XIX TAC (Weyland); and Ninth Army, XXIX TAC (Nugent). In the north, 21st Army Group was supported by the RAF's 2nd TAF, and 6th Army Group to the south had the services of XII TAC (Saville) and the First French Air Force. XII TAC and the French joined together to become the First TAF (Major General Ralph Royce, a celebrated figure from the early days of American air power).

Wehrmacht Defiant

By mid-September 1944, the Allies had freed almost all of France, Belgium and Luxembourg, and they were ready for the next great challenge — reaching and crossing the Rhine. General Eisenhower directed that the main thrust should be made in the north, and that the First Allied Airborne Army should be used in the assault. (The FAAA was formed on August 8, 1944, under the command of Lieutenant General Lewis Brereton. It included the U.S. 17th, 82nd, and 101st Airborne Divisions; the British 1 and 6 Airborne Divisions; and the Polish Independent Parachute Brigade. The air elements were the USAAF's IX Troop Carrier Command, and the RAF's 38 and 46 Groups. Brereton was replaced as Commander Ninth Air Force by Major General Hoyt

The Piper L-4A Grasshopper, the military version of the famous Cub, is typical of the small liaison and observation aircraft used by the USAAF in WWII. Fitted with a 65-horsepower Continental engine, it cruised at 75 mph. This slow speed, combined with the high wing and generous greenhouse windows, allowed the crew to pay close attention to details on the ground. They reported what they saw and could call in artillery fire or air strikes if necessary. Simple and cheap, thousands of Grasshoppers were delivered and saw service in every theater of WWII. The USAF Museum's example is marked as an aircraft flown in Operation Torch, the Allied invasion of North Africa.

Vandenburg.) On September 17, an ambitious operation code-named Market-Garden was launched in a valiant but ill-fated attempt to drive through the German lines and seize bridges in the Netherlands near Eindhoven, Nijmegen and Arnhem. Aircraft of the Eighth and Ninth Air Forces and the RAF prepared the way, and the assaulting airborne forces were dispatched in an armada of 1,546 transports and 478 gliders, reinforced next day with another 1,306 transports and 1,152 gliders. Unfortunately for the Allies, strong German forces were well placed to resist, especially at Arnhem. Even worse, bad weather intervened to deprive the airborne troops of the sort of close support from Allied tactical aircraft they had counted on. After a week of bitter fighting, during which armored spearheads struggled forward through Eindhoven and Nijmegen to relieve the beleaguered paratroops, it was realized that Arnhem was "a bridge too far," and the operation was abandoned.

The European winter of 1944 was one of the worst in living memory. Storms and leaden skies combined to keep the Allied tactical air forces grounded at least half of the time. Taking advantage of the situation, Hitler gathered his reserves and ordered a massive counterattack against thinly held U.S. Army positions in the Ardennes. On December 16, eight Panzer and ten infantry divisions punched through the U.S. front, aiming to split the Allied armies and drive on to the coast, retaking the port of Antwerp and cutting the logistic chain. The "Battle of the Bulge" was on. For once, it seemed that the Luftwaffe was prepared to offer the Wehrmacht some real support, although for a week foul weather hampered both side's air forces in their attempts to intervene. In that time, the enemy penetration was extended for more than 60 miles, although a number of U.S. Army units held out in surrounded strongpoints, notably the 101st Division at Bastogne.

On December 23, the skies cleared, and the full fury of Allied air power descended on the German soldiers in the "bulge" and on their supply lines. Medium bombers attacked roads and railways behind the German columns and struck at Luftwaffe airfields. Transports parachuted supplies into Bastogne. Fighters swarmed over the Wehrmacht, strafing and bombing guns, vehicles and

> *"Anyone who has to fight, even with the most modern weapons, against an enemy in complete command of the air, fights like a savage against modern European troops, under the same handicaps and with the same chances of success."*
>
> FIELD MARSHAL ERWIN ROMMEL

enemy-held buildings. In supporting operations on Christmas Eve, the Eighth Air Force "heavies" pulled out all the stops and launched their largest effort of the war so far. More than 2,000 B-17s and B-24s took off to pound German airfields and communications, greatly hampering the German offensive. (Leading the Eighth on this raid was Brigadier General Fred Castle, a former CO of the 94th Bomb Group revered by his men. His B-17 was shot down on the way to the target and he was killed in the crash, having stayed at the controls to give his crew time to escape. He is the only general officer in American history to die while directly involved in a specific act aimed at saving the lives of his subordinates. His was the last Eighth Air Force Medal of Honor awarded.)

Somewhat to the surprise of Allied airmen, the Luftwaffe had gathered its reserves together too, and it rose in strength, flying as many as 800 sorties on December 23, challenging Allied fighters to combat and inflicting the highest losses ever on the Ninth's medium bombers. From a force of 624 B-26s and A-20s, thirty-five were shot down and over 180 badly damaged. On January 1, 1945, the Luftwaffe did even better, launching nearly 900 aircraft for a sweep against Allied airfields. They achieved considerable success, destroying over 150 Allied aircraft and damaging many others, but it was a costly exercise. Almost a third of the Luftwaffe force was lost.

It was almost the Luftwaffe's last gasp. Hitler's Ardennes offensive was disastrous for the Luftwaffe, which suffered catastrophic pilot losses in the course of the Battle of the Bulge. Among several bad days was December 17, when seventy-nine pilots were killed or wounded. On Christmas Day, there were sixty-two more, and on New Year's Eve, another forty-one, besides smaller numbers on other days. Worst of all, in the Luftwaffe's great sweep of the 1st of January, 237 pilots were killed, missing or taken prisoner, and another eighteen wounded, among them a number of experienced leaders. In its struggle with the Allied air forces, the Luftwaffe was being bled to death. While German industry might be able to supply new aircraft, the men were irreplaceable.

THE STORCH (STORK)

Originally designed in 1935 to perform the roles of casualty evacuation, army cooperation and liaison, the Storch (Stork) was noted for its remarkable STOL (Short Take-Off and Landing) performance. Notable flights that made use of the Storch's ability to operate from very small, unprepared airstrips include the rescue of Mussolini from detention in a hotel in the Italian mountains, and a flight into the center of Berlin made in the last days of the war carrying General von Greim to a meeting with Hitler.

On display at Duxford, England, the Imperial War Museum's Storch was originally a French-built version, a Morane Saulnier MS.502 Criquet. It is finished in the colors of the Storch used by General Erich Hoepner, Commander of the Fourth Panzer Group, during the German invasion of Russia in 1941.

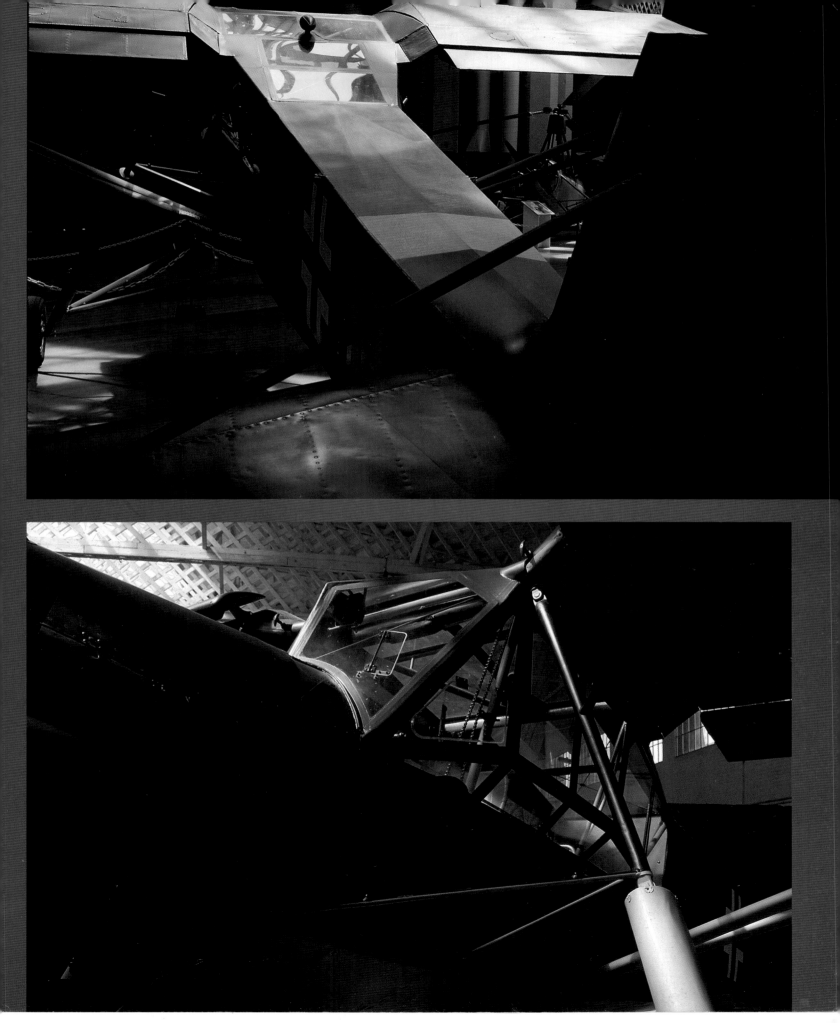

POLISH ALLIES

Photographed in Warsaw in January 2003, Jerzy Szymankiewicz (left) and Jan Janczak are combat aviators who flew with the RAF during the war. Janczak flew with Bomber Command in Wellingtons as well as Mosquitos. He was wounded during combat and crash-landed upon returning to his base. Removed from flying status, he was given a choice of becoming a staff officer in the RAF or joining the infantry: He said that, "It didn't take me very long to make the choice to remain in the RAF." Szymankiewicz, a fighter pilot, flew with the RAF's 317 Squadron (Wilenski) soon after Poland was defeated in 1939.

The Spitfire V on page 56 is painted in the markings of this squadron. Operating Hurricanes and later Spitfires, he flew in most of the major air battles. Wounded in 1945, he was recuperating when the war ended. He was returned to Poland on a Red Cross flight, only to discover that his wife had been murdered by the Nazis in a concentration camp because they knew he flew against them. He quietly told this story, and then smiled. "The Red Cross nurse who took care of me on the flight back has been my wife now for more than fifty years." He went on to continue his flying career and was a test pilot in the Polish Air Force. Jerzy Szymankiewicz died in 2003, a few months after this photo was made.

An offshoot of the USAAF's strategic offensive was a belated agreement with the Soviet government that USAAF aircraft would be allowed to use bases in the Soviet Union for "shuttle" bombing missions, known by the code-word Frantic. Aircraft operating from England and Italy would attack targets in Eastern Europe and fly on to refuel and rearm in the Soviet Union before striking at other targets on the way back. By May 1944, three bases were ready in the Ukraine, and the first of the Frantic missions was flown by the Fifteenth Air Force on June 2. The Eighth Air Force joined in on June 21, when 145 B-17s, escorted by seventy P-51s, bombed oil plants south of Berlin on their way to the Ukraine. The bombing was excellent, but disaster followed. Unseen by the B-17s, a Heinkel He 177 trailed them to Poltava airfield, and that night they were surprised on the ground by the Luftwaffe. Forty-four B-17s were destroyed and twenty-six damaged. Sporadic attempts to use the Frantic bases were made in the months following, but the missions were not very successful. Soviet enthusiasm for the idea was never great, and the results achieved did not match the cost. The last Frantic mission was flown on September 13, 1944, by which time the Soviet Army had advanced so far that the bases in the Ukraine were too distant from likely targets to be of much help.

The advance of the Allied armies in the west to the German frontier had brought all of Germany within reach of tactical as well as strategic aircraft by the beginning of 1945. In a bid to tear out the remaining sinews of the German nation and perhaps stun the enemy population with a massive display of air power before launching troops across the Rhine, Operation Clarion was devised. It was a plan calling for every available Allied aircraft to attack transportation targets — rail, road, canal and river — all over Germany on the same day. On February 22, the weather was favorable and the skies above Germany were filled with over 6,000 Allied aircraft, fighters hunting and strafing at low level, and bombers attacking targets from as low as 10,000 feet or less. The Luftwaffe reaction was feeble and those few enemy fighters that did get airborne were brushed aside. Allied losses were minimal and results so

> *"To use a fighter as a fighter-bomber when the strength of the fighter arm is inadequate to achieve air superiority is putting the cart before the horse."*
>
> LIEUTENANT GENERAL ADOLF GALLAND, LUFTWAFFE

promising that the operation was repeated next day. When the dust from Clarion had settled, it was apparent that the enemy's transport system had been badly hurt. Airmen believed, with some justification, that such severe disruptions of national lifelines, together with the aerial tourniquet they had clamped on the oil supply, had crippled the body of the Third Reich to such an extent that its final collapse must be imminent.

The change in the fortunes of the USAAF and the Luftwaffe in the space of one year had been dramatic. At the end of 1943, the Eighth Air Force gritted its teeth as it struggled to overcome the impact of heavy losses — 45 bombers lost from 262 sent to Stuttgart (17.2 percent); 60 out of 229 at Schweinfurt (26.2 percent); 29 out of 440 at Bremen (6.6 percent); 24 out of 281 at Solingen (8.5 percent); and so on…. In stark contrast, as 1944 drew to its close, the Eighth was nearing omnipotence in German skies. Operations involved huge numbers of bombers and escorts, and American airmen began to feel that they could go where they wished without fear of serious opposition from the Luftwaffe. Flak could still be intense, but loss rates among bomber crews were not as demoralizing as they had been just a year before. As the offensive gathered pace in 1945, the statistics told their own story — one bomber lost from a force of 1,094 sent to Kassel; five out of 1,310 at Chemnitz and Magdeburg; none of 1,219 at Nurnburg.

Even when losses climbed into double figures, as on February 3, when 25 were lost out of 1,370 bombing Berlin, the loss rate was so low that it seemed bearable. The 24 from 281 at Solingen had been nearly 9 percent, a figure that gave aircrews little hope of completing a combat tour unscathed. Twenty-five from 1,370 was well under one percent, and that bred confidence in the prospect of survival, particularly since in 1945 it was a rate that was uncharacteristically high.

As Luftwaffe fighter pilots saw the tide of war turned irrevocably against them, they were left wondering what might have been. Now that Allied aircraft filled the skies over Germany and the Luftwaffe had neither the trained pilots nor the fuel with which to oppose them, German industry was offering aircraft production rates and new aircraft types which, had they been available in the winter of 1943–44, could have tipped the balance of the air war in Germany's favor. Pounded though it was, the German aircraft industry, operating under the dispersal policies of Albert Speer, produced over 40,000 combat aircraft in 1944, almost five times the number made in 1939. (U.S. aircraft production figures rose from 2,100 in 1939 to 96,300 in 1944. It is worth noting that the latter figure, startling enough in itself, includes such large, complex aircraft as the B-29, whereas German industry was driven to produce more and more single-seat fighters.) However, after an encouraging but brief period when the front-line squadrons benefited from the glut by reequipping and being brought up to strength, the relentless attrition of combat took its toll and pilot strengths began to fall. By 1945, fighters sat in rows waiting to be delivered, but their tanks were empty and they outnumbered the pilots produced by the Luftwaffe's flying training program. In many cases, Luftwaffe engineers found that it was no longer worth their while to repair aircraft with even minor battle damage. It was easier to push a damaged fighter to one side and pull out a new one.

The Coming of the Jets

While Speer's production miracles had little apparent effect on Allied airmen, Germany's visionary aircraft designers did manage to take them by surprise. Turbojet engines had been under development in Britain and Germany since the 1930s, but the production of operational jet aircraft had been slowed in both countries by a combination of technical problems and official skepticism. The first jet aircraft to fly was German, the Heinkel He 178 on August 27, 1939, after which progress was anything but swift, and it was the summer of 1944 before the first jets became operational. The Germans introduced the remarkable Messerschmitt Me 262 to the Luftwaffe's front line in July 1944, initially as a high-speed bomber. The RAF's No. 616 Squadron started chasing V-1 flying bombs with its Gloster Meteor jets in the same month. (The Messerschmitt Me 163 was equally remarkable, but flawed in concept. Powered by a rocket engine, it was very fast but its fuel supply was so limited that it could run at full power for only four minutes, after which it became a very ineffi-

cient glider. This limited it to an operational radius of no more than 25 miles and rendered it helpless during its recovery to base.)

Boasting swept wings and two axial-flow jet engines, the Me 262 Schwalbe (Swallow) could reach 540 mph and climb to 30,000 feet in seven minutes. This marked superiority in performance over any Allied aircraft was impressive, as was the Me 262's heavy armament of four closely grouped 30 mm cannon, which could destroy a heavy bomber in one short burst. At a time when the air war seemed all but over, Allied airmen, particularly those in the B-17s and B-24s, might have been faced with a very serious threat. As it was, because of problems with the Junkers Ju Jumo engines and Hitler's initial insistence that it should be brought into service as a fast bomber for use against the Allied invasion force, the first unit of Me 262 interceptors was not declared operational until October 1944. Even then, they were seen by American aircrew only rarely. Me 262s managed to fly more than fifty sorties in one day just once, on April 7, 1945, when the Eighth Air Force alone flew 1,261 bombers and 830 fighters over Germany.

A host of problems combined to ensure that the Me 262 would never play a major role in the air war. There were the teething troubles only to be expected with so revolutionary a design. For example, the running life of the Junkers Jumo engines never exceeded twenty-five hours, and the poor quality tires were inclined to burst under the impact of 120-mph landings. Flying training, particularly at the reduced levels of 1944–45, was soon recognized as being inadequate to prepare a pilot to cope with the Me 262, and it took longer than expected for units to become operational. Then there were the incessant attentions of the Allied air forces. Me 262s and their spares were often stranded in the ruins of the German transport system, and jet airfields became prime targets for the bombers and fighters of both the Eighth and Ninth Air Forces. (It is interesting to speculate on the possibilities if the Me 262 had reached the Luftwaffe just one year earlier, before the appearance of the P-51 as an escort fighter. It is conceivable that the Eighth Air Force would have had to halt its strategic campaign, and that Allied air superiority would then not have been won as it was. In that event, an invasion in 1944 might not have been possible and the war could have dragged on for at least another year, with who knows what long-term consequences for Europe.)

The world's first jet reconnaissance/bomber, the Arado Ar.234 Blitz, first flew in June 1943 and was operational by September 1944. Unconventional in concept and design, the Ar.234 had no defensive armament but could outrun Allied fighters with ease. The single-seat cockpit, placed in the tip of the nose and almost completely glazed, gave the pilot an excellent view to the front, but no view to the rear except through a periscope. The periscope also served as a sight for dive-bombing attacks. The Ar.234 was one of the first aircraft to have a drag chute as standard equipment and some were equipped with an ejection seat.

Knowing that the jets were at their most vulnerable during takeoff and landing, American fighter pilots took to patrolling over their airfields. Lieutenant Urban Drew of the 361st Fighter Group showed the way in his P-51 as early as October 7, 1944, when he caught two Me 262s just after they had taken off and shot them both down before they could accelerate away. Once up to speed, the Me 262 was a more difficult proposition, and an experienced pilot could bank on being allowed to choose or refuse combat as he wished because of his jet's superior performance. Despite that advantage, even the best of them got caught by the persistent and ever-present Mustangs. The redoubtable Walter Nowotny, a Luftwaffe ace with 258 aerial victories, was killed on November 8, 1944, after attacking a B-17 formation and tangling with its P-51 escort. On April 26, 1945, the celebrated fighter leader Adolf Galland was caught napping by a P-51 and forced to put his badly damaged Me 262 down on an airfield that was under heavy attack by P-47s. This was Galland's last operational sortie, and it offered trenchant commentary on the Luftwaffe's problems in the closing days of the war. Even Galland, one of the world's most experienced fighter pilots, flying the most advanced fighter aircraft in existence, could not escape the USAAF's relentless pursuit, either in the air or on the ground.

Mission Accomplished

During the final weeks of the air war in Europe, Germany was hit by a series of hammer blows from massive formations of Allied aircraft. Berlin, Hamburg and Dresden were among cities crushed under immense bomb tonnages intended to complete the dislocation of Germany and its

Bomb doors open, B-17s of the 390th Bomb Group based at Framlingham approach the target.

it involved a jet. Thompson caught an unsuspecting Arado Ar.234 jet bomber near Salzburg and sent it down in flames. These skirmishes concluded, the European air war was over.

From the first, the Allied air forces had taken the war to the enemy. Until 1945, combat aircraft were the only offensive instruments available to the Allies that could strike directly at Germany. Although initially the effects were not great and the costs were sometimes grievous, the air offensive steadily

war machine. On April 16, 1945, General Spaatz sent a message to the Eighth and Fifteenth Air Forces that began: "The advances of our ground forces have brought to a close the strategic air war waged by the United States Strategic Air Forces and the Royal Air Force Bomber Command." In fact, it was not quite over. Strategic missions continued until April 25, when RAF Lancasters bombed Hitler's redoubt at Berchtesgaden, and Eighth Air Force heavies attacked targets in Czechoslovakia and southeast Germany. The last bombs of the 696,450 tons dropped in anger by the "Mighty Eighth" fell from the bomb bays of the 384th Bomb Group. That done, the battle-worn bombers of the USAAF joined with those of RAF's Bomber Command in assuming the quieter occupations of leaflet dropping and delivering food supplies to the starving people of the Netherlands.

Since the ground forces were necessarily in action until all fighting stopped, the tactical air forces retained their combat responsibilities into the last day of the war, and at least some units of the Luftwaffe were ready to oppose them to the end. As late as April 26, Adolf Galland led his Me 262s in an attack on a First TAF formation in which four B-26s were shot down. The last Eighth Air Force fighter pilot victory was claimed the day before by Lieutenant Hilton Thompson in a P-51 of the 479th Fighter Group, and again

gained the initiative and forced the Germans to react by diverting more and more resources to the defense of the Reich. Manpower, aircraft, guns and scientific effort that could have made a difference to the front lines were devoted increasingly to countering the Allied bombers. At the same time, the German people were constantly reminded that they were in a war of their own making, and that their opponents were not about to give up. After the war, Albert Speer (Hitler's Minister of Armaments) noted that, even though there were ways in which the air offensive could have been more effectively conducted, it was Allied air power that had been the principal reason for Germany's defeat. He pointed out that the bomber offensive "opened a second front long before the (Allied) invasion" and drew attention to the enormous efforts made in defending against the bombers, "thousands of guns…tremendous quantities of ammunition…hundreds of thousands of soldiers." There were also squadrons of fighters, and the whole defensive structure was supported by significant elements of German industry and the transportation system. Most of these resources could have been applied elsewhere in the absence of a bomber offensive. By 1945, it was apparent how very significant the effects of the bombing had been. Whatever its shortcomings in its early stages, by the end, the campaign had effectively made it impossible to move goods and supplies within Germany; oil production had all but ceased, and German industry, for all its resilience, was grinding to a halt. The bomber crews paid a terrible price for their achievement, but without their determined courage, the war could have been an even longer and bloodier conflict.

Equally important was the Luftwaffe's defeat, a victory to which the long-range fighters of the Eighth Air Force made a huge contribution. Their efforts over Germany helped to break the Luftwaffe's back and led directly to the achievement of Allied air supremacy. That achievement made the invasion of Normandy possible. Subsequently, it gave the Allied tactical air forces the freedom of action necessary to ensure that the ground forces remained untroubled by the Luftwaffe and had all the support they needed as they drove forward to occupy what was left of Hitler's "Thousand Year Reich."

If further confirmation were needed of air power's decisive role in Germany's defeat, it came from the military men who had been on the receiving end. Agreeing with Albert Speer's views, Field Marshal von Runstedt, C-in-C West until March 1945, listed air power first of the factors that led to the Allied victory. Field Marshal Albert Kesselring, C-in-C Italy and then C-in-C West after March 1945, gave it as his considered opinion that "it was your air force that decided the conflict." General

"The demands on the courage and endurance of the fighting forces were stepped up to the point of ruthlessness.... At the very point when a realistic assessment of military prospects would have readily revealed the inevitability of defeat, calculation and foresight were cast to the winds in favour of that pathetic unknown quantity, sacrifice and heroism, which has played so disastrous a role in German military history."

JOHANNES STEINHOFF,
COMMENTING ON THE CLOSING MONTHS
OF WWII IN *THE STRAITS OF MESSINA*

Alfred Jodl, Oberkommando der Wehrmacht (OKW) Chief of Staff, believed that it was air supremacy that decided the war. Field Marshal Wilhelm Keitel gave the principal credit for the victory in the west to the Allied air forces, and General von Vietinghoff commented similarly about the campaign in Italy.

Even before the final aerial dramas were played out, preparations had been made to conduct an exhaustive evaluation of the air war in Europe by creating an impartial body known as the United States Strategic Bombing Survey. By April 1945, teams of trained investigators were following close behind the Allied armies to begin collecting documents and interviewing prisoners with the aim of assessing the contribution made by air power to the defeat of Nazi Germany. The findings of the USSBS report were detailed and comprehensive. They brought out many of air power's achievements, and they were also sometimes sharply critical of the way in which the air war had been conducted. In later years, some of these criticisms were used selectively by those seeking to denigrate air power's role in WWII, but it should be remembered that the final paragraph of the USSBS report begins by stating an emphatic conclusion: "Allied air power was decisive in the war in Western Europe. Hindsight inevitably suggests that it might have been employed differently or better in some respects. Nevertheless, it was decisive."

PART II

The Pacific, China, Burma and India

"I was in Hanoi the day America declared war with Japan. I heard about it on the radio. I thought war with such a resourceful nation, America, was impossible. I thought I won't be able to go back to Japan alive."
OFFICER AND PILOT SUZUKI, 21ST HIKOTAI, JAPANESE ARMY

General H. H. "Hap" Arnold was Chief of Staff of the United States Army Air Forces during World War II. When the globe from his Pentagon office is turned to show the Pacific theater of operations, the vast scale of the war against Japan is apparent.

CHAPTER 7

Imperial Japan

AS EARLY AS 1924, Billy Mitchell offered his opinion that war between the United States and Japan was almost inevitable. He cannot have been too surprised that his forthright views did little to concentrate American minds on the intentions of a potential enemy. In the 1920s, the horrors of the world conflict just ended rendered the idea of global war nearly unthinkable, and the broad reaches of the Pacific lent an air of unreality to any prospect of a military confrontation between such widely separated nations. The mood of the time was dismissive of defense issues, and Mitchell's somber prediction that the Japanese would strike first at Pearl Harbor was soon forgotten. The awful precision of his prophecy was revealed on December 7, 1941, seventeen years after his visionary warning, when the blow fell just as he said it would, "on a fine, quiet Sunday morning."

The Blow Falls in the Pacific

Launched from six aircraft carriers some 200 miles north of Oahu, Japanese airmen attacked Pearl Harbor in two waves totaling more than 350 aircraft. Surprise was complete. In the years since the attack, the repercussions of the shock felt by the American people at the news from Pearl Harbor have never ceased to reverberate. How could the United States have been caught so completely off guard? How was it possible that U.S. forces could have been so thoroughly crushed while the attackers escaped almost unscathed? The answers to these questions are complex, but in essence, they reflect the general lack of U.S. readiness to fight a Pacific war, and local convictions in Hawaii that Pearl Harbor was sufficiently remote from Japan to be unlikely as a priority target.

As the principal victim of the well-executed Japanese strike, the U.S. Navy suffered heavily. Most notably, all eight of the U.S. Pacific fleet's battleships were either sunk or badly damaged. It was a stroke of good fortune for the American cause that their aircraft carriers were at sea when the attack took place. Equally damaging attacks were made on Oahu's shore installations, including the airfields. Here the Japanese airmen were presented with ideal targets. Reacting to a message from Washington on November 27 warning of deteriorating relations between the United States and Japan, General Short, the U.S. Army's commander in Hawaii, had judged the most serious threat to be from saboteurs. He had therefore moved all Army aircraft out of protective revetments and massed them in the open or in hangars, where it was believed they could be better protected against sabotage. Many aircraft were also kept unarmed and empty of fuel. Standing in neat rows or huddled together under cover, they could hardly have been better

OPPOSITE PAGE
Pearl Harbor, *by Jim Dietz. Aichi D3A Val dive-bombers over the battleship USS Arizona at Pearl Harbor, December 7, 1941.*

On December 7, 1941, the Japanese devastated the U.S. fleet at Pearl Harbor and also left the USAAF base at Wheeler Field in ruins, with dense smoke pouring from many fires.

were flown against the raiders by USAAF pilots, who claimed ten enemy aircraft destroyed, four of them falling to the guns of Lieutenant George Welch's P-40. Altogether, the Japanese lost twenty-nine aircraft in combat, plus a few more in accidents during recovery to their carriers. Given the scale of their victory, it was a small price to pay. The Japanese exulted, and Americans felt anger and a desperate need to avenge the

prepared as targets for air attack if the Japanese had ordered the arrangements themselves.

By the time the raid was over, widespread damage had been done to Oahu's airfield buildings and support facilities by bombing and strafing attacks, and only eighty-three of the 234 U.S. Army aircraft on strength were flyable. Added to the local survivors were some B-17s that had left California the night before on their way to the Philippines. Their tired crews arrived over Oahu in aircraft fitted for ferrying, with neither guns nor armor in place, to find themselves in the midst of a major battle. Short of fuel and being shot at by both enemy airmen and some now thoroughly aroused "friendly" antiaircraft gunners, the twelve B-17s scattered and landed where they could, one ending up on a golf course. One B-17 was destroyed and another three badly damaged.

The American defensive reaction had been at times courageous, but pitifully ineffective and occasionally indiscriminate. Angry antiaircraft gunners fired at any planes they saw, damaging some that were American and shooting down the P-40 of Lieutenant John Dains. Only twenty-five sorties

humiliation of defeat. Emotions ran high, but beyond the agony and the ecstasy lay hidden ironies. In seeking to secure the eastern flank of their southerly expansion, the Japanese had managed to end American isolationism and so ensure their eventual defeat, and in attacking U.S. battleships they had demonstrated the effectiveness of air power against naval vessels while failing to destroy their enemy's aircraft carriers.

Debacle in the Philippines

Further to the west, a combination of human failings and the vagaries of the weather ensured that the United States would suffer another military disaster. News from Pearl Harbor reached General MacArthur in the Philippines shortly after 3 A.M. local time. Exactly what happened in the next few hours is not entirely clear because the recollections of the principal officers involved differ considerably. It does seem, however, as if MacArthur's capacity for decisive action temporarily deserted him, and that his chief of staff, General Sutherland, denied the air commander, General Brereton, direct access to the Commander-in-Chief. Brereton's request for permission to launch a B-17 strike against Japanese airfields on Formosa was passed through Sutherland, but was not immediately approved. A little after 7 A.M., Brereton was contacted by General "Hap" Arnold from Washington and warned not to let his aircraft get caught on the ground. This was followed by a report that unknown aircraft were approaching Manila, so Brereton scrambled thirty-six P-40s to intercept and ordered the B-17s at Clark Field into the air as a precaution. When it appeared that the alarm was false, the P-40s landed to refuel, but the B-17s remained airborne. Later in the morning, Sutherland called Brereton to authorize both a photographic reconnaissance of Formosa and a late-afternoon attack on the Japanese bases there once the photographs had been evaluated. Accordingly, the B-17s were recalled to be refueled and loaded with bombs.

If Brereton displayed some anxiety over the course of events, it is hardly surprising. He had been living in expectation of a Japanese attack on Clark Field since first light, and his instincts were correct. The Japanese had planned to strike Clark at dawn, but had been frustrated by thick fog covering their airfields on Formosa. They too had suffered agonies of apprehension as they waited for the fog to disperse, expecting the B-17s to arrive overhead at any moment. When the skies cleared, 108 bombers and 84 fighters took off and set course for the Philippines. One formation reached Clark Field soon after midday and the Japanese crews could hardly believe their eyes. The American aircraft were still on the ground, bunched together as they took on fuel and armaments. Mitsubishi G3M "Nells" and G4M "Bettys" bombed without opposition, and A6M Zero fighters dropped down to strafe almost at will, leaving Clark Field a smoking shambles. All the hangars were destroyed and most of the aircraft, including two squadrons of B-17s, were reduced to scrap. Similarly

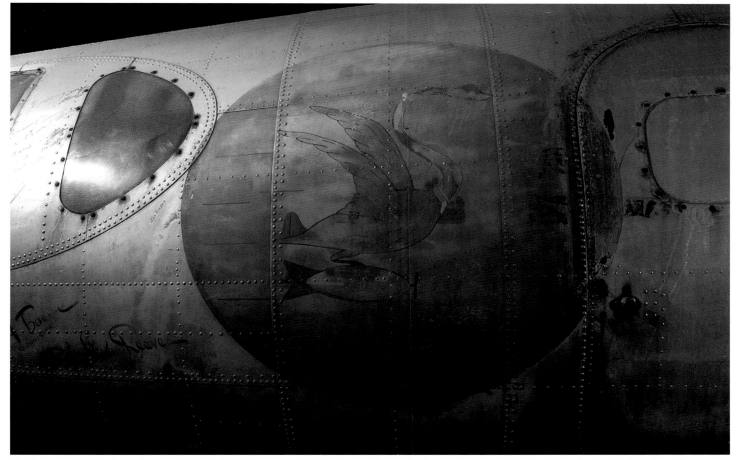

In the year 2000, the only surviving B-17D, known as "The Swoose," awaited restoration at the Smithsonian's Garber site. The original artwork still seen on the bomber's fuselage shows the "swoose" (half swan, half goose) carrying a bomb.

In Alis Vincimus, *by Gil Cohen. Colin Kelly's B-17C of the 19th Bomb Group under attack by Japanese bombers on Clark Field in the Philippines, December 10, 1941. (*In Alis Vincimus *is the motto of the 19th BG, "On Wings We Conquer.")*

catastrophic damage was done to other U.S. air bases on Luzon. At a stroke, U.S. air power in the Philippines, insufficient for its tasks at the outset, lost over half of its strength.

Sixteen B-17s were deployed at Del Monte on Mindanao out of reach of the Japanese, and on subsequent days they and a motley collection of other aircraft did their best to counter the invasion of the Philippines. Courageous though many of these efforts were, they proved to be little more than an annoyance to the enemy. The hard facts of America's lack of preparedness for war were now bitterly revealed — aircraft too few and mostly obsolete, communications facilities unsatisfactory, airfield defenses poor, and intelligence about the enemy inadequate. As a result, a hard lesson about air power was administered to the U.S. forces on the first day of the conflict: air superiority is fundamental to successful military operations. Within a week, it was clear that the Japanese already controlled the air over Luzon, and that their capture of several airfields made the extension of that control over the whole of the Philippines merely a matter of time.

Shocked by the defeats in Hawaii and the Philippines, and facing the prospect of more to come, the American people needed a hero, a symbol of U.S. defiance and fighting spirit. On December 10, a suitably heroic figure emerged. Captain Colin Kelly was pilot of a B-17C that bombed Japanese ships off the coast of Luzon. Early reports of the action claimed that his attack had sunk the battleship *Haruna*, but it subsequently emerged that the warship was most probably the cruiser *Ashigara*, which may have been damaged but not sunk. On the return flight, the B-17 was attacked by enemy fighters and set on fire. Ordering his crew to abandon the aircraft, Kelly remained at the controls to allow them to escape. He died when the B-17 exploded in the air before he could use his own parachute. His was the first B-17 to be shot down, and he was awarded a posthumous Distinguished Service Cross. (After the war, it was discovered that Kelly's B-17 was shot down by one of Japan's greatest aces, Saburo Sakai. In his book, *Samurai!*, Sakai tells of his surprise at the ruggedness of the B-17. After a succession of firing passes from ten Zeros, the bomber

seemed unharmed and full of fight. Sakai says that then, "I decided to try a close-in attack directly from the rear. Greatly to my advantage was the fact that the early B-17s lacked tail turrets.... Pieces of metal flew off in chunks from the bomber's right wing, and then a thin white film sprayed back.... The bomber's guns ceased firing; the plane seemed to be afire within the fuselage.") On December 13, there was something for Americans to cheer about when, during a reconnaissance sortie, Lieutenant "Buzz" Wagner's P-40 ran into a formation of obsolescent Nakajima Ki-27s. He shot down four of them and went on to strafe other Japanese aircraft on the airfield at Aparri. Three days later, he scored another aerial victory to become the USAAF's first ace.

These brave efforts apart, there was little for Americans to savor in the Pacific. The Japanese advance was irresistible, and by December 18, the last of the B-17s in the Philippines had been withdrawn to Darwin, Australia. General MacArthur talked stubbornly of the need for rein-

forcements, and spoke of having 200 fighters and twenty dive-bombers delivered to the Philippines by aircraft carrier. It was all too little, too late. Japanese forces pressed through the islands with great speed and made reinforcement impossible. MacArthur withdrew his troops into the Bataan peninsula and made his headquarters on the island fortress of Corregidor. American resistance there was stubborn, but final surrender came at last in May 1942. The experience of defeat convinced the U.S. ground forces commander, General Jonathan Wainwright, of "the futility of trying to fight a war without an air force."

The Capable Enemy

The Japanese air forces were a revelation to their opponents. Their aircrew were well trained, their tactics sound and their aircraft formidable. The Zero fighter in particular showed that it could outfly anything the Allied air forces had. First blooded over China in 1940, the Mitsubishi A6M, Type O, known as the Zero, should not have come as a sur-

prise to the Allies, but early reports of its performance were treated with skepticism and generally disbelieved. Powered by a 950-horsepower radial engine, the Zero had a maximum speed of 330 mph, which was slower than some of its competitors, but it had an excellent rate of climb and was incredibly maneuverable. Saburo Sakai, the Japanese ace who scored sixty-four victories in Zeros, described it as being "a dream to fly. The airplane was the most sensitive I had ever flown, and even slight finger pressure brought instant response." Its range, too, was extraordinary (with a drop tank, nearly 2,000 miles) allowing Zeros to appear in areas thought to be unreachable by Japanese fighters.

Such outstanding performance came at a price, however. It was largely achieved by keeping the weight of the Zero as low as possible, not much more than 5,000 pounds fully loaded. Japanese fighter pilots were specific in demanding that their aircraft not be encumbered with what they regarded as excessive weight. Above all, they wanted a light, agile aircraft, comparing their fighters with "master

CURTISS P-40

The Curtiss P-40 was used to great effect against the Japanese in China by the American Volunteer Group (AVG), better known as the Flying Tigers.

ABOVE This example, finished in Flying Tiger markings, is displayed at the National Museum of Naval Aviation, Pensacola, Florida. It is a P-40B, one of only two in existence, and nearly identical to those used by the AVG. It was recovered in Russia.

RIGHT The USAF Museum's P-40E was originally a Kittyhawk produced for the RAF. It is now finished in the markings of the Flying Tigers. In the cockpit, most things were controlled electrically, including landing gear, flaps, propeller, and trim. The newfangled gunsight was apparently not so trusted that the external ring and bead could be removed.

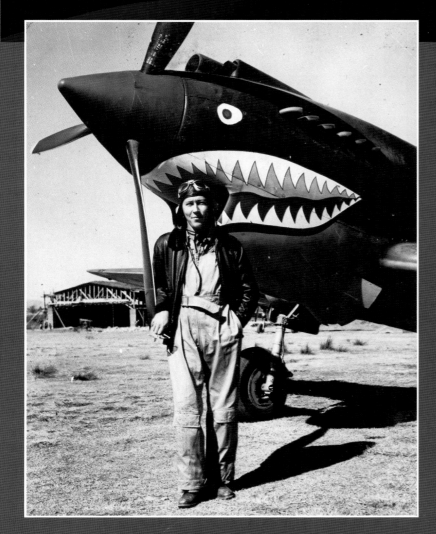

The celebrated tiger shark's teeth painted on Flying Tiger P-40s were an instantly recognizable feature. Standing with his head in the tiger's mouth is Duke Hedman of the AVG's 3rd Squadron — the "Hell's Angels." Hedman left China not quite an ace. The complex rules of air combat scoring awarded him 4.83 aerial victories.

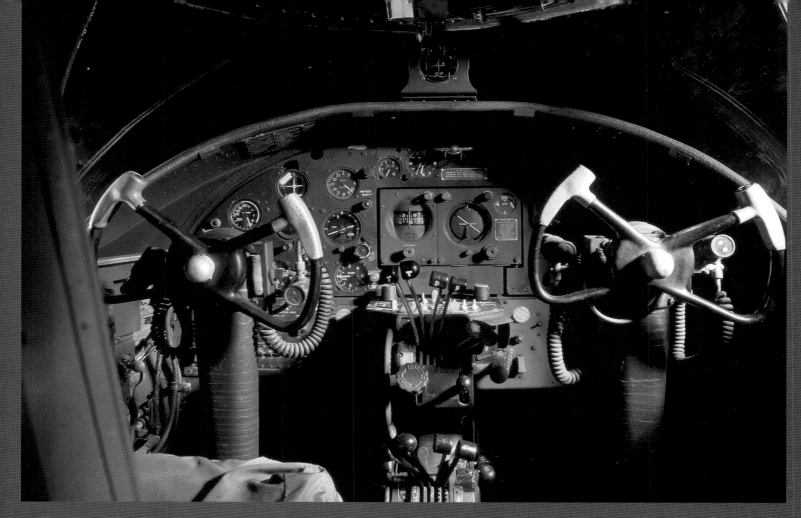

B-25 MITCHELL

The North American B-25 Mitchell was one of WWII's most versatile bombers and was flown by several Allied air forces. The USAF Museum's example is marked as the aircraft used by Jimmy Doolittle on the Tokyo raid of April 1942. The cockpit is functional and uncluttered, with flight instruments duplicated for the benefit of the copilot. The museum's Doolittle collection includes a small piece of a crashed B-25, a simple bombsight, a flight jacket (Tom Griffin, navigator B-25 No. 9), part of a parachute used to make a sleeping bag, raincoat and bandages (Ross Greening, pilot B-25 No. 11), and the camera that took the only photographs of the mission (Richard Knobloch, copilot B-25 No. 13).

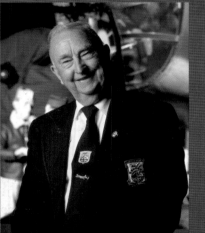 

DOOLITTLE RAIDERS

Most of the surviving Doolittle Raiders gathered at the United States Air Force Museum for their annual reunion in April 1999. Jimmy Doolittle told these men that they would meet every year to celebrate their survival, and established a set of silver goblets and a bottle of 1896 brandy (the year he was born) in a special case. If one of his number is gone, the survivors toast their comrade and his goblet is turned upside down. The last two men alive will open the brandy and toast this unique and very select group of aviators who flew the legendary mission in 1942. They sat for portraits on April 16, 1999, two days before the 57th anniversary of their mission.

LEFT TO RIGHT:

TOP ROW: Colonel Henry A. Potter, No. 1 bomber; J. Royden Stork, No. 10 bomber; Rev. Jake de Shazer, No. 16 bomber; MIDDLE ROW: Lieutenant Colonel Frank Kappeler, No. 11 bomber; Lieutenant Colonel Horace E. Crouch, No. 10 bomber; Colonel Herb Macia, No. 14 bomber. BOTTOM ROW: Nolan Herndon, No. 8 bomber; Lieutenant Colonel Chase Neilsen, No. 6 bomber

In the cockpit of a North American B-25 on display at the U.S. Air Force Museum, restored to the configuration of the Doolittle Raid bombers, Tom Griffin (left) and Colonel Travis Hoover. Hoover flew the No. 2 bomber following Doolittle off the deck of the *Hornet.* Tom Griffin in No. 9 worked out many of the navigational hurdles before the mission and also devised ways of extending the range of the B-25.

LEFT B-25s on the deck of the *Hornet* before the Tokyo raid of April 1942.

LOWER LEFT Jimmy Doolittle's B-25 is first away from *Hornet,* over 600 miles from targets in Tokyo.

The Doolittle Raid

The second gleam of hope in the first half of 1942 came from what might best be described as a gesture of defiance. Wars are not won by being defensive, and Americans were impatient to hear that the United States had demonstrated some offensive spirit by striking back at Japan. President Roosevelt wanted the Japanese home islands attacked both to bolster American morale and to give the Japanese people a sharp reminder that they were not beyond the reach of the war. The operation decided on was fraught with risk. Sixteen modified B-25 Mitchell medium bombers, led by Lieutenant Colonel Jimmy Doolittle, were to be launched from the aircraft carrier *Hornet* to attack Tokyo. To some, with the U.S. task force already plowing through rough seas in the Pacific, such a daring concept stepped beyond the bounds of reason. It seemed that the enemy was also of that view. Listeners heard an English language news report from Radio Tokyo describe as "laughable" the idea that American bombers could attack Japan. "It is absolutely impossible," the announcer told her audience, "for enemy bombers to get within 500 miles of Tokyo."

On April 18, when 650 nautical miles east of Tokyo, the task force was seen by Japanese picket boats. The decision was made to launch Doolittle's aircraft immediately, some 200 miles further from their targets than had been intended. This meant that Doolittle's aircraft would have minimal fuel reserves for their planned recovery to Chinese airfields. All sixteen B-25s took off successfully. Doolittle, in the leading bomber, had no more than 467 feet of deck available. Thanks to the *Hornet* making 20 knots into a 30-knot wind, he later said that he was "off the deck with feet to spare." During the subsequent flight, the B-25 crews saw many Japanese ships and aircraft, and they were engaged by numerous antiaircraft guns, but all dropped their bombs at various points in Tokyo, Kobe and Nagoya. A providential tailwind then helped fifteen of the force to reach the Chinese coast, but from that point on things went less smoothly. Darkness was imminent, the weather was bad, fuel was low, and no radio contact of any kind could be made. All fifteen aircraft were lost when the crews were forced to either crash-land or bail out. Three men were killed and several injured in the process, and eight were captured by the Japanese. Three of the captured were later executed as war criminals, and another died in captivity. The sixteenth B-25 landed without damage near Vladivostok, where it was appropriated and its crew interned by the Soviets.

Depressed by the sight of his aircraft's wreckage the next day, Doolittle convinced himself that the raid had been a failure and that he would face a court martial for the loss of the B-25s when he returned to the United States. The reality was rather different. As the President had believed it would, the raid deeply shocked the Japanese and gave a tremendous boost to American morale

Marc Mitscher, captain of the Hornet, has just handed Jimmy Doolittle some Japanese medals (presented to U.S. Navy personnel during a 1908 goodwill visit) with the instruction from Secretary of the Navy Frank Knox that they be returned to Japan "with interest." They were attached to the fin of the nearby bomb.

at a difficult time. Jimmy Doolittle was rewarded for his efforts with a promotion to Brigadier General and the award of the Medal of Honor.

"Victory Disease"

With the benefit of hindsight, it can be seen that the raid appears to have been the first small link in a great chain of strategic disasters for Japan. The Imperial Japanese Navy had suffered a crushing loss of face. The sacred soil of Japan had been desecrated by enemies, and they had come from the sea. There was an immediate emotional reaction. The views of cautious members of the Japanese high command were brushed aside, and plans to strike back at the American enemy were brought rapidly to fruition. Operations that might better have been separated in time now came together in what was intended to be a massive four-pronged expansion around the extremities of Japan's huge empire. The four prongs pointed at Port Moresby in New Guinea, Guadalcanal in the Solomons, Midway Island and the Aleutians. A dispassionate assessment of the prospects for success in four such widely separated and challenging campaigns at once might have suggested that at least one of them should be delayed, but the Japanese were in no mood to be dispassionate. The Japanese Navy, in particular, needed to expunge its feeling of shame, and in any case, most Japanese at this stage of the war were infected with "victory disease." They had accomplished so much so easily that failure seemed only the remotest of possibilities.

The tremendous flurry of Japanese naval activity that followed the Doolittle raid was also a considerable boon for U.S. intelligence. Thousands of coded radio transmissions were intercepted that gave the analysts their chance to break into Japan's naval code. It became possible to read perhaps 5 percent of Japanese messages, and that was enough to discover that the Japanese were dispersing their superior forces in a way that would allow the U.S. to concentrate its then limited strength against the threats individually. Hope began to blossom in the minds of American commanders.

The Coral Sea

Port Moresby was identified as the target of a major Japanese thrust, and it was found that this was to be a seaborne invasion covered by strong naval forces, including three carriers. To meet the threat in such a remote area,

Nimitz believed that qualities of mobility and long reach were vital. He therefore decided that his battleships would be more of a hindrance than a help, and they were withdrawn to U.S. west-coast ports. This was a farsighted decision, all the more remarkable in that Nimitz had been brought up in a battleship navy and naval air power was still a largely untried instrument of the war at sea. Compounding his gamble, Nimitz went even further by committing all of his available carriers (*Lexington* and *Yorktown*, with *Hornet* and *Enterprise* to follow) to the Coral Sea, leaving Hawaii uncovered.

By contrast, the Japanese were guessing. They thought *Lexington* had been sunk by a submarine in January (*Saratoga* had been torpedoed but had survived), and they believed that the only other U.S. carriers in the Pacific had been involved in the Tokyo raid, and that they were probably back in Pearl Harbor. From his HQ at Truk in the Carolines, Admiral Inouye's last prediction for his task force as they set out for Port Moresby was "It is not likely that powerful enemy forces are in the area." At that moment, converging in the Coral Sea to form Task Force 17 under Admiral Jack Fletcher were the carriers *Lexington* and *Yorktown*, with escorting forces of nine cruisers and thirteen destroyers, including some from the Royal Australian Navy.

The Japanese troop transports had the help of battle groups, including the carriers *Shokaku*, *Zuikaku* and *Shoho*, with a total of ten cruisers and thirteen destroyers. The first hint the Japanese had that there was an American carrier in the area came when Fletcher's aircraft bombed Tulagi in the Solomons. The two large Japanese carriers (*Shokaku*, *Zuikaku*) raced down the eastern side of the Solomons in the belief that the offending U.S. ships would be making for bases in the New Hebrides. Operating in a belt of bad weather, the Japanese reconnaissance probes found nothing and the force came round to the south of Guadalcanal unaware that Task Force 17 was refueling only 80 miles south of them.

During the night of May 6–7, the distance between the opposing fleets opened to 200 miles as Admiral Fletcher set off to the west. He had a sighting report of ships heading south toward the Louisiade Archipelago and he intended to block their advance toward Port Moresby. Believing that the threat would come from that direction, Fletcher detached

his oiler (*Neosho*) and one destroyer (*Sims*) and left them in the rear — for safety. On the morning of May 7, both commanders launched search aircraft in the direction they thought their enemy to be, and both were rewarded by sighting reports. Neither, however, got what they bargained for. At 08:15, a U.S. aircraft claimed contact with "two carriers and four heavy cruisers." Since that was what Fletcher had been expecting to hear, he launched his strike immediately. A total of fifty-three Dauntlesses, twenty-two Devastators and eighteen Wildcats set off to the northwest. Only then did the scouting aircraft land to reveal that there had been an encryption error; the pilot's message should have read "two light cruisers and two destroyers." Fletcher had committed himself against the wrong force.

Although that particular pilot was probably not popular with his admiral, his sortie had another effect. He was spotted by the Japanese, and the admiral in charge of the troop transports rightly guessed that a strike might follow. He therefore reversed his ships until the outcome of the pending battle should be decided. The taking of that decision was to prove historically significant. It would be the first time that a Japanese advance was checked and never subsequently resumed.

With Admiral Fletcher understandably anxious about the turn of events, his opposite number, Admiral Hara, got a sighting report of "a carrier and a light cruiser." He, too, launched a full strike from both his carriers, only for them to discover that they had been aimed at an oiler and a destroyer — *Neosho* and *Sims*, "waiting safely in the rear." They flew on to sniff out the U.S. carriers, but found noth-

OPPOSITE TOP *Production of the Grumman F4F Wildcat was transferred to General Motors in 1942. GM then built the definitive version of the type, the FM-2. As the U.S. Navy's first monoplane fighter with retractable gear, the Wildcat built a reputation at the onset of the Pacific campaign as a rugged, highly maneuverable, hard-hitting little fighter. It continued to fight with distinction until 1945. FM-2 Wildcat JV579 seen here is flown by the Fighter Collection from the Imperial War Museum's airfield at Duxford, England.*
OPPOSITE BOTTOM *The layout of the Wildcat's cockpit is very simple, with only a few essential instruments to distract the pilot from keeping an eye on the world outside. The pilot sits high up and his view is excellent.*

ing. On their way back they vented their fury on the unfortunate American pair, sinking *Sims* in minutes and setting *Neosho* ablaze from end to end. *Neosho* floated for four more days until found by a passing U.S. destroyer. The engagement cost Admiral Hara six aircraft and a great deal of valuable time. He was as confused as ever about the size and whereabouts of his main enemy.

Meanwhile, north of the Louisiades, the Japanese light carrier *Shoho*, with the covering force for the transports, received an accurate sighting report on the two U.S. carriers and prepared to launch a strike. At this point, fate intervened. The U.S. strike was still 50 miles from the position given for their miscoded targets when, through a gap in the clouds, a pilot from the *Lexington* was lucky enough to glimpse what looked like ship wakes some 40 miles away to one side. The formations turned and stumbled on *Shoho*.

Given that this was their first action against a Japanese capital ship, the fire and enthusiasm displayed by the U.S. Navy squadrons was understandable, but it is a pity that almost the whole force directed its efforts against *Shoho* alone. The word "overkill" was never more appropriate. This was a rare (maybe the only) occasion when American bombers and torpedo aircraft successfully coordinated attacks. Both recorded not only hits but also explosions on their target. (For most of WWII, U.S. torpedoes were notoriously unreliable weapons). *Shoho* was comprehensively torn apart by thirteen bombs and as many as a dozen torpedoes. Some twenty minutes after the start of the attack, the battered remains of the carrier sank smoking and hissing out of sight. Just after midday, Lieutenant Commander Bob Dixon of the *Yorktown* put himself in the history books by transmitting a few well-chosen and now-celebrated words to his admiral: "Dixon to carrier — scratch one flat-top!"

The Japanese admirals reacted to these events with shame and alarm. They had lost a carrier and they still had no idea where the enemy was. It was clear that the U.S. ships had managed to get to the west of the Japanese carriers and American aircraft might be pounding the troop transports even now! Admiral Hara fretted impatiently while his strike aircraft straggled back from their extended foray against the U.S. support group, praying that he would get a contact report that would lift the fog of uncertainty. Several reports duly came in during the afternoon, and Hara jumped at the chance to redeem the day. Once again, however, he was misled. It seemed that the Americans were much further west than he had thought.

Various conflicting reports were interpreted by the Japanese as identifying two groups (one including carriers) 330 and 360 miles to the west. Since the "carrier group" had apparently come round on to a southeasterly heading and the distance was therefore shortening, Hara though that a strike might be able to reach them before dark. It was late and the weather was appalling, facing the Japanese pilots with a very difficult recovery problem, but that could not be helped. Twenty-seven aircraft manned by the most experienced crews were launched on a mission induced by desperation. Had they only known that the U.S. carriers were almost on their line of flight and only 150 miles away.

Beset by bad weather, the Japanese aircraft struggled to stay in contact with each other and were completely unprepared for combat when, an hour or so before they should have seen their targets, they ran into the defensive Combat Air Patrol (CAP) of fighters surrounding the U.S. carriers. Nine were shot down and the others scattered into the clouds, jettisoning their weapons as they turned away. Their confusion was complete, and some crews lost their bearings altogether; almost an hour later the U.S. carriers were buzzed by at least three Japanese aircraft looking for their home decks. The mission was the final disaster of the day for Hara. Twelve irreplaceable crews were gone. However, he now learned for the first time exactly where the Americans were. In that, he held a distinct advantage over his adversary. Fletcher still had no idea where to look for the Japanese.

As it happened, probing flights from each side sighted their enemy almost simultaneously the next morning. Opposing

The cockpit of the only known Vought SB2U-2 Vindicator in existence, on display at the National Museum of Naval Aviation at NAS Pensacola, Florida. This aircraft was ditched in Lake Michigan during training operations in WWII. The aircraft was found 130 feet down, then raised and restored in the 1990s. The SB2U was the first U.S. naval divebomber to be designed as a monoplane with retracting undercarriage and folding wings. Vindicators, though outdated, were heavily involved in the early Pacific battles, including the Battle of Midway.

The curtains of flak thrown up by the U.S. task force at the Battle of the Coral Sea were impressive. Even so, Japanese aircraft, flown with great determination, were able to press home their attacks on the U.S. carriers, sinking the Lexington *and damaging the* Yorktown.

strikes were launched, but this time the odds were different. Heavy cloud cover was still shielding the Japanese ships, but the U.S. task force was operating under a clear blue sky. Against *Shoho*, the American airmen had been able to concentrate well and had faced relatively light opposition. In conspicuous contrast to later experience, the torpedo bombers had been able to get in close to their targets and their torpedoes had worked. As they now approached the main Japanese force, the weather made it difficult for them to concentrate and the sky was thick with Zeros. Nearer the targets, the flak was fierce. The vulnerability of the slow, unwieldy torpedo-carrying Devastators was exposed; few of them got anywhere near the Japanese ships and those that did dropped torpedoes that missed or failed. A further problem was that the sights of the dive-bombers misted as they dropped rapidly from the cold of 17,000 feet into warm, moist air nearer the sea.

The attack did not go well, although many of the aircrews thought it did. The difficulty of sifting the truth from the very genuine claims made during a hectic battle was never more evident. For instance, one squadron claimed three hits on a carrier and four Zeros destroyed; another claimed five torpedo hits. It was subsequently shown that none of these was valid. Three bombs saved the day for the U.S. strike, and all of them hit *Shokaku*. The second of these was dropped by Lieutenant "Jo Jo" Powers, a Dauntless pilot from *Yorktown*. Hit early in his dive by 20 mm shells from a Zero, he held his blazing aircraft in the dive to well below 1,000 feet before releasing his bomb. It hit *Shokaku* near the bridge and smashed through two

decks, starting fires that ensured that she was out of the battle. Powers' aircraft hit the sea near his victim. He was awarded a posthumous Medal of Honor.

Back at the U.S. task force, the Japanese were making up for all the mistakes of the day before. They managed to catch the defensive screen of the American carriers in some disarray, with Wildcats on CAP low on fuel, and others still climbing out. They also coordinated their attacks well. *Yorktown*, being the smaller carrier, attracted rather less attention than *Lexington*, whose huge silhouette drew Japanese aircraft like a magnet. Nevertheless, *Yorktown*'s crew saw plenty of action. One blessing from the U.S. point of view was the small number of torpedo aircraft that attacked *Yorktown*. This was a direct result of the abortive Japanese strike of the previous evening. There were not enough torpedo crews left to mount a full strike against both American ships. *Yorktown* was also a more agile vessel than *Lexington*, and she was superbly handled by a very experienced skipper, who adroitly avoided the few torpedoes launched in his direction. He did almost as well against the dive-bombers, successfully weaving his way through falling bombs that covered *Yorktown* in torrents of water as they exploded alongside. One bomb did hit the ship, however. It went through the center of the flight deck,

CHAPTER 8

Turning Point Midway

ADMIRAL NAGUMO WAS NOT too disturbed by the loss of two major fighting units from the list of ships available for the Midway operation. He now believed that not only *Lexington*, but also *Saratoga* and probably *Yorktown* would be missing from the U.S. line of battle. In any case, the Japanese Navy firmly believed that their other carrier task forces, built around *Akagi, Kaga, Hiryu* and *Soryu*, were far superior to those that had just delivered such a stunning blow to the U.S. Navy in the Coral Sea. It is also true that the Japanese did not yet see any evidence to show them that Western forces could defeat them in battle. The Tokyo press referred to the United States sneeringly as "Britain's auxiliary" and taunted that it was Japan's fleet that now ruled the waves since the bulk of both the British and American navies was at the bottom of the ocean. The views of many Japanese military were captured by an admiral who said, "There is no fighting spirit in the American soldier." With this as background, it is perhaps understandable that the Japanese naval staff was not as disciplined in planning the Midway operation as it had been for the attack on Pearl Harbor. Simplicity became elaboration; the main aim was never clearly expressed (was it to capture Midway or to destroy U.S. carriers?); and the strength of the massive forces available was dissipated in pursuing secondary activities.

On the U.S. side, Nimitz sought diligently to make the most of the advantages he had. High among them was the ability of U.S. intelligence to read pieces of Japanese coded messages. He was aware that a major operation was in the offing, and he built up a surprisingly accurate picture of the forces that would be engaged. Then the identity of the target was revealed by an intelligence subterfuge. The Japanese messages constantly referred to their target by the code letters AF. Guessing that this might mean Midway, U.S. intelligence arranged for Midway to report in an uncoded message that their water distillation plant had broken down. Within hours, Japanese messages were decoded that advised the commanders of the various task forces concerned that AF had a water shortage.

With all the basic elements of the forthcoming operation known to him, Nimitz waited only for the messages that would indicate that the Japanese forces were moving. He knew that the Americans would be outnumbered, and his plan depended on getting his fleet close to the Japanese without them being aware of it, and on the U.S. admirals on the spot timing their first strike to catch the enemy by

OPPOSITE PAGE
Old adversaries, the Zero and the Wildcat, meet again at the National Museum of Naval Aviation, Pensacola, Florida.

In Bob Rasmussen's painting, two Dauntlesses of VB-2, USS Lexington, *search for Japanese carriers during the Battle of Midway, June 4, 1942.*

surprise, preferably with aircraft on deck. He had intended that the admirals concerned should be Fletcher and Halsey, but at the last minute Halsey was stricken with a debilitating skin ailment and had to be sent to hospital. His replacement was Admiral Raymond Spruance, a quiet man who was almost as little known in the U.S. Navy as he was in Japan.

Spruance would command Task Force 16, including the carriers *Enterprise* and *Hornet*, while Nimitz intended command of the whole force to pass to Admiral Fletcher on *Yorktown*, since he was determined that the damaged carrier should be patched up in time to join the battle. (Incredibly, *Yorktown* was repaired and made ready in just 48 hours after returning from the Coral Sea.) Both admirals were charged with observing the principle of "calculated risk" during their operations — in risking their ships, they should always be able to inflict greater damage on the enemy than they themselves could receive.

Toward the end of May, the Japanese headed east with a bewildering array of forces. The Midway Invasion Force came on in several groups under Admiral Kondo. The Carrier Strike Force, with four carriers, was under Admiral Nagumo. Following them was what was called the Main Body, with Admiral Yamamoto himself on the huge battleship *Yamato*. On top of this immense collection of nearly one hundred ships, another invasion force was aimed at the Aleutians, including two more carriers among some thirty-four surface ships. They were intended to confuse the Americans into splitting their Pacific forces, but in fact they detracted from the main Japanese thrust.

Against the immense Japanese armada, Nimitz had gathered together a relatively modest collection of ships — three carriers (*Yorktown, Enterprise, Hornet*), with eight cruisers and fifteen destroyers. Midway's own motley assortment of aircraft could be added to the equation. He also sent out a screening force for the Aleutians consisting of five cruisers and thirteen destroyers. Going straight to the heart of the matter, Nimitz asked his intelligence officer to estimate when and where U.S. forces would first sight the Japanese Carrier Strike Force. The answer given was that a U.S. patrol aircraft would sight the carriers at 0600 on June 4 on a bearing of 325 degrees at 175 miles from Midway. Events were to show that this was just 5 minutes, 5 degrees and 5 miles off!

The Japanese believed that the U.S. ships would not leave Pearl Harbor until Midway was attacked. This casual assumption that the Americans would not be ready was typical of the carelessness of the Japanese admirals before Midway. Nagumo, for example, issued a paper summarizing his "appreciation of the situation" before the battle. It included phrases such as "the enemy lacks the will to fight," "the enemy is not aware of our plans," and "it is not believed that the enemy has any powerful unit in the vicinity."

The first exchange of fire came on June 3 when B-17s and Catalinas from Midway attacked Admiral Kondo's transports. Only one hit was recorded and not much physical damage was done. Events served to convince Nagumo that, although the United States might now be aware that an operation of some sort was in motion, American attention would be drawn firmly in the wrong direction, leaving the advance of his carriers undetected. Secure within his forest of false assumptions, Nagumo closed to just over 200 miles from Midway early on the morning of June 4 and launched his first attack. Before 05:00, 108 aircraft were airborne and heading for Midway — thirty-six each of Zero fighters, Kate medium-level bombers and Val dive-bombers. He also sent of a fan of seven search aircraft to cover his flank to the east. Their coverage was less than comprehensive, and this half-hearted effort was a reflection of Nagumo's conviction that there was nothing there for them to find.

Shortly before 06:00, as predicted, Midway's patrolling Catalinas saw the enemy. Reports came in of large formations headed for the atoll and of "Two carriers and battleships bearing 320, distance 180, course 135, speed 25." Both at Midway and

In the vastness of the Pacific, the adaptable Consolidated Catalinas were used in many roles — as bombers, transports, minelayers and reconnaissance aircraft. However, Allied airmen remembered them most for their air-sea rescue work. Hundreds of downed flyers experienced the joy of being saved from capture or a watery grave by the appearance of a lumbering "Cat."

on Fletcher's ships, men were soon running for their aircraft. Midway had eighteen Buffalos and six Wildcats for its defense. They met the Japanese formations some 30 miles out and set about the bombers. The escorting Zeros joined in and the battle broke up into a series of dogfights that clearly demonstrated the superiority of the Zero over the American fighters of the time. For the loss of two bombers and a Zero, the Japanese destroyed thirteen Buffalos and two Wildcats, and damaged most of the others. By the time it was over, Midway had just two serviceable fighters left.

Midway had also launched an extraordinary variety of aircraft to strike at the Japanese carriers. Six of the new Grumman Avenger torpedo bombers, four B-26 Marauders carrying torpedoes, sixteen SBD Dauntlesses and eleven SB2U Vindicator dive-bombers, and fourteen B-17 bombers set out to penetrate the CAP of Zeros over the Japanese fleet. All pressed home their attacks with determination, but their efforts produced no hits, and the Zeros shot down five of the six Avengers, two Marauders, eight Dauntlesses and three Vindicators. Meanwhile, back at Midway, the Japanese bombed and strafed their targets with great success.

It might be thought that the Midway forces had done little to affect the outcome of the battle. They had been conspicuously outfought and they had suffered grievously

Turning Point, *by Bob Rasmussen. Douglas Dauntlesses of VB-6, USS* Enterprise, *start their attacks on a Japanese carrier during the Battle of Midway, June 4, 1942.*

in no position to interfere, Admiral Nagumo made the decision that, more than any other, was to cost him the battle.

Waiting on the decks of his carriers, Nagumo had a second wave of aircraft armed for ship attack with armor-piercing bombs and torpedoes. These were to guard against what he believed to be the remote possibility that U.S. ships would turn up. At 07:15, he ordered them below both to rearm them with high explosive bombs for another attack on Midway and to clear the decks for the returning strike. Now the Japanese carrier crews would have their hands full. They would be dealing with over 200 aircraft, moving some below to hangars, down-loading one set of heavy weapons and preparing another, then landing-on the returning strike and seeing that they, too, were full of fuel and rearmed. In the midst of all this bustle, at about 07:30, Nagumo got the message that began to spoil his day. One of his search aircraft reported "what appears to be ten enemy surface ships bearing 10 degrees distance 240 miles from Midway, course 150, speed over 20 knots." No carriers

in the process. However, such hopeless ventures often prove to have played their part in building eventual victory. The leader of the Japanese bombers had been surprised at the ferocity of the ground fire directed against his aircraft. He was not satisfied that the raid had done enough to reduce Midway's capacity for resistance, so he transmitted his belief that a second strike would be needed. If confirmation of this view were needed, it was delivered by the large number of Midway aircraft that attacked the Japanese carriers. Confronted by evidence that suggested that Midway was still full of fight, and still sure, in the absence of warnings from his search planes, that the U.S. Navy was

were mentioned but, in the name of prudence, Nagumo suspended his previous order. Rearming was stopped about halfway through.

At 08:30, the aircraft of the returning strike on Midway began circling the Japanese carriers, some damaged and asking for emergency landings, all needing fuel. At that moment, Nagumo got the news he least wanted to hear. The search aircraft now reported, "The enemy is accompanied by what appears to be a carrier." This revelation could not have come at a worse time for Nagumo. The right operational response was to launch a strike at the enemy ships immediately, but there were a number of other factors to be taken into account. Half of his available aircraft were not suitably armed for ship attack, none of his fighters had sufficient fuel to escort a strike, and launching now would condemn a large proportion of the incoming wave to ditching in the sea. Given the facts, Nagumo did not hesitate long. He ordered the decks cleared to accept landing aircraft and instructed all carriers to rearm with torpedoes and armor-piercing bombs. Even given the best efforts of their highly trained crews, this was not something that could be done quickly. The hangar parties hurled themselves at the problem, stacking the weapons they removed in piles on the hangar floors rather than wasting time moving them to the magazines. The estimate was that *Akagi* and *Kaga* should be ready to launch at 10:30, with *Hiryu* and *Soryu* following at 11:00.

Battle Is Joined

When the U.S. task force heard the first messages from the Catalinas just before 06:00 that morning, Fletcher used his head. He decided that *Yorktown* should be kept back in reserve, both because he wished to hold position to recover his patrol aircraft and in case there were more than the two Japanese carriers so far reported. He therefore let Spruance off the leash with the signal, "Proceed southwesterly and attack enemy carriers when definitely located." Based on the information he had, Spruance believed that he should launch as soon as possible if he wanted to catch the Japanese with their aircraft on deck. Accordingly, aircraft began to rise from the decks of *Hornet* and *Enterprise* soon after 07:00. It was a formidable array of 116 aircraft. From *Hornet* there were thirty-four dive-bombers, fifteen torpedo aircraft and ten fighters; *Enterprise* added thirty-three dive-bombers, fourteen torpedo aircraft and ten fighters.

Up to now (and indeed for the rest of the action), the American admirals had not put a foot wrong and they would deserve their ultimate success. However, some deep-rooted problems in U.S. military practice now threatened to negate their efforts. For one thing, Spruance launched his attack based on the information in the original messages

> *"Zero Fighters outnumbered our fighters, had greater speed, and vastly greater maneuverability. The Japanese planes were flown with skill and daring. Brewsters and Grummans were no match for the Zero Fighters."*
>
> SECOND LIEUTENANT HYDE PHILLIPS, USMCR, AFTER THE JAPANESE ATTACK ON MIDWAY ISLAND, JUNE 4, 1942

from the Catalinas. He had nothing else to go on, and he heard nothing more until his own aircraft returned, in spite of the fact that Midway aircraft of one sort or another (and a submarine) were in touch with the Japanese ships for several hours. No updated positions or heading changes were passed to the man who was best equipped to win the battle.

At 07:00, as Spruance's aircraft began to launch, it was thought that the Japanese ships should bear about 240 degrees at 155 miles. Although this was the best estimate available (and proved to be reasonably accurate), little attempt was made to ensure that the various squadrons would coordinate their attacks on the basis of these figures. In fact, there was no overall strike plan, no agreement on how the fighters should cover the bombers, and not even a common radio frequency. Each squadron was more or less left to its own devices, and, because of that lack of cooperation, the attack probably cost more American lives than it need have done, and came perilously close to being a disastrous failure.

If the weather had been clear, perhaps none of this would have mattered. The squadrons might have seen that they were on diverging headings and done something about it. As it was, most of them rapidly lost sight of the others, and pressed on, hoping to meet their colleagues again over their targets. The trouble was that the headings varied so much. The Dauntlesses from *Enterprise* set off on 231 degrees, to be followed by the Devastators on 240. The escorting Wildcats, climbing above their charges, lost track of them among the clouds and fastened on to some bombers from the Hornet leaving on 265 degrees — separated by 24 degrees from their most southerly *Enterprise* colleagues! Even among the *Hornet* group, all of whom initially headed off on 265, there was unspoken disagreement. An hour or so after leaving his carrier, the commander of Torpedo Squadron Eight said nothing but left the others and led his aircraft on to a more southwesterly heading, toward where he thought the enemy would be.

An hour and a half after the other U.S. carriers, it was *Yorktown's* turn. Fletcher decided that he should launch at

DOUGLAS SBD-2 DAUNTLESS DIVE-BOMBER

It was in the great carrier battles of the Coral Sea and Midway that the SBD became a legend. It severely damaged one carrier and helped sink another (*Shoho*) during the former and sank four carriers during the latter. The Midway success broke the back of Japanese naval carrier aviation and was the turning point of the Pacific campaign. SBDs in WWII shot down 138 enemy planes and sank 300,000 tons of shipping while losing fewer than 100 to enemy fire — the lowest loss rate of any aircraft of the entire war.

Dauntless Bu 2106, an SBD-2 and the world's only surviving veteran of the Battle of Midway, is preserved at the National Museum of Naval Aviation, Pensacola, Florida.

ABOVE Just seen extended below the wing root are the dive brakes that allowed the Dauntless to attack at very steep dive angles while holding back its speed. Defensive armament was a single rifle-caliber machine gun fired from the rear cockpit.

OPPOSITE The layout of the Dauntless cockpit was influenced by the positioning of the two forward-firing .50-caliber guns, the breeches of which can be seen in the cockpit either side of the main instrument panel. Engine instruments were driven down to just above the rudder pedals and were difficult to see. This is the SBD flown by the Lone Star Museum, Galveston, Texas.

BELOW A Dauntless flies over calm Pacific waters as the sun sets.

Final Hour of Akagi, *by Bob Rasmussen. The Dauntlesses of VB-6, USS* Enterprise, *striking the* Akagi *at the Battle of Midway.*

just when they were between recovering aircraft and launching a new fighter CAP. Several Wildcats nevertheless got in among the Vals during their approach and shot down eleven of them. Soon after midday, seven started dives on *Yorktown.* The first two were blown to pieces in the dive by antiaircraft fire, but one of the bombs broke free of the wreckage and scored a hit near the island. A second hit followed amidships, and a third on the forward elevator. *Yorktown* slowed to six knots and belched black smoke.

Back at *Hiryu,* they had managed to prepare ten torpedo planes and six fighters for a second strike. Yamaguchi now knew that he was facing three American carriers, and he instructed his crews to find and attack one that was undamaged. At 13:30, they set out to do just that. By 14:00, things were looking promising for *Yorktown.* Boilers were back on line, and the damaged carrier was moving forward at 19 knots. Half an hour later, the Val crews saw what they took to be an undamaged carrier and turned to the attack. *Yorktown's* crew, only too well aware that they were again the target, managed to launch eight Wildcats as the Vals closed in.

Admiral Yamaguchi, on board *Hiryu,* was now the standard bearer of Japanese naval power at Midway. *Hiryu* had been ready to launch a strike when the American thunderbolt had blasted the other three carriers. It was meager in terms of what had been planned, but Yamaguchi was determined to turn the tables if he could. He decided to send off his eighteen Val dive-bombers, now standing ready on the deck, immediately, and to follow them with his nine Kate torpedo aircraft once these had been brought up from the hangar. Six Zeros would escort the first wave. As luck would have it, *Hiryu's* dive-bombers caught up with the U.S. ships

In the fierce action that followed, five Vals, two Zeros and four Wildcats were shot down, but *Yorktown* was struck by two torpedoes. Even then, the old ship was not finished. She floated for another two days and was being inspected by a salvage crew when a Japanese submarine appeared to finish off both her and an escorting destroyer.

Hiryu was not long for this world either. It was perhaps grim justice that *Yorktown* crews were in at the destruction of their tormentor. Four of their bombs tore the heart out of *Hiryu* and left her burning furiously. With all four Japanese carriers now doomed, the Zeros of the CAP that had fought so hard to protect them were left with no option but to ditch in the ocean.

The last hours of *Hiryu* were marked by a macabre ceremony. As the carrier burned ever more fiercely forward of the bridge, Admiral Yamaguchi gathered his crew together on the aft end of the flight deck and made a speech. He accepted responsibility for the loss of *Soryu* and *Hiryu*, and told them that, although they must save themselves to fight again for the Emperor, he had decided to remain with the ship. The admiral's staff elected to stay with him, but he ordered them off. His chief of staff asked for a parting gift and was given the admiral's battle cap. The officers then joined in a toast of farewell, drunk in water passed over from the waiting destroyer. Banzais were shouted, and both the admiral's command flag and *Hiryu's* battle flag were lowered for the last time. Forty-five minutes after the order to abandon ship, all was finally ready and *Hiryu's* crew took leave of their admiral. In Japan, he became a national legend. The American reaction was more mundane. Yamaguchi had been a most proficient and aggressive offi-

cer, and the U.S. Navy was glad to hear no more from him.

Immediately after the battle, the initial Japanese reaction was of shocked disbelief, but this was followed by determination to seek a night surface action (in which the overwhelming firepower of their ships would be decisive) and to continue with the Midway invasion. Spruance correctly anticipated Japanese intentions and coolly withdrew eastward during the hours of darkness to hold them at arm's length and preserve his capacity to defend Midway. Once it became clear that they could not catch the American ships and that they would be exposed to air attack again when daylight came, the Japanese prudently reversed course. Even so, fate had not quite finished with the Japanese Navy. Two of their heavy cruisers (*Mogami* and *Mikuma*) had been detached to go off and bombard Midway. During the night, their retreat to the west was slowed when they collided after sighting an American submarine. Next day, U.S. dive-bombers caught up with them, sinking *Mikuma* and damaging *Mogami* so badly that she was out of the war for a year.

There was also some comic relief on this day. A force of B-17s dispatched from Midway to look for a cruiser group were returning from a fruitless search when they saw and bombed what they took to be an enemy ship. Some twenty 1,000-pound bombs were dropped, and the jubilant B-17 crews reported scoring "two hits on an enemy cruiser, which sank in fifteen seconds." Later that day, the airmen were somewhat shamefaced to get a signal from the USS *Grayling*, which asked indignantly why it should be necessary for a U.S. submarine to crash-dive to avoid being plastered by the Army Air Force.

The Japanese aircraft carrier Hiryu *maneuvers to avoid sticks of bombs dropped during a high-level attack by fifteen USAAF B-17 bombers operating from Midway, June 4, 1942.*

CHAPTER 9

Pacific Southwest

AFTER HIS ESCAPE FROM the rampaging Japanese in the Philippines, General Douglas MacArthur assumed command of the Southwest Pacific theater in April 1942 and set up his headquarters in Australia, initially at Melbourne and later at Brisbane. MacArthur's appearance on the scene complicated command responsibilities, and it was never possible to reach agreement on the appointment of a Supreme Allied Commander, as was the case in Europe. The Combined Chiefs of Staff having settled that the Pacific should be an American strategic responsibility, the U.S. Joint Chiefs reconciled the differing opinions of the Army and the Navy by deciding that there should be two principal lines of advance against the Japanese, and therefore two commanders. MacArthur would rule in the Southwest Pacific, and Admiral Chester Nimitz in the Pacific Ocean area. They would be responsible for developing a two-pronged assault, launched through New Guinea and the Solomons, with the initial goal of enveloping the Japanese main base at Rabaul on New Britain.

MacArthur's air commander was Lieutenant General George Brett, whose assets during the summer of 1942 were a motley and scattered collection of American and Australian aircraft, described as being "pitifully inadequate for their task." The few USAAF bomber squadrons on hand were equipped with A-24s and with early models of the B-25, B-26 and B-17. Most of the available fighters were P-40s and P-400s, the latter an inferior model of the P-39 developed for export. Despite the shortcomings, efforts were made to maintain an offensive posture, with the bombers flying unescorted over very long distances against the forward Japanese bases, often suffering significant losses in the process to both the enemy and the elements. For their part, U.S. fighters tackling Japanese raids found themselves consistently outclassed, the P-400s in particular being no match for the escorting Zeros.

Many of the U.S. airmen facing these discouraging operational realities were already war weary, having gone through painful campaigns in the Philippines and the Dutch East Indies, and they knew that their circumstances were not likely to change for the better very soon. The policy of "Europe first" would keep them at the end of the priority list for some time. Their aircraft, most of them recognizably inferior to their enemy's, were also poorly maintained, handicapped by a perpetual shortage of spare parts and trained mechanics. To make matters worse, the units were generally deployed in surroundings that were anything but comfortable. Set in remote areas of Australia, the bases were extremely primitive, with inadequate medical facilities and poor food. Understandably, commanders found it difficult to maintain a high level of morale.

OPPOSITE PAGE
Dawn Operations, *by Robert Taylor. Mitsubishi A6M Zeros fly over a Mitsubishi F1M2 floatplane at Bougainville.*

LEFT *The Bell P-39 Airacobra was unusual for the 1940s in being a single-seat fighter with a tricycle undercarriage. This was possible because the Allison V-1710 engine was mounted behind the pilot. A long driveshaft ran through the cockpit to the propeller. The P-39 was not a good performer at altitude, but was ideal for low-level operations because of its powerful armament — two .50-caliber machine guns on top of the cowling and a 37 mm cannon firing through the propeller boss. It was popular with Soviet pilots for this reason.* BELOW *Another peculiarity of the P-39 was its carlike door entry to the cockpit. The USAF Museum's P-39Q is restored as a P-39J flown by Lieutenant Leslie Spoonts of the 57th Fighter Squadron in the Aleutians.*

New Guinea

Things were not improved when, in July 1942, the Japanese, who were already established elsewhere in New Guinea, beat the Allies to the punch and landed at Buna, on the north coast of Papua and only 100 miles from Port Moresby. From there they launched an overland offensive through the Owen Stanley Range, fighting their way forward in a bloody and relentless campaign until, in late August, overcome as much by the terrain, the jungle and disease as by the desperate opposition of the Allies, the Japanese soldiers reached the end of their tether and began to fall back.

> *"Air power is like poker. A second-best hand is like none at all — it will cost you dough and win you nothing."*
>
> GEORGE KENNEY

At about the same time, Major General George Kenney, one of the most gifted combat commanders of WWII, arrived to take over the Allied Air Forces in the Southwest Pacific Area. He was a man with some claim to being an air power visionary, a leader who encouraged his subordinates to use their imagination and initiative. Under his leadership, Allied air power in the Southwest Pacific was markedly strengthened. It is true that as the U.S. industrial machine gathered pace, more and newer aircraft became available, but that was not the whole story. Kenney's energetic influence pervaded his command, inspiring enthusiasm and determination where none had been before.

Kenney first tackled the maintenance muddle, talking to men on the line to find out what the real problems were first hand. Always prepared to be unconventional if that would get the job done, he quickly improved matters and raised the number of aircraft available to the squadrons. He insisted, too, that maintenance facilities be kept as close to the front line as possible. Jettisonable fuel tanks were found to extend the range of his fighters, and he fostered the development of aggressive low-level attack techniques, including skip-bombing. Kenney was particularly keen on his attack aircraft being able to hit their targets very hard, and he gave one of his protégés, the appropriately named Major Paul "Pappy" Gunn, a free hand to experiment with fitting heavier armament to the A-20 and the B-25. Gunn's modifications turned moderately effective attack aircraft into truly deadly weapons. To make them even better, Kenney himself suggested the use of parachutes on fragmentation bombs so that they could be dropped during low-level attacks without endangering the bomber. Before long, Kenney had molded his air force into a fearsome instrument of war. As if these operational achievements were not sufficient, he was also man enough to stand up to the imperial MacArthur and win his confidence.

In September 1942, the American air force units in the Southwest Pacific were organized as the Fifth Air Force, with Kenney assuming command at his headquarters in Brisbane. A small forward headquarters, tasked with the day-to-day conduct of operations during the New Guinea campaign, was set up at Port Moresby under Kenney's deputy, Brigadier General Ennis Whitehead. Soon after the Fifth Air Force was established, Kenney wrote to General "Hap" Arnold, setting out some of his views on air power and the way it needed to be applied in the special circumstances of the Southwest Pacific. Extracts from his letter give emphasis to the need for close cooperation with ground forces, and include some of the forceful imagery illustrative of his colorful personality:

> Tanks and heavy artillery can be reserved for the battlefields of Europe and Africa. They have no place in jungle warfare. The artillery in this theater flies…
>
> The Air Force is the spearhead of the Allied attack in the Southwest Pacific. Its function is to clear the air, wreck the enemy's land installations, destroy his supply system, and give close support to troops advancing on the ground….
>
> Clearing the air means more than air superiority. It means air control so supreme that the birds have to wear our Air Force insignia. Wrecking the enemy's ground installations does not mean just softening them up. It means taking out everything he has — aerodromes, guns, bunkers, troops. Destroying his supply system means cutting him off the vine so completely and firmly that he not only cannot undertake offensive action but, due to his inability to replenish his means to wage war, he cannot even maintain a successful defense.

A B-25H head-on was a fearsome sight. Inspired by the ideas of the Fifth Air Force's Major "Pappy" Gunn, many Pacific B-25s were modified as heavily armed strafers. This B-25H carries eight .50-caliber machine guns and a 75 mm cannon. Fuselage skin had to be strengthened so that the aircraft could withstand the destructive effects of its own firepower.

Kenney's actions were as good as his words during the New Guinea campaign. Allied infantry slogging up the Kokoda Trail through the Owen Stanley Range were supported whenever possible by low-flying aircraft, the unloved P-39 Airacobras coming into their own as strafers with their 37 mm cannon. The rapid forward movement of troops by air, urged on MacArthur by Kenney, was immensely successful. C-47s shuttled back and forth, both between Australia and Port Moresby, and further forward into areas from which Allied soldiers could surprise the Japanese and threaten their communications and main bases. By the end of 1942, the Japanese had been driven back to the north coast of New Guinea and were desperately defending Buna. Allied ground forces were able to maintain their offensive because of the C-47 lifeline over the mountainous interior, and because the Fifth was growing steadily more effective as a fighting air force. B-24s were arriving to take the load as the region's principal heavy bomber; "Pappy" Gunn's modified A-20s and B-25s were in action; and P-38 Lightnings were replacing the tired P-39s and P-40s.

In Europe, the P-38 was not much admired, but it came into its own in the Pacific. Its twin engines were reassuring to pilots who had to operate over wastes of jungle and ocean, and, with external tanks, it had legs long enough to cope with the scale of the Pacific theater. It was no match for the Zero as a dogfighter, but it was much faster, and could both out-climb and out-dive its Japanese opponent. The P-38 also had an armored cockpit and self-sealing fuel tanks, and its heavy armament of a 20 mm cannon and four .5-inch machine guns made short work of the more lightly built Zero. When American pilots made the most of these advantages, the Zero was outclassed.

Organized Japanese resistance in and around Buna came to an end on January 22, 1943, by which time the Fifth Air Force had long since established air superiority over the Papua region of New Guinea. Among other things, this meant that the vital air transport operations into airstrips on the north coast were never seriously threatened by Japanese aircraft. This not only assured the ground forces of their supplies, but also gave the added comfort of rapid medical evacuation. Allied soldiers suffered over 10,000 casualties in the bloody struggle with their enemies, but, thanks in large part to the tireless efforts of the C-47 squadrons, only 7 percent of these died.

An entry in a Japanese soldier's diary, written in December 1942, graphically underlines the Fifth Air Force's Papuan success: "They fly above our position as if they owned the skies."

General MacArthur, who had been free with his criticism of the Air Force's capabilities at the time of Kenney's arrival, now gave just as freely of his praise in a statement of some architectural confusion: "To the American Fifth Air Force and the Royal Australian Air Force no commendation could be too great. Their outstanding efforts in combat, supply and transportation over both land and sea constituted the keystone upon which the arch of the campaign was erected."

Driven out of Buna, the Japanese strengthened their position further west on the north coast of New Guinea. With that intention, they began to move reinforcements from their main base at Rabaul to the Huon Gulf port of Lae. On December 30, 1942, a Lockheed F-4 Lightning reconnaissance aircraft discovered twenty-one warships and seventy

The Kawasaki Ki-48 Lily light bomber operated mainly in Burma, New Guinea and the Marshall Islands. Slow, capable of carrying less than a ton of bombs, and inadequately equipped with defensive armament, it was not an impressive performer. Toward the end of the war many were used for Kamikaze attacks. This one survived reasonably intact after being shot down.

merchant ships assembled at Rabaul. In a first attempt, the Japanese were successful in getting a small convoy through to Lae and landing some 4,000 troops, but they lost two troop transports and over fifty escorting fighters doing it. Ten Allied aircraft were lost. In his drive to "make the birds wear our Air Force insignia," this sort of exchange rate was welcomed by Kenney. He knew that more convoys would be coming to Lae and that, since enemy fighters had to escort the ships, combat between the air forces was inevitable. The Japanese were caught in a war of attrition Kenney was sure he could win.

At the end of February 1943, five thousand troops of the Japanese 51st Infantry Division set out for Lae from Rabaul in a convoy of seven merchant ships, eight destroyers and a special service vessel. On March 1, the convoy was seen by a B-24 and, over the next three days, the Fifth Air Force and the RAAF hit it in a series of attacks that became known as the Battle of the Bismarck Sea.

DOUGLAS
A-20 HAVOC

The Douglas A-20 Havoc was one of WWII's most effective attack aircraft.

ABOVE AND OPPOSITE The A-20G at the USAF Museum, Dayton, is marked as an aircraft of the 89th Bomb Squadron, 3rd Bomb Group, in the Southwest Pacific. It is armed with six .50-caliber machine guns in the nose, two more in a dorsal turret, and could carry up to 4,000 pounds of bombs.

RIGHT The A-20's single-pilot cockpit was entered through a hatch in the roof. The pilot sat ahead of the propellers, but the cockpit was reputedly still noisy. In British trials, the A-20 was reported to be "an excellent aeroplane, having high maximum speed, manoeuvrability, and excellent fields of view."

OPPOSITE INSET An A-20 of the Fifth Air Force undergoing major servicing at the Eagle Farm depot in Australia.

The Bristol Beaufighter T.F.X was an anti-shipping strike fighter, a late model variant of one of the most versatile and effective combat aircraft produced during WWII. The type was the first high-performance night fighter to be equipped with airborne interception radar, and the formidable gun armament fitted for that role had rockets and torpedoes added for anti-shipping strikes. There were 5,562 Beaufighters produced by the time the last one was delivered in September 1945, and fifty-two Royal Air Force squadrons flew the type. This one is on display at the RAF Museum, Hendon.

Early successes in the battle were claimed by B-17s and B-25s bombing from medium altitude, but most of the damage was done on March 3 by aircraft strafing and bombing from low level. The aircraft modified by "Pappy" Gunn to carry much heavier forward-firing armament came into their own and proved especially destructive. Gunfire from the B-25s, A-20s and Beaufighters swept the decks of the Japanese ships, and 500-pound bombs skipped across the sea to smash into their sides. The attacks, coordinated at first, soon developed into free-for-alls as aircraft separated and maneuvered to take on one ship after another. Aircraft crisscrossed through the convoy and competed for victims, flying at mast-head height and sometimes lower. One A-20 finished off a run by shortening a ship's radio mast with its right wing. Inevitably, attackers wound up aiming at the same target. Out of the corner of his eye, an Australian saw something flying alongside him as his Beaufighter steadied for a strafing run. It was a B-25's 500-pound bomb in mid-skip, heading in the same direction. (The 90th Squadron's aircraft had been modified to become B-25C1s, with forward-firing armament of eight .5-inch guns grouped in the nose, plus two more in the upper turret. Equally effective were the A-20s of the 89th Squadron, with four .5-inch guns in addition to their original armament of four .303-inch, and the RAAF's Beaufighters, which carried four 20 mm cannon in the nose and six .303-inch machine guns in the wings.)

As the low-level attackers approached the convoy, they were startled to find themselves passing through a shower of long-range fuel tanks. Above the smoke and flame of the surface battle, the P-38s of the 35th and 49th Fighter Groups had lightened their load before keeping the covering Zeros occupied. Their efforts were eminently successful. By the end of the battle, more than fifty enemy aircraft had been shot down, at a cost of three P-38s and one B-17, plus one B-25 destroyed in a landing accident. More significantly, twelve ships had been

The USAF Museum supported the restoration of a Beaufighter in the 1990s. When finished, the cockpit was immaculate and remarkably complete. The pilot entered the cockpit from the bottom with the seat collapsed (as in the picture), then stepped over the seat, sat down and pulled the back of the seat up to strap in. It required a certain athleticism.

sunk, including all of the troop transports. Over three thousand Japanese soldiers died, and the 51st Division was effectively destroyed.

General MacArthur later spoke of the Battle of the Bismarck Sea as "the decisive aerial engagement" in his theater of the war. Kenney's airmen had demonstrated their ability to obliterate a convoy with aircraft, and by so doing, created an aerial blockade of Japanese forces around the Huon Gulf. Never again did the Japanese attempt to run large ships into Lae, and the troops there were left to subsist on a meager resupply from those few submarines and

On outdoor static display at the National Museum of Naval Aviation, Pensacola, is a Consolidated PBY-5A Catalina. This is the amphibious version of the aircraft, fitted with a tricycle undercarriage that retracts into the hull. Apart from their normal duties of long-range scouting, convoy escort, bombing, and search and rescue, some PBY squadrons were equipped with magnetic anomaly detection gear to locate submerged submarines. Retro-bombs were also installed which, when fired backward at a velocity equal to the speed of the aircraft, dropped straight down on a target.

barges that managed to break through. In effect, the Japanese had to accept that their hold on the eastern half of New Guinea was broken, and that, in the face of growing U.S. air power, their tenure in the rest of the island would be of limited duration.

As he turned his attention to the next phase of the New Guinea campaign, Kenney believed he could count on having greatly increased air strength. The summer of 1943 saw several more groups join the Fifth Air Force.

Among the new aircraft were the 348th Fighter Group's P-47s and yet another Mitchell variant, the B-25G, equipped with a ship-busting 75 mm cannon. Good though these were, Kenney never stopped being impatient for more of everything. To emphasize his need for troop carrier replacements, he told "Hap" Arnold, "The figures show that between weather and Nips a man lives longer in a P-39 than he does in a C-47 flying the troop carrier supply runs in New Guinea." He added a reminder about the

Angular and ungainly though it could appear from some angles, the Catalina incorporated a host of arcs, sweeps, bends and semicircles. The hull, the fin, the pylon supporting the 104-foot wing, the engine cowlings and the gun blisters were all gracefully curved.

scale of the Southwest Pacific theater, pointing out that the P-47s were not much good without long-range tanks, since they had no more range than was needed "to defend London or to make a fighter sweep across a ditch no bigger than Chesapeake Bay."

Whatever the limitations of their equipment, Kenney's air force did wonders with it. MacArthur now understood that New Guinea's geography defied even rudimentary maneuvers on the ground, and that victory depended on gaining and holding air superiority. The campaign settled into a pattern of using air power to hammer and neutralize enemy forces before bypassing them with troops moved

forward by sea or air transport. The infantry then held the ground while airstrips were constructed, after which the process could begin again.

Gradually overcome by the endless attrition of combat, the Japanese air forces in New Guinea finally succumbed in March and April 1944, when the Fifth Air Force carried out heavy attacks on three air bases in the Hollandia area. The facilities on the bases were wrecked and, counting those destroyed both in the air and on the ground, the Japanese lost more than 450 aircraft. The loss ratio in aerial combat often favored the American pilots by ten to one or more, and it was clear that the caliber of the average Japanese pilot had noticeably declined. Even so, the Fifth Air Force had not escaped lightly. In the two years following September 1942, the Fifth lost 1,374 aircraft to all causes, and more than 4,100 airmen were listed as killed or missing.

By mid-1944, the Thirteenth Air Force in the Solomons found itself underemployed and was moved to join the Fifth Air Force as part of Kenney's command in the Southwest Pacific Area. Kenney became Commander, Far East Air Forces, with Whitehead moving up to take over Fifth Air Force. The Thirteenth's original commander,

Nathan Twining, had long since left for Europe, after surviving an uncomfortable six days in a life raft when his B-17 got lost and ran out of fuel. The new commander, Major General St. Clair Streett, set up his headquarters initially at Los Negros in the Admiralty Islands, northeast of New Guinea, seized as part of the Allied encirclement of Rabaul. The resistance of Japanese ground forces continued in New Guinea until September, by which time the Fifth and Thirteenth Air Forces were preparing for the next big step — MacArthur's return to the Philippines.

A scene from the National Museum of Naval Aviation at Pensacola. In the foreground is a Grumman J2F Duck, one of 544 delivered to the U.S. Navy. The J2Fs were used for anti-submarine operations and as utility aircraft aboard carriers in ship-to-shore links. In the background is a Grumman with entirely different characteristics — an F8F-2P Bearcat. Produced too late to play a part in the Pacific war, the Bearcat was the smallest airframe that could be wrapped around a 2,250-horsepower Pratt & Whitney R-2800-34W engine. The resulting performance was phenomenal. The standard Bearcat had an initial rate of climb of 4,800 feet per minute, and could reach 450 mph. The museum's F8F-2P is a photographic-reconnaissance version, one of only 60 built.

BELOW *A contrast in fins at Pensacola. The high-set tailplane in the foreground belongs to a PBY-5A Catalina. Beyond it is a single-finned variant of the Consolidated B-24 Liberator designated PBY4-2 and named* Privateer. *It was used to destroy enemy shipping and for long range reconnaissance to prevent the undetected approach of enemy forces.* RIGHT *Bulging from the Catalina's fuselage like frog's eyes, the gun blisters each carried a single .50-caliber machine gun.*

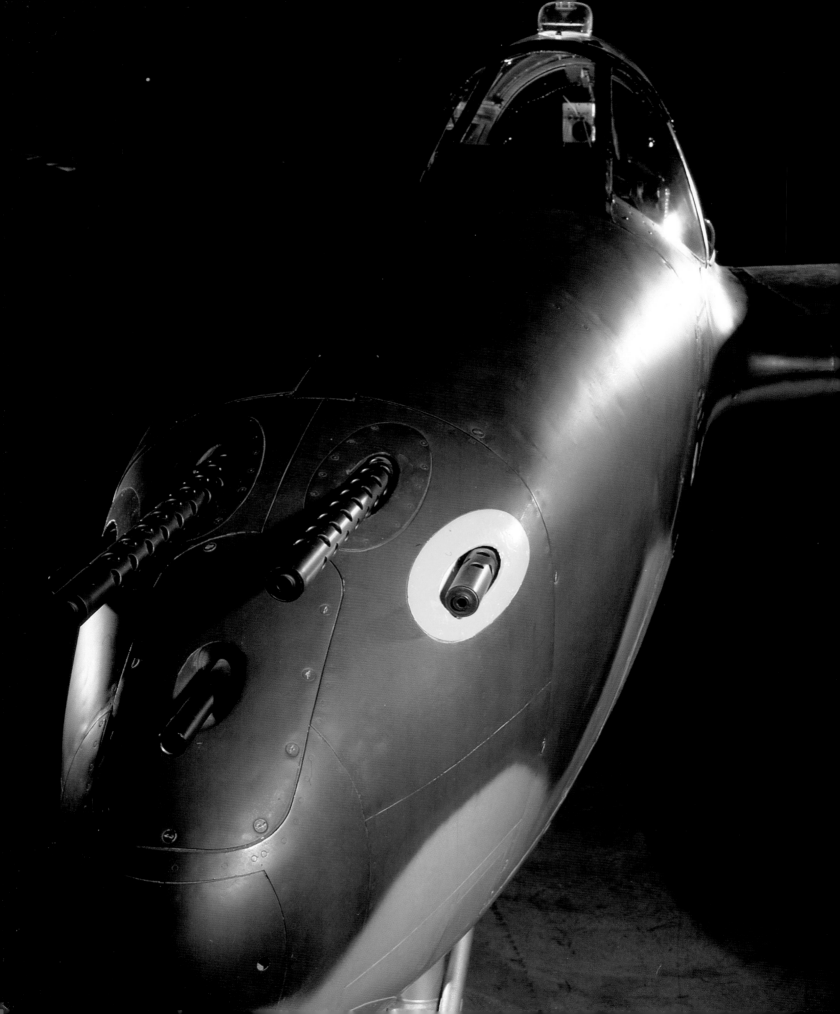

CHAPTER 10

The Islands of the Pacific

AT THE SAME TIME that Japanese troops landed at Buna to start their offensive against Port Moresby, others were building an airfield on Guadalcanal in the southern Solomons. This represented a major threat to the Allies' transpacific lifeline and had to be countered. Operation Watchtower was therefore devised to land U.S. marines on the islands of Guadalcanal and Tulagi. This would be the first U.S. amphibious action since 1898, and the first U.S. offensive of WWII. Air support would have to be provided by the U.S. Navy, since the USAAF's presence in the South Pacific was small and widely scattered, with isolated units operating a total of thirty-three B-17s, twenty-two B-26s and seventy-nine P-39/400s deployed on airstrips as far apart as New Caledonia, the New Hebrides, Fiji and Tonga, covering an area not much smaller than the United States.

The Solomons

The Marines went ashore on August 7, 1942, supported by strong naval forces, including seven cruisers, nineteen destroyers, the battleship *North Carolina,* and three of the four aircraft carriers in the Pacific — *Saratoga, Enterprise* and *Wasp.* Within hours, the partially completed airstrip on Guadalcanal was in American hands, but the Japanese reaction from their main base at Rabaul was swift. Before the day was over, there were raids on the landing forces by Betty and Val bombers escorted by Zero fighters. Naval aircraft from the U.S. carriers engaged the raiders, shooting down sixteen for a loss of twelve.

In the swirling dogfights over Guadalcanal, there was an incident involving one of the war's greatest aces, Saburo Sakai. He added to his score by shooting down two F4F Wildcats, and then dived on what he thought was another flight of Wildcats, only to discover too late that he had committed himself to a stern

The formidable firepower of the Lockheed P-38 Lightning was concentrated in the nose — four .50-caliber machine guns grouped round a 20 mm cannon. The P-38's unorthodox design set it apart among single-seat fighters. The fuselage pod, housing the cockpit and the guns, was relatively small, but the overall dimensions were large for a WWII fighter. Twin nacelles mounted in a wing of 52-foot span held Allison V-1710 engines and were extended into booms to carry the tail. The USAF Museum's example is a P-38L, but is finished as a P-38J of the 55th Fighter Squadron, 20th Fighter Group, at Kingscliffe, U.K.

A flight of Bell P-39 Airacobras poses for the photographer in peaceful skies. The P-39's unique engine location behind the cockpit initially caused some concern among pilots because of the possible hazard during a crash landing. This fear proved unfounded. However, the P-39's spinning characteristics were a problem if the specific recovery techniques approved for the type were ignored.

the U.S. aircraft carriers from the immediate vicinity of Guadalcanal. It was with relief, therefore, that they declared the airstrip (Henderson Field) open on August 20 and welcomed the arrival of nineteen Wildcats and a dozen Dauntlesses, the founding aircraft of what would become known as the "Cactus Air Force." The P-400s of the 67th Fighter Squadron joined them by the end of August. The poor performance of the P-400s made them unsuitable for the daily air battles with Japanese bombers and fighters over the island, but they proved useful in the

attack on what he later believed to be some Grumman Avengers but may have been Dauntlesses, armed with rearward-firing guns. At least one of the American gunners found his mark and the Zero's canopy disintegrated. Sakai was hit in the head, and bullet fragments lodged in his chest, back and thighs. Bleeding profusely and in great pain, he found that he had lost the sight of his right eye and had only partial vision in the other one. He was also paralyzed down his left side. His aircraft was severely damaged and heading for the sea, but he recovered control and turned toward Rabaul. In one of the air war's epic flights, Sakai forced himself to remain conscious and managed to navigate back to his base, nearly 600 miles and over four hours flying away. Left with only half an eye and one arm, he still landed his aircraft safely. Two years later, permanently blind in his right eye, he was sufficiently recovered to become a combat pilot once more. By the end of the war, he had claimed a total of sixty-four victories.

To the dismay of the U.S. Marines ashore, the strength of the Japanese attacks, with land-based air forces by day and powerful naval forces at night, led to the withdrawal of

close-support role, using their cannon to harass enemy troops in contact with the Marines. In the weeks that followed, while the Marines fought vicious close-quarter battles with Japanese soldiers ashore, the seas around Guadalcanal saw numerous actions in which both sides suffered serious losses. Perhaps most significantly, the Japanese carrier *Ryujo* was sunk and the U.S. Navy lost the *Wasp* and had both the *Enterprise* and *Saratoga* severely damaged. Admiral Nimitz in Pearl Harbor had to face the fact that, for the time being, he had only *Hornet* left to confront up to six Japanese carriers in the Pacific. On shore, however, the Marines were well dug in, and were now supported by the 1st Marine Air Wing.

The *Enterprise* returned to the Solomons in October and was soon in action alongside *Hornet*. In a slugging match with four Japanese carriers — *Junyo*, *Shokaku*, *Zuikaku* and *Zuiho* — the U.S. Navy came close to disaster, losing *Hornet* and having *Enterprise* hit hard once again. The U.S. dive-bombers were not so successful, but they damaged both *Zuiho* and *Shokaku*, and the Japanese withdrew. Although seventy-four U.S. aircraft had been lost during the battle, the Japanese had lost 100, together with their crews. Even with two intact carrier decks available, they could not find enough aircraft or crews to use them effectively.

As the year ended, a few P-38s were at last on hand at Henderson to offer both high-altitude and long-range capability. The B-24, too, had made an appearance, and one radar-equipped squadron had demonstrated that it could strike Japanese shipping through cloud or from low level at night. It was a close-run thing, but eventually the Japanese were forced to accept that the cost of supporting their attempt to recover Guadalcanal while operating from a main base over 600 miles away was too high. It was proving almost impossible for their ships to break through the stranglehold of the U.S. naval and air blockade, and their troops on the island were suffering greatly from their enforced isolation. Combat deaths, injuries, sickness and malnutrition had, by November 1942, reduced the original force of 30,000 to little more than 13,000 fit for duty. Early in February 1943, the Japanese bowed to the inevitable, acknowledged the growing imbalance of power, and withdrew the remnants of their Army. The grinding six-month struggle for Guadalcanal was over. The U.S. Navy had suffered some serious losses, but the aerial conflict had been costly, too, even though the numbers involved in combat on any one day were never very great. The Japanese had been especially hard hit, losing almost 2,000 aircraft and their irreplaceable crews.

Admiral Yamamoto

Faced with the fact of defeat both in Papua and on Guadalcanal, Admiral Yamamoto tried to regain the initiative for his forces in the Solomons with a series of air raids in April. They were roughly handled and the ratio of losses greatly favored U.S. fighter pilots. With the momentum of victory building against him, Yamamoto decided to put some steel into the Japanese units by visiting them in person. Unfortunately for him, American intelligence officers were reading his mail.

The code breakers determined that Yamamoto would be visiting Ballale, off the southern tip of Bougainville, on April 18, 1943. His detailed itinerary, complete with timings, was known. Since Ballale was just within the reach of P-38s fitted with drop tanks, Major John Mitchell of the 339th Squadron was given the job of planning an interception and an assassination. From every point of view, the operation was a long shot, following a curving track for nearly 500 miles over water, and flying at low level the whole way to avoid detection. With no radio navigation aids, the navigation had to be by dead reckoning, relying on notoriously suspect aircraft compasses and primitive weather forecasting. Even if the P-38s made an accurate landfall and got there on time, it was by no means certain that Yamamoto's aircraft would be there, too. Mitchell made a number of assumptions about the route and airspeed of

The 347th Fighter Group was assigned to the Fourteenth Air Force in 1943 and was sent to Guadalcanal, where it used its P-39s to attack Japanese ground forces and shipping.

LEFT *Three of the P-38 pilots from the attack section that shot down Admiral Yamamoto's Mitsubishi Betty over Bougainville on April 18, 1943: Thomas Lanphier, Besby Holmes and Rex Barber. A fourth, Raymond Hine, was lost during the attack.*

BELOW *The Smithsonian's G4M3 Model 34 Betty is not complete but it is the best-preserved example in the world. Four major portions survive: the nose including the entire flight deck, 10 feet of the fuselage, and the two engines and their cowlings. The Japanese crews called the bomber Hamaki (cigar) after its cigar-shaped fuselage. Allied pilots had another name for it. The Betty was so prone to ignite when attacked that they nicknamed it "the flying lighter."*

the Japanese formation on the basis of the decoded itinerary, but there were no guarantees.

On April 18, sixteen P-38s from the 339th, 12th and 70th Fighter Squadrons set course for Ballale. Four were selected as an attack section to concentrate on Yamamoto's transport, while the rest of the P-38s took on his escort and whatever other fighters appeared from the nearby base. Much to the jubilation of the Americans and the shocked surprise of the Japanese, the sixteen P-38s ran into two Betty bombers and six Zeros at exactly the appointed time and place. In the ensuing melee, Lieutenant Thomas Lanphier and Lieutenant Rex Barber between them managed to shoot down both Bettys. Next day, the body of Japan's premier admiral, architect of the attack on Pearl Harbor, was found in the jungle.

Rabaul

Throughout 1943, as Marine soldiers forced their way up the chain of the Solomon Islands toward Bougainville and Rabaul, aircraft moved with them and maintained a relentless pressure on the enemy. Wherever possible, Japanese strongholds were pounded from the air, then left behind to become prisons for their isolated garrisons. In November, American troops landed in a lightly held area of Bouganville, established a perimeter,

The Lockheed P-38 Lightning was ideally suited for operations in the Pacific theater. It had a better range than the P-39s, P-40s and P-47s available in 1942, and its twin engines offered an additional safety factory when flying over long stretches of water and jungle. Missions lasting up to twelve hours became routine, and many wounded Lightnings were able to limp home on one engine. The maneuverability of the Lightning was inferior to that of its nimble Japanese opponents, but by avoiding dogfights and making the most of their superior speed and heavy armament in diving attacks, the P-38 squadrons achieved impressive results.

built airfields, and did their best to ignore the 60,000 Japanese elsewhere on the island. Cut off and overmatched, enemy units struggled fitfully on, some soldiers persisting until the end of the war and beyond. Just over 200 miles away, on their airfields near Rabaul, the Japanese steeled themselves to oppose the U.S. buildup on Bougainville, denuding several carriers and main bases to gather together a force of some 550 aircraft. It was a move welcomed by American airmen, who relished the chance of bringing large numbers to battle. Heavy bombers from Kenney's Fifth Air Force joined the Thirteenth for raids against Rabaul, and fighters harassed the Japanese unceasingly, both on the ground and in the air. By March 1944, the Japanese air forces based at Rabaul were effectively destroyed and Rabaul harbor wrecked, with many ships sunk. Few ground installations were intact, and most of the town's buildings were in ruins. Rabaul, with its 100,000-man garrison, was rendered helpless, and there was no longer any need for a direct assault. U.S. commanders left it behind, cocooned in its uselessness, and turned their attention to the Philippines.

Central Pacific

While the Fifth and Thirteenth Air Forces were building their combat reputations far to the southwest, Major General Willis Hale's Seventh Air Force remained quietly in Hawaii, regularly being asked to release units for service with its more heavily engaged cousins. In the fall of 1943, the Seventh's decline was halted by an infusion of fresh units as U.S. forces prepared for their offensive in the Central Pacific. By November, Hale's B-24s were striking Japanese strongholds in the Gilberts and Marshalls from forward bases in the Ellice Islands. The combat record of the Seventh is possibly the least well known of any numbered air force. In the Central Pacific theater, the stars were the U.S. Navy's carriers. Nevertheless, the Seventh Air Force played an essential role for Admiral Nimitz as he drove his forces forward in a series of huge leaps, taking some islands and bypassing others. Nimitz knew that local air superiority was essential to the success of an invasion. The Seventh's bombers were used to batter enemy air bases in the area before an island assault, and Nimitz made it a priority to establish new bases for the USAAF's long-range aircraft as soon as possible so that they could begin reaching out to soften up the enemy for the next jump ahead. The Seventh also paid regular visits to bypassed Japanese garrisons, ensuring that they remained powerless to intervene in a war that had left them behind, frustrated and impotent. In the three months following November 1943, U.S. amphibious forces swept forward through the Gilberts and the Marshalls, taking such key atolls as Tarawa, Kwajalein and Eniwetok in fierce fighting against fanatical Japanese defenders. Moved to bases on Kwajalein and Eniwetok, the Seventh's bombers then joined the U.S. Navy in the reduction of Truk, one of the strongest Japanese naval bases in the Pacific. It was a task that occupied the Seventh until the end of the war, but by then Truk had been rendered ineffective by constant battering from the air.

The successor to the Wildcat, the Grumman F6F Hellcat was a superb fighter, credited by war's end with destroying over 5,000 enemy aircraft in air-to-air combat — 75 percent of all U.S. Navy aerial kills. The F6F-3 seen here at Pensacola was recovered in 1970 from 3,400 feet of water off the coast of California where it had crashed in 1946. The aircraft, painted in the colors of VF-31 assigned to the USS Cabot, *records the fourteen aerial kills made by Lieutenant Ray Hawkins before his twenty-second birthday.*

The cockpit of the Hellcat is large, comfortable and logically arranged. At a time when USAAF aircraft were still registering speed in miles per hour, the Hellcat's airspeed indicator was marked in knots, as befitted a naval fighter. This aircraft is an F6F-3 flown by the Fighter Collection at Duxford, England.

major warships, and the striking arm of the fleet (Task Force 58, commanded by Vice Admiral Mitscher) included fifteen aircraft carriers and seven of the new, fast battleships. The amphibious ships were covered by a force including eight of the small escort carriers and several old battleships, three of which had been recovered from the wreckage of Pearl Harbor. This immense concentration of power was achieved only eighteen months after the U.S. Navy in the South Pacific had been reduced to one operational carrier — the indestructible but damaged *Enterprise* — and two battleships.

The first job for Mitscher's TF58, which included a rejuvenated *Enterprise*, was to clear the way for the assault by neutralizing Japanese land-based air power in and around the Marianas. On June 10, the approaching American ships were seen by Japanese patrol aircraft. Admiral Toyoda, the Japanese commander-in-chief, prepared to annihilate them in the Philippine Sea with the help of some 500 land-based aircraft based in the Marianas area. Mitscher did not give him the chance. Charging straight at the southern Marianas, he launched a 200-aircraft strike from 200 miles out on the afternoon of June 11. Airfields on Guam, Saipan and Tinian were hit, and the attacks were devastatingly effective. Similar sweeps were made during the following days. Airfields already attacked were hit again, and a number of others were added to the target list. The Japanese aircraft losses mounted dramatically, and the airfields were rendered almost unusable.

In the two years following the great carrier battles of the Coral Sea and Midway, the U.S. Navy in the Pacific rebuilt its strength and helped the U.S. Army and Marines to slog their way through a blood-and-guts island-hopping campaign that pushed the Japanese back through the Solomons, Gilberts, and Marshalls. By mid-1944, the decision was made to gamble on taking a great leap forward of 1,000 miles, bypassing the Carolines to tackle the Marianas. In particular, the offensive was to be directed against Saipan, Tinian and Guam — islands from which an air assault against the Japanese mainland could be launched.

The Great Marianas Turkey Shoot

In early June, the U.S. Pacific Fleet, commanded by Admiral Spruance, set out for the Marianas. It was an impressive armada of several task forces, comprising some 535 vessels and carrying 130,000 troops. There were 106

It was by now apparent to everyone that Saipan must be the next target for U.S. troops. The Marine infantrymen were not particularly happy at the news. During a preparatory briefing for the amphibious assault, an officer on one ship described the dangers the troops must face. Besides some 30,000 determined defenders, there were other hazards. The waters around Saipan were polluted and there were "sharks, barracuda, sea snakes, razor sharp coral, poison fish, and giant clams waiting to shut on a man like a bear trap." Once ashore, the marines were told to expect "leprosy, typhus, typhoid, yaws, dengue fever, dysentery, sabre grass, biting and stinging insects, snakes and giant lizards."

"Eat nothing on the island," the officer warned, "don't drink any water and don't approach the inhabitants. Any questions?"

A hand went up at the back of the room. "Sir — why don't we let them keep the place?"

The U.S. infantry went ashore on Saipan on June 15. The Japanese defended ferociously, but they were forced to fight without air cover as U.S. aircraft swarmed over the beaches. Meanwhile, the First Mobile Fleet under Admiral Ozawa was instructed to proceed with all speed toward the Marianas, where it was given

Pugnacious-looking, fast and heavily armed, the Hellcat was designed for carrier operation with good low-speed handling in mind, and it handled well at any speed. It proved to be more than a match for the Japanese opposition and was the dominant fighter of the Pacific war. On one legendary occasion, a flight of Hellcats joined the landing pattern with forty-nine Japanese aircraft returning to their base at Guam. Thirty of the Japanese were shot down and the rest crashed on landing.

the task of crushing the American assault and destroying the invasion fleet. With the benefit of hindsight, that may seem to have been asking too much, but Ozawa did not think it was an unreasonable order. Even though the U.S. fleet opposing him was impressively large, his own was by no means puny, and there were a number of other factors in the equation.

Ozawa sailed with nine carriers, five battleships, thirteen cruisers and twenty-eight destroyers. One carrier was the new 30,000-ton *Taiho*, and two of the battleships were *Yamato* and *Musashi*, the world's largest warships. Ozawa knew he was outnumbered in aircraft by almost two to one — he rightly assumed some 900 U.S. aircraft against fewer than 500 on the Japanese carriers — but at this stage, he was confident he could count on adding the 500-plus land-based aircraft he thought were available. He also knew

RIGHT TOP *Alex Vraciu ended WWII as the U.S. Navy's fourth-ranking ace with nineteen enemy aircraft shot down and twenty-one more destroyed on the ground. On June 19, 1944, he engaged a Japanese air group about twenty-five miles west of the USS* Lexington. *In the subsequent action he shot down six Judy dive-bombers in just eight minutes using only 360 rounds of ammunition. He is seen here after landing with six fingers extended.*

RIGHT BOTTOM *David McCampbell is the U.S. Navy's top ace with thirty-four aerial victories. He was awarded the Medal of Honor while serving as commander, Air Group 15, USS* Essex *(CV 9), during the Battle of the Philippine Sea (June 19, 1944) and the Battle of Leyte Gulf (October 24, 1944). During the first encounter, McCampbell's group took on a force of eighty Japanese carrier-based aircraft, of which he personally shot down seven. In the Battle of Leyte Gulf, he attacked a formation of some sixty aircraft and shot down nine.*

BELOW *Built in response to a 1939 requirement for a carrier-based torpedo-bomber to replace the TBD Devastator, the Grumman TBF/TBM Avenger proved one of the most versatile aircraft of WWII. It was also one of the toughest, often able to absorb battle damage and get back to its carrier. This Avenger has clearly taken several hits.*

Equipped with an electrically powered gun turret and an internal bomb bay, the Avenger carried a crew of three — the pilot, in a cockpit that was almost too big; a gunner manning twin .50-caliber machine guns in a turret; and a bombardier/gunner, who had to lie down to fire the single .30-caliber machine gun in the aircraft's belly. A total of 9,842 Avengers were built. The example on display at Pensacola is a TBM-3.

that his aircraft had longer reach and that he could therefore count on getting off the first strike. He knew, too, that he would have the advantage of coming to battle into the wind (the easterly trades would be in his face) and so could launch his aircraft without changing course. The U.S. ships would have to turn away to launch theirs.

Another plus was the fact that at least half of the Japanese aircraft were new types, much improved over their predecessors. Ozawa believed that the D4Y Judy dive-bomber, the B6N Jill torpedo-bomber, and the latest Zero, the A6M5, would be more than a match for his enemy in the coming battle. Unfortunately for him, there was one factor that was heavily against him from the start. The Japanese naval air arm was no longer the highly trained, competent force that had attacked Pearl Harbor. In the two and a half years since, the Japanese Navy had lost the majority of its best pilots in battles of attrition all over the Pacific. The young aviators now in Ozawa's ships were eager for action but they were poorly trained and few had any significant experience in the aircraft they were flying.

On June 16, Admiral Spruance positioned his forces some 200 miles to the west of Saipan. His message to the U.S. ships concluded with the instruction "Action against the enemy must be pushed vigorously by all hands to ensure complete destruction of his fleet." Even so, he knew that his first responsibility was the protection and support of the U.S. invasion force. As he brought the Imperial Navy to battle, he had to be certain that there was no risk of

Japanese ships getting in behind him to attack the American bridgehead on Saipan.

The morning of June 18 opened with Spruance ordering a precautionary strike against Guam. Then Ozawa launched his first strike against the U.S. fleet from some 300 miles. He knew that he was still beyond the reach of the Americans and was confident that the U.S. ships were by this time being pounded by aircraft from the Marianas. He might have been less sure of himself if he had known that the 500 land-based aircraft on which he was relying had already been reduced to not more than thirty available for combat. The second Japanese wave was sent off half an hour after the first. Almost 200 aircraft headed for the U.S. fleet. Warned by radar contact at 150 miles, Admiral

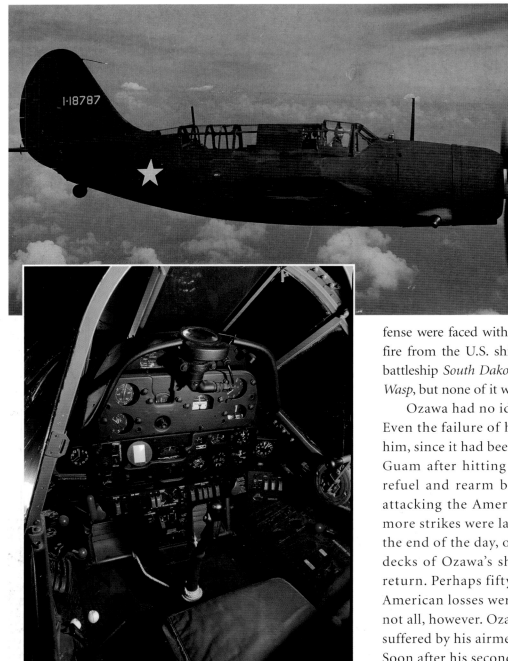

Mitscher had 140 Hellcats in the air to meet them. It was now that the change in the relative experience levels of the opposing pilots since the days of the Coral Sea and Midway became only too apparent. Surviving Japanese have said that, in the Battle of the Philippine Sea, their aircraft "fell like leaves." Forty-two were shot down from the first wave, and ninety-seven more were lost from the second. Those few aircraft that broke through the swarming fighter defense were faced with an unprecedented wall of antiaircraft fire from the U.S. ships. Some damage was caused to the battleship *South Dakota*, and to the carriers *Bunker Hill* and *Wasp*, but none of it was serious.

Ozawa had no idea that things were going so badly. Even the failure of his aircraft to return did not alarm him, since it had been expected that they would fly on to Guam after hitting the U.S. ships. There they would refuel and rearm before returning in the afternoon, attacking the Americans again on the way back. Two more strikes were launched as the day wore on, and by the end of the day, over 370 aircraft had risen from the decks of Ozawa's ships. Of that number, 244 did not return. Perhaps fifty more were lost on or over Guam. American losses were just thirty-one aircraft. That was not all, however. Ozawa, still unaware of the catastrophe suffered by his airmen, had other things to worry about. Soon after his second wave left the decks, his main force was sighted by American submarines, and the USS *Albacore* fired a fan of six torpedoes at an aircraft carrier. Warrant Officer Komatsu had just taken off when he saw a torpedo track heading for his ship, the *Taiho*. In an extraordinary act of self-sacrifice, he dived into the weapon's path, so (he must have hoped) saving his ship. Unfortunately for the Japanese, another torpedo struck home near the *Taiho*'s bow. At first, it seemed that the damage was no more than an inconvenience. *Taiho* was

Top *The Curtiss SB2C Helldiver was known as "the Beast" by both aircrew and mechanics. Its basic handling characteristics and stability were poor, and its performance in combat was sometimes less than impressive. This was especially so during the Battle of the Philippine Sea, when forty-four of fifty-two Helldivers failed to return from a night attack on the Japanese fleet.*
Above *Cockpit of the Curtiss SB2C Helldiver on display at Pensacola.*

thought to be unsinkable, and she steamed on apparently unconcerned.

Just after midday, the USS *Cavalla* also found the main force. Three of her torpedoes struck *Shokaku*, one of the carriers that had attacked Pearl Harbor. Some two hours later, *Shokaku* blew up and sank, taking 1,263 men with her. Appalled as he was by this loss, Ozawa was even more horrified only half an hour later when a violent explosion ripped *Taiho* apart and the flagship also went down, together with over 1,500 of her crew. Fumes from a ruptured fuel line had seeped through the ship, turning the "unsinkable" *Taiho* into a floating bomb merely waiting for the spark of detonation.

Even so, when evening came, Ozawa was on board the cruiser *Haguro*, licking his wounds and not yet beaten. He had not seen an American aircraft all day, and the few pilots who had returned were reporting success against the U.S. carriers. He hoped that many of his aircraft were on Guam, and that they would be resuming their attacks on the Americans in the morning. As darkness fell, Ozawa withdrew to the northwest to refuel his ships and consider his options. Among his surviving carriers, he could still raise about 100 combat aircraft, and he intended to return to the fray. At midday on June 20, Ozawa transferred his flag to the carrier *Zuikaku*, and there, with the help of better communications and news from the aircrew who had survived the previous day's struggle, he began to understand the extent of the Japanese defeat. Nevertheless, it was apparent that the Americans had not yet located his ships, and he determined to strike at them again the following morning with everything he had.

Meanwhile, Admiral Spruance had come to the conclusion that the risk to

An Avenger in serious trouble. The touchdown was hard, it bounced, missed the arrester wires, stalled and dropped the port wing. The engine is roaring at full power as the pilot desperately tries to pull away from a hopeless situation. Note the spirals of vapor trailing from the tips of the racing propeller.

the U.S. beachhead on Guam was small enough to allow at least some of his carriers off the leash. Admiral Mitscher set off west with three of the four carrier groups, but his reconnaissance aircraft had difficulty finding the Japanese fleet. Finally, that afternoon at 16:00, Mitscher had the position report he wanted — the enemy was 220 miles away to the northwest. Twenty minutes later, 216 aircraft were airborne and on their way. The circumstances were far from ideal. It was soon discovered that the original estimate of the distance had been too low. The Japanese were in fact 280 miles away, and that was at the outer edge of the U.S. aircraft's radius of action. It was also obvious that it would be dark when the American pilots got back to where they hoped to find their home decks. This was no small problem since, for all their combat proficiency, few of the American aviators had any experience of operating at night.

The strike was delivered just as the sun had begun to sink below the horizon, and hits were scored on a number of ships. The carrier *Hiyo* and two fleet oilers were sunk, and three other carriers (*Junyo*, *Zuikaku* and *Chiyoda*), a battleship and a cruiser were badly damaged. The aircraft exchange further favored the attackers; sixty-five Japanese were destroyed for the loss of twenty Americans shot down. However, the day was far from over. By the time the first of

Vought F4U-1 Corsairs of VMF-224, U.S. Marine Corps, on Majuro in the Marshall Islands early in 1944. Among the best piston-engined fighters ever designed, the Corsair was distinctive in many ways. Its bent wing allowed for a relatively short undercarriage while giving clearance to the largest propeller (13 feet in diameter) ever fitted to a single-engined aircraft. The long nose housing the huge Pratt & Whitney R-2800 radial pushed the cockpit back to behind the wing, and the air rushing into the wing-root intakes at high speed produced a sound that led to the aircraft's nickname of "Whistling Death." In the Pacific war, Corsairs downed 2,149 enemy aircraft while flying 64,051 missions and losing only 189 of their own in combat.

the returning raiders reached the area of the U.S. ships, it was pitch dark, and many American aircraft were on their last reserves of fuel. They needed all the help they could get, and Mitscher, gambling the security of his ships, ordered the lights of the task force turned on. Lit up like Christmas trees, the ships became beacons but, even so, a number of pilots, desperately short of fuel, crashed on carrier decks or ditched in the sea nearby. Eighty U.S. aircraft were lost in this way, by far their greatest loss of the battle.

Ozawa now commanded a seriously damaged fleet and he was down to his last thirty-five aircraft. Faced with such stark reality, he turned and ran for Okinawa. Mitscher's

ships were slowed by search-and-rescue activity, and he regretfully recorded in his battle report that, by the time that was taken care of, "the enemy had escaped." Mitscher and others, advocates of aggressive action, felt that Spruance had been overcautious in waiting for the enemy to come to him in front of Saipan, and that the Japanese had been let off the hook as a result.

There was no question, however, that the Japanese had suffered a crippling defeat. They had not been able to disrupt the landings on Saipan, and in the course of the battle, their losses had included three carriers and almost 500 aircraft. The U.S. ships were hardly scratched and 130 aircraft had been lost. On paper, the Imperial Navy still looked as if it had the capacity to be a formidable force, but in fact it was a shadow of its former self. In particular, replacements for its shattering aircrew losses were not available. Although it was not yet fully realized by the American admirals, their victory in the Philippine Sea had been one of the most complete of the war at sea. After June 20, 1944, the U.S. Navy effectively reigned supreme in the Pacific, whether they knew it or not.

Assault on the Mariana

Meanwhile, the USAAF's Seventh Air Force supported the assaults made on Saipan, Tinian and Guam. Only one week after the first Marines hit Saipan's beaches, with savage fighting still going on close by, aircraft of the Seventh Air Force were ashore. In a first for the USAAF, P-47s of the 19th Fighter Squadron were catapulted from the light carriers *Manila Bay* and *Natoma Bay* to land at Aslito (Isley) Field. Within days, they were joined by a second P-47 squadron, the 73rd Fighter Squadron, and the 6th Night Fighter Squadron, newly equipped with the P-61 Black Widow. The 333rd Fighter Squadron (P-47s) arrived the following month, bringing the 318th Fighter Group up to full strength.

During the hours of daylight, the P-47s were occupied with standing air patrols, close-support missions and fighter sweeps over neighboring Tinian and Guam, while the P-61s filled in by night. This was the first Central Pacific operation in which land-based fighters were used for close support of ground troops, and they proved to be particularly versatile. From the outset, they could strafe with their .5-inch machine guns, drop 500-pound bombs, and launch 4.5-inch rockets. In the later stages of the struggle they introduced a new weapon of fearful effect. Wing tanks filled with a petroleum mixture (napalm) dropped from 50 feet could each clear an area 200 feet long by 75 feet wide.

Although the last Japanese outpost on Guam did not fall until early September, the Marianas were declared secure by mid-August. American airfield construction crews were already at work building unusually long runways. The new B-29s were on the way, and, from bases in the Marianas, these very heavy bombers would be able to raid the home islands of Japan. Another opportunity would be at hand to test strategic air power theories about defeating an enemy nation by bombing it into submission.

The "Second Pearl Harbor"

However, there were several acts of the Pacific naval drama still to be played. Four months after the sensational events of the "Turkey Shoot," the notorious Tokyo Rose made an astonishing radio announcement. On October 15, 1944, she crowed: "All of Admiral Mitscher's carriers have tonight been sunk!" The Japanese people were told that the "Wild Eagle" pilots of their navy had won a "second Pearl Harbor" in the waters off Formosa, and the Emperor went so far as to announce the first public victory holiday in

An aircraft associated with famous squadrons such as the Black Sheep and Jolly Rogers, the F4U Corsair began development at Vought in 1938. Now remembered as a superb combat aircraft, it was not at first accepted by the U.S. Navy as suitable for the war at sea. The aircraft's poor visibility during landing approaches, adverse stall characteristics at slow approach speeds, and tendency to bounce on a hard landing initially prevented its service aboard carriers, leaving it to land-based squadrons to introduce the aircraft to combat in February 1943. It was not cleared for the U.S. Navy's deck operations until 1944. A total of 12,582 Corsairs was built between 1942–1952, giving it the longest production run of any propeller-driven fighter.

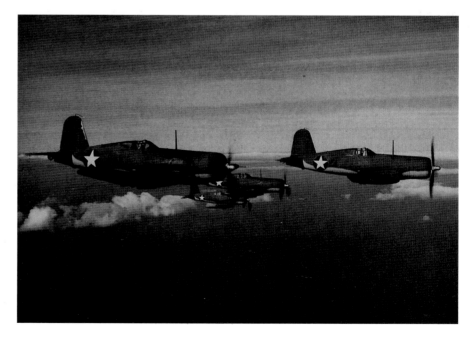

more than two years. Sadly for the Japanese, the truth was somewhat different.

In September, the command of the U.S. fleet had passed from Spruance to Halsey, under the Nimitz policy of "changing drivers" periodically. By October, Halsey was engaged in a campaign to "destroy enemy naval and air forces capable of threatening the area of the Philippines." On October 12, one thousand American aircraft began three days of attacks against the airfields on Formosa. By the time it was over, the U.S. fleet had lost seventy-nine aircraft and had two cruisers badly damaged. Young Japanese pilots came back from their first taste of combat full of tales about sinking U.S. ships. The story of a spectacular victory was built on their glowing reports, but their commanders must have wondered about the facts behind the propaganda. They knew that they had again lost well over 500 aircraft. Irritated by the Japanese victory news, Halsey sent Nimitz a historic signal: "All ships recently reported as sunk by Radio Tokyo have been salvaged and are retiring at high speed toward the Japanese fleet."

> *"All ships recently reported as sunk by Radio Tokyo have been salvaged and are retiring at high speed toward the Japanese fleet."*
>
> ADMIRAL WILLIAM "BULL" HALSEY, SIGNAL TO ADMIRAL CHESTER NIMITZ, OCTOBER 15, 1944

Leyte Gulf

To prepare for MacArthur's next move, U.S. forces established themselves on islands to the south and southeast of Mindanao, the southernmost main island of the Philippines. By October 1944, USAAF aircraft were operating from both Morotai and the Palaus. It had been intended that these bases would support MacArthur's invasion of Mindanao, but intelligence reports now suggested that the weakest point in the Japanese defense of the Philippines would be Leyte, in the center of the archipelago. Admiral Halsey, mixing metaphors in his enthusiasm, said that he believed the Japanese air force in the Philippines to be "a hollow shell operating on a shoestring." He suggested dropping all intermediate plans and going straight for Leyte. The scene was set for MacArthur's return to the Philippines. On October 20, the ships of the General's own navy, Admiral Kincaid's Seventh Fleet (157 combat ships and 581 other vessels) arrived in Leyte Gulf to begin the assault. The 106 warships of Halsey's Third Fleet stood guard in the open

ocean to the northeast, hoping that they could engage the main Japanese fleet in a final decisive battle.

Desperate Japanese measures were called for to defeat the American invasion of the Philippines, and so an audacious (even reckless) plan was devised. The Japanese Navy organized three forces for an attack. Two were striking forces sailing from Brunei and intended to break up the American landings. Center Force, with Admiral Kurita in command, consisted of five battleships (including *Yamato* and *Musashi*), twelve cruisers and fifteen destroyers. Southern Force, under Admiral Nishimura, initially had just two battleships, a cruiser and four destroyers, but before going into battle, he was to be joined by Admiral Shima, sailing from Japan with three cruisers and seven destroyers. One remarkable aspect of the overall plan was that it appeared to have been devised to take account of the temperament of the U.S. commander. Ozawa knew that he was up against the fiery Halsey rather than the prudent Spruance, and he therefore decided to use his Main Force (four carriers, three cruisers, eight destroyers and two hybrid battleship-carriers) as bait. The idea was to entice Halsey away from Leyte for long enough to allow the big guns of Kurita and company to get in among the U.S. invasion fleet. Ozawa knew his opponent and read his mind very well.

As was usually the case with a Japanese naval plan, this one was full of complexity. It depended on widely separated ships approaching the theater of action from several directions, each group arriving on stage at precisely the right time to achieve the desired effect, and also on the American players reacting to the Japanese entrances in a predictable way.

The Americans, although immensely powerful, had their Achilles heel. The twin thrusts across the Pacific had come together in the Philippines, but there were still two commanders-in-chief. Kincaid's Seventh Fleet belonged to MacArthur, but Halsey answered to Nimitz. Kincaid assumed that the principal aim of the American operations was to put ground forces ashore on Leyte and support them once they got there. He further believed that principal responsibility for the protection of his fleet and the landing area lay in the hands of Halsey, who commanded most of the

The cockpit of the Vought FG-1D flown by the Old Flying Machine Company at Duxford, England. It is more complex than the majority of WWII fighters, but is typical of U.S. combat aircraft design in being roomy and comfortable.

naval firepower available, both at sea and in the air. Halsey, however, had orders from Nimitz that allowed him to interpret his responsibilities differently. He was to "cover and support [MacArthur's] forces of the Southwest Pacific," but "in case opportunity for destruction of a major portion of enemy fleet offers or can be created, such destruction becomes primary task." The ambiguity of these orders was to have alarming consequences.

The first act of what became the largest naval battle in history opened on October 23, a much earlier date than what the Japanese had hoped for. Kurita's Center Force was seen north of Borneo by the U.S. submarines *Darter* and *Dace*. Carefully arranging their ambush, they combined to sink two cruisers and cripple another. Kurita was already down three major warships, and the U.S. Navy knew he was on the move, but he pressed on and entered the Sibuyan Sea at the heart of the Philippines early on October 24. He knew that he would be vulnerable to air attack, but he was counting on air cover from Japanese squadrons operating in the Philippines. Despite the carnage of the air battles around Formosa, there were still some 600 Japanese aircraft to take on the Americans.

Unfortunately for Kurita, Halsey's ships were sighted by a patrol aircraft as he entered the Sibuyan Sea, and all available Japanese aircraft were dispatched against the U.S. fleet. Some 200 Japanese naval aircraft aimed their attack at a group of ships including four carriers — *Essex, Lexington, Langley* and *Princeton*. In one and a half hours of combat, the attackers lost almost half their number, mostly to

Hellcats. In other strikes on the invasion beachhead, Japanese army aircraft were given similar treatment. As much as in any engagement of war so far, these relatively ineffective attacks revealed how far the combat proficiency levels of Japanese squadrons had fallen. Only one aircraft managed to penetrate the American defensive screen. A Judy dive-bomber put a bomb through the *Princeton*'s flight deck before being shot down. The carrier's fires soon became uncontrollable, and she blew up while the *Birmingham* was alongside trying to help. The *Princeton* sank and the cruiser took heavy casualties.

That single success apart, the Japanese airmen were on the receiving end of the exchange as the U.S. Navy pilots savaged their formations. Two Americans in particular had

Curtiss Helldivers over the USS Ranger, *March 6, 1945. Corsairs and Avengers on deck.*

a memorable day. Commander David McCampbell and his wingman, Lieutenant Roy Rushing, were the first pair among seven Hellcats scrambled from the deck of the Essex at the approach of the Japanese strike. Detailing the other five to tackle the incoming bombers, McCampbell led Rushing against the escort of forty Zeros. Over the next ninety minutes, the Essex seven accounted for no fewer than twenty-seven Japanese shot down. Of these, nine fell to McCampbell and another six to Rushing. There was no damage to any U.S. aircraft and none of the enemy reached the fleet. David McCampbell's performance stands as the highest number of victories ever achieved by an American airman in a single sortie. He was subsequently awarded the Medal of Honor.

The Japanese attacks had been repulsed, and it was time for the riposte from Halsey. Kurita's force had been spotted by reconnaissance planes in the Sibuyan Sea making for the San Bernadino Strait. At mid-morning on October 24, his ships were hit by the first of a series of attacks. It came as a nasty surprise to Kurita to find that, because of the effort expended against the U.S. fleet, he

would now have to do without air cover. He plowed grimly on, enduring the attentions of wave after wave of American aircraft. Avengers, Helldivers and Hellcats from six U.S. carriers converged on Kurita's ships throughout the day. When evening came, the cruiser *Myoko* was badly damaged and limping away west, three battleships were nursing wounds, and a fourth — the indestructible superbattleship *Musashi* — had finally succumbed after absorbing nineteen torpedoes and seventeen bombs. As night fell, Kurita appeared to have had enough. His ships turned away and withdrew to the west.

To the south, American reconnaissance had found Nishimura's little armada of seven ships as well. They were in the Mindanao Sea and heading for the Surigao Strait. Nishimura was sticking to the plan but he had no idea of what was happening elsewhere. There was no sign of Shima's ten ships, which were supposed to accompany him through to Leyte Gulf, and he had heard nothing from either Kurita or Ozawa. If he was concerned by any of this, Nishimura did not show it. His ships kept on steadily toward the Surigao Straits.

Nishimura's appearance confirmed to Halsey that the Japanese were mounting a big operation. He was sure that they would not do so without carriers. Where were they? Much to Ozawa's consternation, the Japanese deception plan had misfired. Halsey's attention had been drawn to the west by the early contact with Kurita, and airborne scouts had then uncovered the approach of both Japanese surface action forces. Infuriatingly (for both Ozawa and Halsey), the Americans had completely missed the juicy carrier bait being trailed to their north.

Late on the afternoon of October 24, as Kurita's battered force was seen to be in retreat, Ozawa and Halsey got their wish. An aerial search stumbled onto the Japanese carriers. Halsey, determined to destroy the Japanese naval menace once and for all, was sure where the threat lay. Kincaid's ships were guarding the Surigao Strait against Nishimura, and Kurita was beaten. The four carriers to the north had to be engaged. Halsey would make sure that he could not be accused, as Spruance was after the Philippine Sea battle, of being overcautious. He forthwith turned his whole task force north and raced off into the night after Ozawa. Unknown to Halsey, by this time Ozawa's force was capable of being no more than a decoy, whether it wanted to or not. Even when it left Japan, its carriers could muster a total of only 108 aircraft, and now, after Ozawa's efforts to draw attention to himself by intervening in the day's battles, there were just twenty-nine left.

However, even if Halsey's assumption that the Japanese carriers were a real threat is accepted as reasonable, his abandonment of all other tasks to pursue them with his whole force is less easily understood, particularly since such overwhelming strength was hardly necessary and he himself had apparently recognized the possibility of a threat developing through the San Bernadino Strait. He had already earmarked a force of four battleships, five cruisers and fourteen destroyers as Task Force 34 under Admiral Willis Lee. A signal from Halsey, given wide distribution, including Nimitz and Kincaid, stated that TF34 was intended to cover the San Bernadino Strait. A second signal said that TF34 was to form on Halsey's order. When Halsey signaled that he was proceeding north to attack Ozawa's carriers, both Nimitz and Kincaid assumed that he would not leave the Strait unguarded. Halsey, however, saw no need for that and did nothing to form TF34.

Meanwhile, Kincaid, secure in the thought that his northern flank (and the U.S. beachhead) was secure, prepared to receive Nishimura. Six battleships and eight cruisers were placed in a double line blocking the 16-mile-wide entrance to the Surigao Strait. Ahead of them were twenty-eight destroyers and then thirty-nine Patrol Torpedo boats stationed in the shadows of small islands at the other end of the Strait. This was to be a scene to gladden a warrior sailor's heart — a night action in the classic naval style, with not an aircraft in sight.

As midnight drew near, Nishimura entered the Surigao Strait, brushing aside the PT boats as he came. The U.S. destroyers offered more resistance; they sank three Japanese destroyers and hit both battleships with torpedoes. Thus blooded, Nishimura's force presented itself to Kincaid for destruction in naval textbook style. The U.S. ships "crossed the T" of the Japanese advance, pouring multiple broadsides into the oncoming ships. It was over in fifteen minutes. One Japanese destroyer and the seriously damaged cruiser *Mogami* were left to retreat through the Strait. It was at this point that Shima chose to turn up with his supporting force. In the darkness, his flagship, the cruiser *Nachi*, collided with the fleeing *Mogami*. Shima reviewed the situation and decided to retire. It did him little good — both *Mogami* and *Nachi* were later caught and sunk by American aircraft.

Kurita was made of sterner stuff than Shima. Once darkness had fallen on his westward retreat, he turned again to run through the San Bernadino Strait. He emerged from it early on the morning of October 25, hardly daring to believe that he was unopposed. The Japanese appearance coincided with Kincaid's horrified realization that his northern flank was unprotected. His tentative query to Halsey: "Is Task Force 34 guarding San Bernadino Strait?" produced an abrupt "Negative" in response. Soon after, Kincaid's worst fears were realized when he heard that the little escort carriers and destroyers cruising to the north of Leyte Gulf were under attack by Japanese battleships and cruisers.

Directly in the path of Kurita's ships was the escort carrier group known as "Taffy 3," commanded by Rear Admiral Clifton Sprague. His six escort carriers and seven destroyers were all that stood between Kurita and his objective of Leyte Gulf. The escort carriers were primarily intended to provide close support for forces ashore. They were lightly built, capable of only 17 knots, and carried fewer than thirty aircraft.

For the most part, their aircraft weapons were those suitable for use against ground forces, and of little use against armored ships. This small force of slow, fragile ships was now face to face with a fleet that had a speed advantage of at least 10 knots and included ships equipped with 18-inch guns — the most powerful naval weapons in existence.

The course followed by events now depended on the perception of the battle as seen in the minds of a number of admirals. Sprague knew that he could not outrun his enemy and that his ships were overmatched. He did not, however, collapse in despair. He yelled for help and he made up his mind to fight as hard as he could before he died. Kincaid's old battleships were low on fuel and ammunition and three hours away, but he sent them north. He, too, yelled for help. A string of signals went to Halsey, spelling out the danger and urging him to send strike aircraft and warships to Leyte without delay. A plain language broadcast was added to underline the plight of the baby flattops. Sprague was in no doubt that the situation was serious.

However, Halsey had the bit between his teeth. He believed that he was on the heels of the most important force left to the Imperial Navy and that its destruction was within his grasp. With this thought dominating all other considerations, he found it difficult to believe that the Japanese threat to Leyte could possibly be beyond the capabilities of the Seventh Fleet to handle. He was in no hurry to call off his pursuit of Ozawa.

Perhaps the most significant perception of events was in the mind of Kurita. He was astonished to find that he had penetrated so far without opposition. Minute by minute, he

Admiral William F. "Bull" Halsey, Commander, Third Fleet, reading at his desk on board USS New Jersey, *his flagship, while en route to raiding the Philippines, December 1944.*

had expected to run into Halsey's battle fleet. It is, then, not surprising that when U.S. ships hove into view he saw what he expected to see and believed them to be Halsey's. The flattops on the horizon were identified as full-sized fleet carriers, and this conviction drastically affected the way he approached the battle.

Just before 07:00 on the morning of October 25, Kurita's battleships opened fire on Sprague's ships from nearly 20 miles away: 14-, 16- and 18-inch projectiles began to fall among the escort carriers. For a time, fortune favored the little ships. As they ran before the storm of shells, they were into wind and so were able to launch such aircraft as they had on board. They were also able to take cover for a few moments at a time in rain squalls. More important, in his excitement, Kurita had rushed his attack. Not recognizing the vulnerability of his opponents, he had not taken the time to organize a battle line, and so his ships were released to charge into the fight as individual units. Kurita's capacity to influence the course of the battle was thereby limited.

Within minutes, aircraft from Sprague's mini-carriers were attacking the Japanese with whatever weapons they had available. Most were armed with anti-personnel bombs that merely rattled the steel plates of the warships. A precious few Avengers had torpedoes, but others took off carrying depth charges. Some aircraft had no weapons at all, but flew at the Japanese anyway, in the hope of adding to the confusion. Meanwhile, the destroyer escorts turned to face their tormentors. They closed to 10,000 yards to fire spreads of torpedoes, forcing the big Japanese ships to take evasive action. Kurita's flagship, the superbattleship *Yamato*, reversed course to avoid them, taking Kurita several miles to the rear and effectively denying the Japanese commander any lingering hope of being able to control the battle.

The heroic fight of "Taffy 3" was not undertaken without cost. Kurita's big guns had their effect. Three destroyers and the escort carrier *Gambier Bay* were sunk, and all of the U.S. ships engaged were damaged to some degree. However, the Japanese did not escape punishment. Before the day was over, three of their heavy cruisers had been sunk. Some two hours into the battle, Kurita still had not realized the weakness of the forces in front of him. Indeed, his conviction that he was engaging Halsey was confirmed by the fact that the air attacks on his ships were increasing in intensity. The other escort carrier groups to the south of "Taffy 3" were hurling all their available aircraft forward to join the struggle. With his forces disorganized and taking losses, Kurita came to the conclusion that worse was to come as the full weight of Halsey's firepower was brought to bear. Unaware that he was on the verge of breaking through to Leyte Gulf, he ordered his forces to withdraw. His American opponents watched them turn away in astonishment, but the spirit of "Taffy 3" was heard in the voice of a signalman on the bridge of Sprague's flagship *Fanshaw Bay*: "Godammit, boys," he yelled, "They're getting away!"

Far to the north, Halsey had begun the day jubilant at the prospects before him. The first of six successive waves of strike aircraft was launched against Ozawa at dawn. The tiny remnant of the once-formidable Japanese naval air arm was swatted aside in the opening minutes of the attack, and Ozawa's ships began to take a terrible beating. When it was over, Japan had lost four more carriers, including *Zuikaku*, the last survivor of the Pearl Harbor raid, and *Zuiko*. All of this should have made Halsey very happy, but other events had intervened to spoil his day. Kincaid kept asking, "Where is Lee?" and then came the last straw. Admiral Nimitz, growing increasingly anxious as he tried to make sense of the rush of signals arriving in his command center asked simply: "Where is Task Force 34?"

To complicate the job of the Japanese code-breakers, all signals were transmitted with padding phrases. These phrases, which began and ended the text, were supposed to be nonsense and to have no connection with the subject of the real message. Unfortunately, it happened that the yeoman on duty that day was a literate man. He knew that October 25 was Balaclava Day and he remembered a phrase from Tennyson's poem about the sacrificial charge of the British Army's Light Brigade during the Crimean War.

"When can their glory fade?
O the wild charge they made!
All the world wonder'd."

He must have thought it appropriate material in the circumstances. With Tennyson's epic running through his mind, the yeoman sent the following message to Halsey. It began: "Turkey trots to water." Then came: "Where is, repeat, where is Task Force 34?" And finally: "The world wonders."

On Halsey's flagship *New Jersey*, the communications staff rushed the Commander-in-Chief's message to their admiral, but neglected to remove the unwanted tail. Halsey therefore read what appeared to be a sarcastic comment on his conduct: "Where is, repeat, where is Task Force 34, the world wonders?"

Halsey took this as a monstrous insult which he never forgave. He brooded on matters for nearly an hour after receiving the signal before ordering Lee's battleships to reverse course toward the Philippines. His bitterness over being forced into such a decision was compounded by two things — first, he knew that his fast battleships would be too late to help Kincaid, and that they were being denied the chance of destroying Ozawa's remaining ships when that opportunity was so close; second, he must have been tormented by the thought that none of this need have happened if he had left a few of his vast array of capital ships to guard the San Bernadino Strait.

So the Battle of Leyte Gulf came to a close, with Halsey, the victor, angry and disappointed, and Ozawa, the loser, regretting his own success in luring the American carriers away from his battleships. The last desperate throw of the Imperial Navy included a brief tactical victory, but it led to final strategic defeat. In the course of widely separated battles, the Americans lost a light carrier, an escort carrier and three destroyers while sinking four carriers, one superbattleship, two battleships, ten cruisers and nine destroyers. About 1,500 Americans had died. But the Japanese lost over 10,000, including most of their remaining experienced naval aviators. The Imperial Navy could no longer exert any significant influence on the conduct of the war.

The Philippines

On land, however, the Japanese were still capable of offering a serious threat. At the time of the Leyte Gulf landings, there were some 450 Japanese combat aircraft on the island of Luzon, and reinforcements were being rushed forward from Formosa and Japan. For the first few days after the U.S. troops were ashore, the beachhead was anything but secure. U.S. naval aircraft were there to provide air cover, but a horrifying new development made them understandably anxious about the protection of their own ships. Pilots from specially formed Kamikaze units had begun to sacrifice themselves, deliberately aiming to crash their bomb-laden aircraft into U.S. ships. In their initial operations, they had already sunk one escort carrier and damaged several more, seriously reducing the U.S. Navy's capacity to provide the promised air cover over the troops. Aware of the problem, engineers opened a 2,800-foot airstrip at Tacloban by October 27. Thirty-four P-38s of the 49th Fighter Group flew in that day and were immediately in action.

A Kawanishi H8K Emily being shot down.

Other units came in as the days went by, but until well into December 1944, when more air strips became usable, the situation around Leyte Gulf had the USAAF men gritting their teeth. Japanese air raids on Tacloban were frequent, and they often caught U.S. aircraft on the ground. Losses to strafing attacks were distressingly high and requests for replacements commonplace. Combat also took its toll and, for a while, FEAF's front-line strength declined as losses from all causes exceeded replacements. In the three months from September 1, P-38 holdings fell from 497 to 398; P-47s began with 429 in September, but there were only 257 (plus 95 P-51s) by the end of the year.

The other side of the coin was that the Japanese were much worse off. Loss rates in aerial combat invariably favored the USAAF, and FEAF fighters often wreaked havoc at enemy air bases. On November 1, for example, forty-two P-38s of the Eighth Fighter Group swept over three airfields, shooting down seven enemy fighters in the air and destroying seventy-five more on the ground for the loss of three of their own. This was a period in which many Pacific fighter pilots added dramatically to their scores, with P-38 pilots leading the pack. Before the end of October, the 49th Fighter Group claimed its 500th aerial victory, and by Christmas their leading ace, Richard Bong, raised his personal total to forty. (Major Richard Bong was presented with the Medal of Honor by General MacArthur at Tacloban on December 12, 1944. After his fortieth victory, he was retired from combat and returned to the U.S. Bong was killed only eight months later while testing the new P-80 jet fighter in California.) Major Tommy McGuire of the 475th Fighter Group, who claimed thirty-eight before crashing during low-level combat over the Philippines, scored multiple victories on a single mission eleven times, and he was by no means unique. Robert Aschenbrenner, John Dunaway, William Dunham, and Gerald R. Johnson were among those who shot down four enemy aircraft in one sortie. (Major Gerald R. Johnson was credited with twenty-two victories and survived the war. Shortly afterward, on October 7, 1945, he was in a B-17 on his way to Japan when it was damaged in a violent storm. He gave up his parachute to a passenger and was lost with the aircraft.) Even more remarkable was the achievement of Captain William Shomo and Lieutenant Paul Lipscomb of the 82nd Reconnaissance Squadron. Flying F-6s (P-51s) as a pair on January 11, 1945, they attacked a formation of twelve fighters escorting a Betty bomber. Neither had been in combat before, but when the fight was over Shomo had shot down the Betty and six fighters, and

Lipscomb had added three more. (Shomo was awarded the Medal of Honor and Lipscomb the Distinguished Service Cross.)

With FEAF units established on Leyte, MacArthur's next move, to the island of Mindoro in December1944, followed the reassuring pattern of the New Guinea campaign, with the ground forces fighting under the umbrella of their own air forces. Even so, since the Japanese still had ships and aircraft operating in the area, they were occasionally able to make things difficult. On December 26, the U.S. beachhead on Mindoro would have been seriously jeopardized but for the determination of the 310th Wing squadrons, which had just arrived on rudimentary strips nearby. As night fell, a Japanese naval unit comprising two cruisers and six destroyers appeared offshore with the intention of sinking the Allied transports and shelling the beachhead area. Every aircraft on strength was hurled into a low-level assault on the ships — thirteen B-25s, forty-four P-38s, twenty-eight P-47s, and twenty P-40s. Attacks in the darkness were necessarily uncoordinated, and in the glaring confusion of gunfire and bomb-bursts, pilots flashed navigation lights in the hope of avoiding collisions. By the morning, the badly mauled Japanese force was withdrawing, minus one destroyer, having sunk one transport but failed to disrupt the landing operations. A victory had been won and the troops protected, but at considerable cost to the airmen. Lost during the action were three B-25s, seven P-38s, ten P-47s, and six P-40s. A grateful Brigadier General Dunckel, commander of the task force, wrote: "The action of our air units on that night will stand forever as one of the most gallant deeds to be established in the traditions of American fighting men."

Mindoro was a staging post for the later invasion of the main island of Luzon. The landing was the largest American amphibious operation of the war, with 175,000 men covering a beachhead 20 miles wide. Aircraft of the fleet's escort carriers did their best to counter the threat from Kamikazes, but even so, many got through, sinking an escort carrier, a destroyer and ten other vessels, and damaging sixty-seven more. The Kamikaze onslaught eased off only when the Japanese ran out of resources. Their own self-destructive methods, together with a combined USN and USAAF campaign against airfields on Luzon, reduced Japanese air power in the Philippines to impotence.

MacArthur's troops went ashore in Lingayen Gulf on January 9, 1945, with the reassuring presence of Kenney's fighters overhead. Although the struggle for Luzon proved a long and bloody one, U.S. soldiers were never again unduly bothered by Japanese aircraft. FEAF was able to concentrate on providing the ground forces with the support they needed to win the land battle. The campaign was characterized by overwhelming U.S. air power. B-24s hammered strongpoints; B-25s, A-20s, P-38s, P-40s, P-47s and P-51s strafed, rocketed, bombed and napalmed Japanese troops; L-5s marked targets; P-61s harassed by night; C-47s kept forward units supplied and dropped paratroops to speed the ground offensive. It was a virtuoso performance, later singled out for comment by the Joint Chiefs of Staff: "Of the many Pacific tactical air operations, we think the most striking example of the effective use of tactical air power…to achieve decisive results at a minimum cost in lives and material was the work of the Far East Air Forces in the Lingayen Gulf – Central Luzon campaign."

The embers of Japanese resistance smoldered on in the Philippines until the end of the war, and many of MacArthur's troops were kept occupied in operations that, in terms of the strategic aim of defeating Japan, were not strictly necessary. Having bypassed many enemies and left them isolated, U.S. and Australian troops now found themselves turning aside to engage in bitter battles to crush Japanese dug in on Borneo and the outer islands of the Philippines. Savage though many of these were, they were sideshows. The eyes of the Pacific theater's commanders now turned to the north, where the curtain-raisers to the main event were being prepared, with strategic air power moving toward center stage.

> "Oh, Hedy Lamarr is a beautiful gal,
> and Madeleine Carroll is too,
> But you'll find if you query, a different
> theory amongst any bomber crew
> For the loveliest thing of which one could
> sing (this side of the pearly gates)
> Is no blonde or brunette of the
> Hollywood set — but an escort of P-38s."
>
> FREDERIC ARNOLD, KOHN'S WAR,
> FIRST VERSE FROM "ODE TO THE P-38."

CHAPTER 11

War on the Asian Mainland

FOR REASONS BOTH GEOGRAPHICAL and political, the China-Burma-India theater of the war was not given the same priority by the Allies as Europe and the Pacific. It was the most difficult region to reach and supply, and Allied leaders did not always feel entirely comfortable in dealing with the Chiang Kai-shek regime. For the United States, the idea of being involved in a struggle that seemed likely to return a number of colonial territories to their former European rulers was not appealing. Nevertheless, there was general agreement on the importance of keeping China in the war, and of preventing the Japanese from pursuing their expansionist ambitions into India.

The fall of Burma, and particularly the loss of the northern base of Myitkyina in May 1942, effectively cut China off from the Western Allies. The only way of supplying the Chinese was by air from bases in India, with transport aircraft flying across the Himalayas to Kunming. With Myitkyina in enemy hands, this aerial supply route was forced further north over (and between) much higher mountains, and heavily laden aircraft were often wallowing along at heights up to 18,000 feet. The contrast between the steamy heat of the Indian plains and the freezing temperatures at altitude was hard on both men and machines. For much of the year, crews faced violent storms, heavy rain, and the threat of ice along the route, sometimes flying blind for hours in aircraft fitted with the most basic of instrument panels and radio aids. Icing or loss of power spelled disaster, and even a successful crossing could precede a perilous arrival if, as was frequently the case during the monsoon, the destination airfield was covered with water. Flying "the Hump," as it was known, was recognized as being among the most hazardous of occupations for a military airman.

To begin with, the airlift for the Chinese was handled by a few transport aircraft organized into what was known as the Assam-Burma-China Ferry Command, the last stage in the longest supply chain in the world. It started in Miami and traveled via the Atlantic, North Africa, and the Middle East to Karachi and Assam. By the end of 1942, the responsibility for controlling the increasing numbers of aircraft crossing "the Hump" had passed to Air Transport Command. This was in recognition of the dominant role of air supply in a theater of operations that lacked all but the most basic systems of communication yet exceeded the size of the United States by a considerable margin.

OPPOSITE PAGE
Silver Wings, Douglas C-47, Over the Hump, *by R.G. Smith, from the United States Air Force Art Collection. A C-47 flying supplies to the Chinese over the dangerous "Hump" route between Burma and China during WWII.*

Don Lopez, Deputy Director of the Smithsonian's National Air & Space Museum, photographed in front of the Spirit of St. Louis *in 2002. In October 1943, a the age of nineteen, he was assigned to the 75th Fighter Squadron, 23rd Fighter Group, in Hengyang, China, flying P-40s. He scored a victory in his first air combat, surviving a midair collision with a Japanese Zero after achieving strikes on the enemy aircraft during a head-on attack. He completed his tour in 1945 as Squadron Operations Officer, with five aerial victories.*

Meanwhile, Major General Lewis Brereton had been ordered to India in March 1942 to establish the Tenth Air Force. It was the latest stage in Brereton's westward progress. He had spent the war so far retreating through the Philippines and the Dutch East Indies in front of the victorious Japanese and he must have felt a little discouraged at the scale of the problems he faced in his new command. The Tenth was intended to supply the Chinese (until ATC assumed responsibility at the end of 1942), defend the "Hump" route and its airfields, and help the British fight the Japanese in Burma. To tackle this monumental task, he had an air force only on paper. The combat aircraft available were a few aging B-17s and P-40s, and

there seemed little prospect of getting more in the near future. Brereton wrestled with the problem until June, when he was told to pack his bags again and move on to Egypt, this time to take command of U.S. air forces in the Middle East and help the British against the Germans. He duly left, taking his B-17s with him. The Tenth reverted to being an air force without teeth.

The China Air Task Force

A few teeth were inherited by the Tenth Air Force in July 1942 when Chennault's American Volunteer Group was transformed into a regular element of the USAAF. However, the ex-"Flying Tigers" added to the bite of the

Tenth in name only. Although on its strength, they remained in effect independent, forming the core of a new organization called the China Air Task Force (CATF). Commander of the CATF was the AVG's Brigadier General Chennault, recalled to duty with the USAAF. A few of his pilots elected to join him in the move, and they brought their battered P-40s and the benefit of their combat experience to the newly arrived 23rd Fighter Group. Seven B-25s of the 7th Bomber Group gave the CATF a little striking power.

The CATF was never very big, but the challenges and hardships it faced must have been fertile ground for developing remarkable characters, because it seems to have had more than its share. The 23rd Fighter Group was commanded by Colonel Bob Scott, later author of the book *God Is My Co-pilot*. Two of the squadrons were commanded by aces from the AVG, "Tex" Hill and Ed Rector. In 1943, "Tex" Hill, then commander of the 23rd Fighter Group, led one of the most successful raids of the war in China, striking Shinchiku airfield on Formosa with a force of fourteen B-25s, eight P-38s and eight P-51s, and destroying over forty Japanese aircraft without loss. Later members of the 23rd Fighter Group included Don Lopez (later the long-serving Deputy Director of the National Air & Space Museum in Washington, D.C.), who gained his first aerial victory over a Zero by surviving a head-on attack driven through to collision, and John Alison, who decided to experiment with night interceptions in his P-40 and succeeded in destroying two bombers and damaging another at his first attempt. Badly shot up and with the P-40 on fire, Alison lived through a night ditching in a river and swam ashore.

General "Hap" Arnold (left) visited China in 1943 and met Claire Chennault. He judged Chennault to be a formidable fighting man but a poor administrator. He also believed that the prickly leader of the Flying Tigers too often put the interests of Chiang Kai-Shek's China above those of the United States.

Chennault lost no opportunity to say that air power was the only practical way to fight the Japanese in China. This put him at odds with the senior U.S. officer in the theater, Lieutenant General "Vinegar Joe" Stilwell, an infantryman, who insisted that the Allied cause would profit by concentrating on a ground offensive into Burma. As the Allied Chiefs preferred to continue with both options, resources were split between the two, and neither was given what he considered adequate for the tasks at hand. However, Chennault's persistence, and his use of political channels via Chiang Kai-shek, led to the formation of the 14th Air Force from the elements of the CATF, at the direction of President Roosevelt and against the advice of Generals Marshall and Arnold. In the process, Chennault advanced to Major General.

Reorganization and Complexity

Following the constitution of the Fourteenth Air Force in March 1943, the fortunes of American airmen in China gradually began to improve. Combat units, equipment and supplies began to flow more generously across the "Hump." Even so, apart from the Eleventh in Alaska, the Fourteenth remained the smallest of the U.S. numbered air forces throughout the war, reaching a maximum strength of a little over 700 combat aircraft early in 1945. As the Fourteenth grew in size, it acquired P-38s, P-51s, B-24s and more and newer B-25s. Chennault established a series of bases in southern China and adopted an aggressive operational policy. The Fourteenth struck at Japanese ports and bases in China and Indo-China, harassed shipping along the Asian coast, mined harbors, attacked enemy airfields, supported Chinese troops, interdicted Japanese supply lines, and fought the Japanese Air Force for air superiority over

China. Badly hurt by these efforts and fearing further expansion of U.S. air power, the Japanese launched a massive assault into southern China in 1944 to deny the Fourteenth its airfields and open up internal communications between Southeast Asia and Japan. By the end of the year, they had rolled over the demoralized Chinese armies facing them and had taken thirteen of the U.S. bases, forcing the Fourteenth back toward Kunming and limiting its operations in East China. Japanese troops suffered badly under air attack during the offensive, but never enough to stall their advance.

Seriously concerned, Chiang Kai-shek appealed for help to Stilwell, who was heavily occupied with his Burma campaign. The General was reluctant to leave Burma, and his intransigence led to his being recalled to Washington. His replacement as Commanding General, U.S. Forces China Theater, was Lieutenant General Albert Wedemeyer. He took

over at the end of October 1943, and agreed to return Chinese troops from Burma in preparation for a counteroffensive in the spring of 1945. From May 1945, the reorganized Chinese Army, closely supported by American tactical aircraft, first checked the Japanese and then drove them back. Napalm and the concentrated fire of .5-inch-caliber machine guns were the most effective methods of reducing Japanese strongpoints. By the end of July, central China and the coast were almost completely free of Japanese forces, and thought was being given to continuing the offensive to the north. Within days, however, the need disappeared with the surrender of Japan. As the fighting in China ground to a halt, the men of the Fourteenth were left with the feeling that they had fought their war on the fringes. Hard as they had struggled to overcome the enemy, the elements, their living conditions, the convoluted command chain, and the low priorities accorded them by their friends and allies, it was clear that they had not occupied center stage. The core of the Allied

British Major General Orde Wingate, eccentric leader of the "Chindits" in Burma, with Phil Cochran (right) and John Alison of the Air Commandos. On March 5, 1944, Alison led the glider force carrying the "Chindits" into Japanese-held territory.

The "Chindit" force landed at Broadway, a clearing 150 miles behind Japanese lines in Burma. Waco CG-4 gliders were used, most of which were destroyed or severely damaged in the operation. This one came to rest reasonably intact.

victory over the Japanese was in the Pacific. They gained their satisfaction from the knowledge of a job well done, an achievement recognized in an accolade from an enemy soldier, General Takahashi, who said that, but for the Fourteenth Air Force, "we could have gone anywhere we wished."

Chennault was not there to join in the victory celebrations with his airmen. General Arnold's patience with his unconventional subordinate had come to an end. In June 1945, Arnold wrote to General Wedemeyer, saying: "General Chennault has been in China for a long period of time fighting a defensive air war with minimum resources. The meagerness of supplies and the resulting guerilla type of warfare must change to a modern type of striking, offensive air power. I firmly believe that the quickest and most effective way to change air warfare in your Theater, employing modern offensive thought, tactics and techniques, is to change commanders. I would appreciate your concurrence in General Chennault's early withdrawal from the China Theater."

At the same time, Arnold offered a plan for reorganizing the air forces in China. Chennault entered a vigorous protest against the whole idea, but the die was cast and he

grudgingly put forward his request for retirement on July 6.

While Chennault had been creating his own air force and fighting his own kind of war, the Tenth Air Force had been wrestling with equally challenging problems. Shortly after the CATF was formed as an element of the Tenth to give Chennault his freedom of action, Brigadier General Clayton Bissell, the Tenth's new commander, created a similar organization for the India-Burma region. The India Air Task Force was activated on October 3, 1942, and immediately had to face the fact that not one of its nine allocated squadrons was capable of combat operations. Several either had no aircraft or were not yet even in the theater. Matters improved very slowly, and it was not only a matter of supply. Throughout their time in the CBI, USAAF commands and units operated under a tangled web of national and service rivalries as well as suffering the handicap of being at the bottom of a long priority list. Chains of command were duplicated and tasks complicated to a degree unknown in other theaters. In 1943, it was decided by Generals Marshall and Arnold that a senior airman should be appointed to the CBI to straighten things out in the theater generally. Almost

The Curtiss Commando is best known for transporting desperately needed supplies to troops in China from bases in India and Burma. It carried all kinds of cargo — light artillery, fuel, ammunition, parts of aircraft and, occasionally, livestock. The Marines used the Commando in the Pacific island-hopping campaigns, flying supplies in and wounded soldiers out of numerous island landing strips. The Commando on display at the USAF Museum is painted as a C-46D that flew "the Hump" in 1944.

immediately, objections from Chiang Kai-shek led to the concession that there would be no interference in his direct relations with Chennault, and it had to be accepted that the new commander would have only advisory responsibility toward the Fourteenth Air Force.

In August 1943, Major General George Stratemeyer assumed command of all USAAF units in the India/Burma Sector (IBS) of the CBI. At the time, this amounted to little more than the Tenth Air Force, then commanded by Brigadier General Howard Davidson. Recognizing the limitations of the position and the complexity of the overlapping organizational arrangements and regional politics, Arnold warned Stratemeyer: "This new command setup

and your relationships…are somewhat complicated and will have to be worked out to a great extent among yourselves…. If a true spirit of cooperation is engendered throughout this command, it will work. If the reverse is true, it is doomed to failure." (The limitations of his position having been revealed to him, Stratemeyer also discovered that no less than seven lines of command had found their way to his chair from above — Roosevelt, Marshall, Arnold, Stilwell, Chiang Kai-shek, Mountbatten (Supreme Commander, Southeast Asia), and Peirse (Air Commander, Southeast Asia) were all entitled to give him orders.)

As 1943 drew to a close, there were more organizational changes. To rationalize the operations of USAAF and RAF units in the IBS, they were integrated under a new headquarters called Eastern Air Command, with Stratemeyer as the commander. All Allied air force combat units in the IBS having been joined together, he separated them again, this time functionally under strategic, tactical, troop carrier, and reconnaissance headings. Davidson of the Tenth drew the strategic force, while the tactical aircraft, as the Third Tactical Air Force, went to his RAF opposite number, Air Marshal Baldwin. Addressing his new command, Stratemeyer emphasized the need for them to "merge into one unified force in thought and deed — a force neither British nor American, with the faults of neither and the virtues of both."

The second half of 1943 had seen a marked increase in the number of combat units available to the Allies in the IBS. The American contribution in 1943 had risen to include five complete groups — 80th Fighter Group, 311th Fighter/Bomber Group, 7th Bomber Group (Heavy), 341st Bomber Group (Medium), 5306th Photographic Reconnaissance Group — and four troop-carrier squadrons, and more groups arrived in 1944. As Allied air power grew, so did the determination to use it to wrest the initiative from the enemy. Bombers struck at transportation targets, military airfields, ports and supply dumps, and fighters strafed Japanese forward airfields and began to inflict serious losses in the air. The struggle in the air shifted in the Allies favor in early 1944, and by the spring Allied air superiority was an accomplished fact.

> "We have the enemy surrounded. We are dug in and have overwhelming numbers. But enemy airpower is mauling us badly. We will have to withdraw."
>
> JAPANESE INFANTRY COMMANDER'S SITUATION REPORT TO HEADQUARTERS, BURMA, WWII

riers from as far away as the European theater, and a total of more than 20,000 tons was delivered, plus the better part of two divisions of infantry. By June the British Army was strong enough to go over to the offensive. With the constant support of EAC tactical aircraft, the British Fourteenth Army under General Sir William Slim broke out and inflicted a decisive defeat on the enemy, driving them into a retreat that degenerated into a rout. Before the assault, Slim announced that his whole plan of battle was based on Allied air support, and Japanese radio broadcasts later openly attributed their difficulties in Burma to Allied air supremacy and to the work of the troop carrier squadrons.

At almost the same time that the Japanese struck at Imphal, the Allies launched a very different offensive of their own. In early 1943, Brigadier Orde Wingate, a British officer who specialized in unconventional operations, had led a force of 3,000 men into the jungles behind Japanese lines, causing confusion and disrupting communications for four months. The experiment was now repeated, but on a much larger scale and this time supported by aircraft. The proposal for Wingate's Long Range Penetration Group (the "Chindits") was accepted by the Allied leaders at the Quebec conference in August 1943, and General Arnold had agreed that the USAAF would provide the necessary air power. Colonels Philip Cochran and John Alison were given a free hand to form a special air task force, and they put together the First Air Commandos to operate under the control of General Stratemeyer's EAC.

Ground Offensives

Without Allied air superiority, two major campaigns by ground forces in March 1944 would probably have had very different conclusions. On March 10, a Japanese offensive against the British Army near Imphal and Kohima on the Indian-Burmese border threatened to overwhelm the defenders. Large numbers of British and Indian troops were surrounded and were able to hold out only because reinforcements and essential supplies were flown in daily for weeks. The air transport force was augmented by troop car-

The Commandos

The First Air Commando Force was tailored for the task with a remarkably varied collection of aircraft — thirteen C-47s, twelve C-46s, 150 CG-4 gliders, seventy-five TG-4 gliders, a hundred L1/L5s, six YR-4 helicopters, thirty P-51As, and twelve B-25Hs. The operation began on the evening of March 5, 1944, when the transports and gliders took off to deliver soldiers to a large jungle clearing, code-named Broadway, over 100 miles deep into Japanese-held territory. Each transport had to act as tug for two gliders,

Two potent symbols of the Fourteenth Air Force in China. A C-46, mainstay of the aerial supply line over "the Hump," lands near a P-40 of the 23rd Fighter Group, the unit that inherited the mantle of the AVG's Flying Tigers.

and that led to early problems. The gliders were overloaded and the C-47 tugs struggled up to 10,000 feet to haul them over the rugged Naga Hills. Turbulent conditions compounded the difficulties, and several gliders parted from their tugs, either having broken their tow ropes or been cast adrift by alarmed C-47 pilots. Less than half of the sixty-seven gliders dispatched arrived at Broadway, and most of those crashed in the process of making a landing after dark on a very rough surface. Of the men who got there, thirty-one were killed and thirty injured. Nevertheless, 539 men, three mules, and nearly 66,000 pounds of stores arrived safely. Among them was John Alison, who had set aside his fighter background to become a glider pilot for the operation. His cargo included the flying control equipment he needed for handling later flights and a bulldozer for leveling an airstrip. L-5s came in the next morning to collect casualties, and by the following night the strip was cleared; a procession of C-47s began

flying in with many more men and much more equipment. A second strip, named Chowringhee, was opened a few miles away, and by March 11, the Air Commandos had delivered over 9,000 men, nearly 1,400 mules, and almost 260 tons of stores to set Wingate's offensive in motion.

By any standards, it had been an extraordinary achievement, but one that Wingate did not live to see. On March 25, he was killed in the crash of a B-25 flying from Broadway back to Imphal. For the next few weeks, his "Chindits" roamed the jungle and, supplied by air, harassed and confused the Japanese, cutting supply lines to their forward units. Cochran's P-51s and B-25s operated on call for close-support missions and raided Japanese forward airfields, taking a heavy toll of enemy aircraft on the ground. The B-25Hs were impressive, firing their 75 mm cannon and dropping parafrag bombs on Japanese soldiers in close contact with British troops. A British patrol found a message written by a

Japanese officer that recorded his despair over the relentless attentions of the Air Commandos. Unless something was done about the U.S. aircraft, he said, his operation was doomed. Flesh and blood, he insisted, could not stand up to them.

The Soldiers' Victory

Meanwhile, Stilwell drove his "New China Army" down the Hukawng Valley into northern Burma and a unit of U.S. special forces known as "Merrill's Marauders" accomplished an astonishing forced march through jungles and over mountains to take the airfield at Myitkyina. For their success, both advances were heavily dependent on air supply, a luxury not available to their often starving and poorly equipped enemies. By mid-1944, the Japanese armies in Burma were reeling back on all fronts. Monsoon weather and the stubborn endurance

of the Japanese soldier prolonged the war in Burma into 1945, but the final result was never again in doubt. In the end, the campaign was a triumph for the foot soldiers, who overcame appalling hardships to defeat their enemy. However, it was clear that their victories had been built on air power, notably on the achievements of the air transport force. Nowhere else had C-47s and C-46s so obviously turned the tide of battle. Allied commanders began to realize that even large forces, isolated by facts of geography or cut off by the enemy, could survive if supplied by air. When counter-air operations denied the enemy the same facility, victory was only a matter of time. An entry in a Japanese officer's diary put it most succinctly: "Enemy aircraft are over continuously in all weather. We can do nothing but look at them. If we only had air power! Even one or two planes would be something. Superiority in the air is the decisive factor in victory."

A B-25H of the Air Commandos after attacking Wunto, Burma, on March 18, 1944.

CHAPTER 12

Kamikaze and Firestorm

IN THE PACIFIC, THE Japanese commanders quite rightly regarded the U.S. carriers as being at the root of their problems. The American forces could depend on having air superiority wherever they went, and any attempts at counteroffensive moves by the Japanese were hammered unmercifully and without pause by U.S. aircraft. It had been found out the hard way that conventional air attacks against the U.S. carriers were no longer a reasonable proposition. The air umbrella over the U.S. fleet was awesome and almost impossible to penetrate with the standard tactics of dive-bombers or torpedo aircraft.

The Divine Wind

It was therefore almost inevitable that the Japanese should be driven to take what Western people generally regard as extreme measures. Japanese servicemen believed that there could be no greater honor than to die for their Emperor. It was evident from the way they fought that this was true. They were unflinching in the face of death; indeed, they often seemed to seek the opportunity of dying in battle. A warrior's death assured them of their place of honor in the life hereafter. What more natural, then, for them to welcome the chance to offer their lives in exchange for striking a mighty blow at their country's enemy. The proposal for Japanese pilots to do just that was made by Admiral Ohnishi soon after his arrival in the Philippines on October 17, 1944, to take over the First Air Fleet. Others had made similar proposals earlier in the war, but Ohnishi would see it to fruition. His command had fewer than 100 operational aircraft at that time, and he knew that, even with reinforcements, it could not be expected to stop the American invasion of the Philippines — unless most of the attacks mounted against the enemy got through to the U.S. carriers, and every single attack was made to count.

Ohnishi visited the 201st Air Group in Luzon and told the group commander that there was only one way that the available strength could be fully used — Zero fighters armed with 250-kilogram bombs should be sent to crash into the enemy carriers. The commander agreed with the admiral. In the circumstances, that is hardly surprising. Not only was he driven by the Japanese code of honor; he knew that the chance of his pilots coming back alive from any mission against the U.S. fleet was very slim. Since death was highly probable, why not make sure that each man died effectively, at great cost to the enemy?

OPPOSITE PAGE
Looking up at the bombardier's position of the Boeing B-29 Bockscar *at the USAF Museum. Dressed in authentic clothing, a 21st-century reenactor adopts the pose of* Bockscar's *bombardier, Kermit K. Beahan, during the approach to Nagasaki on August 9, 1945.*

In every culture, individuals who sacrifice their lives for their companions or their country are considered the bravest of the brave and are highly respected. Nevertheless, most non-Japanese people in WWII recoiled from the idea of forming units with the intention of having every member committed to an act of suicide. The difference is that even death-defying acts of courage usually carry a slim possibility of survival. Posthumous winners of the Victoria Cross or the Medal of Honor probably did not begin their action certain that they would die. The Japanese proposal was for premeditated and unavoidable death. The units selected for this honor were to be known as the Special Attack Force, and the name chosen for them reflected the desperation of Japan's situation.

In the year 1281, Kublai Khan approached the islands of Japan with an armada just as irresistible as that of the United States in 1944. As the great Mongol army stood ready for invasion, a typhoon swept over their fleet and destroyed it as an effective force. The Japanese people considered this to be a heavenly intervention, and they credited their survival to the Kamikaze — the Divine Wind. Faced once more with an irresistible military machine, the Japanese turned to a few dedicated young airmen for their salvation, and appointed them elements of the new Kamikaze, which would once more sweep away the threatening fleet.

On being briefed by their commander, the pilots of the 201st Air Group reacted to Admiral Ohnishi's proposal for suicide attacks with enthusiasm. According to Japanese historians, there was a roar of approval for the idea and every man stepped forward without hesitation. The rush to volunteer was so great the commander had to tell the most insistent pilots not to be selfish — everyone wanted to go.

A Nakajima B5N Kate breaks up and trails fire after being hit by gunners on the USS Yorktown *near Kwajalein in the Marshall Islands on December 3, 1943.*

Admiral Ohnishi issued an order bringing his ideas into effect on October 20, 1944. The 201st Air Group was to organize a Special Attack Force to destroy the U.S. carriers to the east of the Philippines. Twenty-six aircraft were allocated, half as Kamikazes and half as escorts. The force was to be commanded by Lieutenant Seki and divided into four sections with names taken from a celebrated poem that compared the Japanese spirit to cherry blossoms radiant in the sun: Shikishima, a poetic name for Japan; Yamato, an ancient name for Japan; Asahi, the morning sun; and Yamazakura, mountain cherry blossoms.

Ohnishi's speech to the pilots before their first mission is reputed to have included the following: "Japan is in grave danger. The salvation of our country can only come from spirited young men like you. On behalf of your hundred million countrymen, I ask of you this sacrifice, and pray for your success. You are already Gods, without earthly desires, but one thing you will want to be assured of is that your last flight is not in vain. Regrettably, we will not be able to tell you the results. But you can be certain I will watch your efforts to the end and report your deeds to the Emperor. I ask you all to do your best."

We are told that the pilots heard these words with composure and that they looked forward to their missions with eagerness. One determined young man was Lieutenant Kanno. He knew that it was the custom for servicemen killed in action to be given a posthumous promotion, so he had the bag in which he carried his belongings clearly marked: "Personal effects of the late Lieutenant Commander Kanno."

Lieutenant Seki's Shikishima unit was alerted for its first mission on October 21. They wrote their letters home and cut off locks of their hair as mementos for their families. Then they gathered for a farewell toast in water and heard the words of an ancient song before they set off to die. The sentiment of the song leaves no doubt about the Japanese warrior's code:

> If I go away to sea, I shall return a corpse awash;
> If duty calls me to the mountain, a verdant
>   sward will be my pall;
> Thus, for the sake of the Emperor, I will not die
>   in peace at home.

The Kamikazes did not get off to a good start. They were launched several times only to be defeated by the weather or by poor intelligence on the whereabouts of the U.S. ships. Having said their farewells, they had to fly back to base, full of abject apologies for their failure. They were also harassed by American strafing attacks on their airfields. Many of their carefully prepared Kamikaze aircraft were caught on the ground and destroyed, much to the distress of the young volunteers, who could see their chances of dying for the Emperor diminishing as each day went by. As it was rather quaintly put by Japanese commentators, some of them were doomed to miss their Kamikaze opportunity.

Their morale was not improved by the fact that the Japanese warships hurrying to intervene in the Leyte Gulf invasion were being terribly mauled by aircraft from the U.S. carriers. When the incredible news came that the "unsinkable" superbattleship *Musashi* had been sunk by relentless air attack, the Japanese pilots were appalled. They held themselves responsible for the disaster because they had been tasked to destroy the enemy carriers and so remove the threat to the Japanese fleet.

On October 25, Lieutenant Seki and his unit took off on their fifth attempt to find the U.S. ships, and this time they were successful. They came across the force of little escort carriers and destroyers that had just performed the impossible in turning Admiral Kurita's battleships away from the U.S. transports in Leyte Gulf. The big battle over, the Americans were just indulging their euphoria when Japanese aircraft were seen overhead. Lieutenant Seki and his team caught the American ships by surprise. The aircraft from the little "jeep" carriers were recovering from their efforts against the Japanese big ships, and they were certainly not prepared for attacks in which the enemy aircraft was itself the weapon. All five of Seki's Kamikazes struck home. The escort carriers *Kalinin Bay*, *Kitkun Bay* and *White Plains* were damaged, and the *St. Lo* was sunk. Further south, Kamikazes from another unit damaged the *Santee* and the *Suwannee*.

The pilots of the escorting Zeros gave glowing reports of the action when they got back. At that time, the Japanese had not appreciated that the U.S. Navy had several sizes of aircraft carrier. They therefore claimed that a number of full-size fleet carriers had been hit, and that one of them had been sunk. The next day saw more success for the Kamikazes. *Kitkun Bay* and *Suwannee* were hit and damaged again. The smoke of battle led to Japanese claims of having sunk another fleet carrier and damaged a second. The truth was bad enough from an American point of view — one escort carrier sunk and five more damaged by suicides in two days. As far as the Japanese were concerned, the Kamikaze idea had been fully justified. They believed that they had destroyed two fleet carriers and put several others out of action for the cost of eight aircraft and their pilots. A surge of hope went through the Japanese High Command. With results like that, they could stop the Americans after all. There was just a hint that the Emperor was not so sure about the tactic.

Ohnishi's message to the Kamikaze units after Lieutenant Seki's attack included remarks about the Emperor's reaction: "When told of the special attack, His Majesty said, 'Was it necessary to go to this extreme? They certainly did a magnificent job.' His Majesty's words suggest that he is greatly concerned. We must redouble our efforts to relieve His Majesty of this concern. I have pledged our every effort toward that end."

> *"It is a great honour for me, aged eighteen, to die as a suicide attack pilot. I know that my spirit will live for ever as I am about to do my duty for my country. I shall die smiling…."*
>
> TOSHIROU OHMURA IN A LETTER TO HIS PARENTS BEFORE DYING IN AN ATTACK ON THE BRITISH FLEET, JULY 26, 1945

USS Belleau Wood *(CVL-24) burning after being hit by a Kamikaze while operating off the Philippines on October 30, 1944. The ship's crew fight the fires and drag undamaged TBMs of VT-21 away from the flames. Smoke from the USS* Franklin *(CV-13), also hit during this Kamikaze attack, can be seen in the distance.*

finally withdrew from the Philippines, the Kamikazes had sunk two escort carriers and damaged thirteen more, and had also damaged seven fleet carriers and two light carriers. Altogether, they sank sixteen ships and damaged eighty-seven. It cost them 378 aircraft and pilots.

Between Admiral Ohnishi's escape from the Philippines in January 1945 and the U.S. invasion of Okinawa in April, the conviction that only Kamikaze units could stop the Americans gained general acceptance among the Japanese. The three air fleets based in the home islands of Japan had some 1,800 aircraft available between them for operations against the Americans at Okinawa. Almost 600 of them were set aside for suicide attacks. The Japanese wished there were more, but there were other problems besides the limited number of aircraft. They were running out of pilots, and many of those they had were very young and inadequately trained. Some could barely fly the aircraft in which they were to die. But if the Japanese were disappointed with the scale of their efforts, the U.S. Navy at Okinawa viewed the Kamikazes as a very serious threat.

At about this time, the Kamikazes were joined by other units equipped with a weapon specially designed for suicide attack. This was a tiny wooden aircraft, rocket-propelled and consisting mostly of a two-ton warhead. It was carried under a twin-engined bomber and released within 20 miles of the target. Its Japanese name was Ohka (Cherry Blossom), but the Americans christened it the Baka (Foolish) bomb.

The suicide operations from the Japanese mainland were flown by both the army and the navy. To begin with, the Zero was the chosen aircraft, but in time the missions were flown by whatever was available — twin-engined bombers, dive-bombers, fighters or trainers. The major raids were named Kikusui (Floating Chrysanthemum) and there were ten between April 6 and June 22. The first Kikusui attack, begun on April 6 and continued into the next day, was a massive affair aimed at the U.S. Fifth Fleet

Whether the Emperor was concerned or not, there was now little opposition to adoption of the Kamikaze tactic as standard. In their first two days, the Kamikaze units appeared to have done more damage to the U.S. fleet than the combined efforts of the Japanese big ships and conventional aircraft. More units would be formed and bigger efforts made.

It may be that the U.S. Navy would have suffered rather more than it did in the following months if, as the Kamikaze effort multiplied, the Japanese had stuck to their original intention to concentrate on the carriers. Instead, the High Command allowed the already small resources of the Kamikazes to be dissipated by attacking other targets. In the Philippines, the army was desperate for air support, and much of the Kamikaze effort was directed against the transport vessels in Leyte Gulf. Even so, by the time the Japanese

off Okinawa. In all, 355 Kamikazes took part, plus an equal number of conventional aircraft. The targets were 1,500 American ships, among them forty aircraft carriers. For the first time, a British carrier task force was on hand. They had some 250 aircraft, while the U.S. ships had almost 1,000. The fleet was also defended by many thousands of antiaircraft guns.

The Japanese attacked in aircraft ranging from the newest fighters to old fabric-covered biplanes. The majority never got anywhere near their targets. The carrier fighters accounted for 288 and the guns got most of the others. Sheer weight of numbers, however, allowed more than twenty to get through. In a pattern that was to be maintained throughout the Kikusui campaign, the picket ships around the fleet bore the brunt of the successful attacks. Two destroyers were sunk and eleven others seriously damaged. The carrier *Hancock* and the battleship *Maryland* were also hit.

All this was remarkable enough, but it was made even more extraordinary by the extension of the Kamikaze principle to include ships. The Japanese fleet had been reduced to a shadow of its former self. However, the greatest battleship ever built was still afloat. The *Yamato*, escorted by a light cruiser and eight destroyers, steamed out of the

Inland Sea to add its 18-inch guns to the Kikusui attack. The *Yamato* had fuel sufficient only for the passage to Okinawa. If she survived that, the intention was to beach her and use her guns for bombardment. Admiral Ito, commanding the *Yamato* force, sent a message to his crews before they left: "The fate of the homeland rests on this operation. Our ships have been organized as a surface special attack force. [In other words, this is a suicide mission.] Every unit is expected to fight to the bitter end. Thereby the enemy will be annihilated and the eternal foundations of our motherland secured."

The great ship never reached Okinawa. She was met by hundreds of dive-bombers and torpedo planes and endured continuous air attack for over an hour. Hit by dozens of bombs and at least ten torpedoes, the *Yamato* finally rolled over and sank, taking almost 2,500 men with her, including Admiral Ito, who chose to go down with the ship. The cruiser and four of the destroyers escorted him to the bottom. The U.S. Navy lost ten aircraft and crews. The Japanese Navy lost over 3,500 men and had effectively ceased to exist.

As the Kikusui attacks continued, at intervals of about a week, the numbers of planes involved diminished from the 355 of the first to only forty-five for the tenth and last.

LEFT *USS* Bunker Hill *(CV-17), flagship of Task Force 58, pouring smoke from raging fires after being hit by two Kamikaze aircraft off Okinawa on 11 May 1945.* RIGHT *The scene on the flight deck of the carrier* Bunker Hill, *looking aft. Fire hoses lie across the deck and damage control teams fight the fires caused by two Kamikaze hits. Almost 400 crewmen were killed in the attack. Despite severe damage, the carrier was able to return to the United States for repairs.*

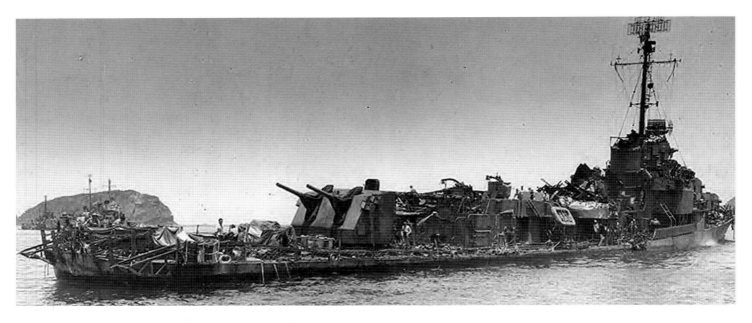

ABOVE *USS* Aaron Ward *(DM-34) in the Kerama Retto anchorage on May 5, 1945.* Aaron Ward, *a mine warfare ship, was wrecked when hit by several Japanese suicide planes off Okinawa two days before. Note the three-bladed aircraft propeller lodged just forward of the gun turret. The crew managed to keep the ship afloat, an effort that was recognized by the award of a Presidential Unit Citation. Following temporary repairs, the* Aaron Ward *was able to steam across the Pacific and through the Panama Canal, arriving in New York in August 1945.* LEFT *The 65,000-ton Japanese super-battleship* Musashi *surrounded by the explosions of bombs dropped by U.S. aircraft from the Task Force 38 carriers* Essex, Enterprise, Intrepid, Franklin, *and* Cabot. *In the Battle of the Sibuyan Sea on October 24, 1944, the* Musashi *was under continuous attack for nine hours. The battleship was struck by nineteen torpedoes and seventeen bombs before sinking. Of the* Musashi's *2,399 sailors, 1,023 were lost, including Rear Admiral Inoguchi.*

Nearly 1,500 Kamikazes took part in the Kikusui raids, and there were smaller attacks in between. It was a terrifying ordeal, particularly for the picketing destroyers. Before it was over, eleven were sunk and sixty-one seriously damaged. One destroyer, after enduring many attacks, put a sign up that read: "That way to the carriers!" Of all the little vessels, the mine warfare ship *Aaron Ward* suffered the greatest ordeal. During Kikusui 5, on May 3, the *Aaron Ward* was hit by Kamikazes eight times. When it was over, the ship was dead in the water, with her engine rooms flooded and her deck only inches above the water — but she was still afloat.

The Kamikazes were frightening weapons, but they never slowed the U.S. offensive and, given the resources available to the Japanese, they could not have saved them from defeat. From the launching of the first Kamikazes in the Philippines until the defeat of Japan, over 1,200 pilots gave their lives in suicide attacks. The claims made on their behalf of ships sunk and damaged are interesting. Their most important targets were the carriers. They claimed to have sunk seven and damaged forty-three. The true figures were three sunk (all small escort carriers) and thirty-six damaged. The claims for all classes of ships were eighty-one sunk and 195 damaged. U.S. records show that thirty-four were sunk and 288 damaged. This reveals the surprising fact that, although the Japanese thought they were sinking more than they were, they actually claimed a total of 276 hits, which is less than the true figure of 322.

Japan surrendered on August 15, 1945, and Admiral Ohnishi committed hara-kiri. Even then, it was not quite over. In a bizarre postscript to the Kamikaze story, Admiral Ugaki, of the Kikusui campaign, chose to ignore his Emperor's efforts to end the fighting. In an extraordinary broadcast to the Japanese people, the Emperor avoided any mention of defeat or surrender, but admitted "the war situation has developed not necessarily to Japan's advantage," and said that "We have resolved to pave the way for a grand peace for all the generations to come by enduring the unendurable." Ugaki reacted to this by ordering three aircraft prepared for a suicide mission that he elected to lead. In the event, eleven aircraft took off to find the U.S. fleet with Ugaki in the rear seat of the leading bomber. To be precise, he was sharing the rear seat, since the young observer refused to be displaced and insisted on sharing the admi-

ral's fate. Some time later, messages were received that said that the admiral would "crash into the conceited enemy in the true spirit of Bushido," and then that he was "plunging on the target." It was all very strange. No attacks on U.S. ships were detected. Ugaki and his aircraft just disappeared and no trace of them was ever found.

The Destruction of Japan

In the late 1930s, a few visionary air planners were already thinking of a strategic bomber that would be a generational improvement over the B-17 and the B-24. In November 1939, General Arnold formally proposed the development of such an aircraft, and in September 1942, two contenders took to the air. The Consolidated XB-32 was the first to fly, but design difficulties and an early crash prevented the B-32 from seeing combat until the closing days of the war, and then only in very small numbers. The other prototype was Boeing's XB-29, which had problems enough of its own, but was nevertheless the first step toward the production of the B-29 Superfortress, one of the war's most significant aircraft.

The only flyable Boeing B-29 in the world at the end of the 20th century was Fifi, *operated by the Confederate Air Force (since renamed the Commemorative Air Force).*

Boeing B-29s in tight formation for mutual protection during a daylight raid on Japan. General Curtis LeMay introduced attacks by night using incendiaries from much lower altitudes.

Urgency brought priority to the bomber's development, and that forced a compression of the program, with the result that the B-29 was ordered into production with more than its share of teething troubles. Before the XB-29 even flew, 1,664 aircraft had been ordered on the strength of blueprints and a wooden mockup. Pressurized crew compartments, new construction techniques, remotely controlled guns and, most critically, new radial engines of unprecedented power — all were rushed into front-line service harboring problems for aircrew and mechanics to overcome in the field.

In 1940, air force planners believed that VLR (Very Long Range) bombers would be primarily engaged in bombing Germany by 1944. Positive developments in Europe and the relatively poor situation of the Allies in the CBI brought about a shift in policy by late 1943. Japan became the more likely target for the B-29, situated as it was in a region of few bases and vast distances. As the date of the B-29's operational debut drew nearer, USAAF headquarters was besieged by requests from commanders worldwide who believed that the new bomber's capabilities would be best exploited in their theater. To avoid argument and recrimination, and to prevent B-29s being wasted on missions for which they were not designed, General Arnold decided to form a new air force specifically for the B-29, and to keep it under his own command. Accordingly, the Twentieth Air Force came into being on April 4, 1944.

The organization of the B-29 front line began somewhat earlier, in June 1943, with the formation of the 58th Bomb Wing at Salina, Kansas. In November, XX Bomber Command followed, with Brigadier General Kenneth Wolfe, the officer responsible for the B-29 production program, as its commander. Operational deployment had to wait as solutions were sought to training and logistical problems. The sheer size of a B-29 unit gave an indication of what had to be faced. A B-29 had a crew of eleven, and there were up to 180 aircraft in a wing. With a double crew allocation and full maintenance establishment, the total personnel in a wing reached 11,112, including 3,045 officers. When XX Bomber Command went to war, it moved with more than 20,000 officers and men. Accommodating and feeding them on the far side of the world was difficult enough, and the added challenge of operating and maintaining over a hundred very large and untried bombers from a deployment base produced a truly monumental task for a wing.

Matterhorn was the code name for the planned bombing offensive against Japan, which was to use B-29s based in India and operate through forward airfields in China. The first of the big bombers arrived at its base near Kharagpur, India, on April 2, 1944. There followed long weeks of preparing the Chinese airfields near Chengtu for opera-

tions. Fuel, armaments and spares had to be pre-positioned, and since transport aircraft were scarce, the crews of the 58th Bomb Wing (VH, for Very Heavy) found themselves doing their own airlift. On average, it took eight B-29 "freighter" flights into Chengtu to support one operational sortie. When all was ready, the first combat mission was flown on June 5 — but it did not go through China. The target was a railway repair shop in Bangkok.

The Bangkok mission was flown as a dress rehearsal for what was to follow. It was not a polished performance. Of the ninety-eight B-29s that set out at dawn, one crashed on takeoff, fourteen aborted, and several others failed to find the target. Cloud defeated attempts to fly any sort of formation and many aircraft made their way to Bangkok separately. One hour and forty minutes went by between the passage of the first and last of the seventy-seven crews claiming to have bombed the target. Forty-eight of those crews bombed through cloud by radar, and the accuracy was poor. The Japanese defense was feeble and there were no combat losses. On the return trip, however, mechanical

Bombs cascade from B-29 bomb bays during an attack on a Japanese target. A B-29 had the capacity to load up to 20,000 pounds of bombs internally.

failures took their toll before bad weather and fuel shortages combined to scatter B-29s over a wide area, two in the Bay of Bengal and more than forty at airfields other than their own. Five B-29s were lost and fifteen crewmen killed, a high cost for placing fewer than twenty bombs within the target area. Given the results, XX Bomber Command put on a brave face, saying that a great deal of experience had been gained from operating the B-29 under combat conditions. Any thought of being more critical was swept aside by an urgent message from Arnold. A maximum effort was required for a raid on Japan. It was time for the B-29 to get on with the real war.

Strenuous efforts were made by all parties concerned to turn Matterhorn into a success, but the conditions under which the operation labored were too difficult. The first B-29 raid on Japan was indicative of the problem. Eighty-three bombers were gathered at Chengtu, China, for a mission to strike the Yawata steelworks. Sixty-eight got airborne on the evening of June 15,

> "Where the Raiden shone against the B-29, it was helpless before the swifter, more maneuverable Mustang. Almost every day our new fighters plunged burning from the sky, their wings torn off, their pilots dead."
>
> SABURO SAKAI, SAMURAI!

aiming to be over the target close to midnight. Forty-seven of them bombed Yawata and seven more unloaded elsewhere. Seven B-29s were lost, only one of them to enemy activity, and fifty-five men died. Just one bomb hit the target area, and that was over half a mile from the aiming point. If concrete results were poor, there were some intangibles to consider. American bombs had fallen on Japan for the first time since the Doolittle raid more than two years before, and, if their strident reaction was anything to go by, the Japanese were deeply concerned. In the United States, the news was received enthusiastically, and the B-29s competed with the Normandy beachheads for the front pages of the newspapers.

Matterhorn struggled on for the rest of the year, with the B-29s striking both at Japan and at a number of targets in Southeast Asia. Wolfe, an excellent logistician and engineer, returned to the United States to sort out B-29 production problems, and in September, Major General Curt LeMay arrived from Europe to grip the problem of making XX Bomber Command more effective. Squadrons were reorganized, tactics were changed, and occasionally results

were good, but aircraft losses continued and there were times when results were abysmal. By October 1944, airfields in the Marianas were ready for B-29s, and with that preferred alternative available it became possible to accept that the operations through Chengtu were a poor return on the investment of men and materials. Weather, geography and logistics had limited the 58th Bombardment Wing (VH) to forty-nine missions, less than half of them against Japan, and an average of only two sorties per aircraft per month. Of course, there were some positive aspects to Matterhorn. Operational lessons had been learned, crews had become familiar with the B-29, and many bugs had been driven from the aircraft. On the other hand, the support costs had been prohibitive, and so had the loss of 147 B-29s by the end of the year, the majority of them not attributable to enemy action. (At least three B-29s survived emergency landings in the USSR. The aircraft were not returned and were copied as the Tu-4 bomber and the Tu-70 transport.)

On October 12, 1944, Brigadier General Haywood "Possum" Hansell brought the first B-29 into the Marianas, landing Joltin' Josie, the Pacific Pioneer on the vast new Saipan base. Hansell had been one of the principal planners of the air assault on Japan, and he was now to lead XXI Bomber Command, spearheading the offensive. The 73rd Bomb Wing (VH) provided XXI Bomber Command's cutting edge. Training missions were flown against Truk and other Japanese held islands, and, after some preliminary photographic sorties by F-13s (a strategic reconnaissance version of the B-29), the 73rd aimed its first bombing mission at Japan on November 24. The target directive from the Joint Chiefs of Staff put aircraft assembly and engine plants at the top of the priority list, and the Nakajima engine factory in Tokyo was the first selected. As had been the case with the raids by the 58th Bomb Wing (VH), weather and mechanical problems had their effect on the raid and the results of the bombing were disappointing. Only two B-29s were lost, but, ominously, one of them went down after what appeared to be a deliberate ramming by a Japanese fighter pilot.

B-29

RIGHT Twin .50-caliber machine guns in the tail turret of B-29 *Enola Gay*. From here, gunner Staff Sergeant George R. Caron watched the mushroom cloud rise from Hiroshima on August 6, 1945.
BELOW The seat occupied by the B-29's central fire controller. From here he coordinated the aircraft's defense, assigning targets to the gunners as necessary.
BOTTOM The gunsight in a side blister of a B-29. Each gunner could control two turrets from a single sight. Both photographs are of the interior of *Fifi*, the Commemorative Air Force's restored B-29.

OPPOSITE AND BELOW The Wright R-3350 Cyclone used in the B-29 was one of the most powerful radial aircraft engines produced in the United States. The first R-3350 was run in May 1937, and later versions remained in production into the 1950s. The R-3350 is a twin-row, air-cooled, supercharged, 18-cylinder radial engine producing from 2,200 to over 2,800 horsepower, depending on the model. These huge engines enabled the B-29 to operate well above 30,000 feet, although that proved unnecessary once General LeMay introduced bombing from much lower levels. Operating at the outer limits of reciprocating engine technology, the R-3350s were never free of problems. Flying from hot Pacific islands in WWII exacerbated some existing overheating difficulties with the big Wright engines, and B-29 crews learned to keep engine runups to a minimum before takeoff. The cooling system was poor, there were numerous fuel leaks, and engine fires were frequent.

ABOVE B-29s being serviced on the ramp at Guam between bombing missions against Japan. The Wright R-3350s took more than their share of maintenance time and ground crews spent many hours on ladders.

With few exceptions, the B-29 raids followed strategic bombing's conventional wisdom for the next three months. Attacks were generally made in daylight from high altitude, and they were planned as precision strikes on specific targets, mostly in the aircraft industry. Reconnaissance revealed that very little damage was being done, and XXI Bomber Command reported a now-familiar list of shortcomings, among them the slow buildup of the B-29 force, bad weather, poor bombing accuracy, mechanical problems leading to a high abort rate and to aircraft losses, and a lack of escort fighters. Nevertheless, the raids had disturbed the Japanese sufficiently for them to strike back at Isley Field on Saipan with aircraft from Iwo Jima, destroying several B-29s on the ground.

Impatient for better results, Arnold intervened, sending LeMay to replace Hansell as commander of XXI Bomber Command in January 1945. LeMay brought his usual energy to making changes aimed at improving aircraft maintenance and aircrew training, but initially the operational pattern remained the same. Daylight precision attacks continued to drop high-explosive bombs from above 20,000 feet, and the results were little better than before. At the request of Twentieth Air Force, a couple of experimental raids were made with the B-29s carrying

A B-29 strike on Japan in progress. Bombs can clearly be seen falling. It is to be hoped that the bombardier of the photographer's aircraft is keenly aware of the B-29 immediately below.

only incendiaries. These were also made from high altitude with not much more encouraging results, although a few promising fires were started. By the time February arrived, XXI Bomber Command was nearing a crisis. Two things happened to deflect it. The first was another island assault by the U.S. Marines some 725 miles north of Saipan, and the other was a radical change in B-29 bombing tactics.

Japanese aircraft on Iwo Jima had posed a threat to the U.S. bases in the Marianas from the start. Raids were launched from there against B-29s on the ground, and Iwo's fighters intercepted the bombers on their way to Japan or forced them to dogleg, thereby using more fuel and reducing bomb loads. Even if no interception took place, radar on Iwo still gave early warning to the Japanese mainland of the B-29's approach. The threats were not really critical, but the benefits to U.S. forces of taking the island were considerable. If U.S. fighters could be deployed on Iwo's airfields, that would allow the B-29s to operate over Japan under escort, and the runways there would be available for emergency use by bombers either damaged or struggling home with a mechanical failure. Equally important, Iwo would be a forward base for air-sea rescue units, which had already proved an essential element of B-29 missions against Japan.

The Marines went ashore at Iwo Jima on February 19, 1945, and the battle raged until the island was declared secure in the middle of March. On March 6, P-51s of the Seventh Air Force's 15th Fighter Group began arriving on Iwo's South Field, and were soon in action, often taking off under fire to give close support to the nearby Marines. Later in the month, they were followed by the 21st Fighter Group, and by the P-61s of the 548th and 549th Night Fighter Squadrons. (During the later part of 1944, the Army Air Forces, Pacific Ocean Areas, had been formed under General Harmon, who was also Deputy Commander, Twentieth Air Force. Harmon's new headquarters provided the support services for XXI Bomber Command as well as being the superior headquarters for Seventh Air Force, the latter nearing the end of its island-hopping progress across the Pacific. Harmon himself disappeared without trace into the Pacific on February 25, 1945, while on a flight to Washington. He was succeeded by Major General Willis Hale.) As it happened, the fighter squadrons did not contribute as much as had been expected as escorts for the B-29s. By the time they were ready to fly escort missions, the air defense of Japan was already deteriorating, and in any case, the B-29s were operating much more frequently by night. Iwo's true value proved to be as an emergency way station for ailing bombers, and as such it was in frequent use.

Early in March, LeMay defied conventional theory. The B-29 had been designed to conform to the ideas of those dedicated to daylight precision bombing, and plans for its employment against Japan had naturally been based on classic AAF doctrines. LeMay himself had fought under those doctrines in Europe, but his mind was not closed to other ways of doing things. His observations since taking command of XXI Bomber Command convinced him that B-29 operations had to change if they were to play a decisive part in the defeat of Japan. In his view, the B-29's ineffectiveness was the result of several factors, most of them attributable to flying at high altitude in daylight. If the missions went in at lower levels at night, it seemed to him probable that a number of benefits would follow. Elimination of the climb to maximum altitude would save fuel, reducing the weight of fuel carried and increasing the bomb load. Operating at low altitude would save wear and tear on the engines and perhaps cure the engine fires that were one of the B-29's greatest problems. It was also true that Japan's day defenses had been improving and the B-29 loss rate was rising. Japan's night defenses were thought to be poor, and LeMay believed that even flak would not offer a serious threat. He also felt that, in spite of the inconclusive results from the experimental raids flown so far, Japan's wood-and-paper cities ought to be susceptible to incendiary attack, and that the quickest way to destroy many of the Japanese war industries would be to burn

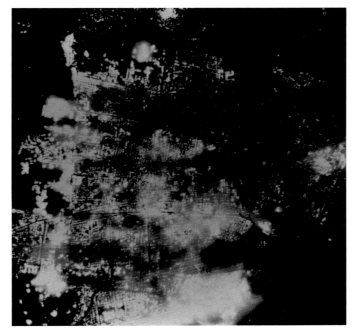

Toyama, a Japanese aluminum manufacturing center of 130,000 people, was subjected to a B-29 fire raid on the night of August 1, 1945. It was one of the war's most punishing attacks, destroying more than 90 percent of the city.

them out, since most of them were integral parts of built-up areas.

Having reached these conclusions, LeMay showed his decisiveness. He issued a field order for an operation to take place on March 9. It was to be a maximum effort, flown by night at much lower altitudes than before. Fuel was to be limited, to take account of the new flight parameters, and gun ammunition was not to be carried, so allowing bomb loads (exclusively incendiary) to increase to about six tons per aircraft. The order raised expectations (and pulse rates) throughout LeMay's command. Even he must have felt a tremor of nervous excitement. He had turned the B-29 world upside down, and the responsibility for the risks of the operation rested squarely on his own shoulders. General Arnold was not consulted; he was merely informed of LeMay's intentions on the day before the raid.

By this time, three wings of B-29s were operating from Saipan, Tinian and Guam — the 73rd, 313th and 314th Bomb Wings. A force of 334 bombers was assembled, and Tokyo was attacked from altitudes between 4,900 and 9,200 feet. The first bombs fell just after midnight and fires started immediately, spreading quickly in a brisk surface wind. As the B-29s fanned out to cover unburnt areas, new fires sprang up and merged with those already blazing. Later aircraft reported having difficulty because of flying through dense smoke and severe turbulence generated by the intense heat. The fire grew into one of the greatest urban conflagrations in history, consuming vast areas of the city and destroying over a quarter of a million buildings. For the Japanese, the scale of the catastrophe defied belief. More than a million people were homeless and over 80,000 dead. It was the most destructive air raid of the war, unsurpassed in the

European or Pacific theaters. The official history of the Army Air Forces in WWII describes it thus:

> The area attacked was densely populated, with an average of 103,000 people per square mile. It bordered the most important industrial section of Tokyo and included strategic targets. Its main importance lay in its home industries and feeder plants. Being closely spaced and predominantly wood, bamboo, and plaster construction, these buildings kindled easily and flames spread with the rapidity of a brush fire in a drought. The high concentration of bombs started so many fires that the situation was out of control within thirty minutes. The flames, fanned by a brisk wind, caught and destroyed 95 fire engines and the antiaircraft barrage fell off sharply as the fire overran gun positions. Police records show that over 267,000 buildings were destroyed (about one quarter the total in Tokyo) and that more than 1 million persons were rendered homeless. The official toll of casualties listed 84,000 dead and 41,000 injured. Panic had been partly responsible for the heavy casualties, since people trapped by the spreading fires had tried to run through the flames. Many found safety in rivers and canals, but in the smaller canals the water was actually boiling.

It was the greatest conflagration ever suffered by a city, vastly exceeding those experienced by Nero's Rome, London in 1666, Napoleon in Moscow, or San Francisco in 1906. Sixteen square miles of Tokyo were reduced to ashes. The effect on Japanese morale was profound.

Fourteen B-29s were shot down and forty-two damaged by flak during the Tokyo raid, which LeMay, remembering the severity of his European experience, felt to be a moderate price to pay for striking such a heavy blow. He felt his judgment had been justified, and he immediately ordered a similar strike against the city of Nagoya. Before the end of March, Osaka and Kobe had also been incinerated by fire raids, and the damage inflicted was such that LeMay knew he was right. He had in his hand a weapon capable of realizing the apocalyptic strategic air power theories of Douhet, Mitchell and Trenchard, one that could indeed destroy the fabric of an enemy nation.

Plans were made for the burning of Japan to continue, and a list of cities intended for systematic destruction was prepared. The need to defeat Japan as quickly as possible was paramount and, since precision bombing had failed, it was, for the time being, set aside in favor of area attack. LeMay was impatient to get the job done, and he drove his crews harder than ever, raising their combat flying hours to eighty per month, a far greater rate than had ever been attempted in Europe.

By the middle of 1945, the Japanese were desperate to produce as many fighters as possible to defend against the USAAF's B-29s. They had plenty of Kawasaki Ki-61 airframes but none of their intended in-line engines. It was decided to use Ha-112 radials instead, and the result was an exceptional fighter. The Ki-100 was simple to fly and maintain, and the Ha-112 engine proved reliable. In combat, the Ki-100-Ia was a revelation, especially at low altitudes. In one encounter over Okinawa, a Ki-100-equipped unit destroyed fourteen F6F Hellcats without loss. Combat with the P-51D Mustang was on more or less equal terms at low or medium altitudes, but at altitudes above 26,000 feet, the maneuverability of the Ki-100 became noticeably worse.

TOP *The elegant Mitsubishi Ki-46 Dinah was one of the most impressive machines operated by the Japanese during WWII, and a superlative reconnaissance aircraft. The Ki-46 served from the beginning to the end of the war in the Pacific, and was a constant thorn in the Allied side. For most of the war, the Japanese knew that they could count on the Ki-46 being able to fly over Allied territory and obtain information with impunity.*

BOTTOM *The cockpit of the Dinah was reasonably conventional, and the pilot was afforded an excellent all-round view through the elongated glass canopy. This Dinah is on display at the RAF Museum at Cosford.*

In April 1945, a pause in the fire-bombing campaign was forced on LeMay. The B-29s were diverted to operations in support of the invasion of Okinawa, attacking Japanese airfields from which Kamikaze missions were being flown against the U.S. fleet. B-29s of the 313th Bomb Wing also began the specialized work of mine-laying, sowing thousands in harbor approaches and in the waterways most used by Japanese shipping. Unheralded though it was, the mine-laying was a conspicuous success, accounting for approximately half the Japanese tonnage sunk in this closing stage of the war.

In May, the incineration of Japan was resumed. The B-29s worked their way through the major cities, and then started on a list of smaller urban areas with populations between 100,000 and 200,000. One refinement was that leaflet dropping was introduced. The leaflets listed the cities scheduled for attack and told the Japanese population: "In accordance with America's well-known humanitarian principles, the American Air Force, which does not wish to injure innocent people, now gives you warning to evacuate the cities and save your lives." It proved to be an effective measure, later characterized by a high Japanese official as "a very clever piece of psychological warfare, as people in the affected regions got extremely nervous and lost what faith they still had in the Army's ability to defend the mainland."

His eagerness was at least in part sparked by the thought that his B-29s could ensure victory not only over Japan but also for the concept of strategic air power. In a letter to Brigadier General Lauris Norstad, Chief of Staff at Twentieth Air Force, he wrote: "I am influenced by the conviction that the present stage of development of the air war against Japan presents the AAF for the first time with the opportunity of proving the power of the strategic air arm. I consider that for the first time strategic air bombardment faces a situation in which its strength is proportionate to the magnitude of its task."

OPPOSITE *The nose of* Bockscar, *the USAF Museum's B-29. It was from this position that Captain Kermit Beahan saw a hole in the cloud covering Nagasaki and dropped the atomic bomb Fat Man on August 9, 1945.*

OPPOSITE INSET *The crew of* Bockscar *on August 9, 1945. Standing L to R: Captain Kermit Beahan, Captain James Van Pelt, Lieutenant Charles Albury. Lieutenant. Fred Olivi, and Major Charles Sweeney; Kneeling L to R: Staff Sergeant Edward Buckley, Master Sergeant John Kuharek, Sergeant Raymond Gallagher, Staff Sergeant Albert DeHart, and Sergeant Abe Spitzer.*

ABOVE *The pilot's seat in a B-29 seems almost too exposed. The general roominess is emphasized by the huge expanse of glass on every side.* LEFT *Charles W. Sweeney piloted* Bockscar *over Nagasaki on August 9, 1945. More than fifty years later, in 1996, he once more took his place in the left-hand seat.*

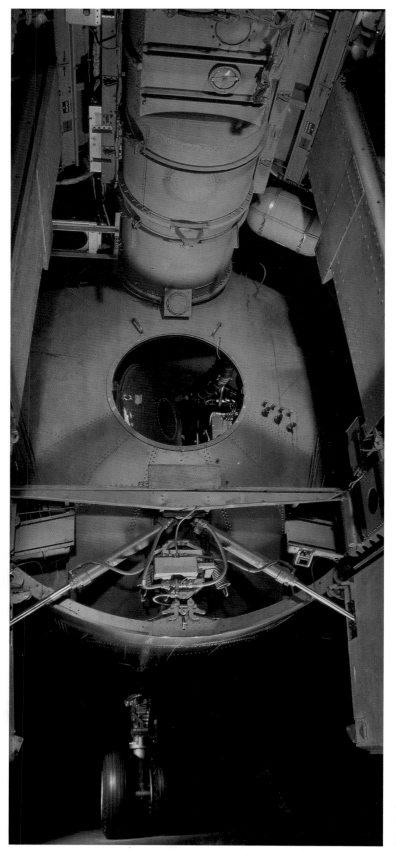

By August, the B-29s were running out of large places to burn, and towns with populations of less than 40,000 were being attacked. Much of Japan's urban area lay in ruins, and some places were almost totally obliterated. Among them, reconnaissance recorded that the cities of Namaza and Fukui were almost 90-percent destroyed, and Toyama, with a pre-raid population of almost 130,000, had effectively ceased to exist. In all, some sixty-six urban centers were attacked, and about 178 square miles of Japan's built-up area had literally gone up in smoke. The morale of the people declined and the number who expected Japan to lose the war rose sharply. Industrial production fell to one-third of capacity. LeMay was certain that the B-29s had the capability to force surrender without any recourse to an invasion of Japan by ground forces. He may have been right; the Emperor told his government as early as April (after the March fire blitz) that a way should be found to end the war as quickly as possible.

With so much destruction already accomplished, there was no thought of reducing the scale of the bombing offensive. On the contrary, extensive plans were made to build up the USAAF's striking power in the Pacific and to restructure command arrangements to take account of a massive increase in strength. General Arnold advocated the appointment of a Supreme Commander for the final offensive against Japan, with senior and equal commanders from the army, navy and air force responsible to that officer for operations in their own spheres. Given the sensibilities of the individual services, the question of a Supreme Commander could not be resolved, but agreement was reached by the Joint Chiefs of Staff that General MacArthur should command all land operations, and that Admiral Nimitz should be the commander at sea. Those decisions made, it was further agreed that there should be an air commander who would take charge of land-based strategic aviation and have broad administrative and logistical responsibilities for all AAF forces in the theater. The senior airman selected to be Commander, U.S. Army Strategic Air Forces, Pacific, was General Carl Spaatz.

Inside the forward bomb bay of B-29 Bockscar, *looking toward the nose. The open hatch into the crew compartment is at the center of the picture.*

ABOVE *B-29* Enola Gay's *tail-gun fire controller with a reflector sight. As the gunner manipulated the controls and aligned the sight, a fire control computer analyzed the signals and sent electrical impulses to move the guns.*
RIGHT *A dense column of smoke gives rise to the distinctive mushroom cloud reaching more than 60,000 feet into the air over the Japanese port of Nagasaki, after the B-29* Bockscar *dropped the atomic bomb* Fat Man *on August 9, 1945.*

Spaatz arrived from Europe to set up his new head-quarters on Guam at the end of July 1945. With Germany defeated, the "Mighty Eighth" was already on its way from Europe to add its strength to the air forces facing Japan. In a letter to Spaatz in May 1945, General Arnold explained his plans for the build up of strategic air power in the Pacific, and gave an indication of the politics lurking behind the command appointment. He said that the Eighth would operate from Okinawa with 720 B-29s, and that the Twentieth would remain in the Marianas with 720 more, a combined striking force more than twice as powerful as that ranged against Japan so far. In nominating Spaatz for command of USASTAF, Arnold wrote: "I believe we need somebody who can work more nearly on parity and have more influence with MacArthur and Nimitz...I can see

The Mitsubishi G4M Betty's last wartime mission was to carry the Japanese surrender delegation to Ie Shima, a small island in the Ryukyu chain to the west of Okinawa. Two G4Ms, hastily painted white with green crosses over Japan's national markings, flew there on August 19, 1945, with envoys from Japan, who were then transferred to a USAAF C-54 and flown to Manila, where they received instructions concerning the surrender and occupation.

nobody else who has the chance to save for us a proper representation in the air war in the Pacific...." As these ideas were being considered, a revolutionary event changed the nature of global war for ever.

Apocalypse Now

On June 11, 1945, some specially modified B-29s began arriving at Tinian's North Field. They were aircraft belonging to the 393rd Bomb Squadron, the combat element of the 509th Composite Group. Externally, they were distinguished by a lack of gun turrets, apart from the two gun positions in the tail. They were parked in their own part of the airfield, a complex of heavily guarded buildings and hard standings. Once settled in, the crews followed normal practice and completed a few training missions to well visited islands such as Truk before flying several more to selected targets in Japan. The curiosity of the other B-29 units was aroused because the 393rd never flew as part of a wing operation. They went off in small formations of their own, sometimes only two or three aircraft at a time, apparently following the discredited tactics of penetrating Japanese airspace in daylight at high level. Over the targets, however, their tactics

were anything but standard. At the release point, a single bulbous bomb fell from the lead aircraft, which immediately broke into a steep diving turn, aiming to get as far away as possible before the bomb exploded. Even to the crews performing these maneuvers, it was all very strange.

During the training period, the commander of the 509th was the only member of the unit who knew that his group had been formed for the specific purpose of dropping the first operational atomic bomb on Japan. He was Colonel Paul Tibbetts, an exceptional pilot with a distinguished B-17 record in Europe and North Africa, who had recently been testing B-29s in the United States. On July 18, he received a coded message that told him that an atomic bomb had been detonated at Alamagordo, New Mexico. He was pretty certain then that his months of preparatory work had not been in vain, and that the next atomic explosion would take place over Japan with him and his crew as witnesses.

The Allied powers issued an ultimatum on July 26 calling for the Japanese to surrender or suffer "prompt and utter destruction." President Truman had decided that the "special bomb" would be used if the Japanese refused to comply, and the anticipated rejection came from Premier Suzuki on

July 28. A directive had already been issued to General Spaatz on July 25 in the expectation that the Japanese would refuse to cooperate. In it, Spaatz was instructed that the 509th was to deliver its first special bomb, visually aimed, on or after August 3, 1945, "on one of the targets: Hiroshima, Kokura, Niigata, and Nagasaki." The field orders for the attack were signed on August 2 by Lieutenant General Twining, who, in the reorganization of the Pacific air forces had become commander of the Twentieth Air Force. Hiroshima was selected as the primary target.

The fissionable material for the core of the bomb arrived at Tinian on board the cruiser *Indianapolis* on July 26, and by August 1, both the weapon and the 509th were ready to go. Weather forecasts for the period after August 3 were promising and led to final briefings being given. On August 4, the crews of the 509th at last learned that their special bombs were expected to explode with a force equal to 20,000 tons of TNT.

At 02:45 on August 6, 1945 Paul Tibbetts lifted his B-29, *Enola Gay*, off the Tinian runway and headed north. Two other B-29s, *The Great Artiste* and *No. 91*, followed with official observers on board. Approaching Japan, Tibbetts received a report from weather reconnaissance aircraft indicating that the skies over Hiroshima were almost clear of cloud. By then, the weaponeer had made the bomb live, and all was ready for the drop. Navigator "Dutch" van Kirk brought the *Enola Gay* accurately to the initial point for the attack, and at 09:11, Tibbetts steadied at 31,600 feet on the final heading for the target and handed the aircraft over to bombardier Tom Ferebee. At 09:15, the bomb, a uranium device known as *Little Boy*, fell from the bomb bay toward the aiming point of Hiroshima's Aioi Bridge. Tibbetts immediately broke hard right and dropped the nose, gathering speed to escape the coming blast. Fifty seconds after release, *Little Boy* detonated and Hiroshima was transformed into a scene of utter devastation.

The official Japanese communique minimized the disaster at Hiroshima. It mentioned a new bomb which had caused "considerable damage" and "should not be made light of," but there was no hint of a Japanese surrender. The decision was therefore made to use the second bomb, *Fat Man*, which had a plutonium core. The mission was flown on August 9, led by Major Charles Sweeney in a B-29 called *Bockscar*. (Sweeney's own B-29, *The Great Artiste*, was the principal observation aircraft and was loaded with monitoring instruments. Sweeney therefore exchanged aircraft with Captain Fred Bock, whose usual B-29 was the appropriately named *Bockscar*. It is *Bockscar* that is preserved as an exhibit in the USAF Museum, Dayton, Ohio.) The primary target selected was Kokura, but that city was saved by the weather. Complete cloud cover defied Sweeney over Kokura, and *Bockscar* was turned toward the secondary target, Nagasaki. With the cloud cover persisting, the approach to the target was made on radar, but at the last moment the city was seen through a break and the bomb was released visually. The blast from the explosion caught up with the aircraft about a minute later. The crew felt "it was as if the B-29 were being beaten by a telephone pole."

"To the Japanese people: America asks you to take immediate heed of what we say on this leaflet.

We are in possession of the most destructive explosive ever devised by man. A single one of our newly-developed atomic bombs is actually the equivalent in explosive power to what 2,000 of our giant B-29s can carry on a single mission. This awful fact is one for you to ponder and we solemnly assure you that it is grimly accurate.

We have just begun to use this weapon against your homeland. If you still have any doubt, make inquiry as to what happened to Hiroshima when just one atomic bomb fell on that city.

Before using this bomb to destroy every resource of the military by which they are prolonging this useless war, we ask that you now petition the Emperor to end the war. Our President has outlined for you the thirteen consequences of an honorable surrender. We urge that you accept these consequences and begin work of building a new, better and peace-loving Japan.

You should take these steps now to cease military resistance. Otherwise, we shall resolutely employ this bomb and all our other superior weapons to promptly and forcefully end the war.

Evacuate your cities now!"

TEXT OF A LEAFLET PREPARED BY THE U.S. OFFICE OF WAR INFORMATION AND DROPPED ALL OVER JAPAN AFTER THE DESTRUCTION OF HIROSHIMA.

At Hiroshima, the area destroyed covered nearly 5 square miles. Almost 80,000 people died and those injured numbered about the same. Nagasaki was to some extent protected by its hilly terrain, and the area destroyed was less than one and a half square miles. The dead and injured figures could not be precisely determined, but they were approximately 35,000 and 60,000 respectively.

The Japanese were in desperate straits. Their armies were defeated, their naval and air forces destroyed, their sea lanes closed, their cities burned, and now they had felt the impact of two terrible new weapons. As if that were not enough, on August 8, the USSR declared war on them, and Soviet armies swept into Manchuria. Yet Japanese militarism remained strong and there were still those in the leadership who opposed any move for peace. Deadlocked, the Japanese government turned to Emperor Hirohito. On August 10, he gave his view that "the time has come when we must bear the unbearable." Papers flew between Japan and the Allies, but it was August 14 before the Emperor's will prevailed. While intense internal struggles were going on in Tokyo, the USAAF resumed conventional operations, culminating in a "1,000 plus" grand finale on August 14, when 828 B-29s and 186 escorts attacked various targets. Before the last B-29 landed, President Truman was at last able to announce the unconditional surrender of Japan.

The formalities ending the Pacific War were concluded by General MacArthur on board the battleship *Missouri* in Tokyo Bay on September 2, 1945. The Army's senior soldier and the Navy's battlewagon occupied center stage, but overhead the Air Force made its point with a flypast of 462 B-29s. In view of recent events, it was a display of strength that could hardly fail to draw the eye.

With Hindsight

Generally speaking, the Allied cause was served even more effectively by air power in the Pacific and CBI theaters than in Europe. This was possible because, for one thing, the discrepancies in strength between the two major combatants were more obvious. In terms of population and industry, Japan was greatly inferior to the United States. In the air, that was evidenced by the Japanese air forces becoming increasingly outnumbered and being unable to keep up in the race to produce not only more aircrew and aircraft, but better versions of both. One of the most extraordinary

aspects of the war was the speed with which the United States was able to mobilize and organize its forces in the Pacific while still committing huge resources to the Allied policy of "Germany first."

The growth of the USAAF's six air forces in the Pacific and CBI theatres was typical of what was accomplished. In 1942, the USAAF in the Pacific was an operator of small, scattered collections of outdated aircraft. Little more than three years later, it was a mighty assembly of air power capable of dominating any confrontation anywhere in the world. The overwhelming nature of U.S. air power was emphasized when it became possible to mount an aerial offensive against the main islands of Japan. The emphasis was marked because Japanese air defenses were found to be relatively poor and the cities that housed the principal industries proved to be particularly susceptible to incendiary attack. In Europe, on the other hand, the Luftwaffe was always a ferocious adversary and German industry more robust.

Another factor was the geography of the region. The vast distances and frequently rudimentary national infrastructures emphasized the need for reach and flexibility in air power, and the United States employed its assets far more effectively than did its enemy. The Japanese understood the importance of air power, but were limited in their view of how to use it. It was primarily for the support of their Army and Navy, and those two services generally kept the efforts of their air forces well separated. The U.S. services used their aircraft in every role imaginable — strategic bombing, interdiction, close support, artillery spotting, reconnaissance, air defense, fighter escort, ship attack, maritime patrol, air-sea rescue, troop and freight transport, glider assault, casualty evacuation — and became highly effective in them all.

At the war's end, it became clear that the immense amount of destruction effected during the fire-bombing campaign had reduced Japan's already declining industrial capacity dramatically. By mid-1945, Japan's production was down to about one-third of that reached during the previous year, and this was the result of both the loss of factories and a lowering of the morale of the Japanese people, who had become noticeably more defeatist and less willing to work. The evacuation of large numbers of people into the countryside had also had its effect.

The first series of incendiary attacks on the major cities in March 1945 shocked some of the Japanese leaders sufficiently to make them think about how they might initiate peace negotiations. Indeed, well before the dropping of the atomic bombs, the members of the "peace party" in the Japanese government were predicting that the bombing would force an end to the war by September and were arguing that further resistance was pointless. Their reaction to the aerial threat was understandable, but, in its postwar examination of the air war against Japan, the United States Strategic Bombing Survey took care not to attribute Japan's defeat to any single factor, preferring to mention "the numerous causes which jointly and cumulatively were responsible for Japan's disaster." The USSBS report pointed out that the final air assault on Japan had not been feasible until bases had been secured within reach of the main islands, and that the history of the war in the Pacific was largely one of surface forces seizing territory with the support of air forces. It went without saying that the surface campaigns would have been unlikely to succeed in the absence of air support.

The USSBS comments were more than justified. By the time the B-29 offensive began, Japan was in decline as a result of calamitous defeats for its armed forces and the strictures of a relentless naval blockade. Nevertheless, it is interesting to speculate on how the war might have gone had there been no strategic bombing campaign. Given the nature of their society in 1945 and the military domination of their government, the Japanese would probably have been prepared to endure the sufferings of total isolation and would have fought to the death against invasion. The B-29s made such stoicism impossible by bringing the war home to the Japanese people in a form so irresistible and so horrifyingly destructive that increasing numbers of them lost the will to fight on. Even military fanatics who refused to think of surrender no longer talked of victory but of "finding life in death."

In reaching the point at which they felt driven to seek the intervention of their Emperor, the Japanese leaders would undoubtedly have been keenly aware that Japan was facing inevitable defeat. Their military reverses and the naval blockade had created that situation, but had not forced them to consider surrender. They were unequivocal in testifying later that the bombing campaign had done that. Prince Konoye said, "Fundamentally the thing that brought about the determination to make peace was the prolonged bombing by the B-29s."

Premier Suzuki agreed: "It seemed to me unavoidable that in the long run Japan would be almost destroyed by air attack so that merely on the basis of the B-29s alone I was convinced that Japan should sue for peace."

Suzuki and others mentioned the atomic bombs and the Soviet declaration of war as additional factors, but suggested that, significant though these events were, they were not the real roots of the drive to end the war. They served to bolster the arguments of the members of the "peace party," but the difficult decision to face the terrible disgrace of surrender had already been made. They had no idea what kind of bomb had destroyed Hiroshima and did not particularly care. B-29s had shown that they could eradicate cities just as effectively with incendiaries and the distinction between one kind of bomb and another did not seem to them significant.

By 1945, the inevitability of Japan's defeat, with or without a strategic bombing offensive, was not in doubt. The fact remains that the blows that precipitated the end of the war and obviated the need to consider a costly invasion of Japan were delivered by the USAAF's B-29s. It was their demonstrated destructive capacity that most affected the states of mind of the Japanese leaders in 1945 and led them to sue for peace. Early air power strategists who had theorized that bombing an opposing nation's heartland would, among other things, "destroy the enemy's will to fight" might at last have claimed justification for the thought.

In 1947, General Carl Spaatz looked back on WWII and delivered the airmen's verdict on the role of air power in the Pacific: "In our victory over Japan, air power was unquestionably decisive. That the planned invasion of the Japanese Home islands was unnecessary is clear evidence that air power has evolved into a force co-equal with land and sea power, decisive in its own right and worthy of the faith of its prophets."

REMEMBRANCE

RIGHT Larry Pisoni was a schoolboy in the village of Vezzano near Trento in northern Italy in 1945. German forces were retiring northward toward the Brenner Pass, harassed in their retreat by the aircraft of the USAAF. A B-24 was shot down and crashed into a mountainside above Larry's village. Several of the crew survived, some fortunate enough to be spirited away by Italian partisans, but two were captured by the Germans and fell into the hands of the SS. Later, Larry saw these two marched through the village. He remembers being surprised that they looked like other young men and not like the monsters of Nazi propaganda, and was shocked to hear that they had been executed at the side of a road not far away.

BELOW LEFT Larry never forgot the incident and, half a century later, collaborating with the local Italian government, he arranged for a small park to be set aside on the road where the Americans were killed. A stone placed on the spot carries a plaque that names the victims and tells the story.

BELOW RIGHT Back in the village, Larry likes to draw attention to the gates of a villa. They are largely made of panels taken from the wings of the B-24.

THE ALLIED FORCES LANDING ON THIS SHORE WHICH THEY CALL OMAHA BEACH LIBERATE EUROPE JUNE 6TH 1944

This stone monument seems out of place along this tranquil stretch of Normandy coast, now known as Omaha Beach. These photographs were made on June 6, 1999, and the view here was far different fifty-five years earlier. It was to the right of this marker that the 116th Infantry Regimental Combat Team, 29th Division of the U.S. Army, came ashore leading the division. The aerial and naval bombardments of the defenses behind the beaches failed to disrupt the carefully planned German defense along this part of Hitler's Atlantic Wall. The 116th suffered enormous casualties in the first ten minutes of the invasion.

Dedicated in July 1993, the Battle of Britain memorial on the cliffs near Folkestone is in the shape of a giant three-bladed propeller carved into the ground, with the statue of a lone airman sitting on the propeller-boss looking out across the English Channel. Carved on the boss are the squadron badges of the RAF units that took part in the battle. The surrounding grassy area features a series of raised banks that give the impression of a pilot's leather flying helmet and earphones.

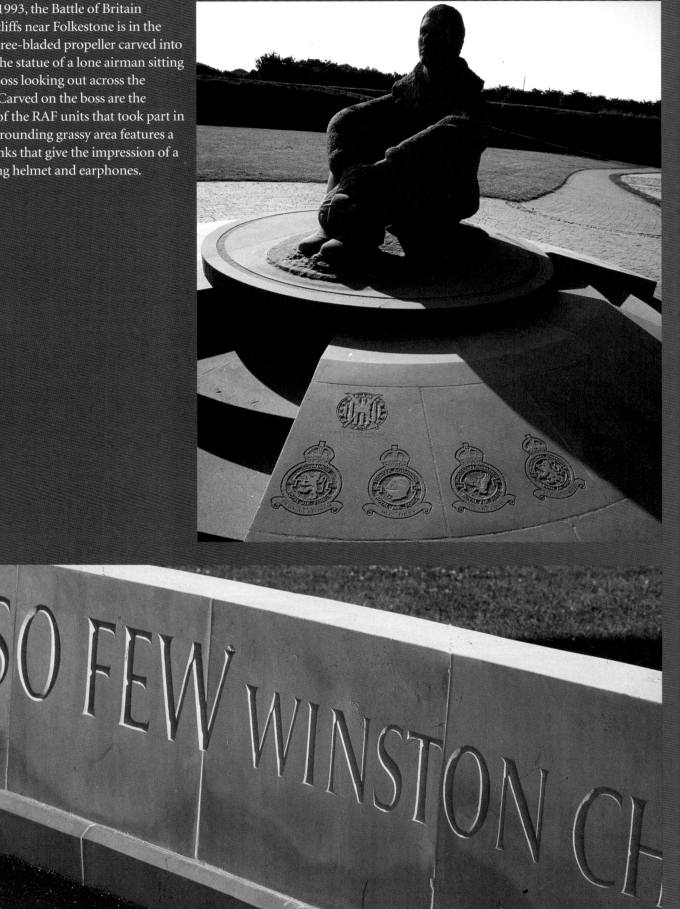

One of the most moving of the American cemeteries in Europe is at Madingley, near Cambridge, England. There are 3,812 American military dead buried there. On the wall running from the entrance to the chapel are inscribed the names of 5,126 Americans who gave their lives in the Battle of the Atlantic or in the strategic air bombardment of Northwest Europe, but whose remains were never recovered. The mosaic ceiling in the chapel is a memorial to those Americans who died while serving in the U.S. Army Air Force. Beside and above the main door, stained-glass medallions represent the seals of the War and Navy Departments, as well as the principal decorations awarded by the U.S. armed services.

Greenwood, John T., ed. *Milestones of Aviation.* New York: Hugh Lauter Levin Associates, 1989

Griehl, Manfred. *German Night Fighters in World War II.* Westchester, PA: Schiffer Military History, 1990

Gunston, Bill. *The Development of Piston Aero Engines.* Yeovil, UK: Patrick Stephens Ltd., 1993

Gunston, Bill. *Fighting Aircraft of World War II.* New York: Prentice Hall Press, 1988

Gunston, Bill. *The Illustrated Encyclopedia of Aircraft Armament.* New York: Orion Books, 1988

Gunston, Bill, ed. *Chronicle of Aviation.* London: Chronicle Communications, 1992

Haining, Peter. *The Spitfire Summer.* London: W.H. Allen, 1990

Hall, Grover C. Jr. *1000 Destroyed.* Fallbrook, CA: Aero Publishers, 1978

Halley, James J. *The Squadrons of the Royal Air Force.* Tonbridge, UK: Air-Britain, 1980

Hallion, Richard P. *Legacy of Flight.* Seattle, WA: University of Washington Press, 1977

Hallion, Richard P. *Strike from the Sky.* Washington, DC: Smithsonian Institute Press, 1989

Hardesty, Von. *Red Phoenix.* Washington, DC: Smithsonian Institution Press, 1982

Harris, Arthur. *Bomber Offensive.* London: Greenhill Books, 1990

Harris, Stephen K. *The B-17 Remembered.* Seattle, WA: Museum of Flight, 1998

Harrison, James P. *Mastering the Sky.* New York: Sarpedon, 1996

Harvey, A.D. *Arnhem.* London: Cassell, 2001

Hastings, Max. *Bomber Command.* New York: The Dial Press/James Wade, 1979

Haugland, Vern. *The Eagle Squadrons.* New York: Ziff-Davis Flying Books, 1979

Hawkins, Ian L., ed. *B-17s over Berlin.* McLean, VA: Brassey's, 1990

Held, Werner. *The Day Fighters.* West Chester, PA: Schiffer Military History, 1991

Held, Werner. *The German Fighter Units over Russia.* West Chester, PA: Schiffer Military History, 1990

Held, Werner, and Holger Nauroth. *The Defense of the Reich.* New York: Arco Publishing, 1982

Hendrie, Andrew. *Flying Cats.* Annapolis, MD: Naval Institute Press, 1988

Henshaw, Alex. *Sigh for a Merlin.* Wilmslow, UK: Air Data Publications, 1996

Heppenheimer, T.A. *A Brief History of Flight.* New York: John Wiley & Sons, 2001

Herrmann, Hajo. *Eagle's Wings.* Shrewsbury, UK: Airlife, 1991

Hess, William N., and Thomas G Ivie. *Fighters of the Mighty Eigth.* Osceola, WI: Motorbooks International, 1990

Hess, William N., and Thomas G. Ivie. *P-51 Mustang Aces.* Osceola, WI: Motorbooks International, 1992

Hibbert, Christopher. *Anzio.* New York: Ballantine Books, 1970

Hough, Richard, and Denis Richards. *The Battle of Britain.* New York: W.W. Norton, 1989

Hoyt, Edwin P. *Carrier Wars.* New York: Paragon House, 1992

Hughes, Thomas Alexander. *Over Lord.* New York: The Free Press, 1995

Jablonski, Edward. *Flying Fortress.* New York: Doubleday, 1965

Jablonski, Edward. *Air War.* New York: Doubleday, 1979

Jablonski, Edward. *America in the Air War.* Alexandria, VA. Time-Life Books, 1982

Jacobs, Peter. *Hawker Hurricane.* Malmesbury, UK: Crowood Press, 1998

Jarrett, Philip, ed. *Biplane to Monoplane.* London: Putnam, 1997

Jarrett, Philip, ed. *Aircraft of the Second World War.* London: Putnam, 1997

Johnson, J.E. "Johnnie." *The Story of Air Fighting.* London: Hutchinson, 1985

Josephy, Alvin M. *The American Heritage History of Flight.* New York: American Heritage Publishing, 1962

Kaplan, Philip, and Richard Collier. *Their Finest Hour.* New York: Abbeville Press, 1989

Kaplan, Philip, and Andy Saunders. *Little Friends.* New York: Random House, 1991

Keen, Patricia Fussell. *Eyes of the Eighth.* Sun City, AZ: CAVU Publishers, 1996

Kennedy, Ludovic. *Pursuit.* London: Collins, 1974

Kennedy, Ludovic. *The Death of the Tirpitz.* Boston, MA: Little, Brown & Co., 1979

Knight, Dennis. *Harvest of Messerschmitts.* London: Frederick Warne, 1981

Knott, Richard C. *The American Flying Boat.* Annapolis, MD: Naval Institute Press, 1979

Koc, L.W., and E. Quirini. *The Polish Army & the Polish Navy.* Central Warsaw: Military Booksellers Magazine, 1939

Lamb, Charles A. *To War in a Stringbag.* New York: Doubleday, 1980

Lande, D.A. *From Somewhere in England.* Osceola, WI: Motorbooks International,1990

Larkins, William T. *Battleship & Cruiser Aircraft of the United States Navy.* Atglen, PA: Schiffer Military/Aviation History, 1996

Lee, David. *Never Stop the Engine When It's Hot.* London: Thomas Harmsworth, 1983

Leuthner, Stuart, and Oliver Jensen. *High Honor.* Washington, DC: Smithsonian Institution Press, 1989

Lopez, Donald S. *Into the Teeth of the Tiger.* Washington, DC: Smithsonian Institution Press, 1997

Lucas, Laddie, ed. *Wings of War.* London: Hutchinson, 1983

Lucas, Laddie, ed. *Out of the Blue.* London: Hutchinson, 1985

Lundstrom, John B. *The First Team.* Annapolis, MD: Naval Institute Press, 1984

Lyall, Gavin. *Freedom's Battle (Vol 2).* London: Hutchinson, 1968

MacIntyre, Donald. *Aircraft Carrier.* New York: Ballantine Books, 1968

MacIntyre, Donald. *Leyte Gulf.* New York: Ballantine Books, 1970

March, Daniel J., and John Heathcott, eds. *The Aerospace Encyclopedia of Air Warfare (Vol. 1).* London: Aerospace Publishing, 1997

Mason, Francis K. *Battle Over Britain.* London: McWhirter Twins, 1969

Mason, Francis K. *Aces of the Air.* New York: Mayflower Books, 1981

Mason, Francis K. *The British Bomber since 1914.* London: Putnam, 1994

Mason, Francis K. *The British Fighter since 1912.* London: Putnam, 1992

Mason, T. *IX Squadron.* Lincoln, UK: The Lincolnshire Chronicle, 1965

Maurer, Maurer. *Air Force Combat Units of World War II.* Edison, NJ: Chartwell Books, 1994

McAulay, Lex. *Battle of the Bismarck Sea.* New York: St. Martin's Press, 1991

McFarland, Stephen L., and Wesley P. Newton. *To Command the Sky.* Washington, DC: Smithsonian Institution Press, 1991

Middlebrook, Martin. *The Nuremburg Raid*. London: Fontana, 1975

Middlebrook, Martin. *The Battle of Hamburg*. New York: Charles Scribner's Sons, 1981

Middlebrook, Martin. *The Shweinfurt-Regensburg Mission*. London: Allen Lane, 1983

Middlebrook, Martin, and Patrick Mahoney. *Battleship*. New York: Charles Scribner's Sons, 1979

Middlebrook, Martin, and Chris Everitt. *The Bomber Command War Diaries*. London: Penguin Books, 1990

Millbrooke, Anne. *Aviation History*. Englewood, CO: Jeppesen Sanderson, 1999

Miller, Russell. *The Soviet Air Force at War*. Alexandria, VA. Time-Life Books, 1983

Mitcham, Samuel W. *Eagles of the Third Reich*. Shrewsbury, UK: Airlife, 1989

Mondey, David, ed. *Aviation*. London: Octopus Books, 1980

Moolman, Valerie. *Women Aloft*. Alexandria, VA: Time-Life Books, 1981

Morley-Mower, Geoffrey. *Messerschmitt Roulette*. St. Paul, MN: Phalanx Publishing, 1993

Morrison, Wilbur H. *Fortress Without a Roof*. New York: St. Martin's Press, 1982

Muller, Richard. *The German Air War in Russia*. Baltimore, MD: Nautical & Aviation Publishing, 1992

Murray, Williamson. *Strategy for Defeat*. Secaucus, NJ: Chartwell Books, 1986

Murray, Williamson. *War in the Air 1914-45*. London: Cassell, 1999

Musciano, Walter A. *Messerschmitt Aces*. Blue Ridge Summit, PA: Aero, 1989

Musciano, Walter A. *Warbirds of the Sea*. Atglen, PA: Schiffer Publishing, 1994

Nalty, Bernard C., ed. *Pearl Harbor and the War in the Pacific*. New York: Smithmark, 1991

Nauroth, Holger, and Werner Held. *Messerschmitt Bf 110*. West Chester, PA: Schiffer Military History, 1991

Nevin, David. *Architects of Air Power*. Alexandria, VA: Time-Life Books, 1981

Nijboer, Donald, and Dan Patterson. *Cockpit*. Erin, Ontario: Boston Mills Press, 1998

Nijboer, Donald, and Dan Patterson. *Gunner*. Erin, Ontario: Boston Mills Press, 2001

Nowarra, Heinz J. *Die 109*. Stuttgart: Motorbuc-Verlag, 1979

Nowara, H.J., and G.R. Duval. *Russian Civil and Military Aircraft*. London: Fountain Press, 1971

Oakes, Claudia, ed. *Aircraft of the National Air & Space Museum*. Washington, DC: Smithsonian Institution Press, 1981

Orange, Vincent. *Coningham*. Washington, DC: Center for Air Force History, 1992

Overy, Richard J. *The Air War*. New York: Stein & Day, 1981

Overy, Richard J. *Bomber Command 1939-45*. London: Harper Collins 1997

Pack, S.W.C. *Operation Husky*. Newton Abbot, UK: David & Charles, 1977

Pape, Garry R., and Ronald C. Harrison. *Queen of the Midnight Skies*. West Chester, PA: Schiffer Publishing, 1992

Parry, Simon W. *Intruders over Britain*. Surbition, UK: Air Research Publications, 1987

Perkins, Paul, and Dan Patterson. *The Lady*. Charlottesville, VA: Howell Press, 1993

Perkins, Paul, and Dan Patterson. *The Soldier*. Charlottesville, VA: Howell Press, 1994

Perkins, Paul, and Dan Patterson. *Mustang*. Charlottesville, VA: Howell Press, 1995

Philpott, Bryan. *RAF Bomber Units 1939-42*. New York: Sky Books Press, 1977

Pimlott, John. *Strategic Bombing*. New York: Gallery Books, 1990

Powell, Robert H., ed. *The Bluenosed Bastards of Bodney*. Dallas, TX: Taylor Publishing, 1990

Prange, Gordon W. *At Dawn We Slept*. New York: McGraw-Hill, 1981

Prange, Gordon W. *Miracle at Midway*. London: Penguin Books, 1983

Price, Alfred. *Luftwaffe*. New York: Ballantine Books, 1969

Price, Alfred. *The Hardest Day*. London: MacDonald and Jane's, 1979

Price, Alfred. *The Bomber in World War II*. New York: Charles Scribner's Sons, 1979

Price, Alfred. *Aircraft versus Submarine*. London: Jane's, 1980

Price, Alfred. *The Spitfire Story*. Poole, UK: Arms & Armour Press, 1987

Price, Alfred. *The Last Year of the Luftwaffe*. Osceola, WI: Motorbooks International, 1991

Price, Alfred. *Aggressors Volume 4*. Charlottesville, VA: Howell Press, 1991

Rabinowitz, Harold. *Conquer the Sky*. New York: Metro Books, 1996

Ramsey, Winston G. *The Battle of Britain Then and Now*. London: Battle of Britain Prints International, 1989

Rawlings, John D.R. *The History of the Royal Air Force*. Feltham, UK: Temple Press, 1984

Redding, Robert, and Bill Yenne. *Boeing, Planemaker to the World*. Greenwich, CT: Bison Books, 1983

Reed, Arthur, and Roland Beamont. *Typhoon and Tempest at War*. New York: Charles Scribner's Sons, 1974

Reynolds, Clark G. *The Carrier War*. Alexandria, VA. Time-Life Books, 1982

Richards, Denis. *The Hardest Victory*. New York: WW Norton, 1995

Richards, Denis. *The Fight at Odds*. London: HMSO, 1974

Richards, Denis, and Hilary St. G. Saunders. *The Fight Avails*. London: HMSO, 1975

Robinson, Anthony. *Nightfighter*. London: Ian Allan, 1988

Rohwer, J., and G. Hummelchen. *Chronology of the War at Sea 1939-1945*. Annapolis, MD: Naval Institute Press, 1992

Ross, Tony, ed. *75 Eventful Years*. Canterbury, UK: Wingham Aviation Books, 1993

Sakai, Saburo. *Samurai!* Annapolis, MD: Naval Institute Press, 1991

Saunders, Hilary St. G. *The Fight is Won*. London: HMSO, 1975

Scott, Robert L. *God Is My Co-Pilot*. Reynoldsburg, OH: Buckeye Aviation Books, 1989

Shepherd, Christopher. *German aircraft of World War II*. London: Book Club Associates, 1975

Sherry, Michael S. *The Rise of American Air Power*. New Haven, CT: Yale University, 1987

Shores, Christopher. *Air Aces*. Greenwich, CT: Bison Books, 1983

Shores, Christopher. *Duel for the Sky*. New York: Doubleday, 1985

Shores, Christoper and Brian Cull, with Yasuho Izawa. *Bloody Shambles (Vols. 1&2)*. London: Grub Street, 1992

Slater, Harry E. *Lingering Contrails of the Big Square A*. Nashville, TN: Harry E. Slater, 1980

Smith, Herschel. *A History of Aircraft Piston Engines*. Manhattan, KS: Sunflower University Press, 1986

Smith, Peter C. *The History of Dive Bombing*. Annapolis, MD: Nautical & Aviation Pub. Co., 1981

Spenser, Jay P. *Focke-Wulf Fw 190*. Washington, DC: Smithsonian Institution Press, 1987

Spick, Mike. *Fighters at War*. London: Greenhill Books, 1997

Stanley, Roy M. Jr. *Prelude to Pearl Harbor*. New York: Charles Scribner's Sons, 1982

Steinhilper, Ulrich, and Peter Osborne. *Spitfire On My Tail*. Keston, UK: Independent Books, 1990

Stern, Donald E. *483rd Bomb Group (H)*. Paducah, KY: Turner Publishing, 1994

Sturtivant, Ray. *British Naval Aviation*. Annapolis, MD: Naval Institute Press, 1990

Swinson, Arthur. *Defeat in Malaya*. New York: Ballantine Books, 1970

Taylor, John W.R. *Combat Aircraft of the World*. New York: Putnam, 1969

Taylor, John W.R. *A History of Aerial Warfare*. London: Hamlyn, 1974

Taylor, John W.R., Michael Taylor, and David Mondey. *Air Facts & Feats*. Enfield, UK: Guinness Superlatives, 1977

Taylor, John W.R., and Kenneth Munson. *History of Aviation*. New York: Crown Publishers, 1972

Taylor, Michael J.H. *Great Moments in Aviation*. London: Prion, 1989

Terraine, John. *A Time for Courage*. New York: Macmillan, 1985

Thetford, Owen. *Aircraft of the Royal Air Force*. London: Putnam, 1988

Thomas, Gordon, and Max Morgan Witts. *Enola Gay*. New York: Stein & Day, 1977

Thompson, R.W. *D-Day*. New York: Ballantine Books, 1968

Thruelsen, Richard. *The Grumman Story*. New York: Praeger, 1976

Tibbetts, Paul, with Clair Stebbins and Harry Franken. *The Tibbetts Story*. New York: Stein and Day, 1978

Toliver, Raymond F. *The Interrogator*. Fallbrook, CA: Aero Publishers, 1978

Toliver, Raymond F., and Trevor J. Constable. *The Blond Knight of Germany*. Blue Ridge Summit, PA: Tab/Aero Books, 1970

Toliver, Raymond F., and Trevor J. Constable. *Fighter General*. Zephyr Cove, NV: AmPress, 1990

Townsend, Peter. *Duel of Eagles*. New York: Simon & Schuster, 1970

Townsend, Peter. *The Odds Against Us*. New York: William Morrow, 1987

Vader, John. *Pacific Hawk*. New York: Ballantine Books, 1970

Vader, John. *New Guinea*. New York: Ballantine Books, 1971

van der Linden, F. Robert. *Aircraft of the National Air & Space Museum*. Washington, DC: Smithsonian Institution Press, 1998

van der Vat, Dan. *The Pacific Campaign*. New York: Simon & Schuster, 1991

Vella, Philip. *Malta: Blitzed But Not Beaten*. Malta: Progress Press, 1985

Wakefield, Kenneth. *Luftwaffe Encore*. London: William Kimber, 1979

Wagner, Ray. *Mustang Designer*. New York: Orion, 1990

Wells, Mark. *Courage and Air Warfare*. London: Frank Cass, 1997

White, Stanley, and Henry Probert, eds. *The Means of Victory*. London: Charterhouse, 1992

Willmott, H.P. *B-17 Flying Fortress*. London: Arms & Armour Press, 1980

Wilmot, Chester. *The Struggle for Europe*. London: Fontana, 1959

Wolfe, Martin. *Green Light!* Washington, DC: Center for Air Force History, 1993

Wood, Derek, with Derek Dempster. *The Narrow Margin*. London: Tri-Service Press, 1990

Wood, Tony, and Bill Gunston. *Hitler's Luftwaffe*. New York: Crescent Books, 1979

Wragg, David. *Wings Over the Sea*. New York: Arco Publishing, 1979

Y'Blood, William T. *Red Sun Setting*. Annapolis, MD: Naval Institute Press, 1981

BOOKS BY CORPORATIONS AND MUSEUMS

Dateline Lockheed. Burbank, CA: Lockheed Corporate Communications, 1982

Forty Years On ... London: Handley Page Ltd., 1949

National Museum of Naval Aviation. Pensacola, FL: Naval Aviation Foundation, 1996

Pedigree of Champions: Boeing since 1916. Seattle, WA: The Boeing Company, 1977

The Pratt & Whitney Aircraft Story. Hartford, CT: Pratt & Whitney Aircraft, 1950

United States Air Force Museum. Wright-Patterson AFB, OH: Air Force Museum Foundation, 1997

ANNUAL PUBLICATIONS

Aviation Year Book. New York: Aeronautical Chamber of Commerce of America

Jane's All the World's Aircraft. London: Jane's Yearbooks

Jane's Fighting Ships. London: Jane's Yearbooks

MAGAZINES

Aeroplane Monthly. London: IPC Media Ltd.

Air & Space Smithsonian. Washington, DC: Smithsonian Business Ventures

Flight Journal. Ridgefield, CT: Air Age Inc.

International Air Power Review. Norwalk, CT: AIRtime Publishing

The Journal of the Royal Air Force Historical Society. London: RAFHS

INDEX BY SUBJECT

Note: Page numbers in bold indicate an illustration.

AIRCRAFT

American

Bell
P-39 Airacobra *99*, *266*, *268*, *281*
P-400 *280*

Boeing
B-17D *The Swoose* *229*
B-17E *127-8*
B-17E *Memphis Belle* *145*
B-17E *Yankee Doodle* *128*
B-17 Flying Fortress *75-7*, *86*, **130-1**, *162-5*, *201*, *213*, *219*, **222**, *228-30*, **230**, *251*
B-17G *Shoo Shoo Baby* **130-1**, **132-3**
B-29 Superfortress *319*, *320-2*, **321**, *325*, **326**
B-29 *Bockscar* *312*, **330-1**, **332**, *335*
B-29 *Enola Gay* *323*, *333*, *335*
B-29 *Fifi* *323*
B-29 *Joltin' Josie, the Pacific Pioneer* *322*
B-29 *No. 91* *335*
B-29 *The Great Artiste* *335*
XB-29 *319-20*

Brewster
239 *Taivaan Helmi* (Pearl of the Skies) *90*
F2A Buffalo *251*

Consolidated
B-24 Liberator *73*, *76*, *128-9*, *146*, **167**, *188*, *211*, *277*
B-24 *The Duchess* **141**
B-24 *Utah Man* **140**
B-24 *Strawberry Bitch* **142-3**
B-24 *Wongo Wongo* *146*
Catalina *188-9*, *251*, *263*, **274**, *277*
PBY4 Privateer *277*
XB-32 *319*

Curtiss
C-46 Commando **308**, *309*, **310**
Hawk *90*
Kittyhawk *71*, *73*
P-40 Warhawk *73*, *75*, *78*, *228-9*, *305*
SB2C Helldiver **290**
Tomahawk *71-2*

Douglas
A-20 Havoc *75*, *183*, *201*, **270-1**
Boston *57*, *127*
C-47 Skytrain *75*, *81*, *200-1*, *267*, *309-10*

SBD Dauntless (A-24) **250**, *251*, **252**, *253-5*, **256-7**, **258-9**, **260**
TBD Devastator *245*

Grumman
F4F Wildcat *243*, **248**, *251*, *254-5*, **260**, *279*
F6F Hellcat **284-5**, **286**, **287**, *290*, *295*
F8F Bearcat **276**
J2F Duck **276**
TBF/TBM Avenger *251*, **288**, **289**, *291*

Lockheed
Hudson *57*, *185*, *187*
P-38/F-4 Lightning *75*, *268-9*, **278**, *283*
P-38J *Texas Ranger IV* *170*

Martin
B-26 Marauder *75*, *86*, **174-5**, **178**, **200-1**, **210**, *251*
Maryland *63*

North American
A-36 Mustang **80**, *85-6*
B-25 Mitchell *73*, *75*, *86*, **236-7**, **239**, *240*, *267*, **268**, *272-4*, *309*, **311**
F-86 Sabre *106*
Mustang I *57*
P-51 Mustang *156*, **159**, *170*, *219*, *221*, *305*, *309*
P-51 *Cripes a Mighty* **154-5**
P-51 *Lil Margaret* **154**

Northrop
P-61 Black Widow *216*, *293*

Piper
L-4 Grasshopper **212**, *216*

Republic
P-47 Thunderbolt *145*, **146**, **152-3**, **154**, *161*, *167*, *180*, *199-201*, *221*, *300*

Sikorsky
YR-4 *309*

Vought
F4U Corsair **292**, *293*
FG-1D **295**
SB2U Vindicator **244**, *251*

Waco
CG-4 Haig *309*
Hadrian *81*

British

Airspeed
Horsa *81*, **199**, *201*
Oxford *79*

Armstrong-Whitworth
Albemarle **201**
Whitley *56-7*, **59**

Avro
Lancaster *109*, *115*, *195*, *222*

Lancaster *Johnny Walker* *123*
Lancaster *Just Jane* **118-19**, *122*
Lancaster *S for Sugar* *125*
Manchester *109*

Blackburn
Roc *31*
Skua *24*, *31*

Boulton-Paul
Defiant *38-9*, **41**, *53*

Bristol
Beaufighter *54-5*, *64*, *73*, *75*, **272**, *272-3*, **273**
Beaufort *73*, *195*
Bisley *75*, *76*
Blenheim *21-2*, **22**, *24*, *26*, *53*, *57*, *60*, *64-5*
Blenheim IV *50*, *68*
Blenheim V (Canadian built) *75*
Bombay *65*
Bulldog *22*

de Havilland
Mosquito *55*, *111*, **176**
Tiger Moth *49*

Fairey
Battle **25**, *26*
Fulmar *80*
Gordon *79*
Swordfish *24*, *186*, **190**, *190-1*, **191**, **192-3**, *194-5*

Gloster
Gauntlet *65*
Gladiator *24*, *29*, *60*, **62**, *65*
Meteor **177**, *220*
Sea Gladiator *Faith, Hope, Charity* *63*

Handley-Page
Halifax *57*, *73*, *109*
Hampden *21*, *24*

Hawker
Audax *79*
Hardy *65*
Hurricane *24*, **29**, *29*, *31*, *32*, *33*, *37*, *39-40*, *45*, *51*, *53*, *60*, *63-4*, *73*, *74*, *77*
"Collie's Battleship" *68*
Hurricane I *44*
Hurricane IIC **74**
Hurricane IID **70**, *74*
losses *47*
"Hurricat" *186*, *187*
Sea Hurricane **188**
Tempest *173*
Typhoon *57*, **172-3**, *210*, *217*

Short
Stirling *57*, *109*
Sunderland *64*, *185*, **186**, *187*

Supermarine
Seafire *83*
Spitfire *31*, *33*, *37*, *39-40*, *45*, *49-51*, **65**, *74-5*, **76**, *78*
Spitfire I *22*
Spitfire IIA **34-7**
losses *47*
Spitfire V *56*, **64**, *73*
Spitfire IX **197**
Walrus **194**, **195**

Vickers
Valentia *65*
Vincent *65*
Wellesley *65*, *79*
Wellington *21-2*, *24*, *63*, *68*, *73*, *76*, *111*, **112-13**

Westland
Lysander *57*, *57-8*, *65*

Dutch

Fokker
C.X *22*
D.XXI *22*

French

Bloch
MB. 151 *60*
Dewoitine
D.520 *26*, *75*, *80*
Morane-Saulnier
406 *80*
Potez
63 *60*

German

Arado
Ar. 234 **221**
Blohm and Voss
Bv 138 *189*
Deutsches Forschungsinstitut für Segelflug (German Research Institute for Gliding)
DFS 230 *61*
Dornier
Do 17 *19*, *24*, *39*, *41*, *190*
Do 18 *189*
Do 217K-2 *84*
Fieseler
Fi 103 (VI flying bomb) *181*, *181*, *182*, *220*
Storch **214-15**
Focke-Wulf
Fw 190 *54*, *56*, *129*, **164**, **200**
Fw 200 *95*, *185*
Ta 152 **182**
Heinkel
He 111 *19*, *24*, *26*, **36**, *37*, **38**, *49*, *64*, *79*, *190*
He 111H-4 *53-4*

He 115 *189-90*
He 162 **216**
He 177 *186*, *219*
He 178 *220*

Henschel
Hs 129 *102*, *103*

Junkers
Ju 52/3m *24*, *61*, *78*
Ju 86 *95*
Ju 87 Stuka *19*, *21*, *24*, **26**, *28*, *39*, *44*, *47*, *64*, *74*, *77*
Ju 88 *39*, *75*, **138**, *190*
Ju 290 *95*
W.34 *22*

Messerschmitt
Bf 109 *19*, *21-2*, *37-40*, *45-7*, *49*, *60*, *73*, *78*
Bf 109E *19*, *21*, *24*, *32-3*, *38*, **39**, *68*
Bf 109F *56*
Bf 109G **151**
Bf 110 *22*, *24*, *26*, *39*, **40**, *40-1*, *45*, *60-1*, *78-9*, **166**
Black Six *75*, **148-9**, *163*
Me 163 **169**, *220*
Me 262 *77*, *158*, **168**, *220*
Me 323 *78*
Me 410 Hornisse **165**

Italian

Fiat
B.R.20 *60*
C.R.42 *60*, **61**, *79*
G.50 *60*
Macchi
MC.200 Saetta *63*, **85**
MC.202 Folgore *78*, **77**
MC.205 Veltro **82**
Savoia-Marchetti
S.M.79 *60*, *63-4*, **66-7**
S.M.82 *78*

Japanese

Aichi
D3A (Val) *251*, **254**, **255**, *260*, *279*
Kawanishi
H8K (Emily) **300**
Kawasaki
Ki-48 (Lily) *232*, **269**
Ki-61 *328*
Ki-100 *328*
Mitsubishi
A6M (Zeke or Zero) *229*, *231-2*, **233**, *245*, **248**, *251*, *260*, *263*, *279*, *283*, *289*
G3M (Nell) *229*, *232*
G4M (Betty) *229*, *232*, *279*, *282-3*, **334**
Ki-46 (Dinah) **329**

GENERAL INDEX